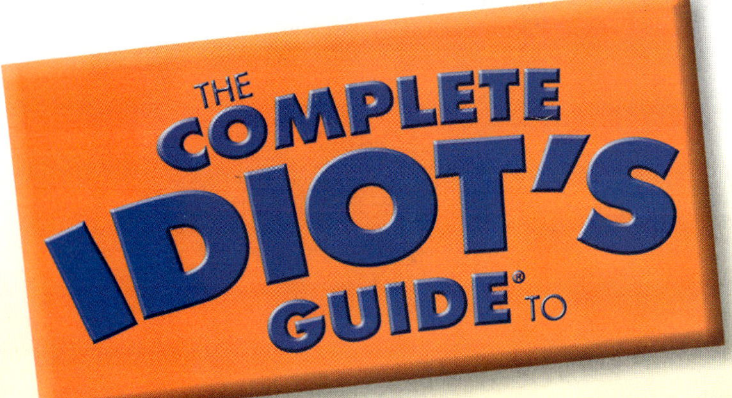

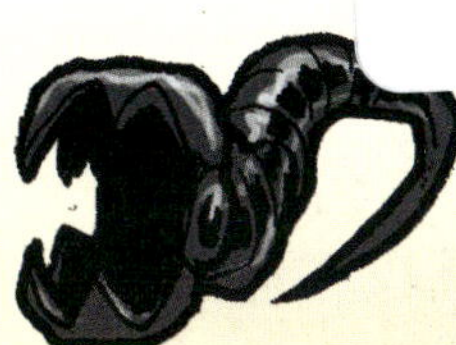

DRAWING SUPERHEROES & VILLAINS Illustrated

Matt Forbeck
and Yair Herrera
for Idea + Design Works, LLC

ALPHA
A member of Penguin Group (USA) Inc.

To my parents—Ken Forbeck and Helen Forbeck—who taught me how to read with comic books. They were the greatest heroes a boy could have had.

—Matt Forbeck

I dedicate this book to my parents—David and Claudia—for the support and the genes, to my brothers—Yago y Ariel—for being the hardest critics and the biggest fans, and to all the people that help me in my dream of becoming a comic artist.

—Yair Herrera

ALPHA BOOKS

Published by the Penguin Group

Penguin Group (USA) Inc., 375 Hudson Street, New York, New York 10014, U.S.A.

Penguin Group (Canada), 10 Alcorn Avenue, Toronto, Ontario, Canada M4V 3B2 (a division of Pearson Penguin Canada Inc.)

Penguin Books Ltd, 80 Strand, London WC2R 0RL, England

Penguin Ireland, 25 St Stephen's Green, Dublin 2, Ireland (a division of Penguin Books Ltd)

Penguin Group (Australia), 250 Camberwell Road, Camberwell, Victoria 3124, Australia (a division of Pearson Australia Group Pty Ltd)

Penguin Books India Pvt Ltd, 11 Community Centre, Panchsheel Park, New Delhi—110 017, India

Penguin Group (NZ), cnr Airborne and Rosedale Roads, Albany, Auckland 1310, New Zealand (a division of Pearson New Zealand Ltd)

Penguin Books (South Africa) (Pty) Ltd, 24 Sturdee Avenue, Rosebank, Johannesburg 2196, South Africa

Penguin Books Ltd, Registered Offices: 80 Strand, London WC2R 0RL, England

International Standard Book Number: 978-1-59257-795-8
Library of Congress Catalog Card Number: 2008922784

10 09 08 8 7 6 5 4 3 2 1

Interpretation of the printing code: The rightmost number of the first series of numbers is the year of the book's printing; the rightmost number of the second series of numbers is the number of the book's printing. For example, a printing code of 08-1 shows that the first printing occurred in 2008.

Printed in the United States of America

Publisher	**Marie Butler-Knight**
Editorial Director/Acquiring Editor	**Mike Sanders**
Senior Managing Editor	**Billy Fields**
Development Editor	**Ginny Munroe**
Production Editor	**Megan Douglass**
Copy Editor	**Mike Dietsch**
Book/Cover Designer	**Kurt Owens**
Proofreader	**John Etchison**

CONTENTS

PART 1: BRAWN

PART 2: BRAINS

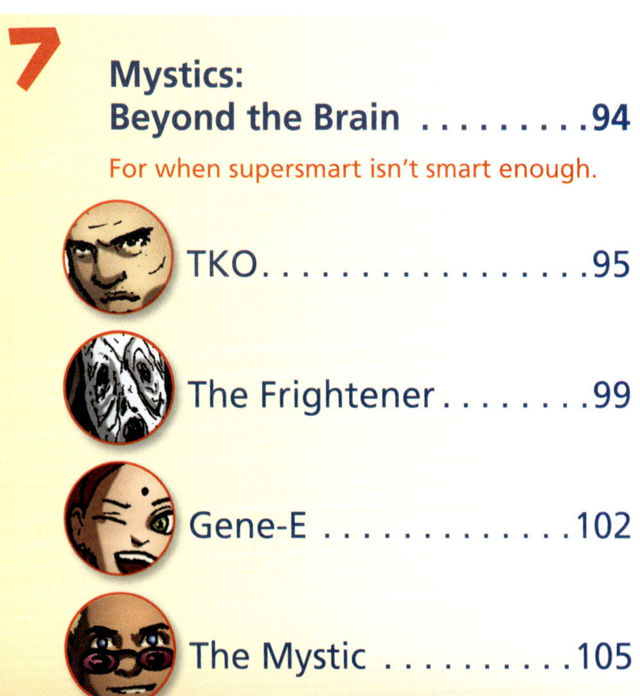

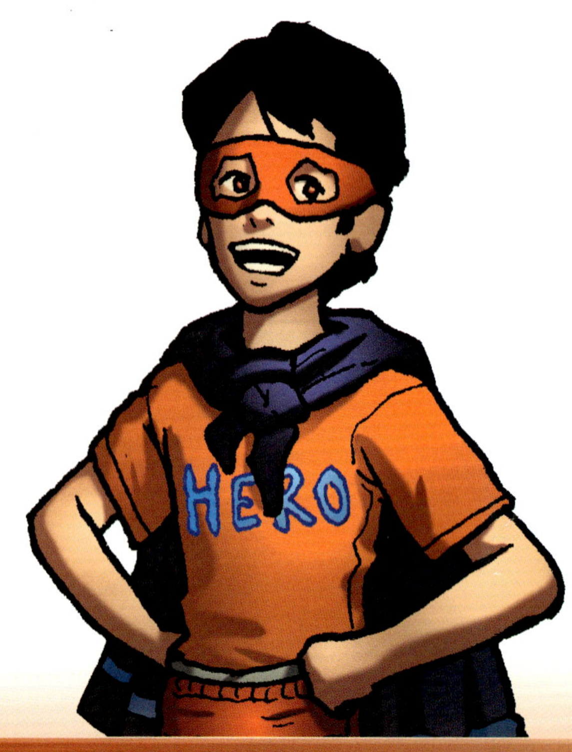

PART 3: MISCELLANEOUS

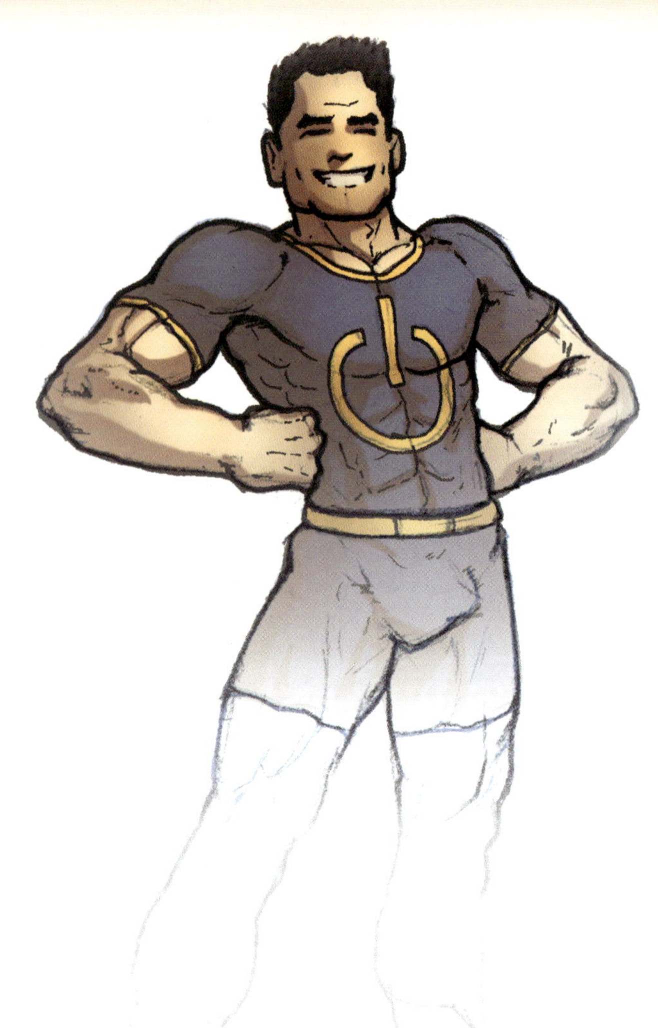

APPENDIXES

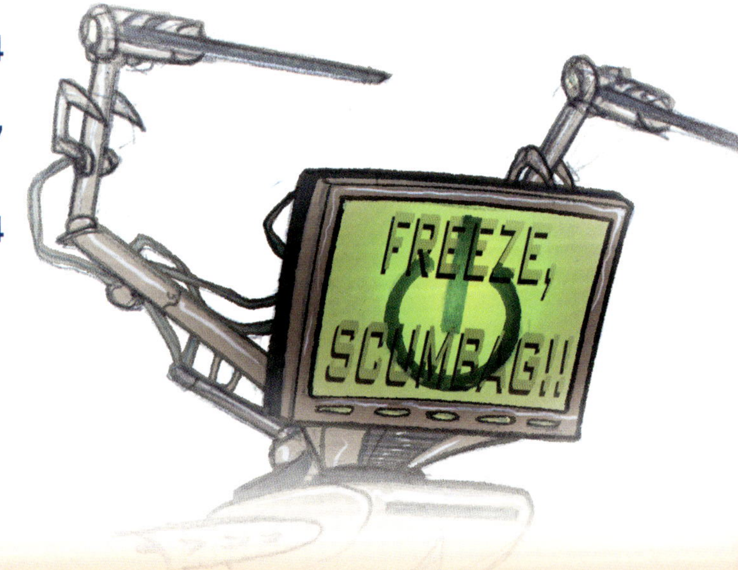

INTRODUCTION

Welcome to *The Complete Idiot's Guide to Superheroes and Villains Illustrated.* Despite that being a mouthful of a title, we hope you'll find the contents of this book easy to swallow.

If you're interested in drawing superhero comics—and you already know your lead from your eraser—you've come to the right place. In this book, we'll show you how to draw a wide variety of different kinds of characters, nearly 50 in all. By the time you're done, you'll have mastered the genre and should be ready to go out and come up with all sorts of characters of your own, too.

HOW TO USE THIS BOOK

This book is broken down into three large sections. We start with the two basic types of superpowered character (brawny or brainy) and then cap it all off with a grab bag of fun.

Part 1, "Brawn." Many superhero stories revolve around massive fights in which characters who could level city blocks have a crack at each other instead. In this part, we tackle the best sorts of fighters and show you how to draw them all.

Part 2, "Brains." Despite what you might see on splash pages, comics aren't all about punching out your foes. Some challenges require a bit of thought, and that's where the brains come in. They range from big-thinking scientists to masters of the mystic arts and everything in between.

Part 3, "Miscellaneous." Once we cover the basics, we move on to everything else. This includes speedsters, shape shifters, robots, sidekicks, and more. If you can't find what you're looking for in the first two parts, be sure to turn here.

EXTRAS

Throughout the book, you'll find snappy little sidebars designed to help answer questions and illuminate the world of superheroes and villains for you.

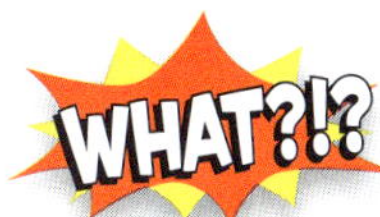

Learn definitions of words that come from the world of superheroes.

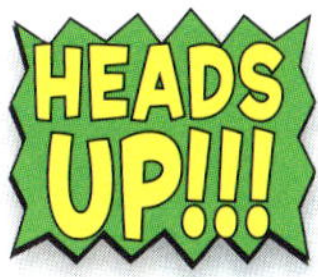

These are miscellaneous pieces of information that don't seem to fit anywhere else—but which we're sure you'll appreciate.

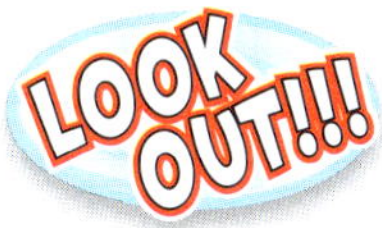

These feature warnings about things that might go wrong with a particular drawing. Pay careful attention here, or you'll end up saying "Ouch!"

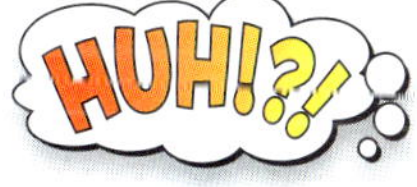

These feature a grab bag of bits of knowledge that you'll want to hold on to like the precious things they are.

ACKNOWLEDGMENTS

We'd like to thank the fine people at IDW for asking us to create this book and giving us the encouragement to finish it. Special thanks go to Kris Oprisko for his wise and steady guidance.

TRADEMARKS

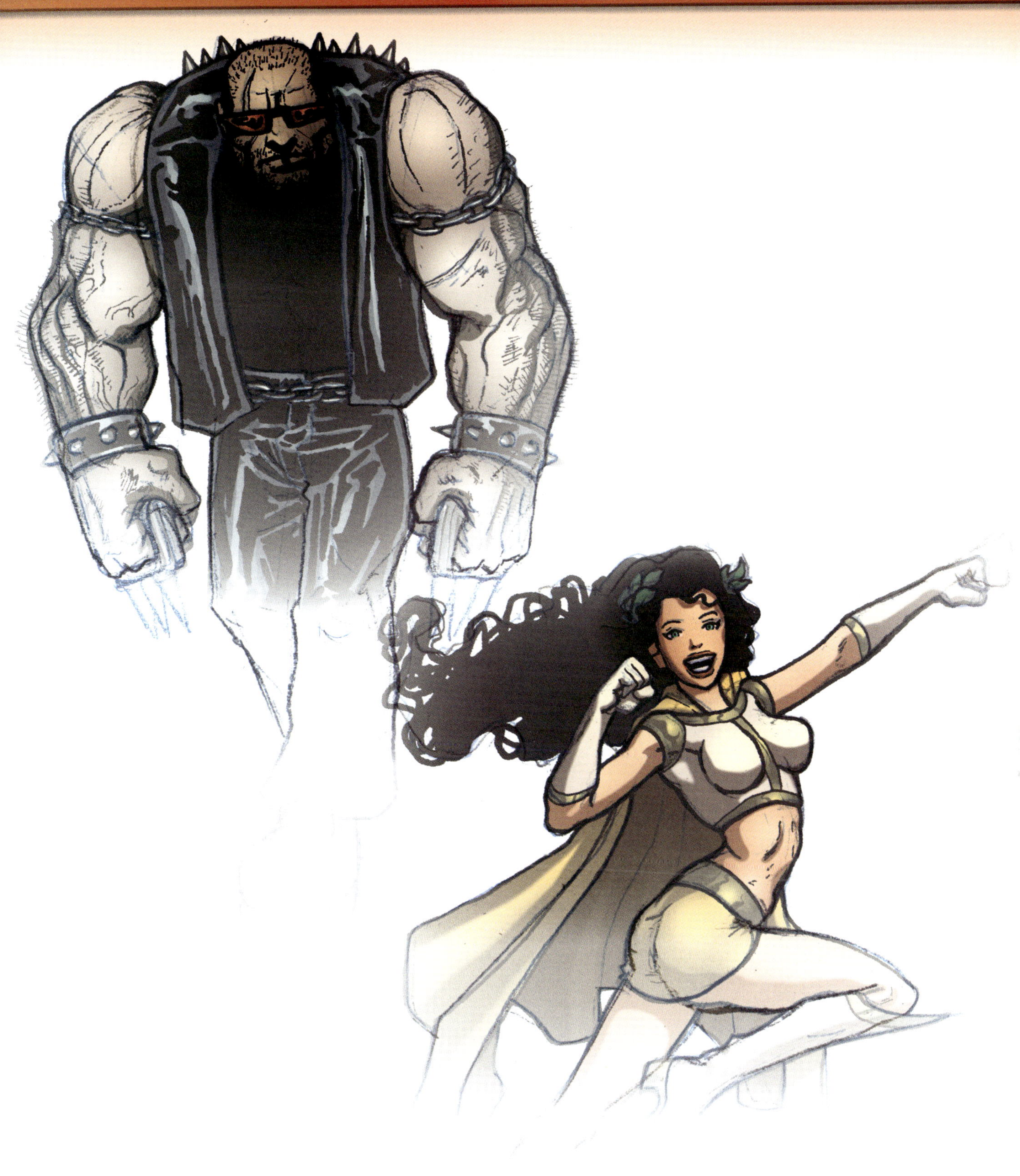

PART 1

BRAWN

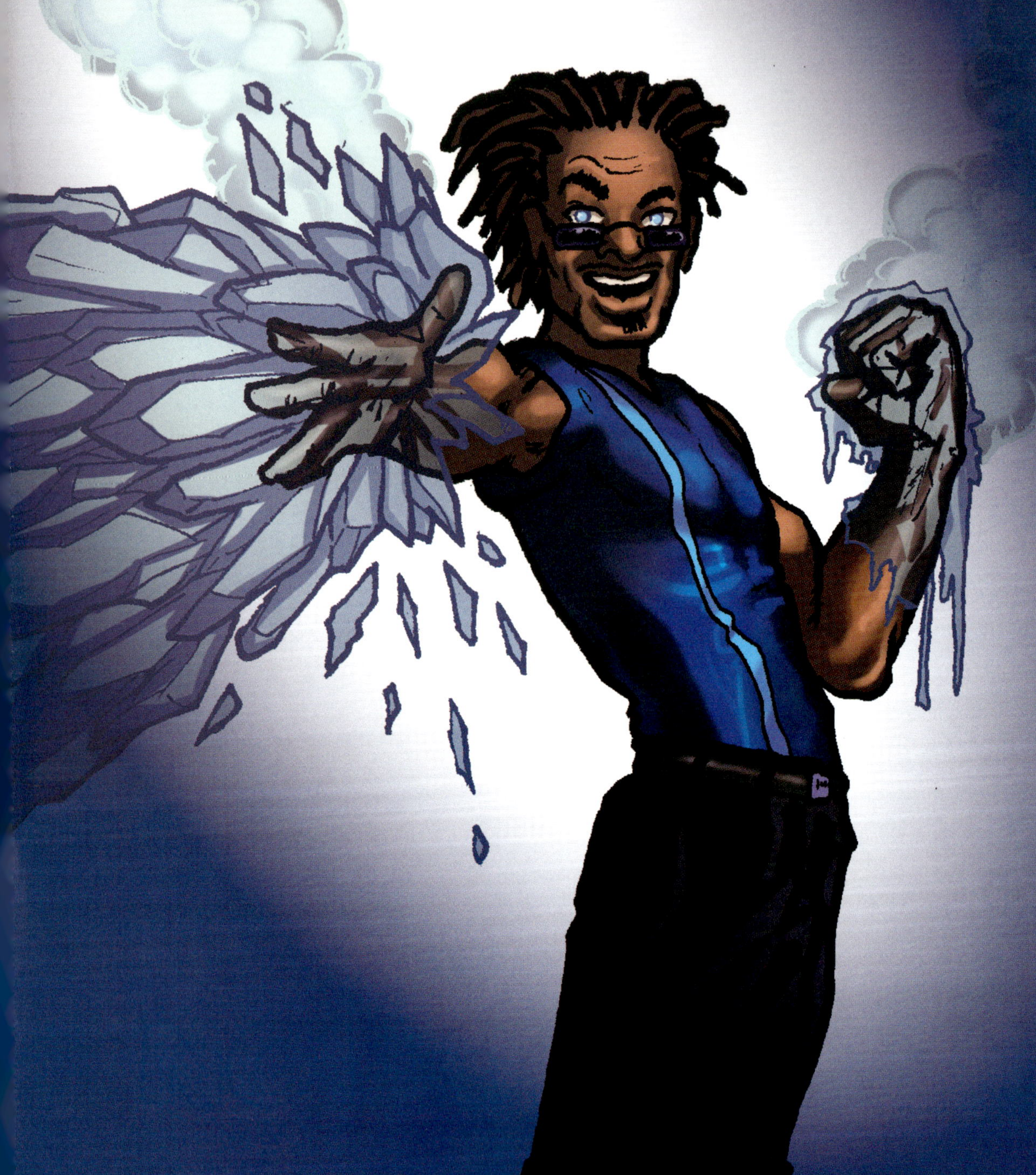

IN THIS PART

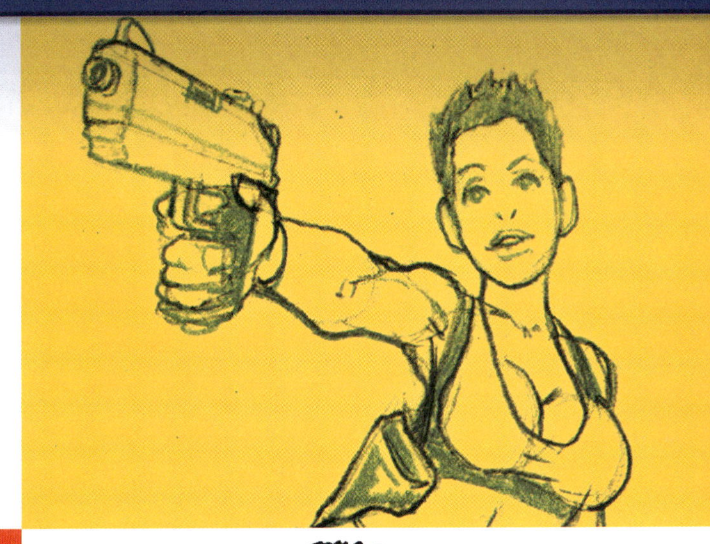

Superhero stories always seem to devolve into a fight at some point. This is, after all, the best way for the hero to stop the villain, since you just can't have a reasonable conversation with most murderous madmen.

The best heroes in such situations are those who let their martial skills do their talking for them. Whether they're throwing buildings at each other or blasting apart boulders with plasma beams, they make the best use of their amazing powers to put the villains behind bars—or to put a more permanent end to them and the threats they represent.

In this part, we start out with blasters, who use blasts of energy to attack their foes from a distance. Then we move on to scrappers, who prefer their battles a bit more up close and personal. After that, we move on to the invulnerable and mighty bricks. From there, it's just a short hop over to examining the shooters who use more mundane tools like bows or guns to make their points in spectacular ways.

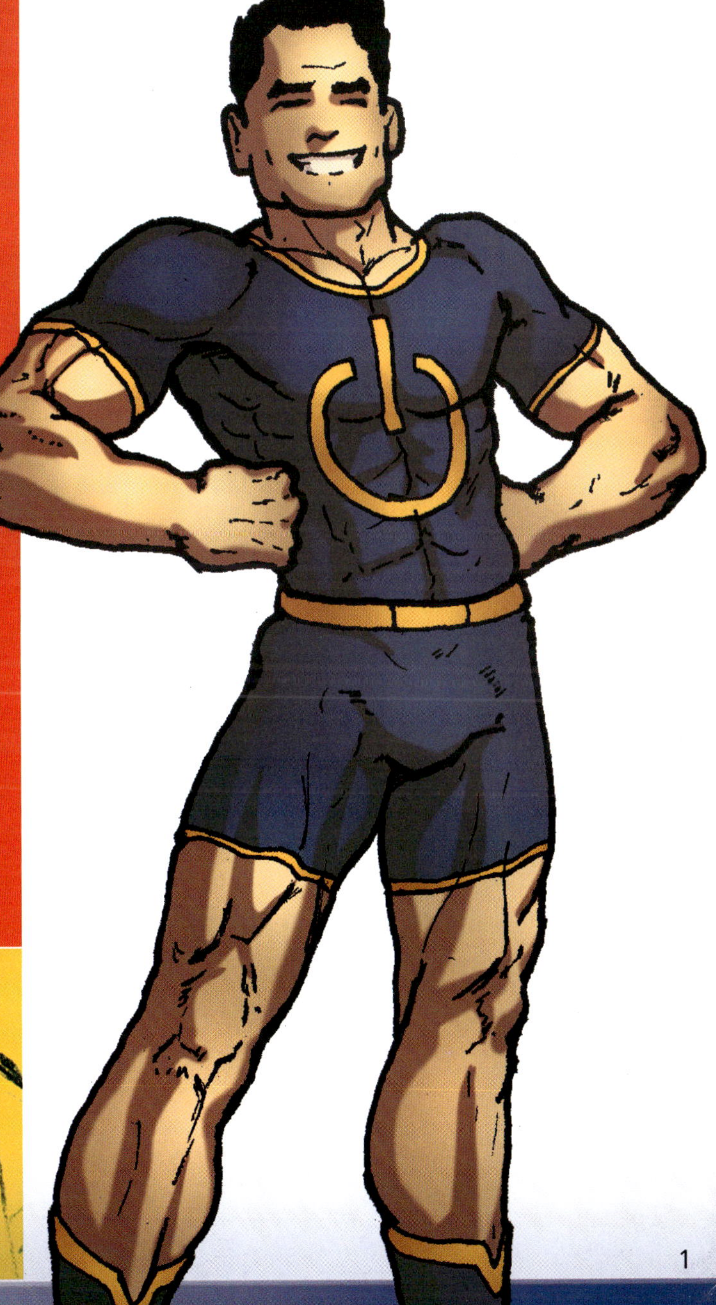

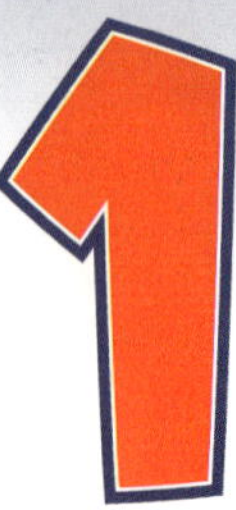

BLASTERS: KA-ZAP!

In This Chapter

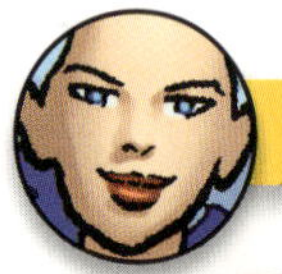

A hot heroine

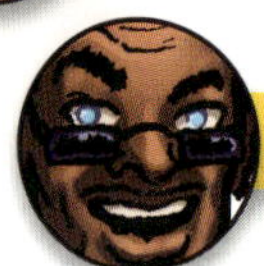

A man who knows how to chill

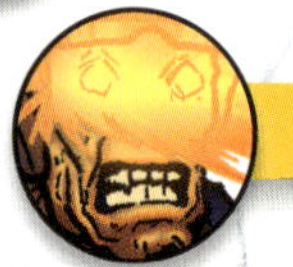

Watch the man with the laser eyes

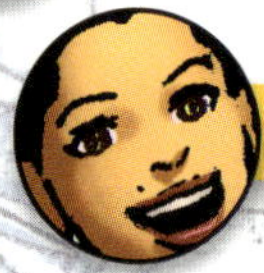

The girl with the electric touch

Blasters make for a straightforward version of the most powerful people in the real world: those with guns. Instead of firing bullets from a weapon, though, they shoot fire—or ice or lasers or electricity from their own bodies. In a superteam, they soften up the enemy from a distance before their teammates meet them toe to toe.

We begin with a hot lady: Blowtorch. She burns so bright you'll have to shade your eyes to look at her. She flies through the air like a flare shot from a gun, and she'll scorch you if you get too close.

Next up is Blowtorch's polar opposite: Chiller. This urban hero is always dressed to kill and ready to chill with his control over frost and ice. That might sound refreshing on a hot day, but getting frozen solid is no fun.

After that we meet a villain with a view to a kill: Lazerize. He fires lethal blasts of solid light from his eyes. Don't let him catch you in his sight.

We wind up with a wild woman who literally crackles with electricity: Zapper. Don't let her clothes (or lack thereof) fool you. She's far more shocking than her fashion sense.

BLOWTORCH

Once a college student by day and welder by night, the woman who would become Blowtorch was nearly killed in a case of industrial espionage that blew up the factory in which she worked. Instead, she rose from the rubble, surrounded by glowing blue flames like those of an acetylene torch.

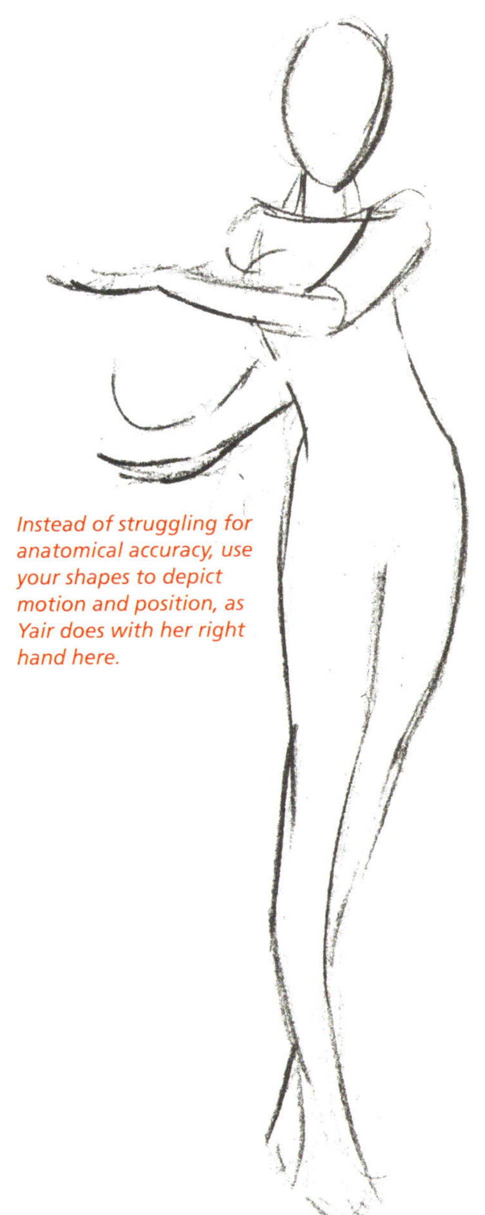

Instead of struggling for anatomical accuracy, use your shapes to depict motion and position, as Yair does with her right hand here.

It's okay to make changes, especially if they make the picture better.

1. Sketch out Blowtorch's figure. She is a slim woman, and she will be holding something hovering between her hands, a blast of flame she's charged up for something really explosive.

2. Rough in some more details. Concentrate on the flames and the costume. Put a ball of fire between her hands. Note how Yair moves her right hand down a bit.

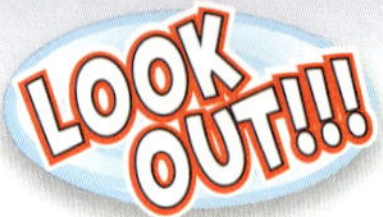

Superpowered characters usually wear skintight clothes. Female characters often seem to wear little at all. If you like this, more power to you. If it offends your sensibilities, feel free to add more clothing to your characters.

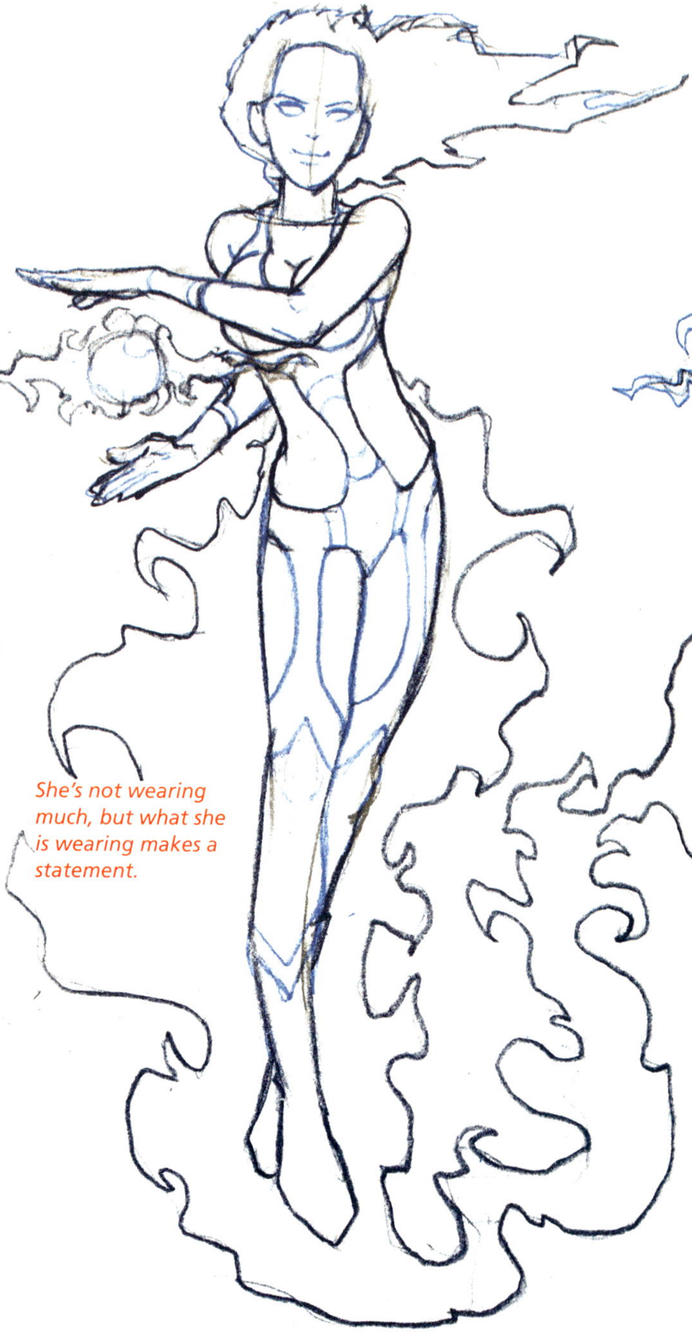

She's not wearing much, but what she is wearing makes a statement.

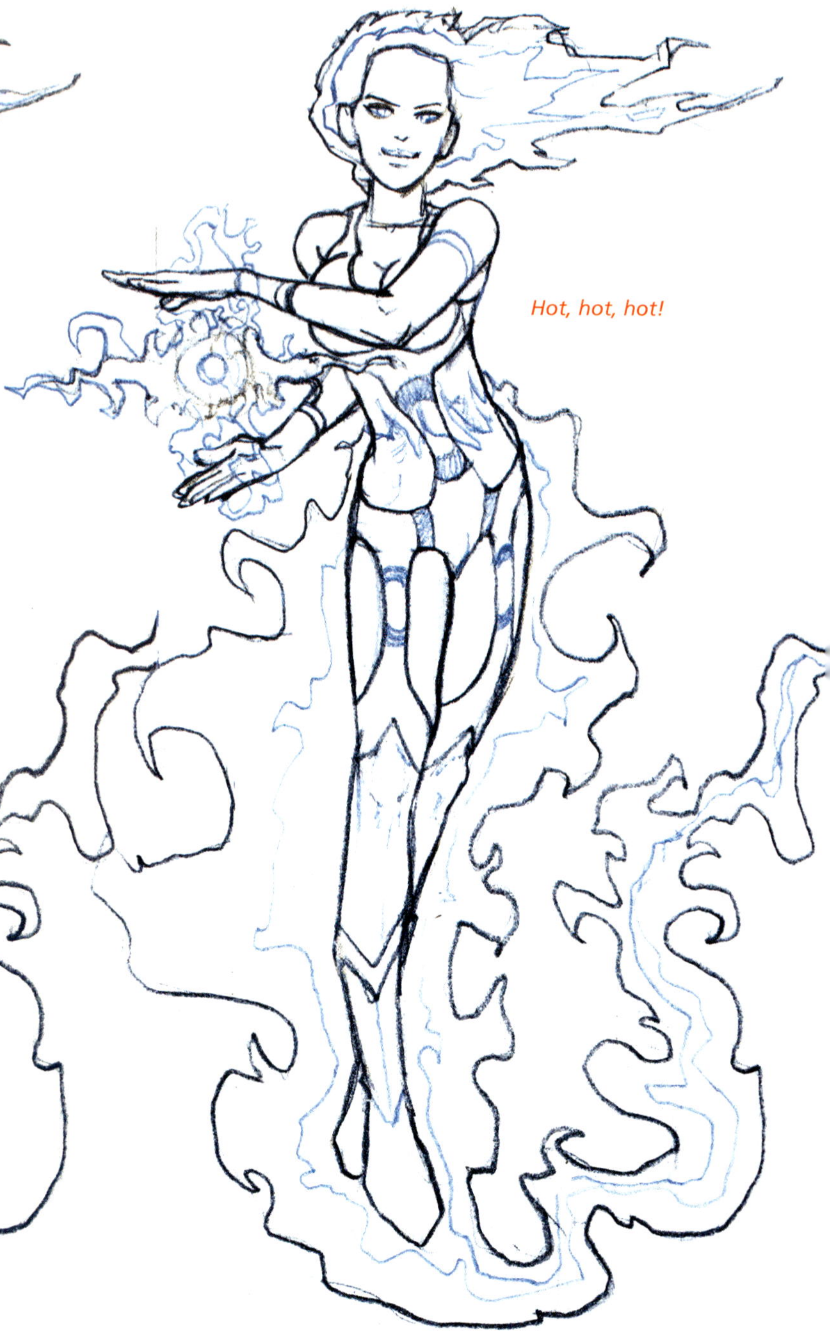

Hot, hot, hot!

3. Focus on the face here, and then work on other details, like adding a bit more to her costume.

4. Add another layer of flame, representing where the flame burns even stronger. Respect the outline of the flame you've already drawn. Also finish off the rest of the picture, especially the face.

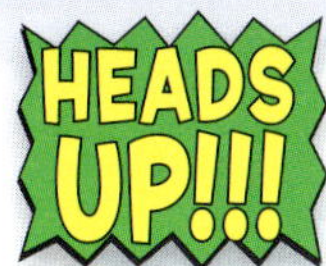

Flames may look tricky to draw, but they're as simple as you let them be. Concentrate on the edges of the flame, which always flicker. Make the flames wider at the bottom and have them narrow to a point, curling in different directions along the way. This isn't realistic, but your viewers will recognize your symbolic flames at once.

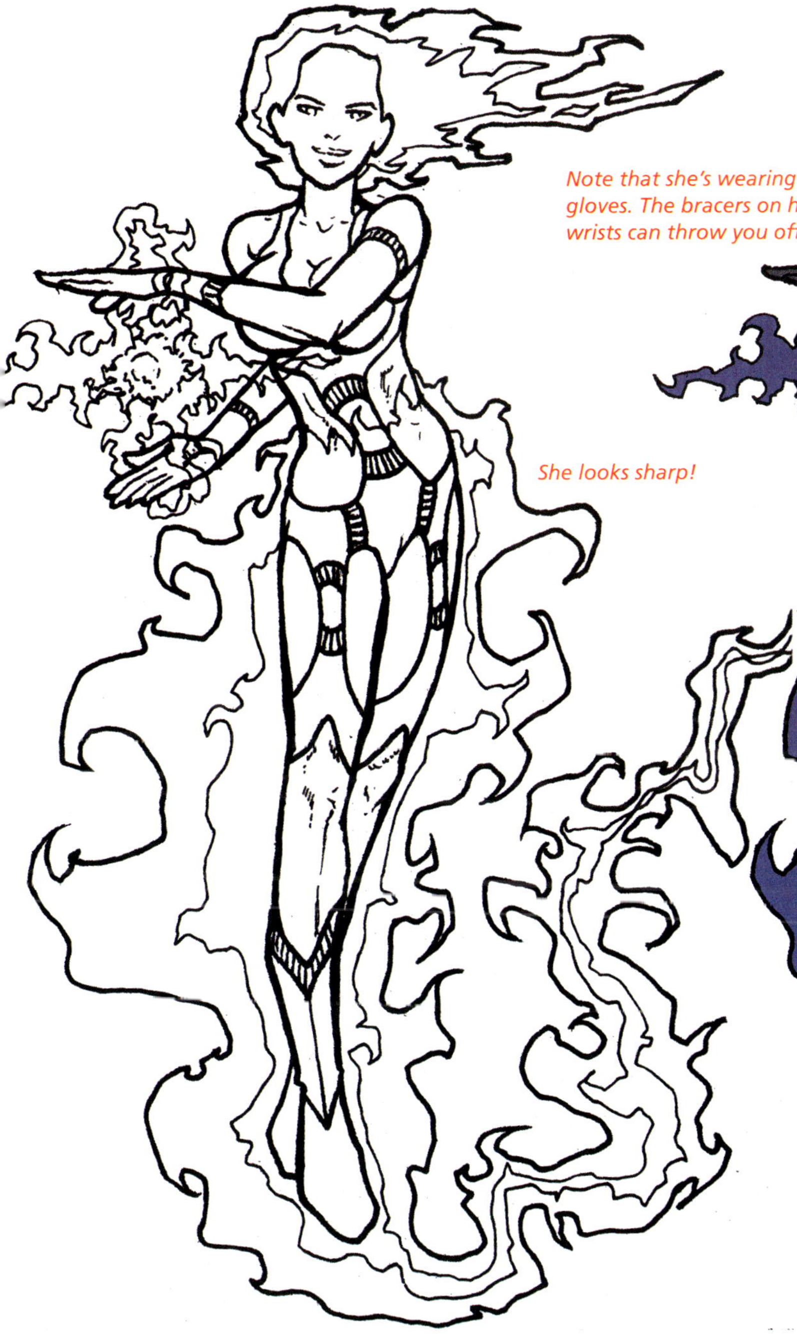

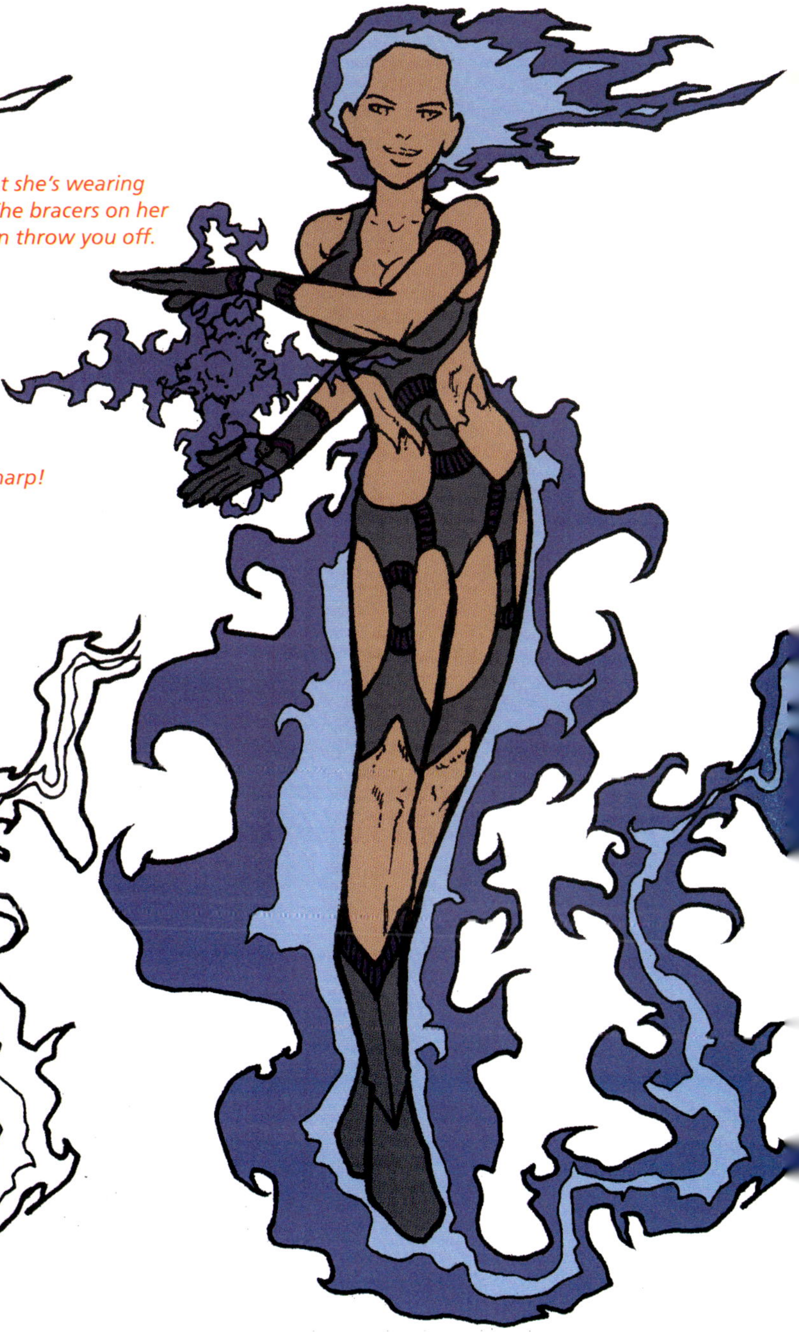

Note that she's wearing gloves. The bracers on her wrists can throw you off.

She looks sharp!

5. Use heavier inks on the figure's edges. Use lighter ones for the interior flames. Otherwise, she'll look like she's banded in flame rather than cocooned in it.

6. Color her skin as you like. Her costume is gray, and her flames are dark blue on the outside and light blue on the inside.

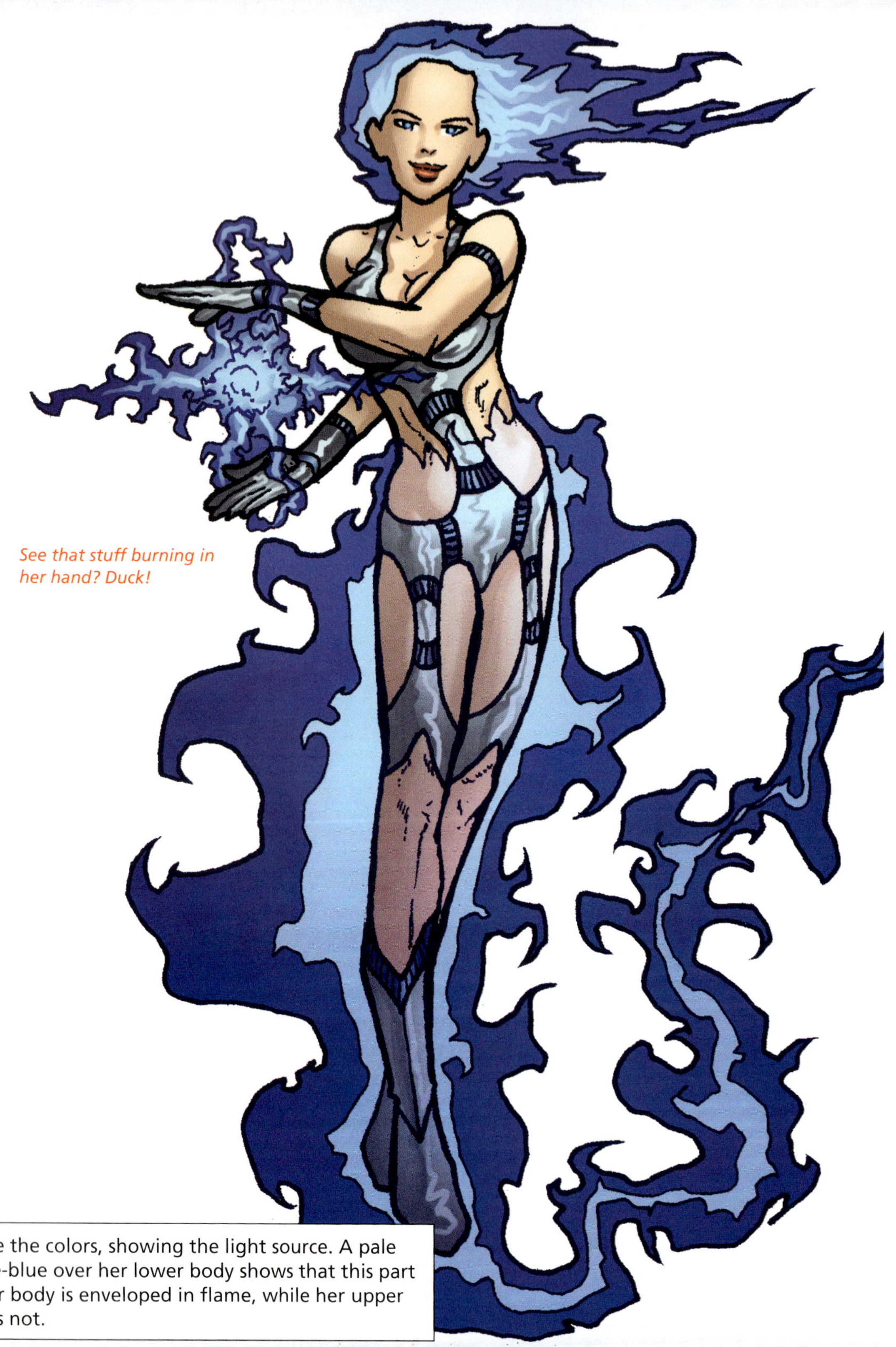

See that stuff burning in her hand? Duck!

7. Shade the colors, showing the light source. A pale white-blue over her lower body shows that this part of her body is enveloped in flame, while her upper half is not.

THE CHILLER

The Chiller started out as a cryogenics researcher by day, DJ by night. While working the club scene in the big city, he ran afoul of a gang that insisted he craft a new designer drug to rule the streets. After he refused, they tossed him in a meat locker overnight. When they came to find his body the next day, they got a face full of ice from the Chiller instead.

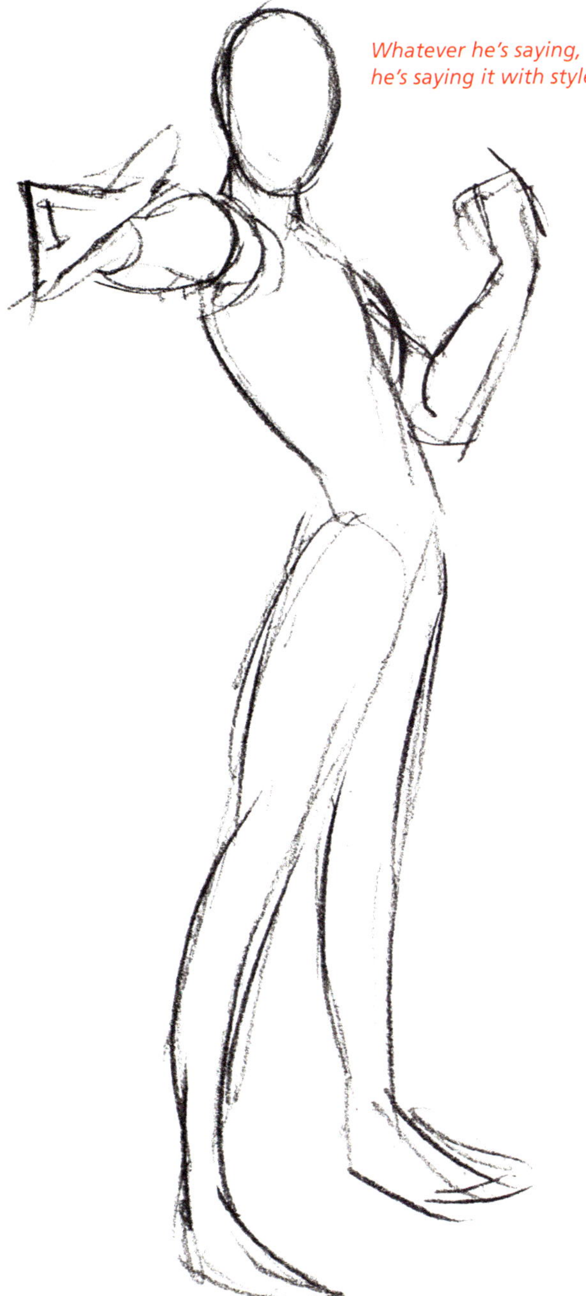

Whatever he's saying, he's saying it with style.

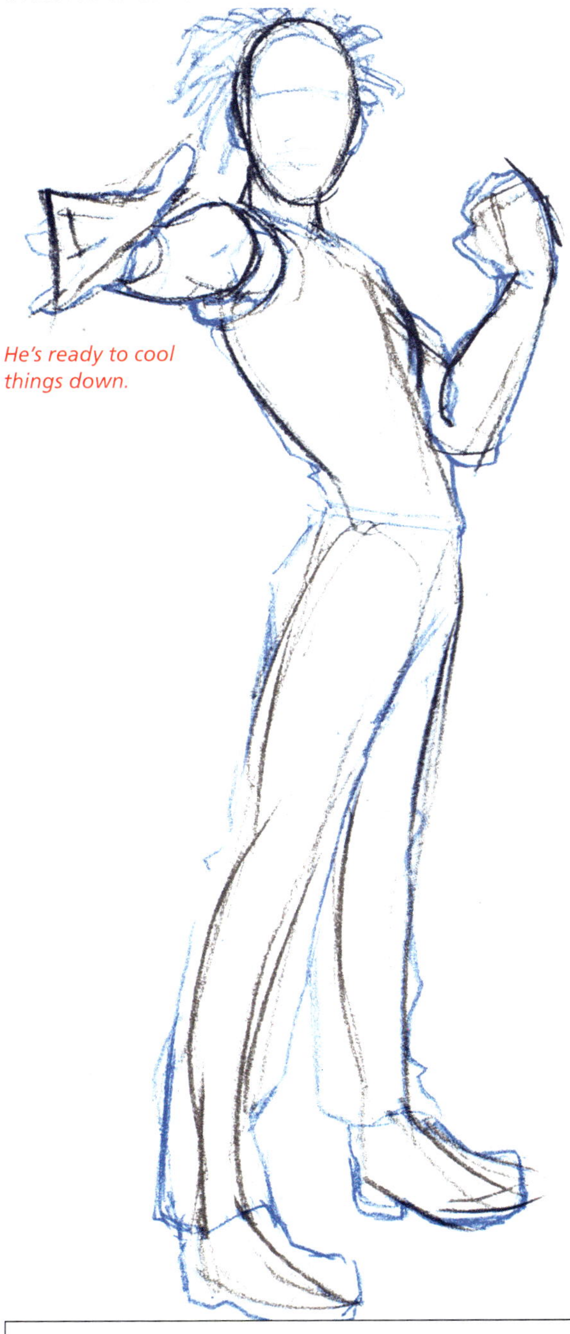

He's ready to cool things down.

1. Rough in the figure. Yair chooses a dynamic pose that features *foreshortening* of Chiller's right arm. The clenched fist of his left hand shows he's in power.

2. Work in the details of his hair and clothing. He wears small and tight dreadlocks on his head, and baggy pants on his legs. The tight shirt shows off his muscles and makes him look more like a traditional superhero.

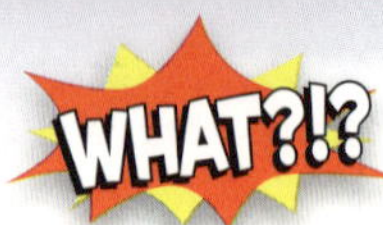

Foreshortening is a trick of perspective that makes something long that's turned toward the viewer seem short. See Chiller's right arm for an example. Notice also that his hand is larger to show that it's closer to the viewer.

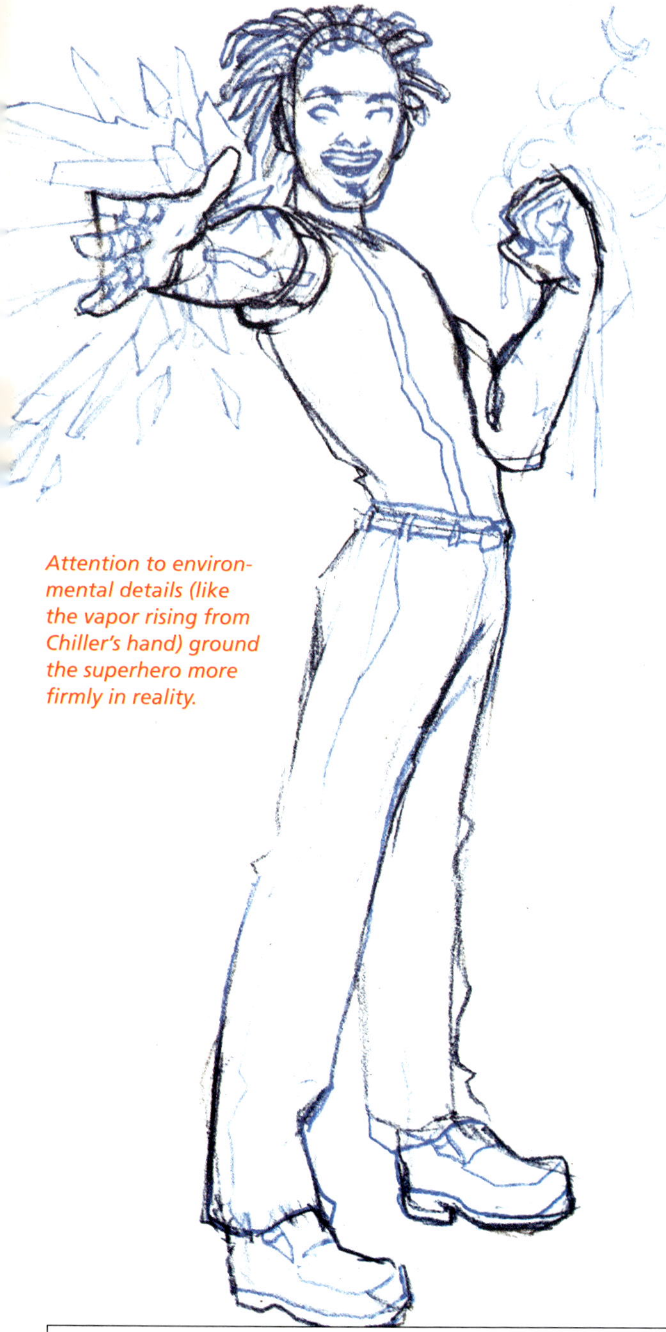

Attention to environmental details (like the vapor rising from Chiller's hand) ground the superhero more firmly in reality.

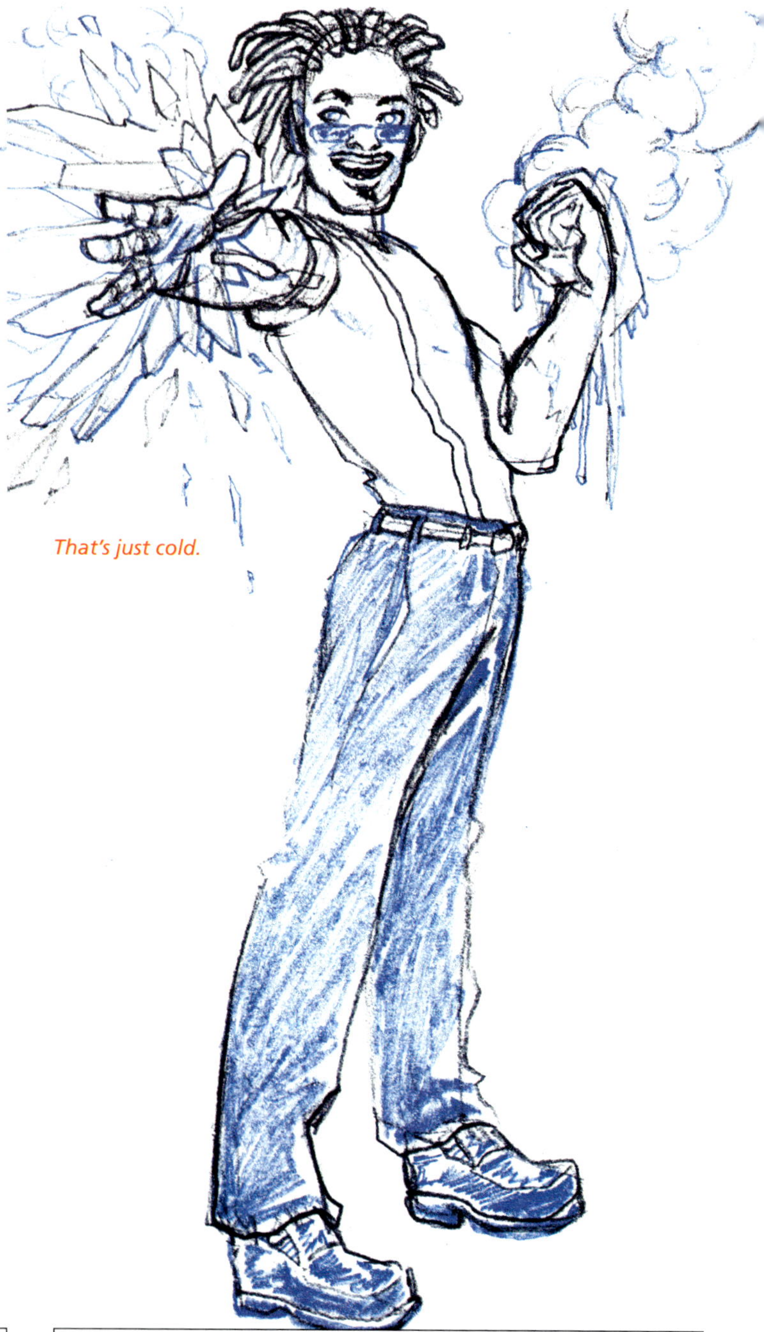

That's just cold.

3. Work on the face first. Expressions mean a lot. Add some ice crystals flying from his hand, and encase the other hand in ice so cold it seems to steam in the warm air.

4. Black in his pants and shoes. Give him a set of shades. Add more ice to his right hand, and trail some vapor from that, too.

It's easy to fall into stereotypes when dealing with characters from cultures that aren't your own. Take care so that your characters don't become caricatures. The easiest way to do this is to work pointedly against the archetype.

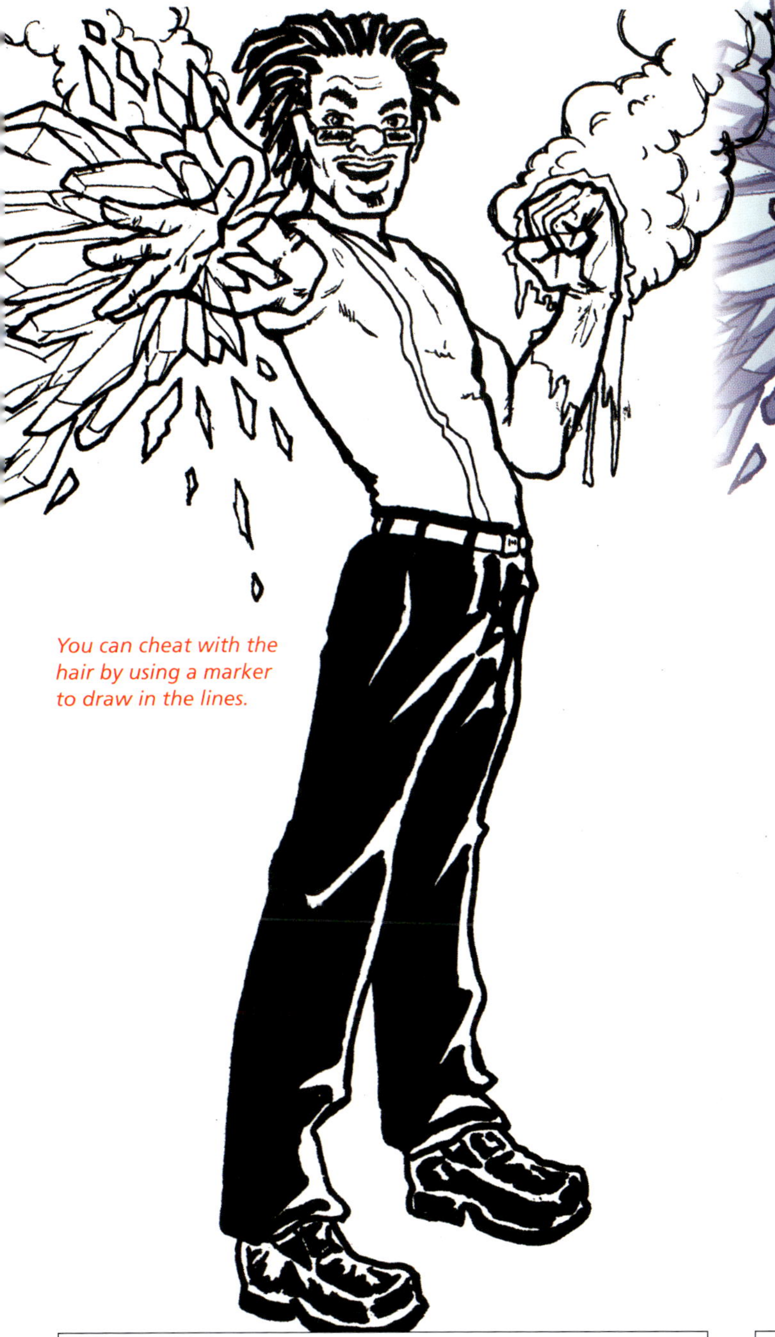

You can cheat with the hair by using a marker to draw in the lines.

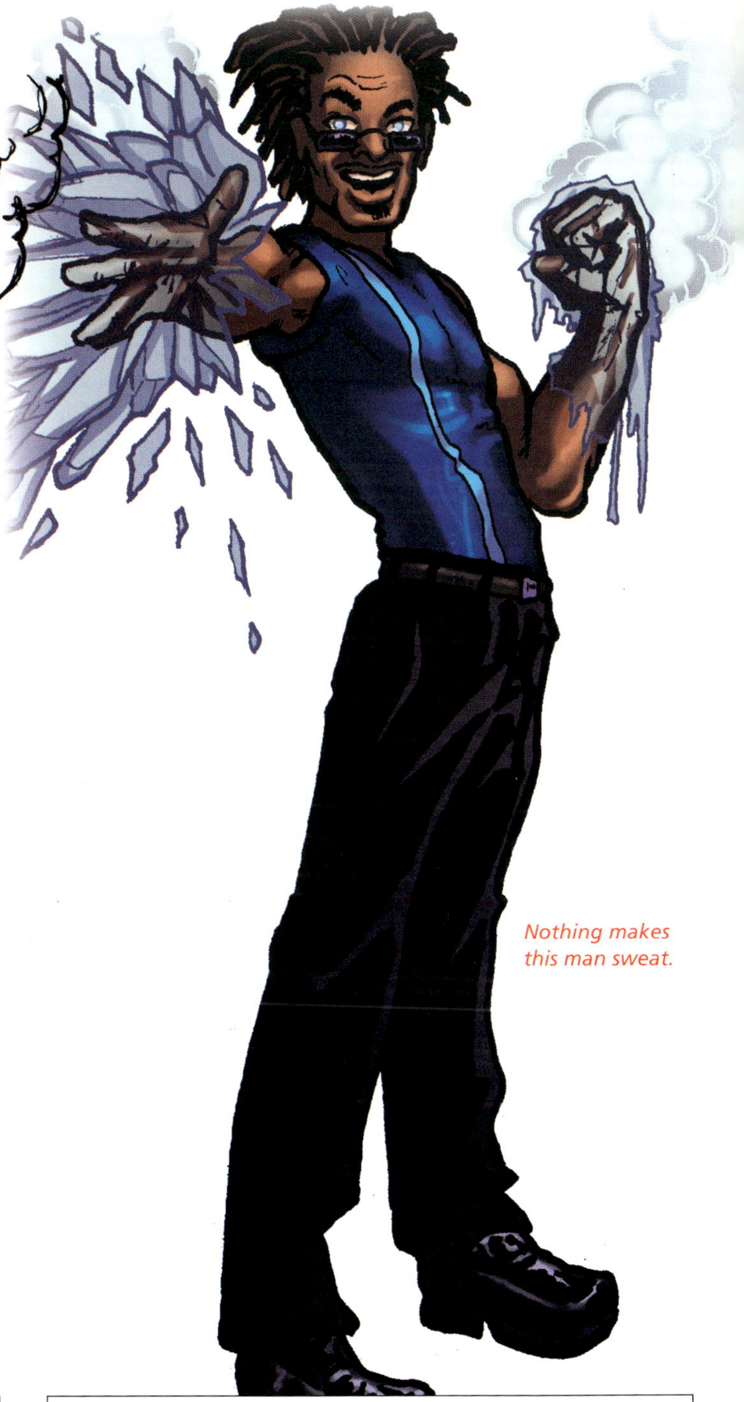

Nothing makes this man sweat.

5. Use heavy blacks on the pants and shoes, leaving white space to define the shiny parts or the folds. Use thinner lines for the ice on his left hand to draw attention more to the fist than the ice. Note that the closer ice crystals use thinner lines, too.

6. Give him brown skin and hair and a bright blue shirt. This contrasts nicely with his skin and his gray pants, and also evokes cold well. Use lighter blues and even violets for the ice, with even lighter blues for the vapor.

LAZERIZE

Lazerize used to like to try to blind airline pilots with a laser pointer. One day his beam reflected off the plane's windshield and bounced right back into his eyes. Instead of blinding him, the laser beam made his eyes throb with power. He found he could charge up his eyes with such energy, amplify it by a thousand, and then blast it back. Soon after, he embarked on his life of crime.

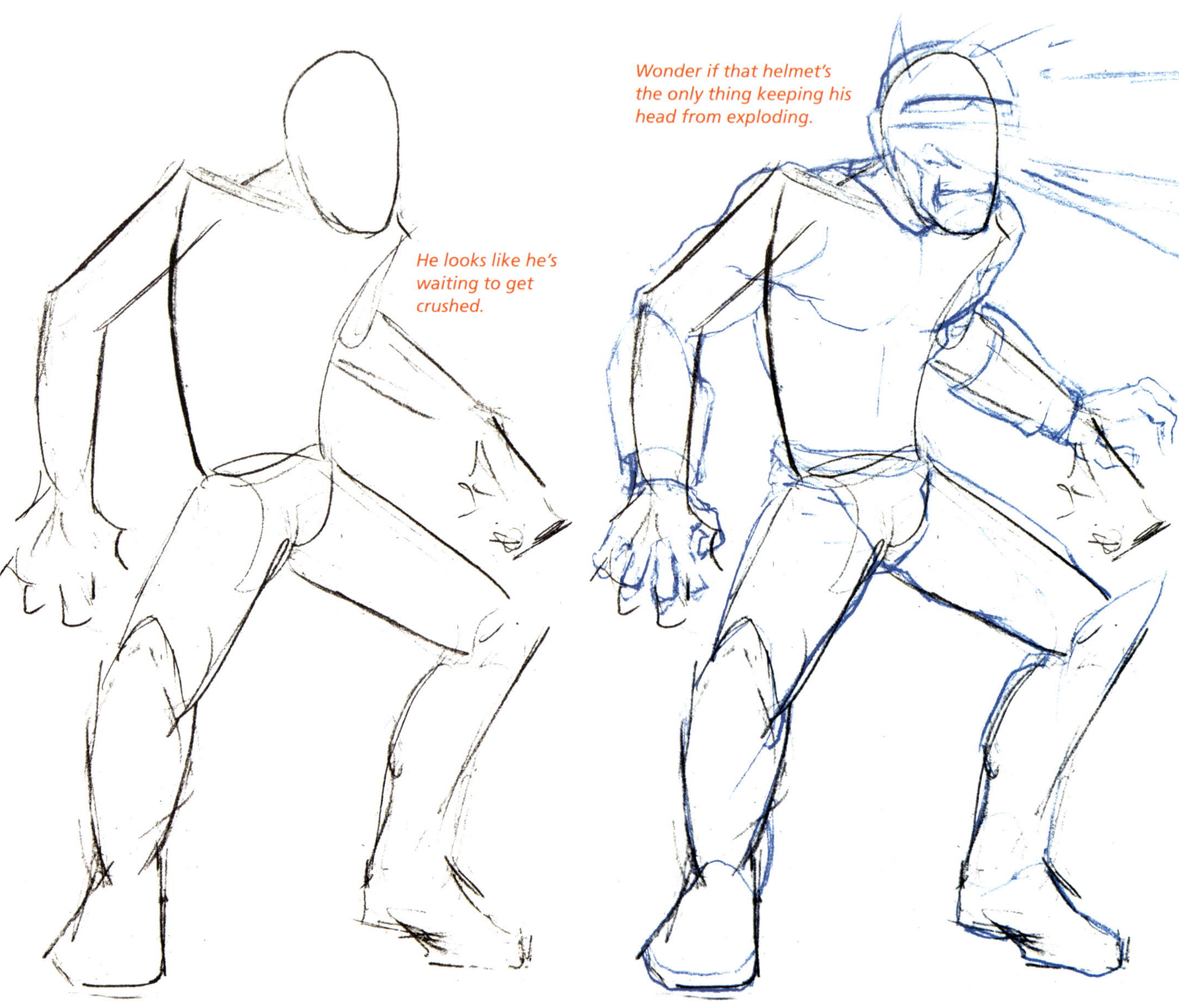

1. Break down Lazerize's basic shape. Since he's the kind of creep who plays with innocent people's lives for fun, Yair puts him in a half-cowering, half-crouching stance. He also exaggerates the hands a bit so he can show the effort it takes for Lazerize to use his powers.

2. Work up Lazerize's musculature and his costume. He wears techy armor on his lower arms and legs, plus a helmet to protect his head. Show the power blasting from his face, too.

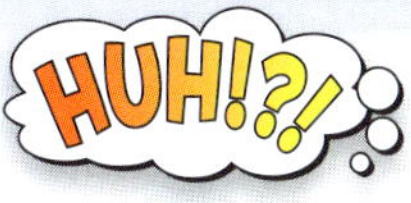

As a visual medium, comics often show the heroes looking great, and the villains as ugly creeps. This implies that the person's exterior mirrors in the interior. Many comics creators like to play with this expectation by introducing ugly heroes and clean-cut villains.

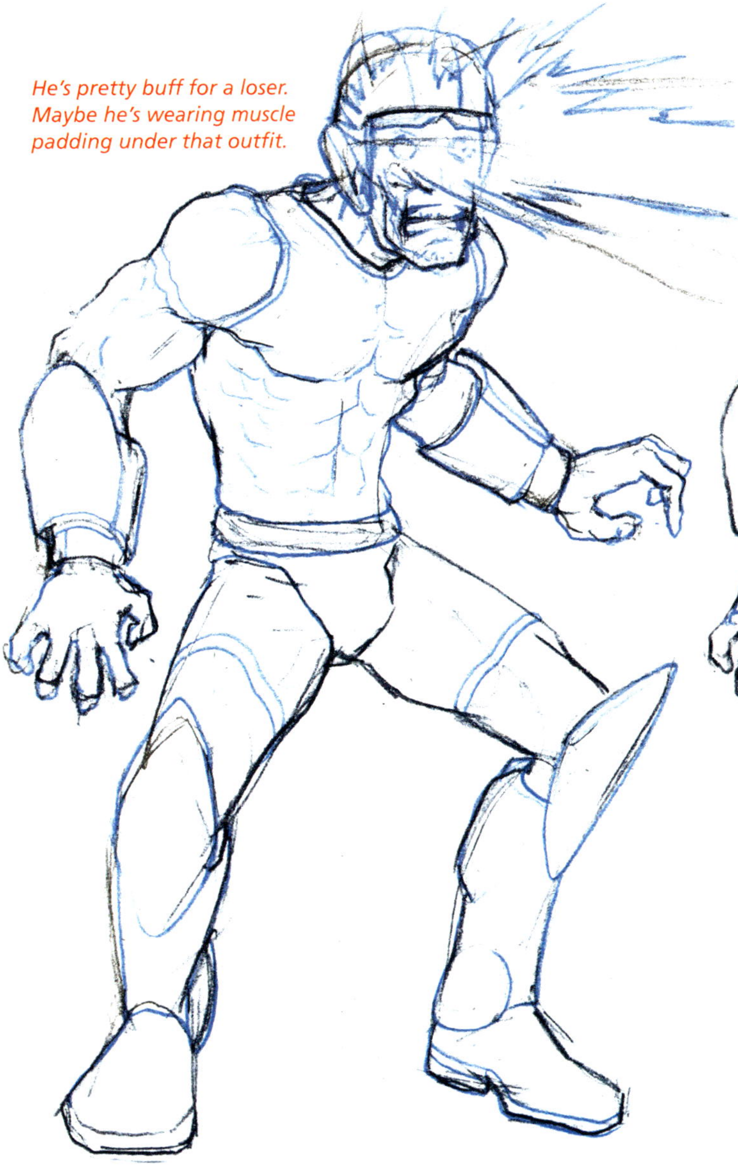

He's pretty buff for a loser. Maybe he's wearing muscle padding under that outfit.

He's gonna blow!

3. Add more details to his face and body. Add in some more muscles. Work at his expression to make him look both angry and scared.

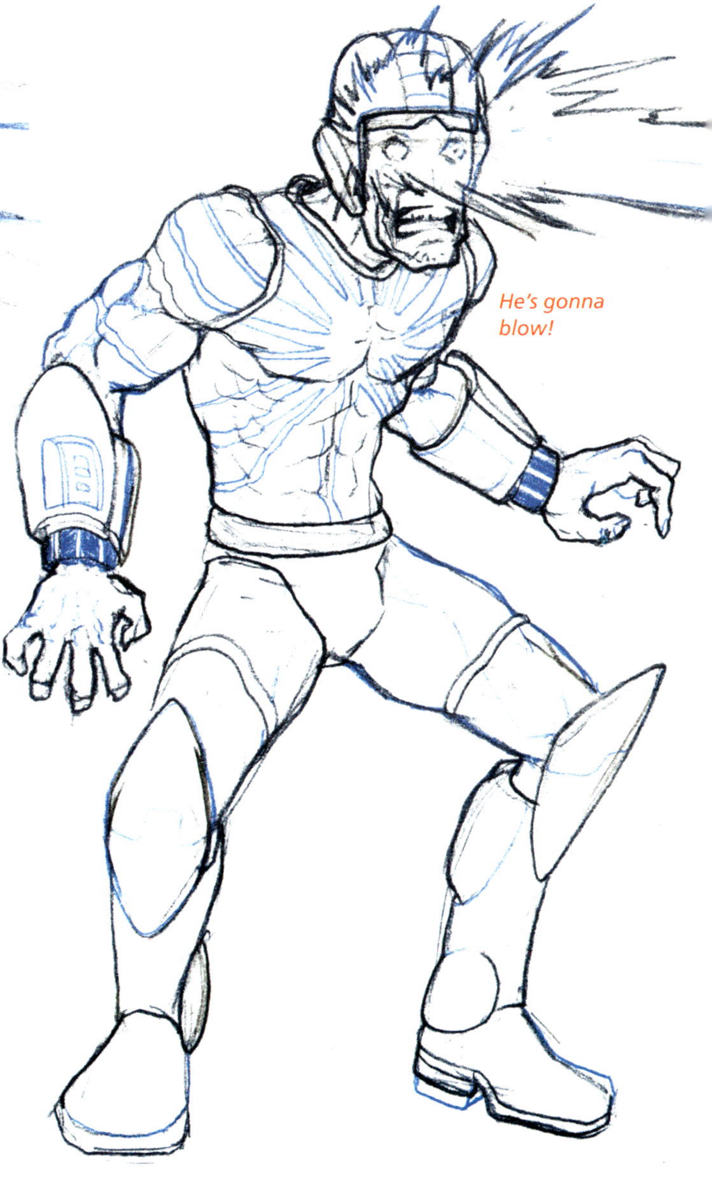

4. A blast pattern on the chest completes the costume, along with a gizmo on his right forearm and a few other details. Some stubble on the chin and lines on the back of his hands make him seem even more tense and desperate.

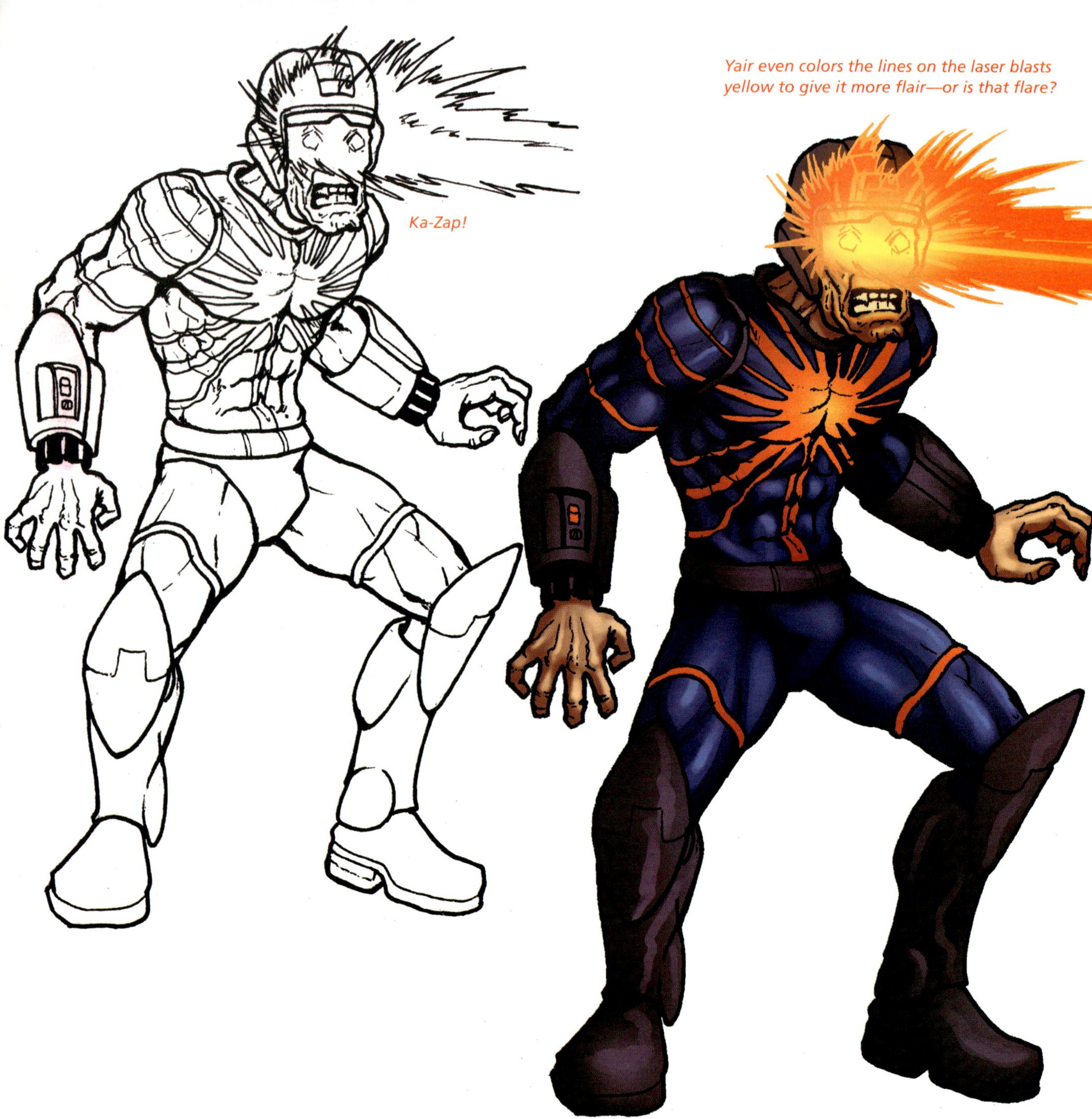

5. For your inks, use thick lines on the outside of the figure and along the edges of the armor. For other details, like the spiky lines along his eye blasts, use lighter lines.

6. Lazerize's costume is blue, with violet-gray armor and orange details. The beams from his eyes are the same basic color as the details, but they run bright yellow through the middle. Using a lighter color against a darker one heightens the contrast and implies that something is glowing.

THE ZAPPER

This daredevil was out parachuting one day when she got her chute caught in a set of high-voltage lines. Rather than getting fried, her body absorbed the electricity, giving her a power as shocking as her costume.

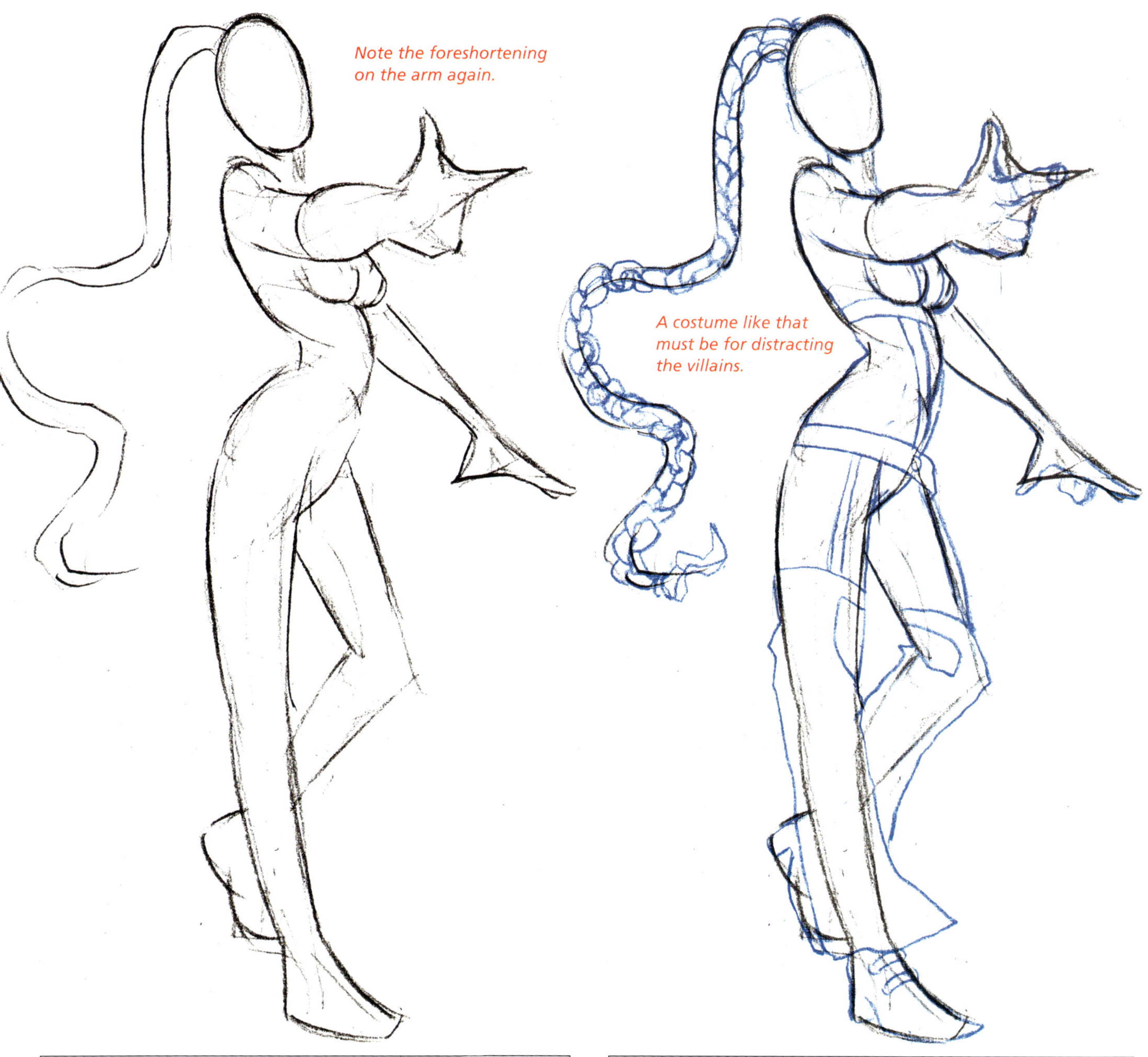

1. Rough out the woman's shape. Yair gives her a dynamic stance, an extra-long ponytail, and a long, trim form. She points her right finger out like she's firing a gun.

2. Add a braid to the ponytail. Put fingers on the hands. Draw in the lines of her costume, including baggy leggings that hang from her mid-thigh.

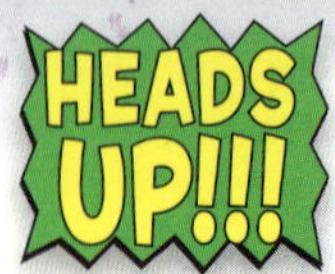

Yair likes to black in parts of the figure with his pencil before he lays down his inks. If that's not your style or you don't care to take the time to manage that, it's fine. Many artists just place large Xs in spaces to be blacked out. When you go back through for inks, you can color in those areas then.

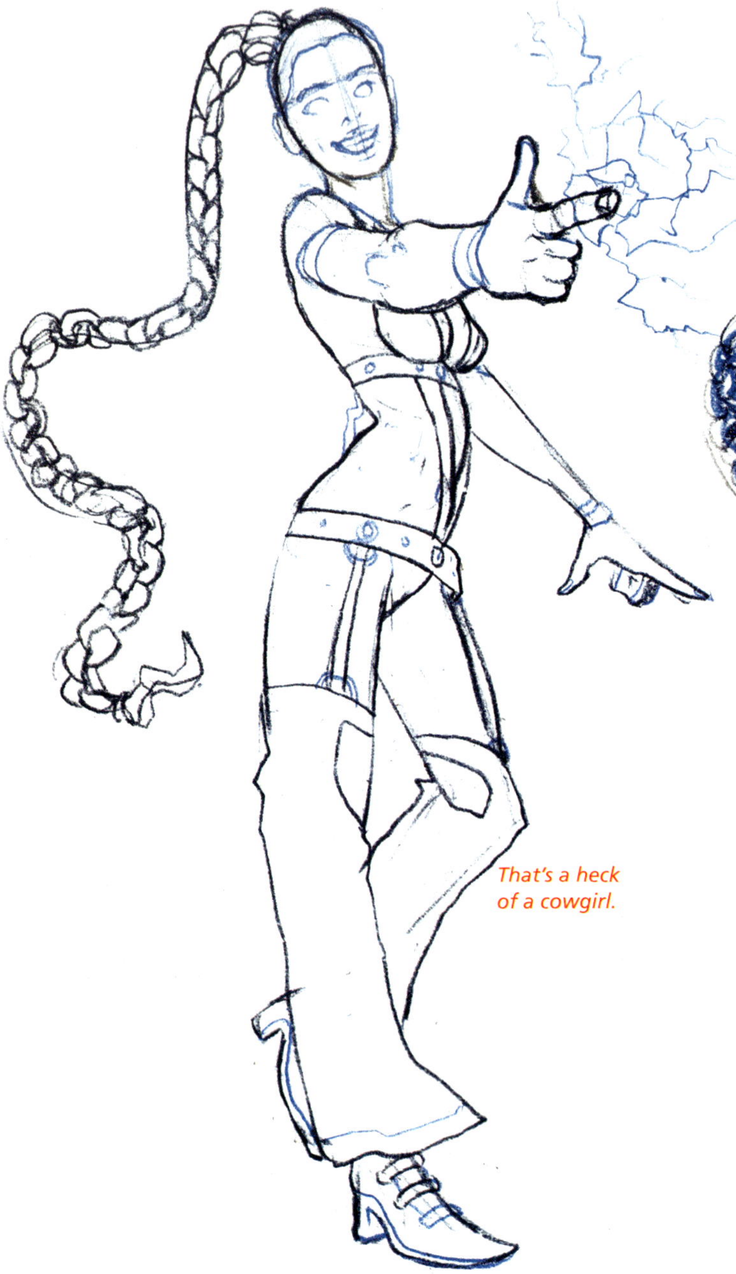

Without any pupils, she looked inhuman.

That's a heck of a cowgirl.

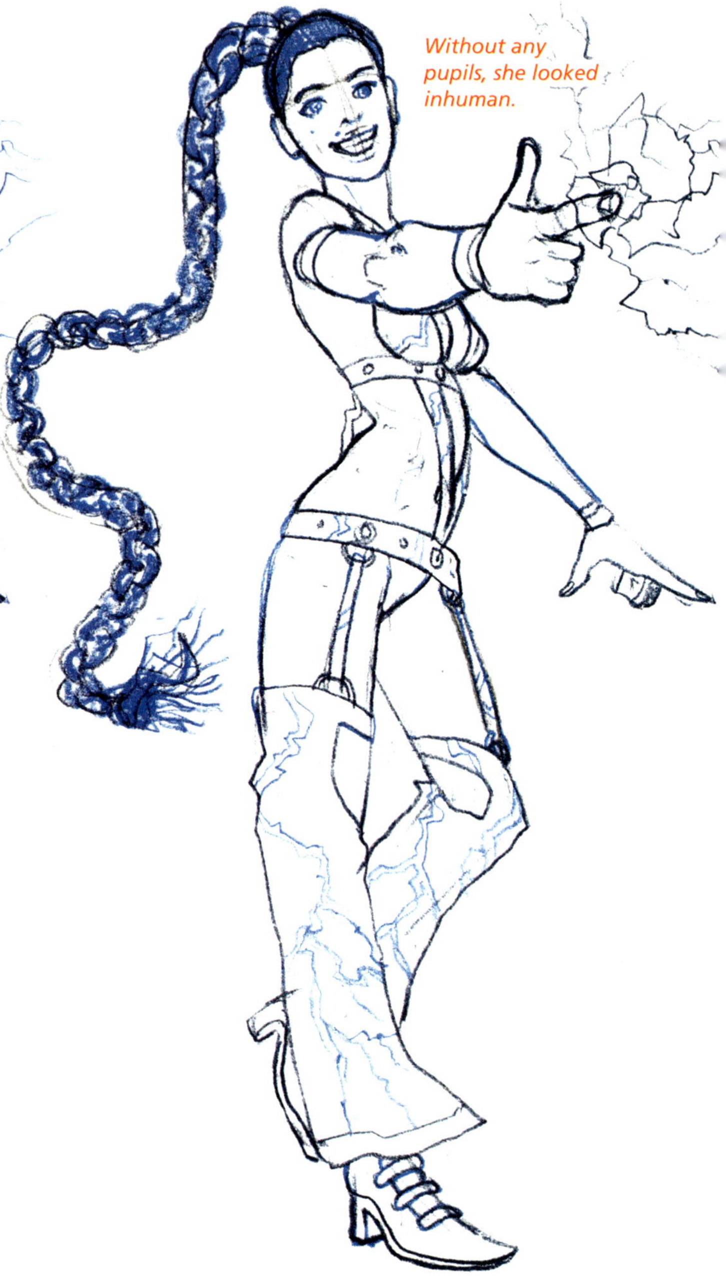

3. Add a hairline and features to her face. She's sassy and confident. More details add texture to her costume. Lightning crackles from her fingertip.

4. Black out the hair. Add lightning patterns to her leggings and the rest of her costume. Draw in her eyes, too.

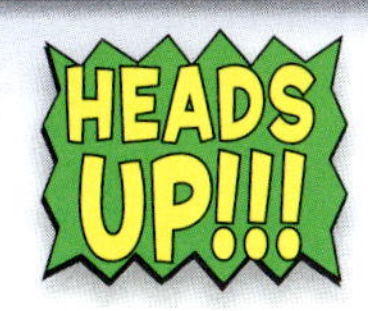

Zapper clearly pushes the boundaries of what's possible to do with a costume. If she had much less on, she'd be naked. While some comics fans appreciate this (it's called "fan service"), it turns others off. Be sure to target your artwork to your audience.

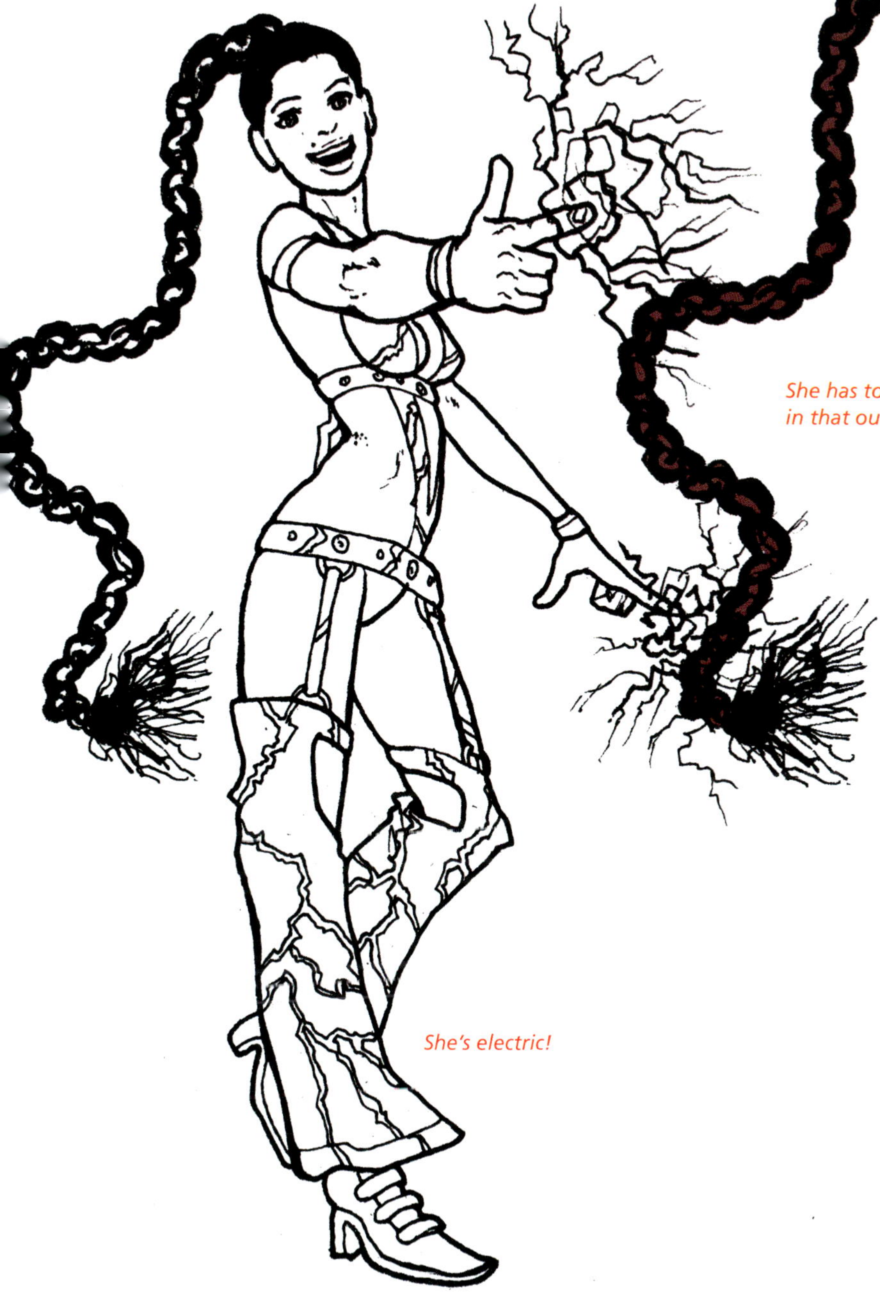

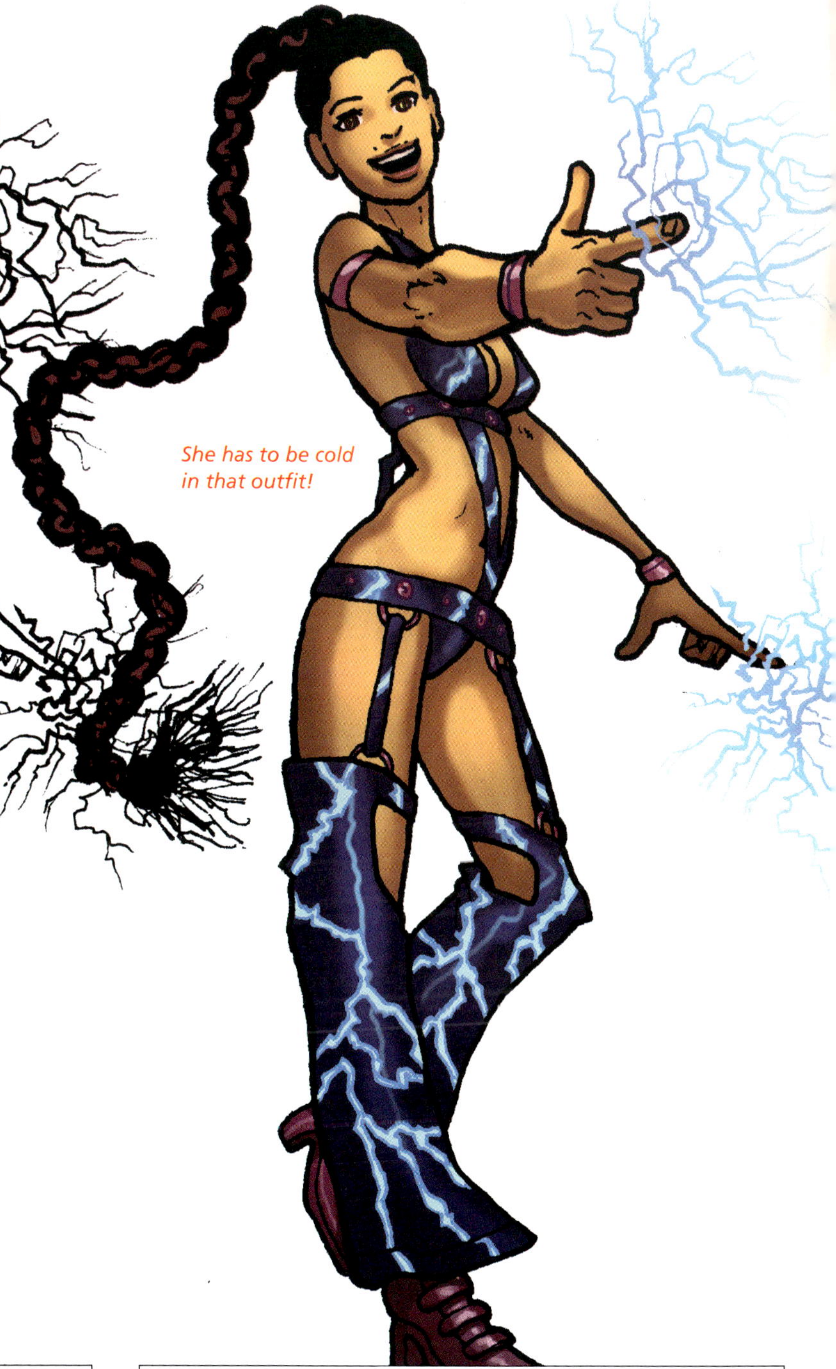

She has to be cold in that outfit!

She's electric!

5. Use dark lines around her body and the edges of her costume. Use thinner lines for the lightning on the costume, but vary the lines for the lightning itself. Use thicker lines near the source of power and branch them out to thinner lines as you go, as with the limbs on a tree.

6. Use brown for her hair, as highlights in the black inks you laid down. She has deeply tanned skin from all that exposure. Her outfit is indigo with electric blue details. The lightning from her fingers is the same color as that on her clothes. Add in some purple boots and accents, and she's ready to get cracking.

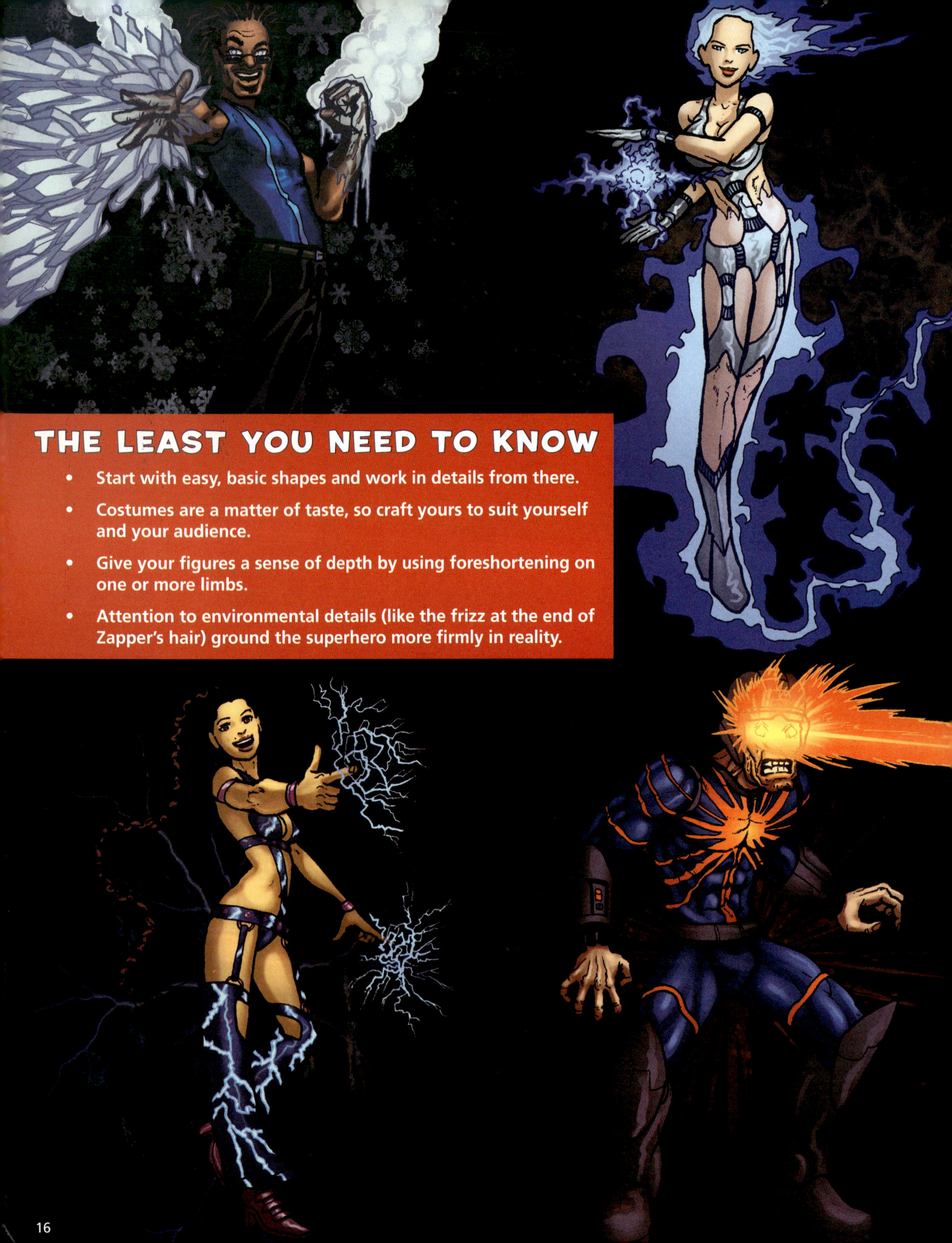

THE LEAST YOU NEED TO KNOW

- Start with easy, basic shapes and work in details from there.
- Costumes are a matter of taste, so craft yours to suit yourself and your audience.
- Give your figures a sense of depth by using foreshortening on one or more limbs.
- Attention to environmental details (like the frizz at the end of Zapper's hair) ground the superhero more firmly in reality.

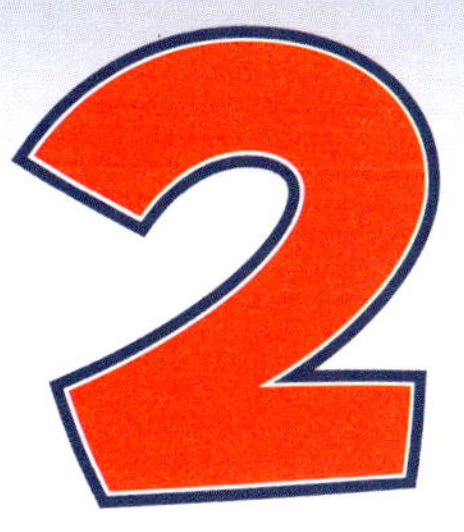

Scrappers: Always Itching for a Fight

In This Chapter

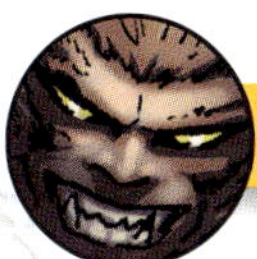

- A real animal

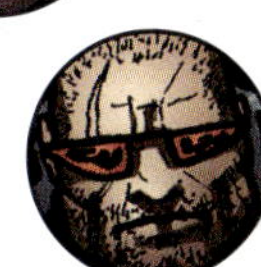

- A very bad man

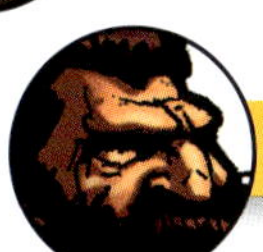

- A hero from the highlands

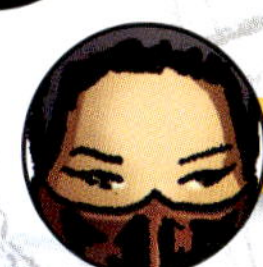

- A Japanese girl

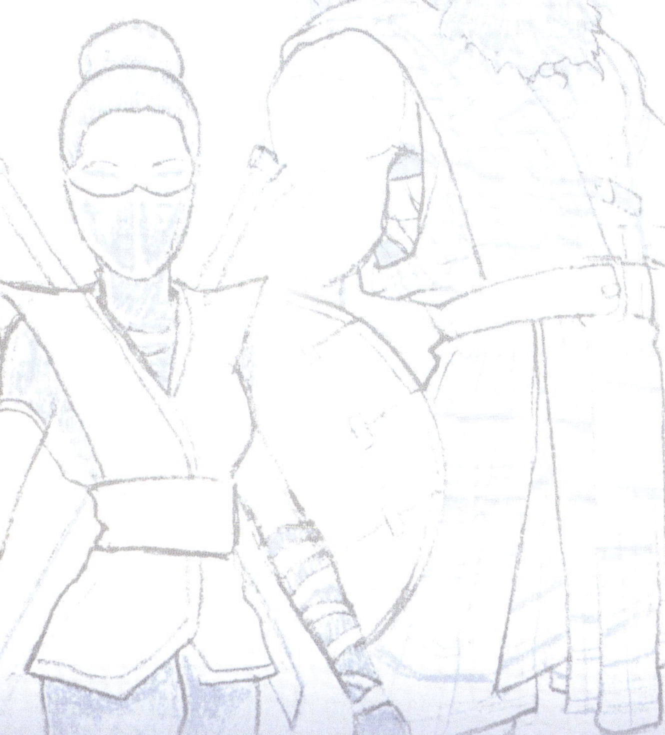

For some reason, most comic book conflicts often devolve into a toe-to-toe fight. That's when it's time to call in the scrappers. This rough-and-tumble crew excels at creating mayhem, up-close-and-personal style.

The Animal charges in as the first in our lineup. He's more savage than any regular person, but his human mind gives him a cunning that no average animal can match. He's an unparalleled hunter, able to track down his prey under even the worst conditions.

Bad Man is a bruiser of the bone-breaking kind. He's hard as rock and just as unforgiving. He wears spikes as mores rather than a fashion accessory. They're part of his way of life.

Claymore hails from the highlands of Scotland, and he wears the warrior garb of a nearly forgotten age. Others might require two hands to wield his massive sword, but he swings it like a baton in one.

Trained as a ninja from birth, Shoujo has chosen to step from the shadows to fight against her former masters. She wears a mask to conceal her true identity while she seeks to tear back the veils that hide her foes.

THE ANIMAL

The Animal spent his days in the north woods of Wisconsin, hunting, fishing, and living off the land. One day, he ran into a party of poachers who tried to hunt him. Nearly dead, he had a vision from the spirit of the woods. He awoke to find himself transformed into the Animal, and he has dedicated himself to defending the woods and finding his killers ever since.

Don't let him sink his teeth into you.

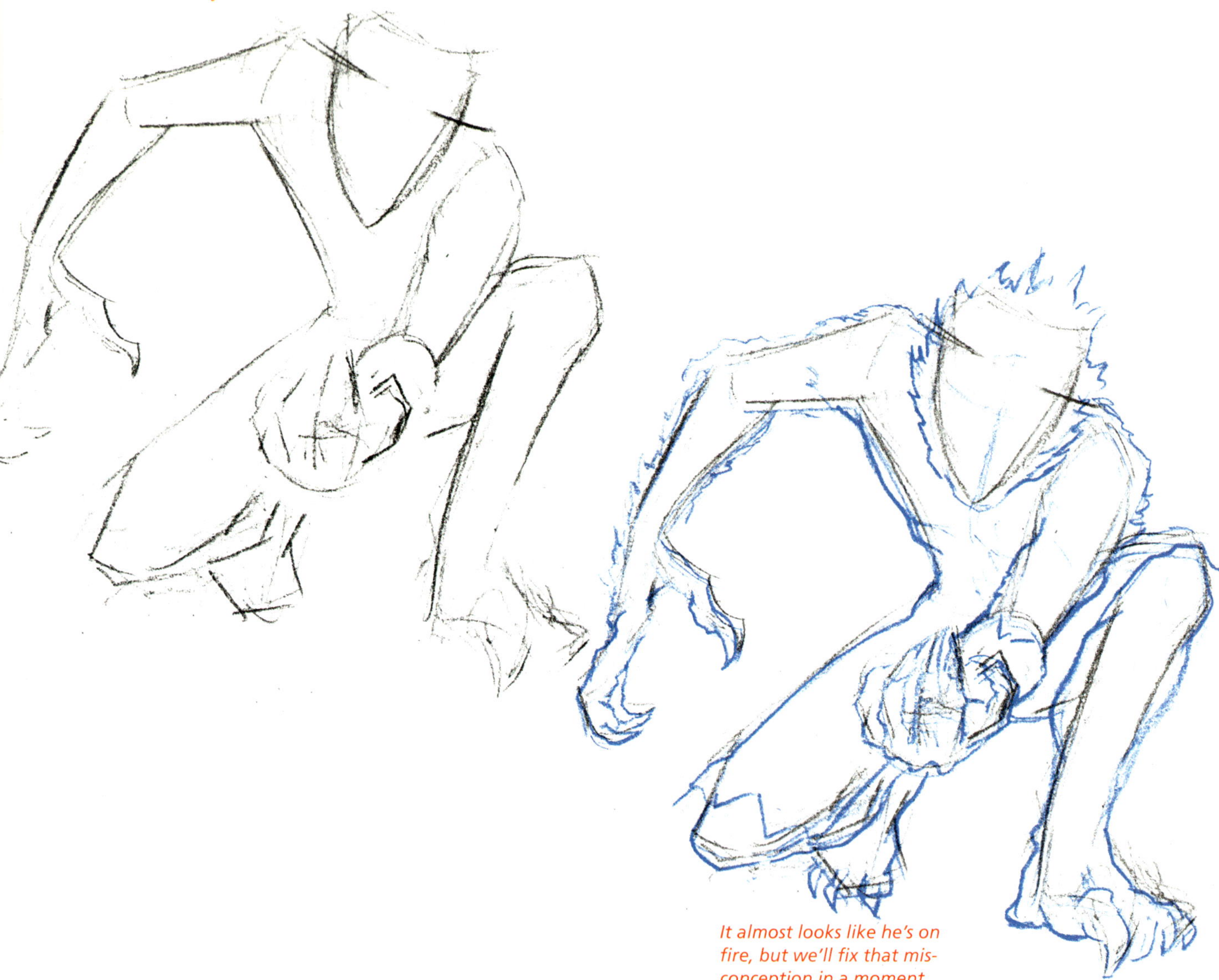

It almost looks like he's on fire, but we'll fix that misconception in a moment.

1. Break down the Animal's figure. Since he's a feral creature, Yair puts him in a crouch, low to the ground, as if he's just stopped walking on all fours. The triangular head and the extra-long hands make it clear at once that this is no normal man.

2. Add fingers and talons to the hands and feet. Give him a ratty pair of pants, for modesty's sake if nothing else. Line his head and limbs with fur.

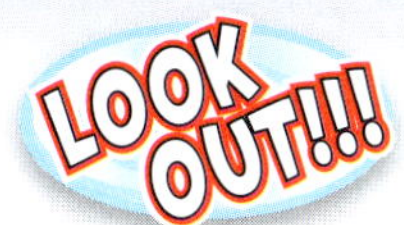

Crouches can be hard to pull off because they involve the foreshortening of multiple limbs all at once. Be sure to study your anatomy to make sure you get it right. A photo reference or a poseable doll comes in handy at such times.

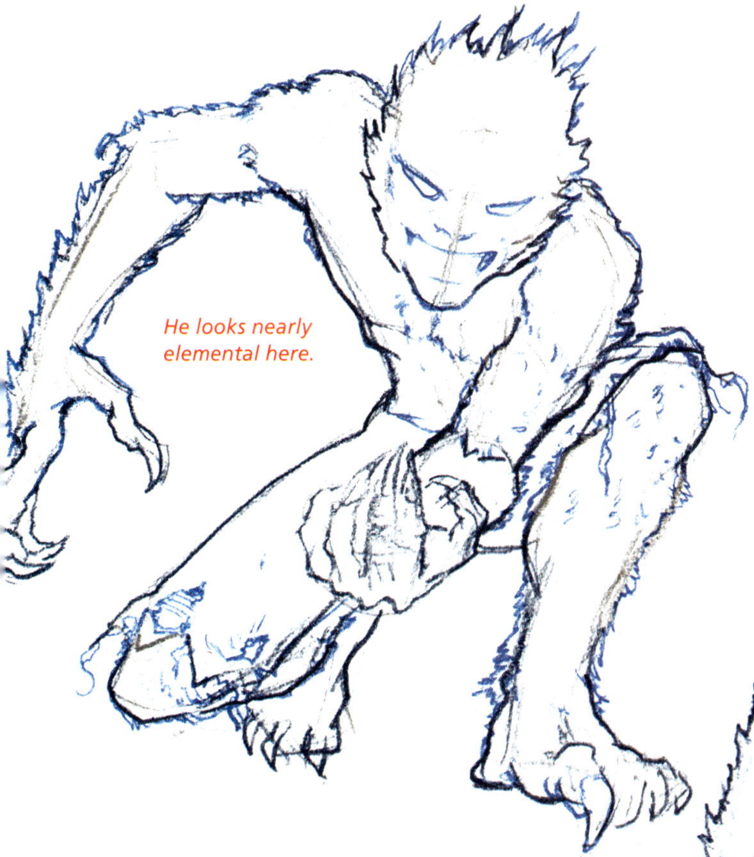

He looks nearly elemental here.

He's so uncuddly, he's the anti-Teddy bear.

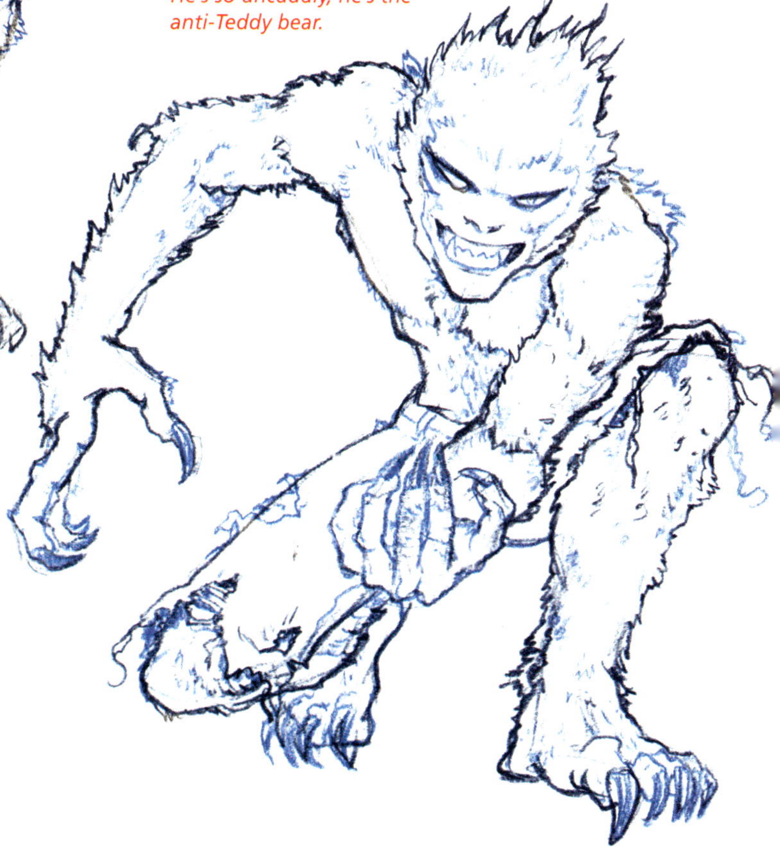

3. Give him tight, slanted eyes and a toothy, feral grin. Tatter the pants a bit more, and add some extra texture to that fur. Show the edges of the talons, right where they grow out of his skin.

4. Sketch in those vicious teeth. Add details to the face (which is hairless, unlike the rest of him), and work in from the edges to show the Animal's fur.

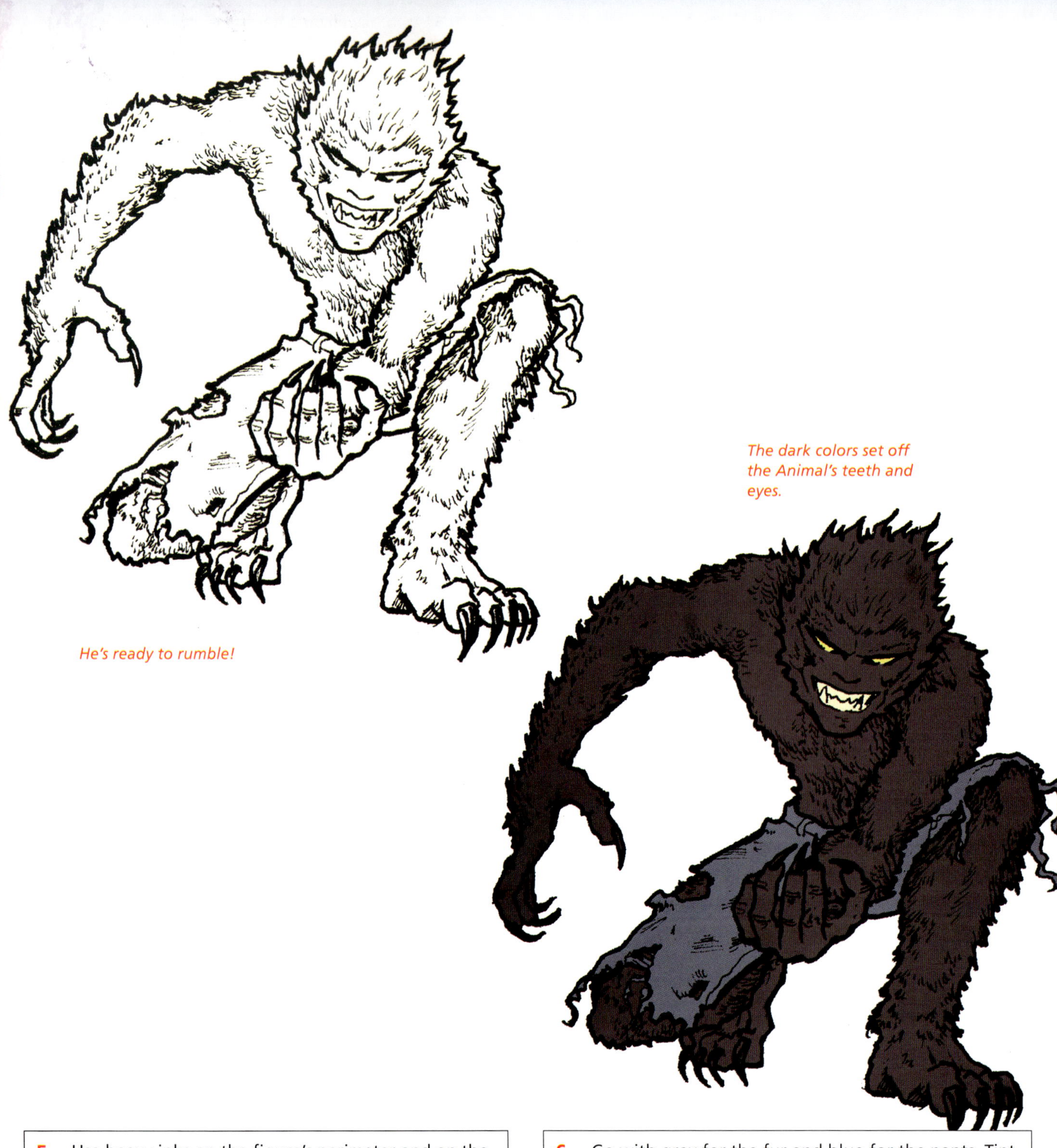

He's ready to rumble!

The dark colors set off the Animal's teeth and eyes.

5. Use heavy inks on the figure's perimeter and on the edges of his pants. For the fur, use short, lighter lines. Apply them as you would cross-hatching for distinctive shades.

6. Go with gray for the fur and blue for the pants. Tint his eyes yellow, and leave his teeth white.

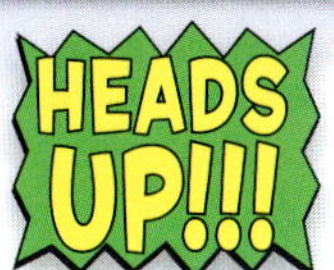

When drawing fur, pick a direction and go with it. Usually the hair is swept back from the figure's front and center. You can play with other configurations, but take care in doing so.

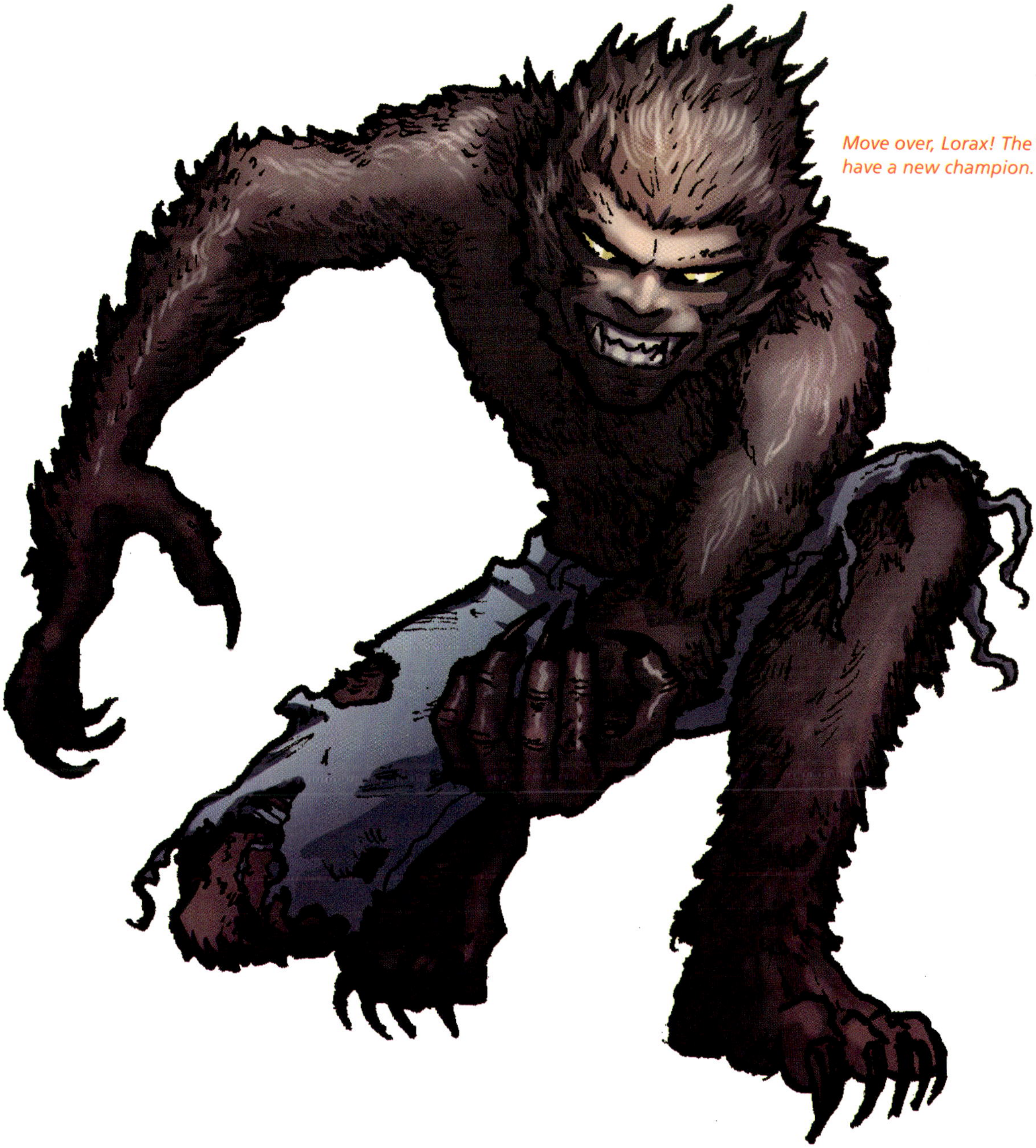

Move over, Lorax! The trees have a new champion.

7. Apply lighter browns to the Animal's fur to provide highlights. Also, draw in lines of fur in an even lighter color. This makes the fur look even more real.

THE BAD MAN

The Bad Man started out as a bodybuilder. After losing a competition, however, he decided to put himself up as a guinea pig for an experimental steroid. It made him larger than ever—more than human—but it also stripped away every emotion he'd ever had. Now he's a remorseless enforcer, ready to tear a foe to pieces at a moment's notice.

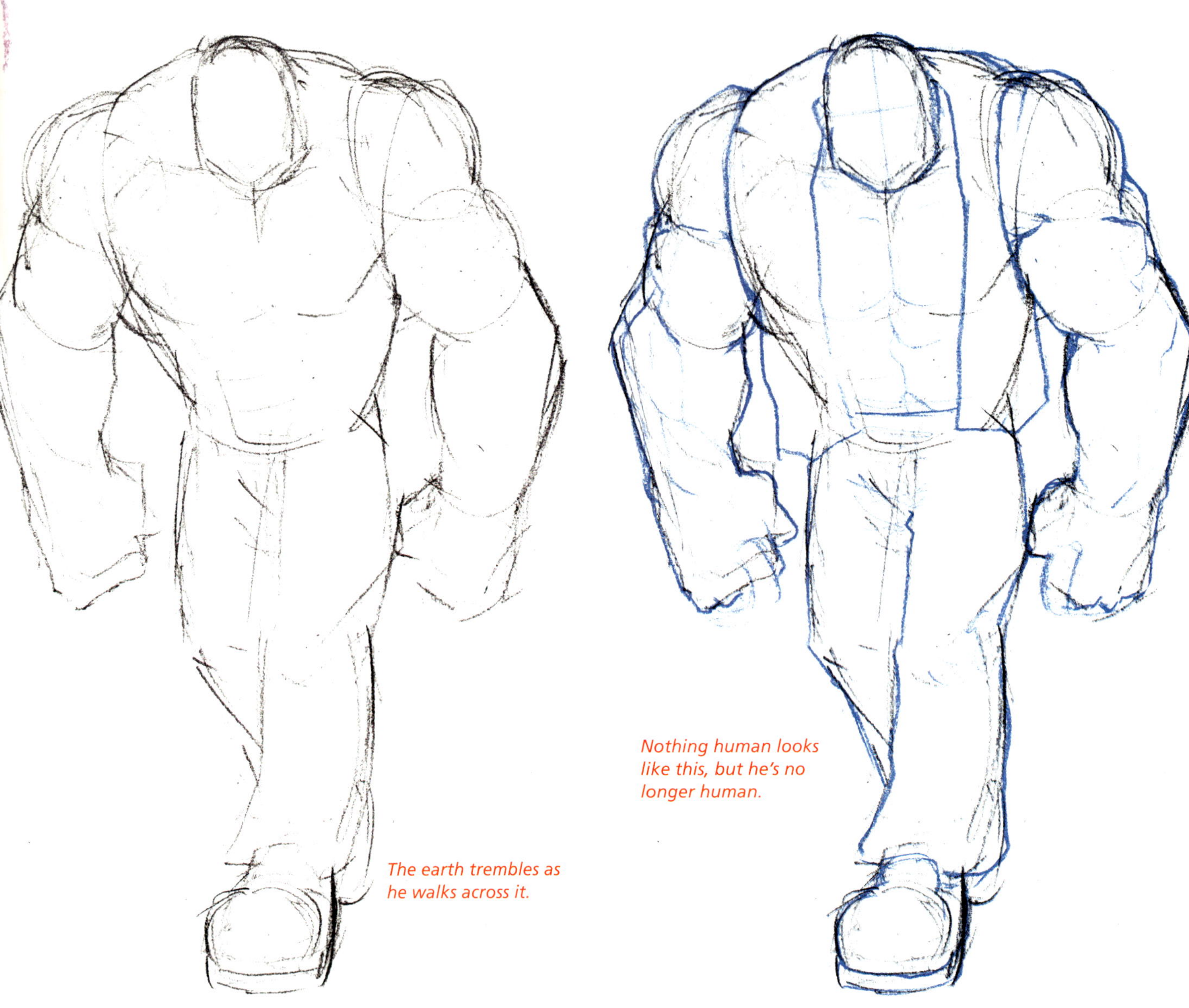

The earth trembles as he walks across it.

Nothing human looks like this, but he's no longer human.

1. Work out the Bad Man's breakdown. He's like a normal human, only thicker everywhere. His shoulders are so large they almost top his head. He's a mountain of a man.

2. Put some clothes on him: pants, a shirt, a vest, shoes. Define his musculature a bit more. When in doubt, make it bigger.

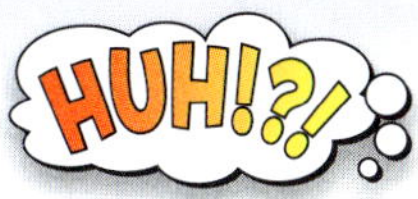

One way to make your characters more interesting is to link them to a current situation in modern life. In the 1960s, all the powers seemed to come from radiation. In the 1980s, it was genetics. The Bad Man's powers come from experimental steroids, an idea ripped straight from today's headlines.

Nothing gets close to him without paying for it in blood.

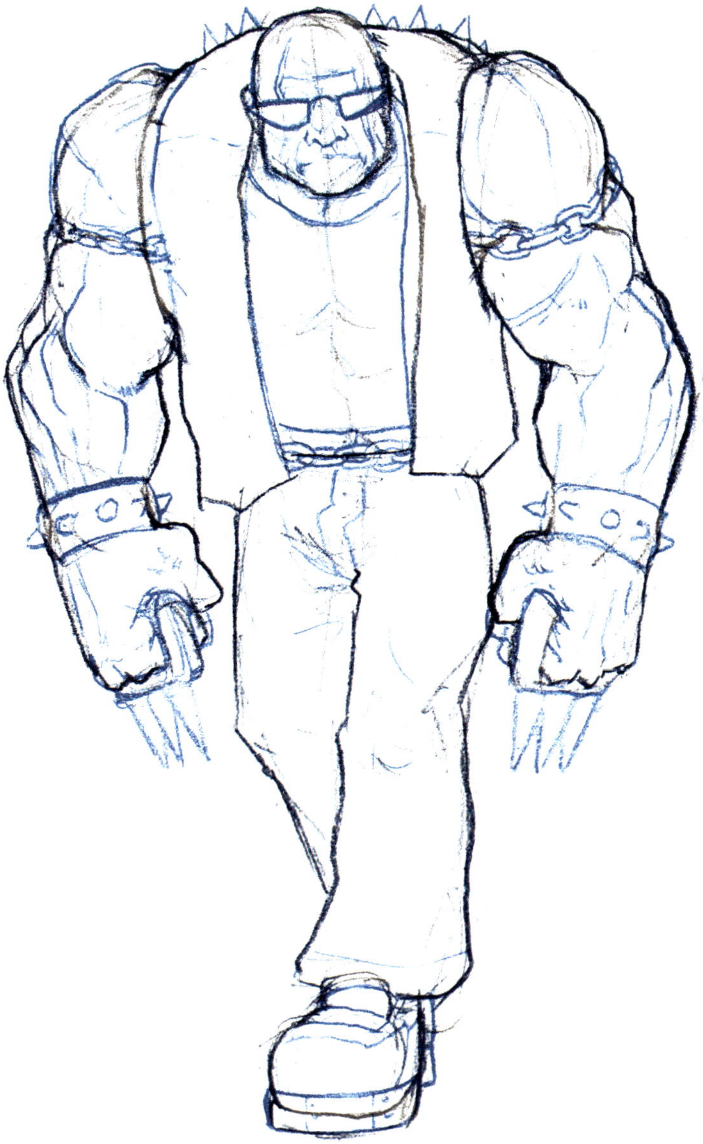

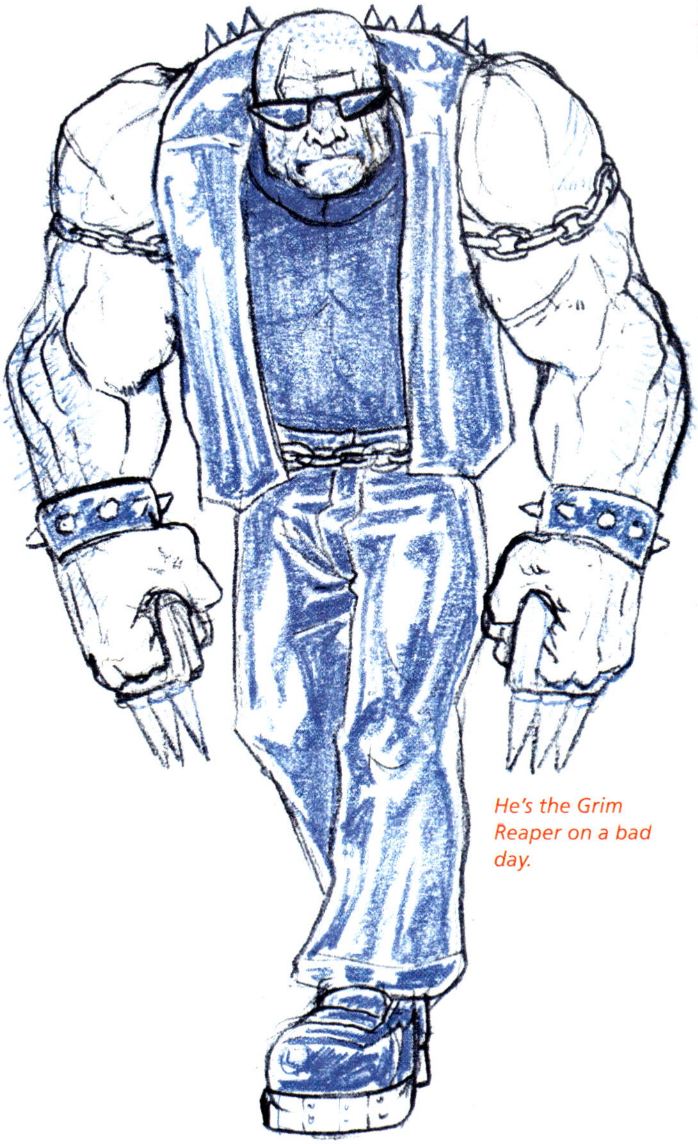

He's the Grim Reaper on a bad day.

3. Put some shades on his face, and wrap some chains and spikes around him. Add some spiked steel knuckles. The eyes are the windows of the soul, and by hiding them away, you dehumanize him further.

4. Black out his clothes. Black is the color of death, and he exudes it. Add some dark hair to his arms and stubble to his face and scalp to emphasize his darkness.

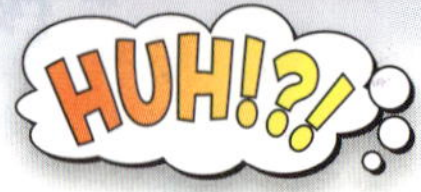

Many of the names of superhero archetypes come from the first superhero role-playing game, *Champions*. This game represented one of the first and best endeavors to classify and name as many types of superheroes as possible, all in the name of making it easier for you to create similar characters yourself.

The hair on his arms is longer than the hair on his face!

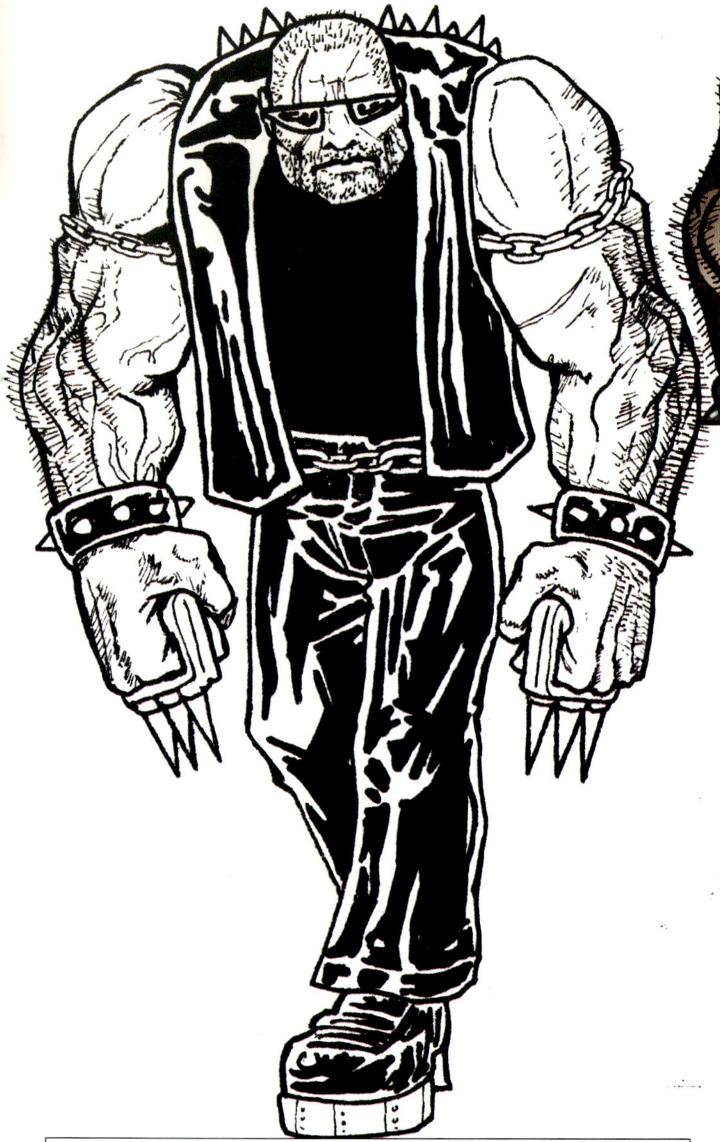

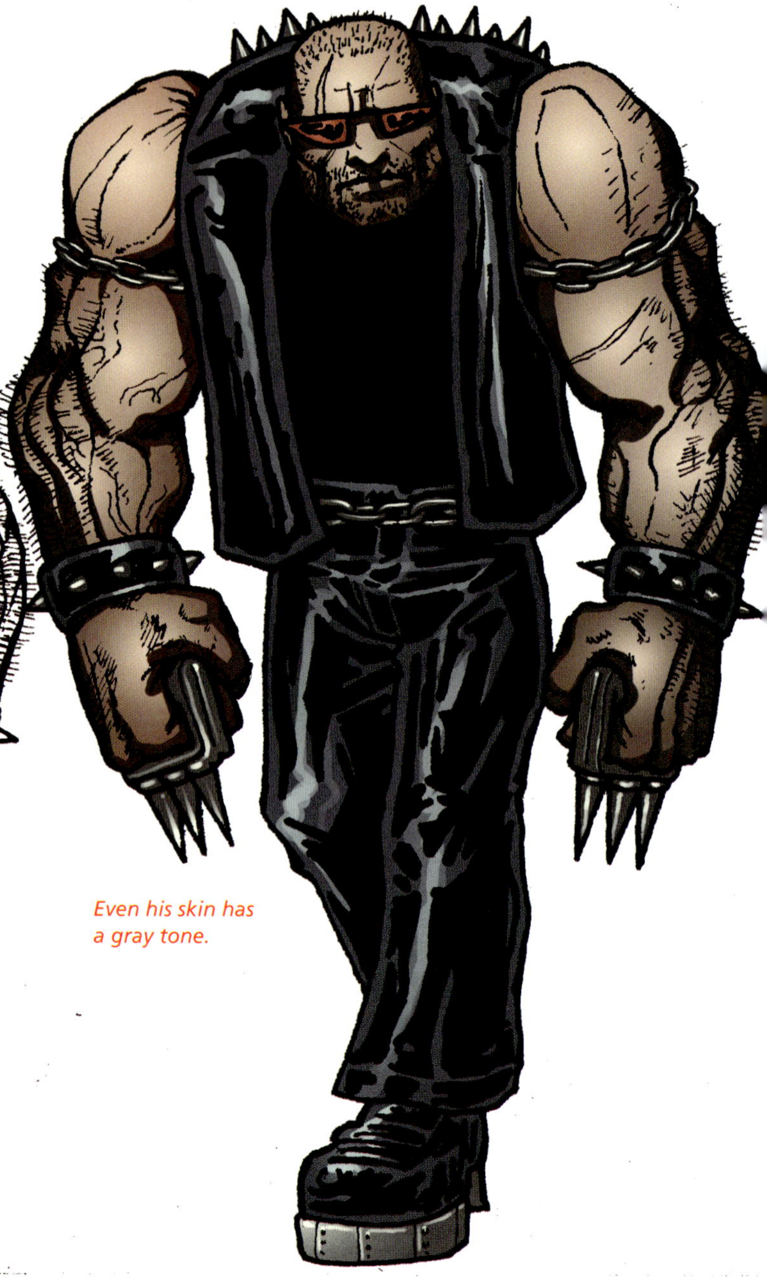

Even his skin has a gray tone.

5. Go mostly with thick, heavy inks here. Leave some white space on the clothes to help define their shape. Use lighter lines for the hair on his arms. Use heavy ones for the edges of his shades.

6. Color his clothes black with gray highlights. Add silvery tones to the metallic bits, but no sparkles. This man does not shine.

CLAYMORE

Claymore—once a mighty warrior in the service of Robert the Bruce—was nearly killed near a loch in the highlands of Scotland in the year 1300. He crawled into the waters to escape his attackers, and darkness took him. He awakened seven centuries later to find the world had changed all around him. Although he does not know it consciously, he can take on the form of a mighty sea monster, the sort of which has long been rumored to inhabit a particular Scottish loch.

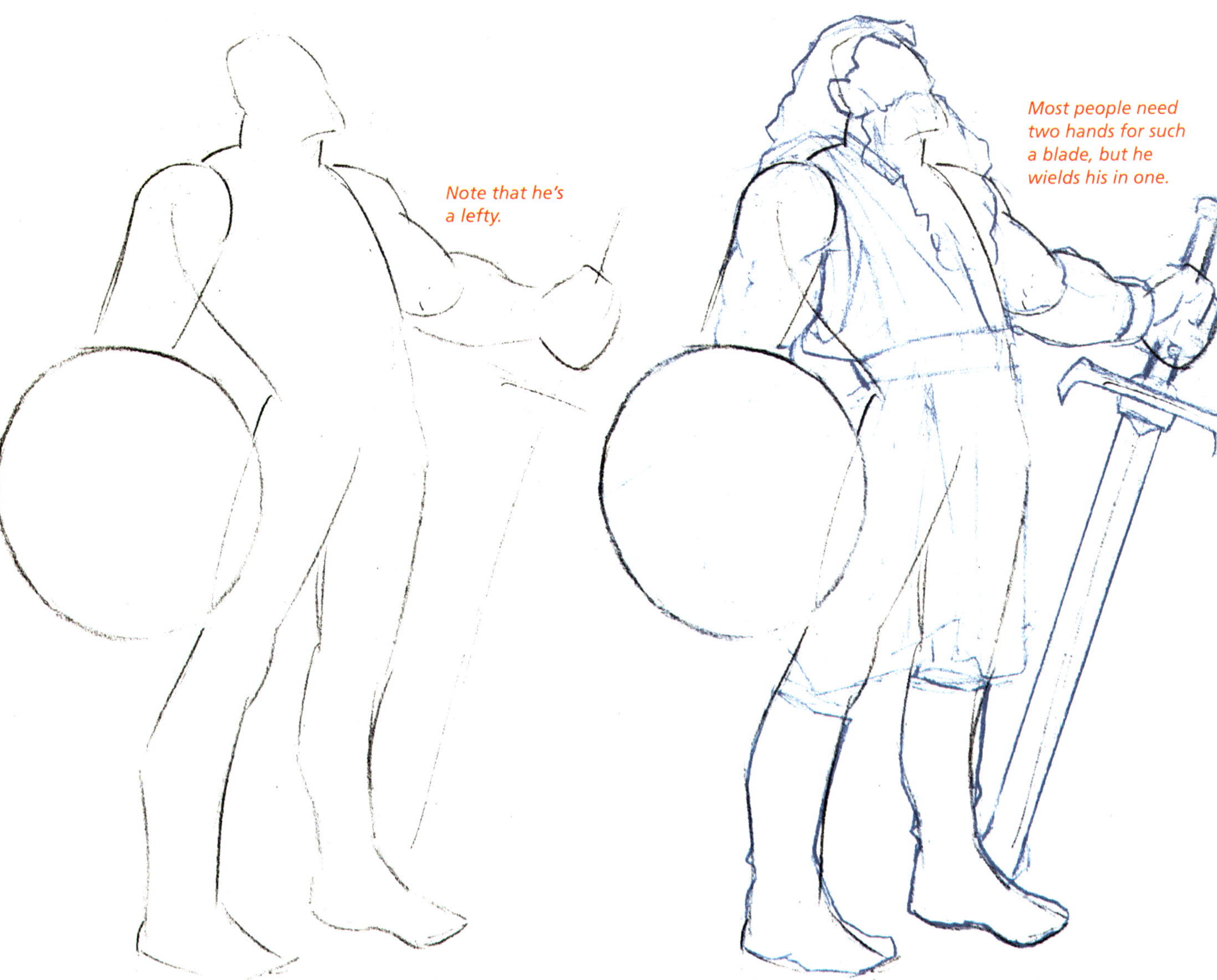

1. Give Claymore a heroic pose. Put a shield on his arm and a sword in his hand. He has a square jaw that could be made of granite.

2. Add some clothing to Claymore. He wears the traditional highlander's kilt (don't call it a skirt!). He wears his hair and his beard long and bushy. His sword is a massive Claymore, from which he takes his nom de guerre.

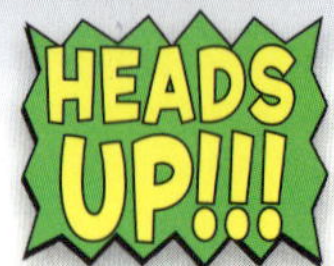

Lots of comic book characters have their roots in history. Be warned, though, that if you use a historical or mythological person for your hero or villain, you may find it hard to defend the originality of your creation. Such characters are in the public domain and are thus free for anyone to use. While Claymore has strong roots in the Scottish wars of independence, he is not a named historical figure and so is protected by copyright laws.

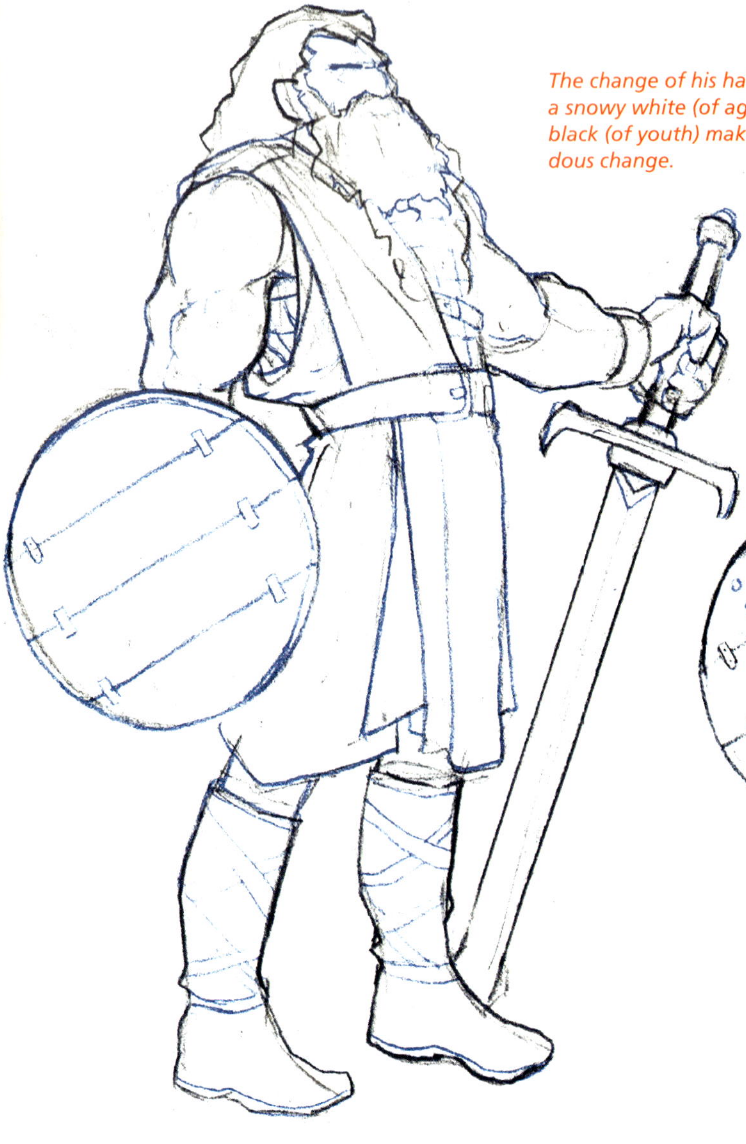

The change of his hair color from a snowy white (of age) to an inky black (of youth) makes a tremendous change.

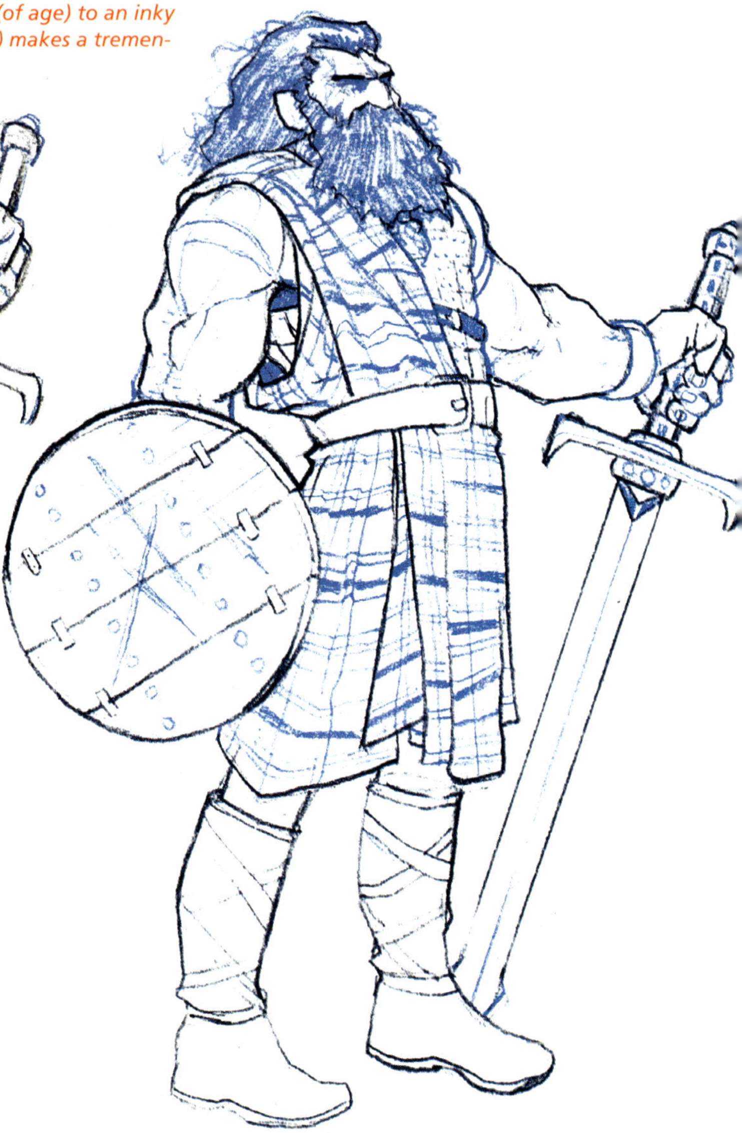

He almost has a godlike quality about him—that of a god of war.

3. Work those details. Add planking to his shield, and place binding straps on his boots. Give him a deep, furrowed brow. Define the folds of his kilt.

4. Go nuts on the details. Add rivets to the shield, and scars, too. Blacken his hair and beard. Add a tartan (plaid) pattern to his clothing. Add a leather wrap to the hilt of his sword.

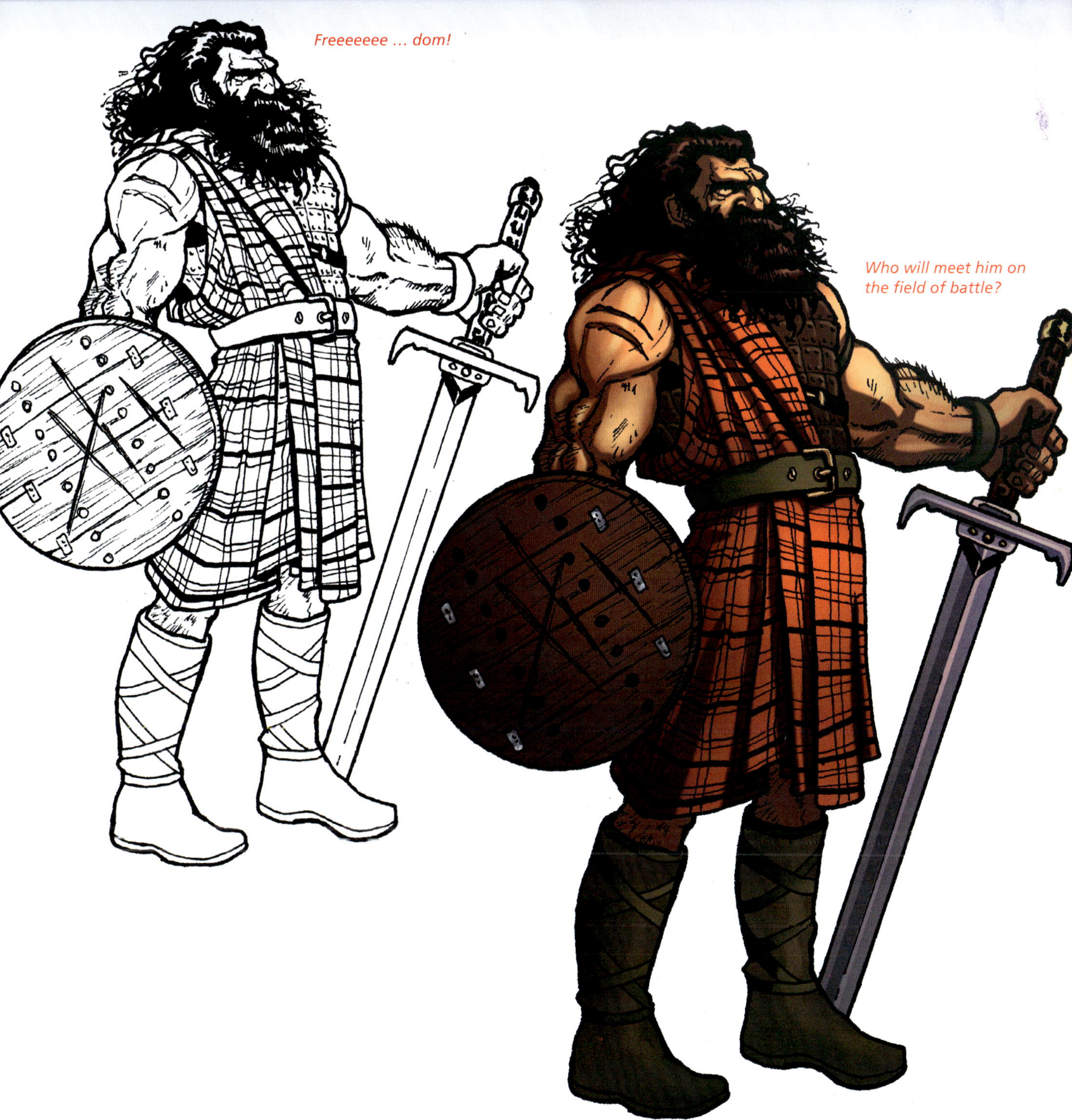

5. Ink like you normally would. Take special care with the tartan, which employs both thin and thick lines in its pattern. Note how the use of several thin lines makes the scars on the shield look more real.

6. Add brown to Claymore's hair, and use a similar shade on his chest armor, hilt wrap, boots, belt, and shield. A bluish gray works well for all the steel bits. You can play with the tartan all you like, and even research historical patterns. Here Yair goes with a simple red and black.

THE SHOUJO

Shoujo was trained from birth to become a ninja. When sent out on her first assignment, though, she discovered she was meant to assassinate her father. Balking at such a charge, she left her trainers and has been fighting a secret war against them ever since.

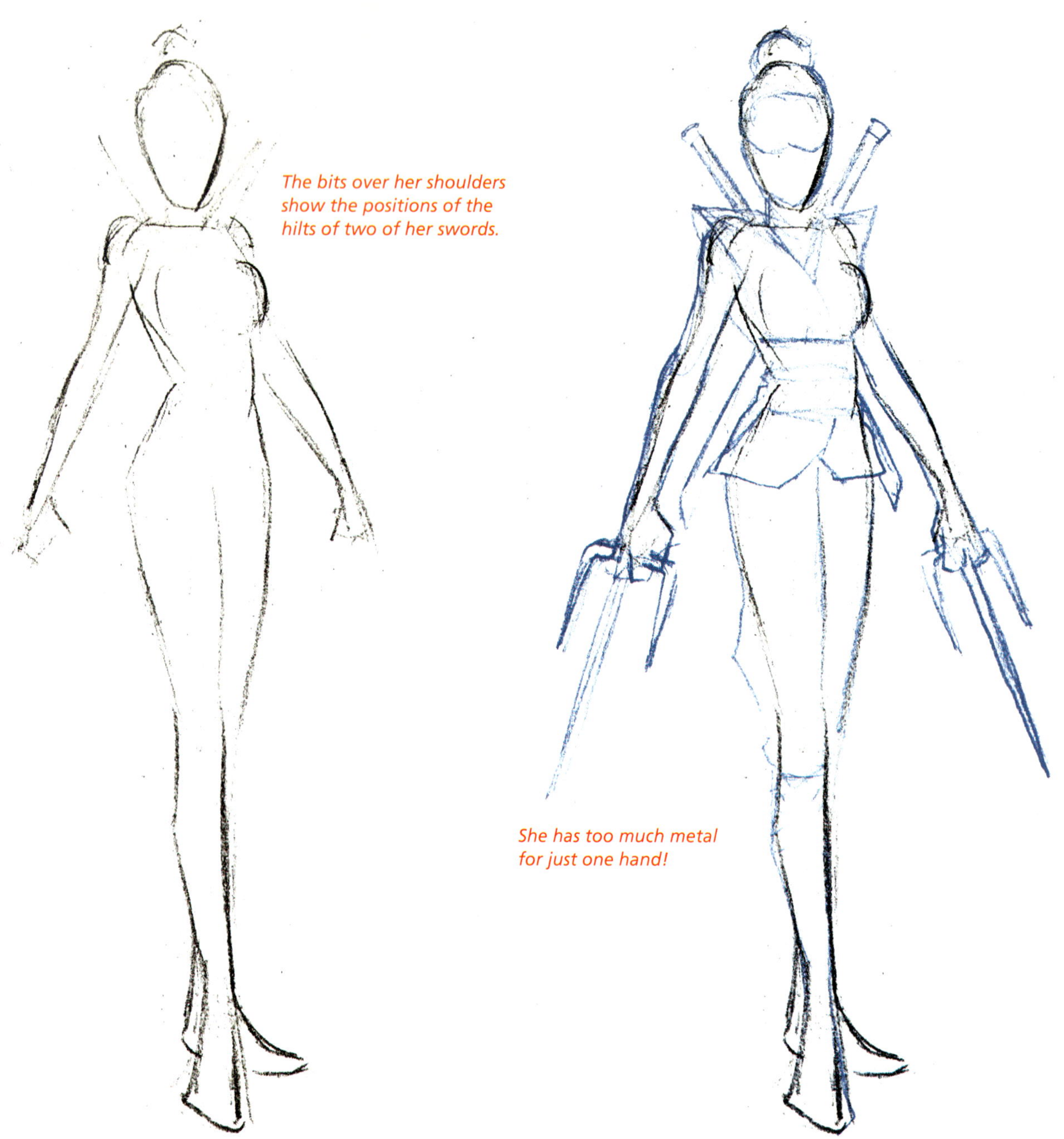

The bits over her shoulders show the positions of the hilts of two of her swords.

She has too much metal for just one hand!

1. Pose Shoujo for the picture. She is a slim and fit Japanese girl, nearly of age but not quite. Yair goes with a long-limbed teenager who stands ready to burst into motion.

2. Add clothing and weaponry. She carries a pair of wakizashi (short, cutting swords) on her back, and a sai (short, stabbing sword) in each hand. She also wears a short robe, boots, and a mask that covers her lower face.

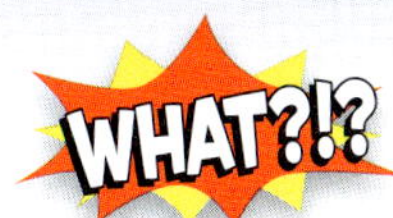

Shoujo is Japanese for "girl." It's also used to refer to Japanese comics (manga) created for an audience of girls. For more details, see *The Complete Idiot's Guide to Drawing Manga Illustrated: Shoujo*, which Matt wrote with Tomoko Taniguchi.

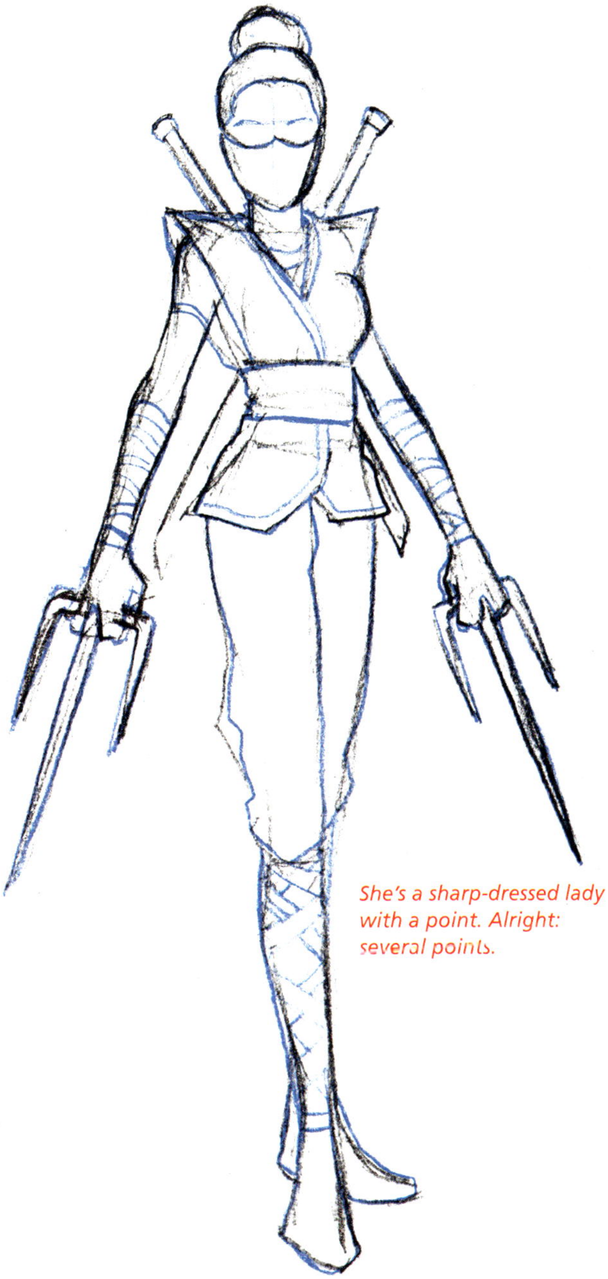

The white of her robe is the Japanese color of death.

She's a sharp-dressed lady with a point. Alright: several points.

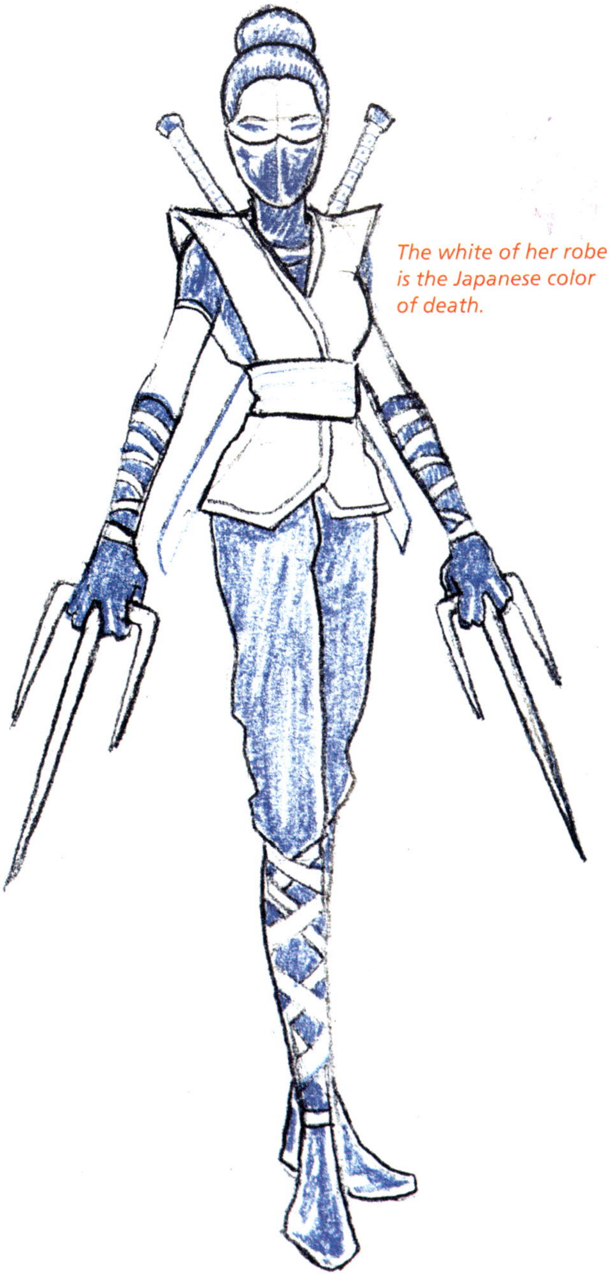

3. Sketch in her eyebrows for placement. Add wrappings to her lower arms and legs, and place some piping on the edges of her robe.

4. Black out her first layer of clothes from her mask to her toes and do the same for her gloves. Black out most of her hair but leave bands of white for highlights. Add wraps to the handles of her wakizashi. Give her a pair of knowing eyes.

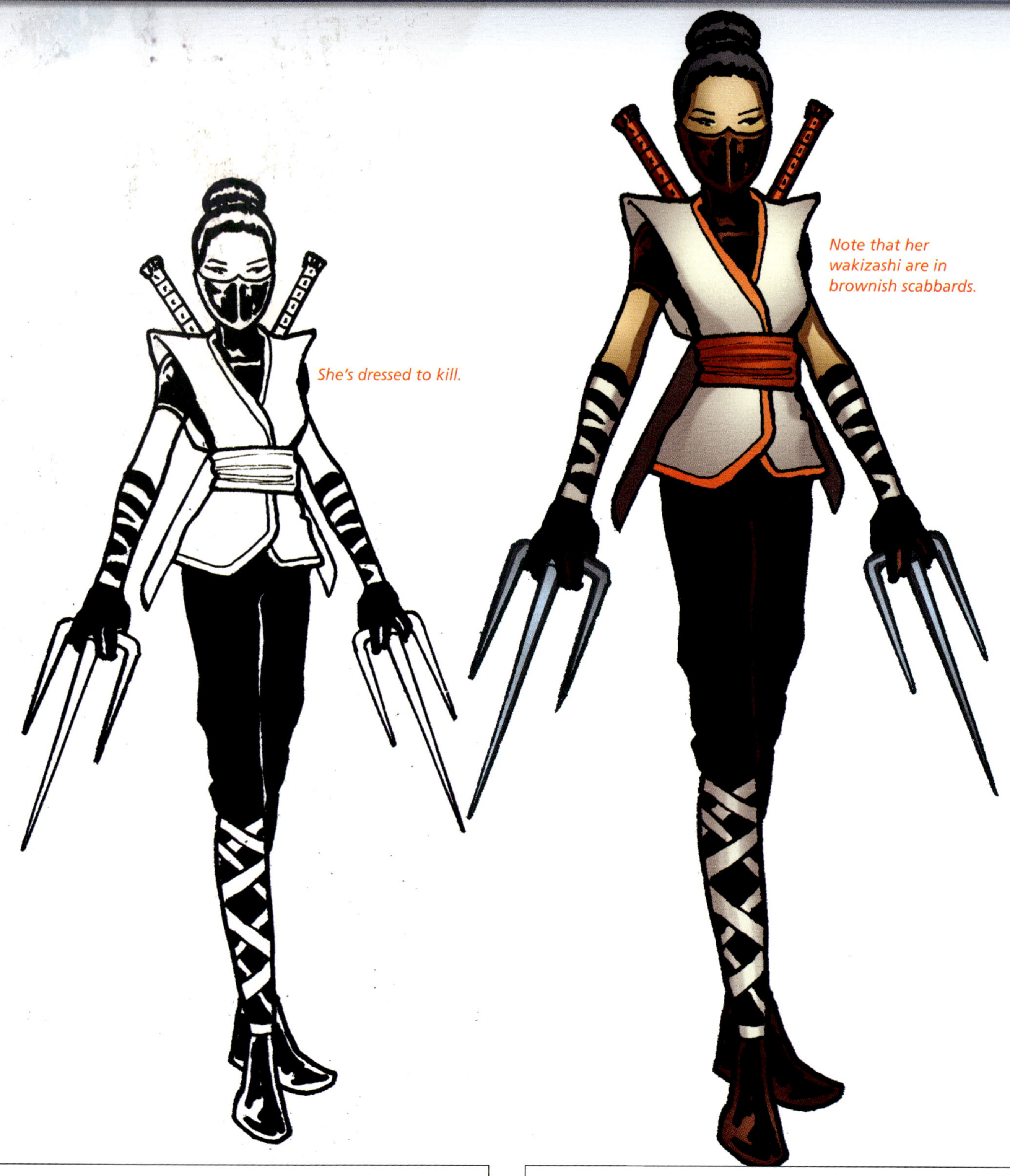

5. Ink her carefully. Use mostly uniform lines. The only exceptions are for the folds of her belt.

6. Use a dark red for the highlights on her black outfit. This implies that it's soaked in blood. Use a brighter red for the piping on her robe and for the handles of her wakizashi. Leave the wraps white, but add a sheen of gray to them to make them seem like satin. The metal of her sai is bluish.

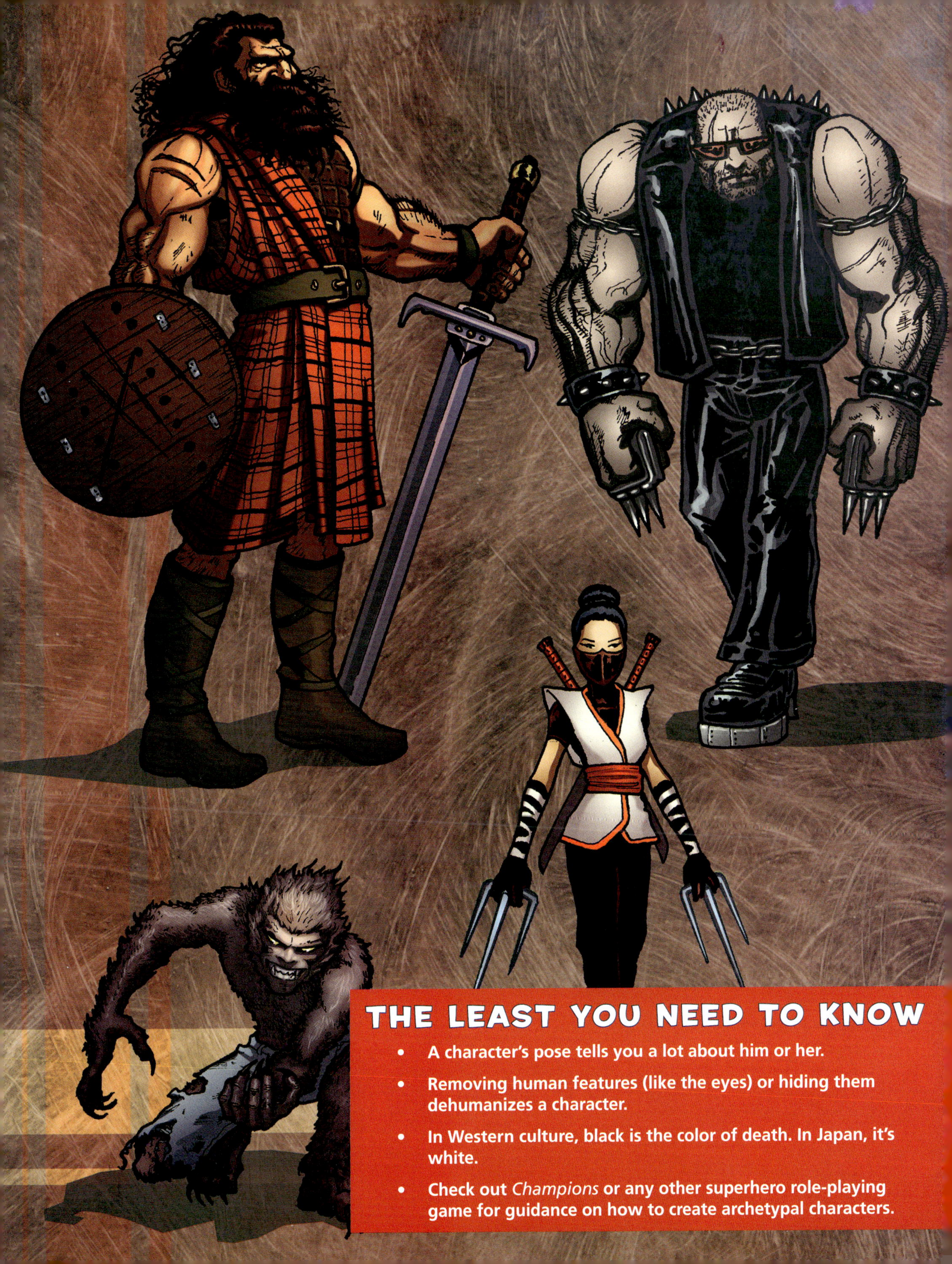

THE LEAST YOU NEED TO KNOW

- A character's pose tells you a lot about him or her.
- Removing human features (like the eyes) or hiding them dehumanizes a character.
- In Western culture, black is the color of death. In Japan, it's white.
- Check out *Champions* or any other superhero role-playing game for guidance on how to create archetypal characters.

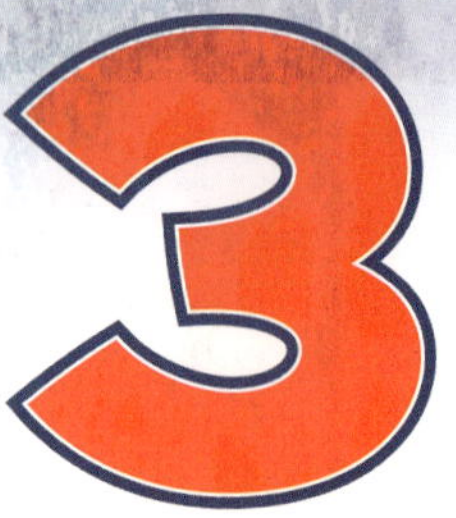

3 Bricks: Hard Targets

In This Chapter

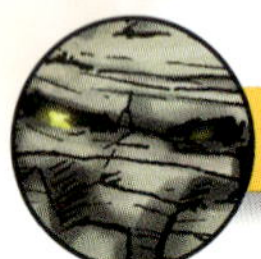

A rocking villain

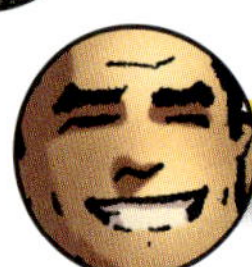

A powerful man

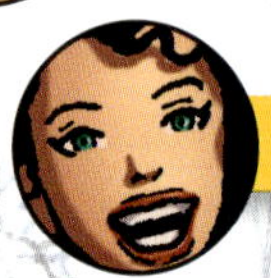

A winning woman

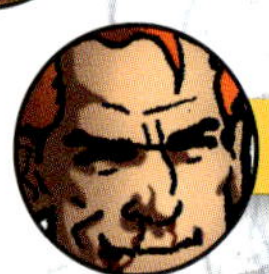

A metal-fisted master

While the scrappers can dish out the damage, the bricks are the ones who can take it. Very little ever bothers them, other than another superpower. They may not always be the strongest people on the planet, but they're by far the toughest.

We start with the Mountain, a man made entirely out of one of the most durable materials around: stone. Nothing gets through his rock-hard skin.

We move on to Power, a hero perhaps a little too proud of his abilities. No one ever poses like that anymore, right?

Then we check out the Champ, the fittest woman alive. She never loses. Never.

We wind up with Punch, the man with the steel fist. All he needs is one good hit, and he can knock anyone out.

THE MOUNTAIN

The Mountain was once an aspiring mobster who stretched himself just a bit too far. The mob tossed his body into a steep canyon and thought that was the end of him. As he died there, though, Mountain's spirit infused the rocks around him, and by sheer force of will, he held together and animated the stones that now make up his form.

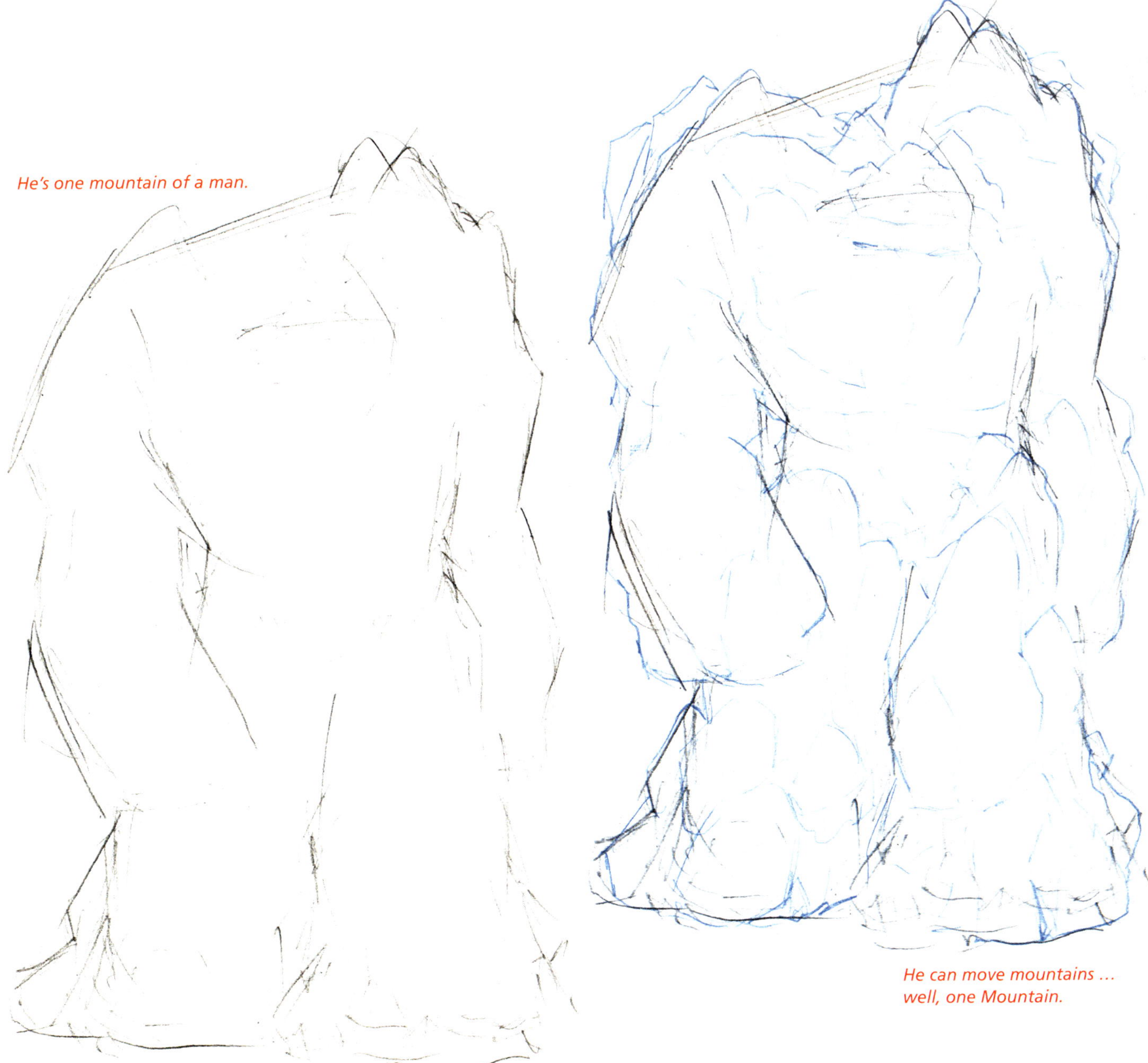

He's one mountain of a man.

He can move mountains ... well, one Mountain.

1. Use craggy forms for this figure. He's shaped roughly human, but just roughly, despite the fact that the Mountain still thinks he's somehow alive. His head sits down below his shoulders, for instance, because it's closer to his original body's height that way.

2. Add in more details. Make his shoulders look like a mountain range. His feet look like the foothills (of course).

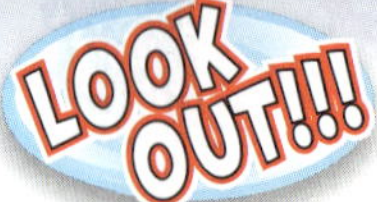

While the Mountain sounds great on paper, and looks great, too, he can be a pain to draw. With regular characters, you have long, smooth lines to lay down. With the Mountain, you have lots of jagged angles, and drawing them takes far more time.

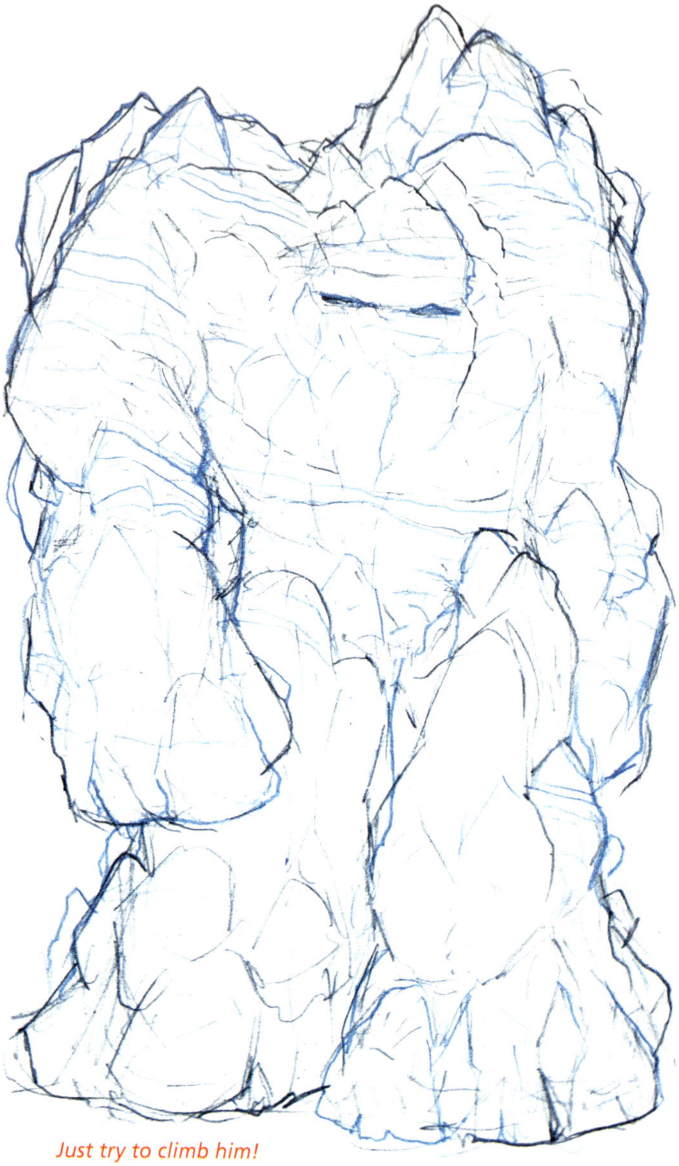

He looks so solid you could add snowcaps to his peaks.

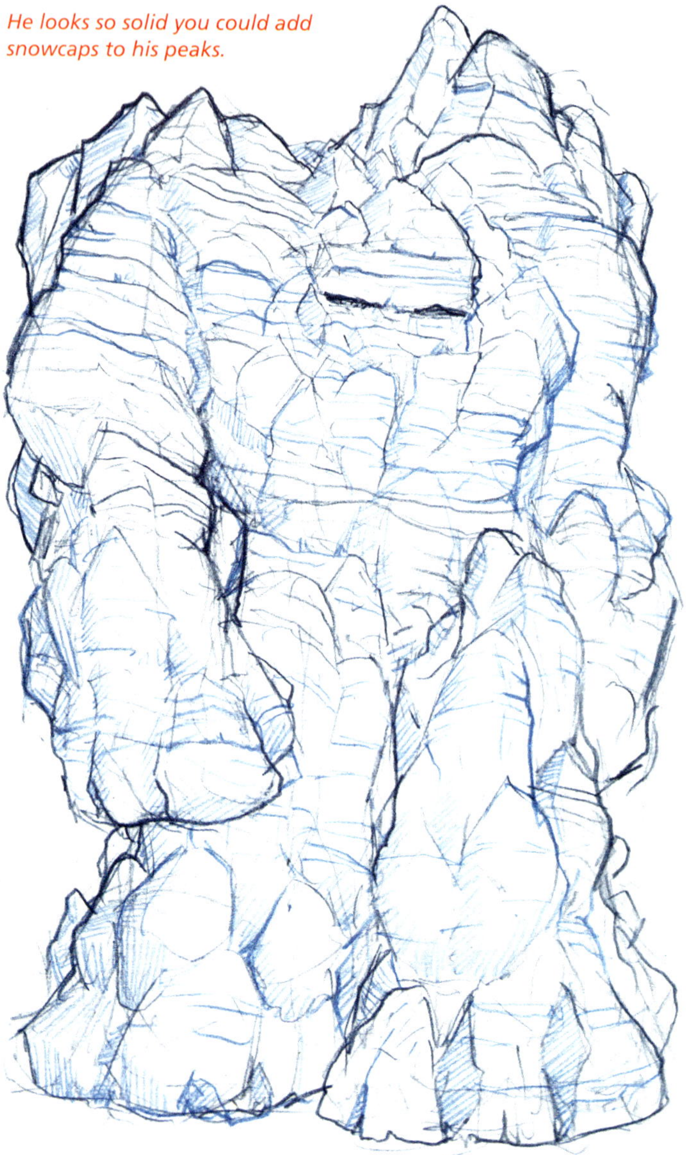

Just try to climb him!

3. Add more rocky texture. Keep stacking rocks on each other until there's no space left for anything else. Remember, still, to follow the basic human shape.

4. Define the rocks everywhere. Cover him with striations (horizontal lines that show layers, just like with real rock). Darken those eyes. Leave off the mouth to make him that much more inhuman.

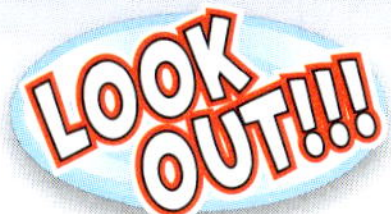

Although the Mountain gives you lots to draw, there are ways to cheat around that if you're short on time. Tight shots that only show part of the creature work great to cut down on your load, and in distant shots you only need to draw the creature's outline.

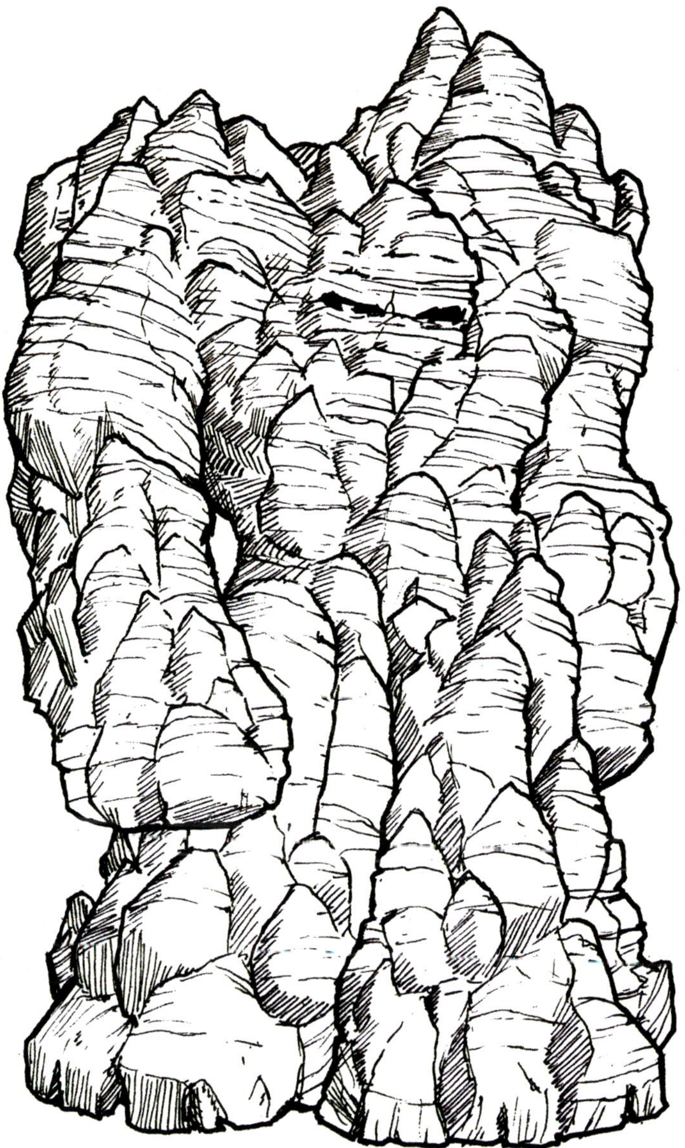

Rock and roll!

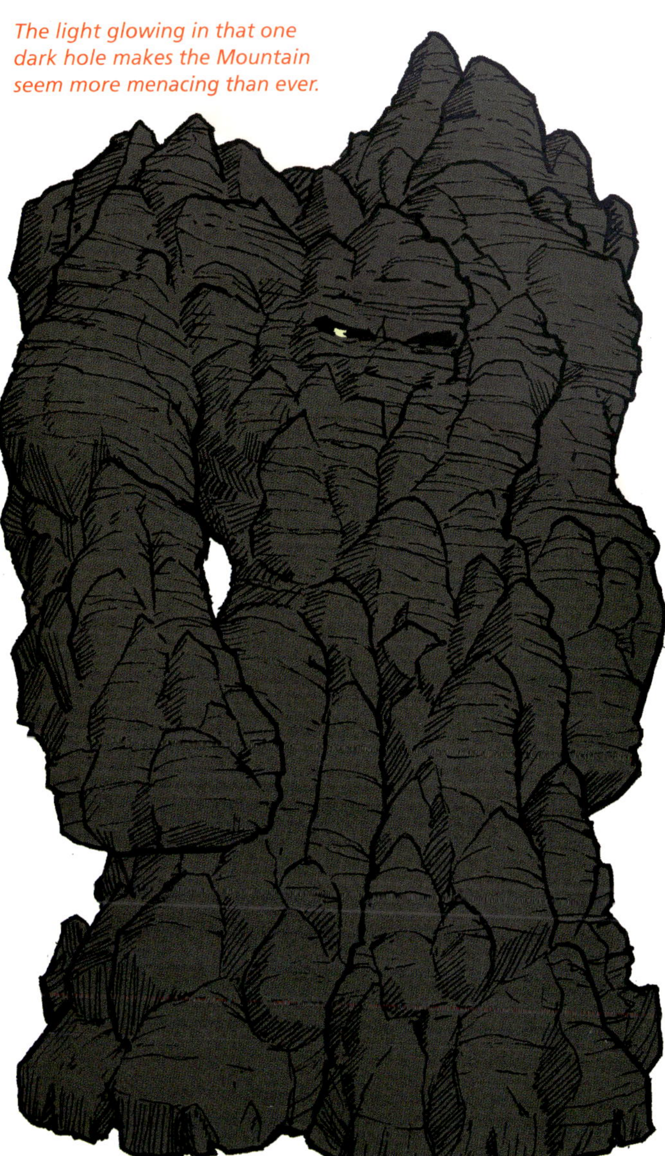

The light glowing in that one dark hole makes the Mountain seem more menacing than ever.

5. Use heavy inks on the figure's perimeter and on many of the vertical lines to differentiate the sections of rock. Use lighter lines on the horizontal lines. Blacken in those eyes.

6. Try a dark gray color for the stony skin. Add a touch of yellow to the center of one of the creature's eyes.

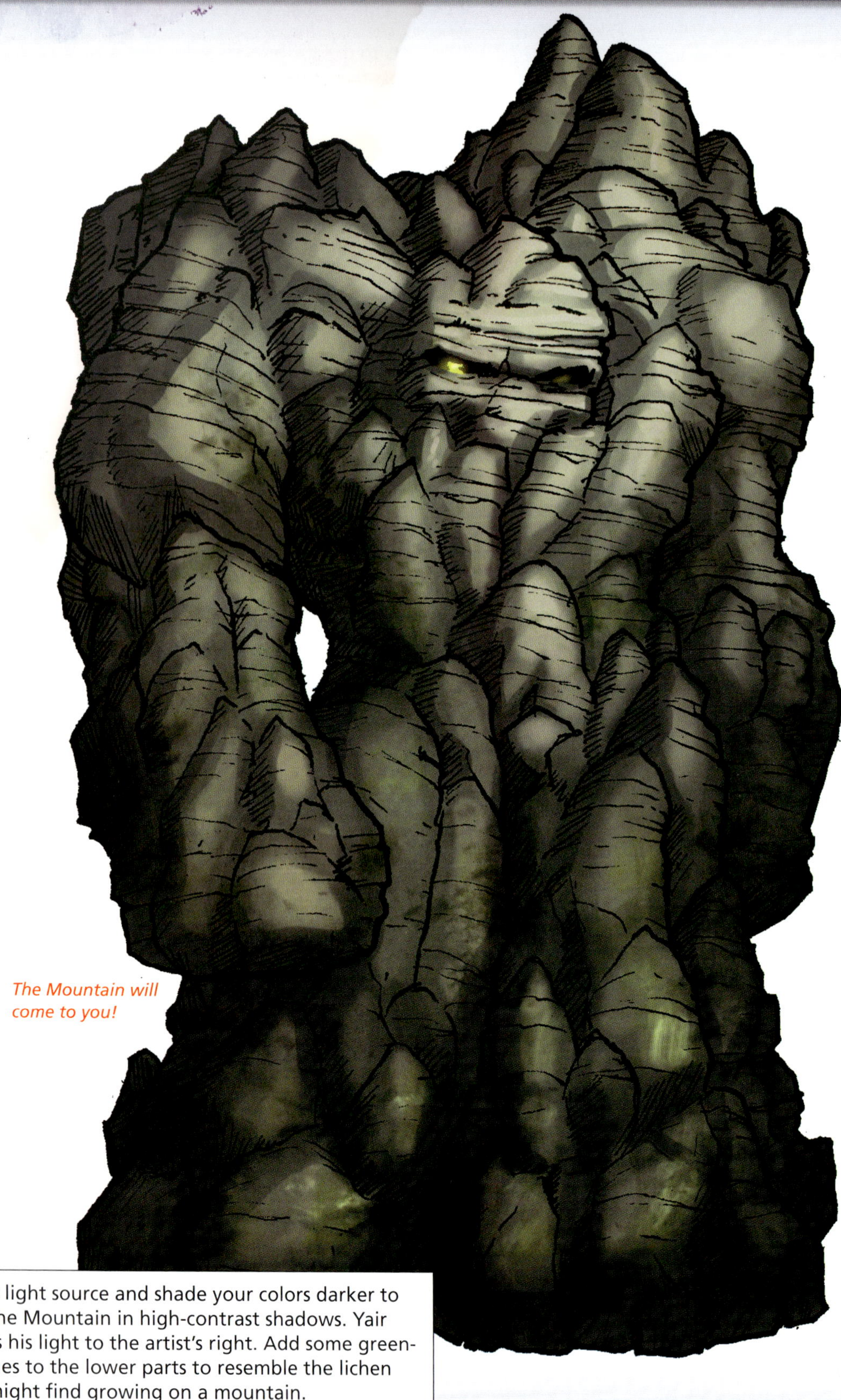

The Mountain will come to you!

7. Pick a light source and shade your colors darker to cast the Mountain in high-contrast shadows. Yair places his light to the artist's right. Add some greenish hues to the lower parts to resemble the lichen you might find growing on a mountain.

POWER

From as early as he could remember, Power always wanted to be a hero. He trained as a Boy Scout and constantly prepared himself to be the kind of morally centered hero he knew he was destined to become. One day—while working as an assistant district attorney—it finally happened, and he knew the time of Power had arrived!

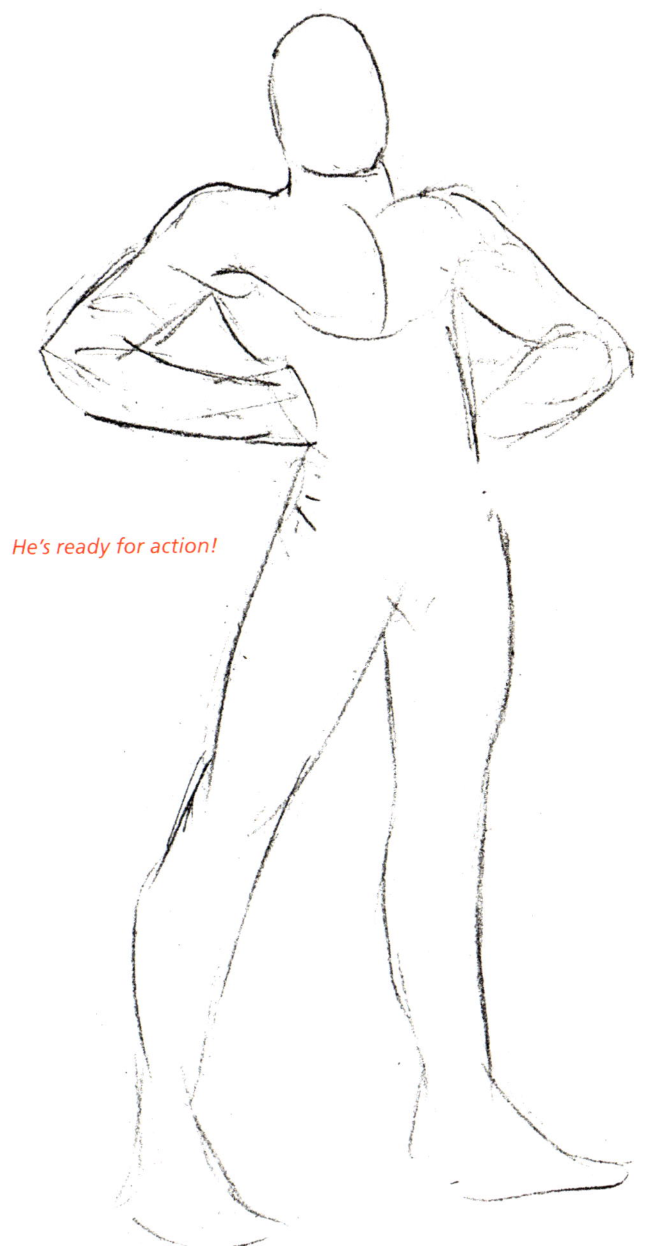

He's ready for action!

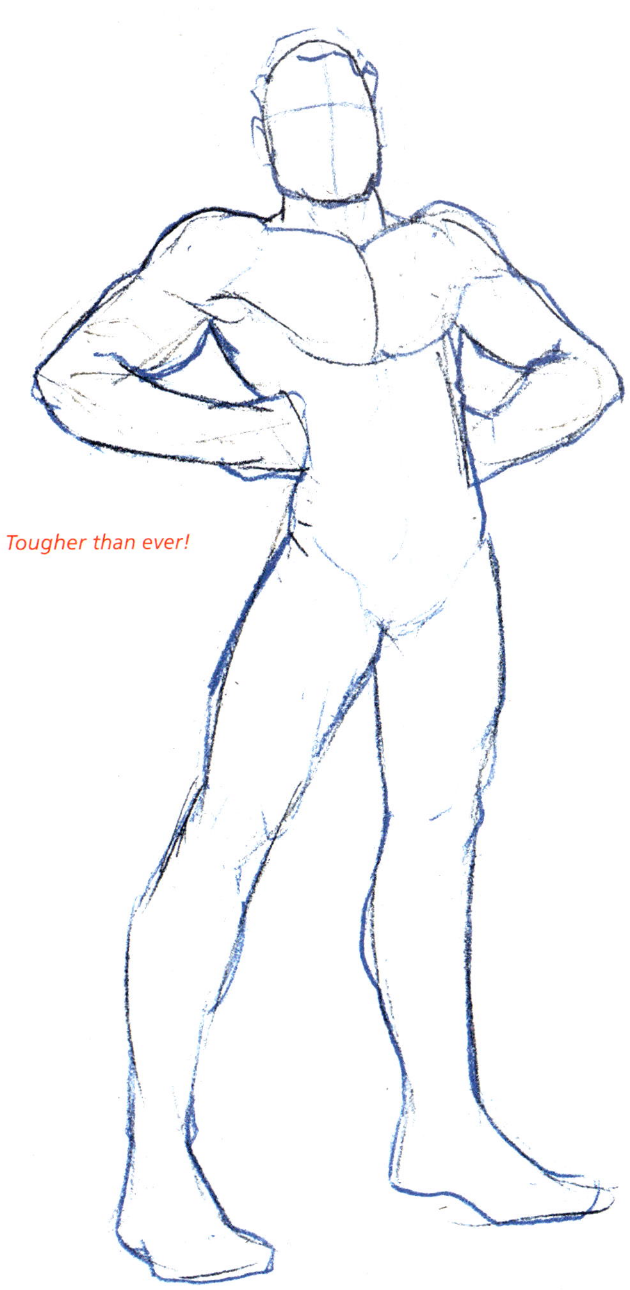

Tougher than ever!

1. Scratch out Power's stance. He has a traditional, 1940s-style superpose, complete with fists on hips. Even with just the oval for a face, you can almost see the grin on his face.

2. Build up his muscles. Define those limbs and his chest. Place his ears on his head. Notice how Yair uses a pair of crossed lines on his face to show the direction in which Power faces.

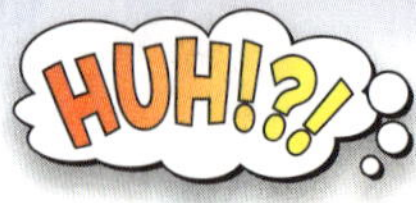

In many comic-book universes, comics don't seem to exist. They have the superheroes right there among them, after all, so they may not need such stories. In others, they have a long legacy of both tales and the heroes who lived through them, and these can offer inspiration to generation after generation.

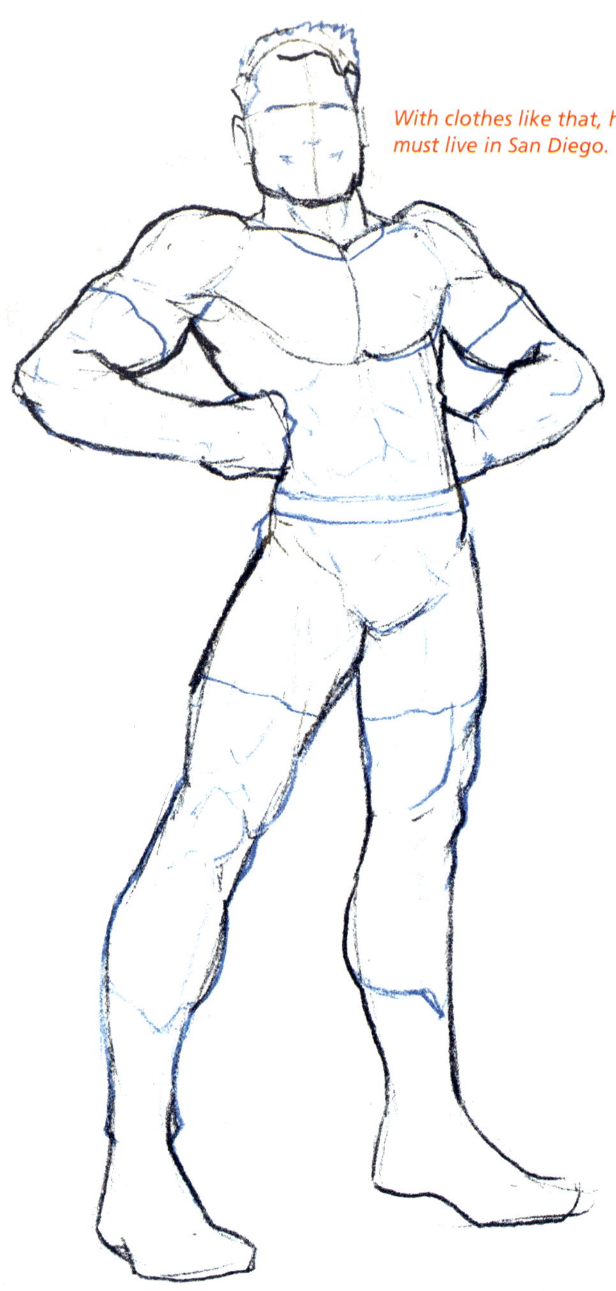

With clothes like that, he must live in San Diego.

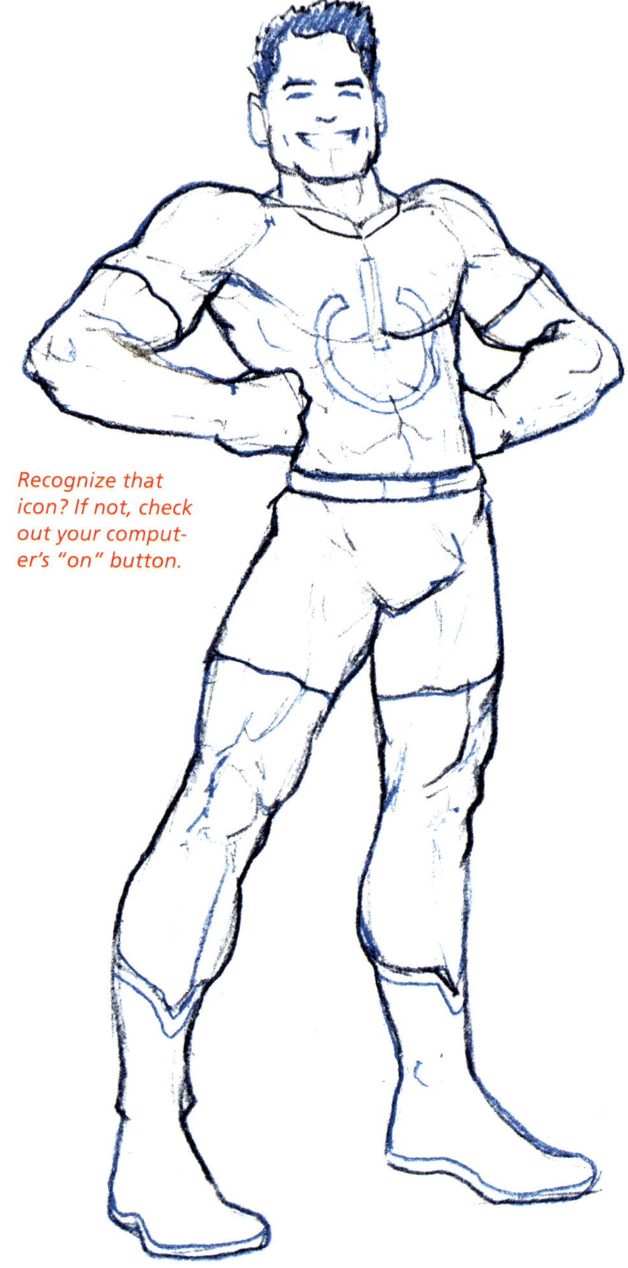

Recognize that icon? If not, check out your computer's "on" button.

3. Dress him in the spandex equivalent of a shorty wetsuit, leaving his arms and legs mostly exposed. Give him a pair of boots and a full head of hair while you're at it. Define the musculature a bit more, too, and place his eyebrows.

4. Slap a big grin on his face and give him happy eyes. Place his icon on his chest. Put dimples on his cheeks. Add piping to his boots.

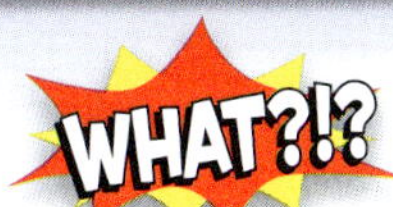

A character's **icon** (also known as a logo, symbol, or insignia) sums up everything about him in a single, sharp image. Often worn on the chest, it can be repeated throughout the character's costume and even appear on vehicles and weaponry.

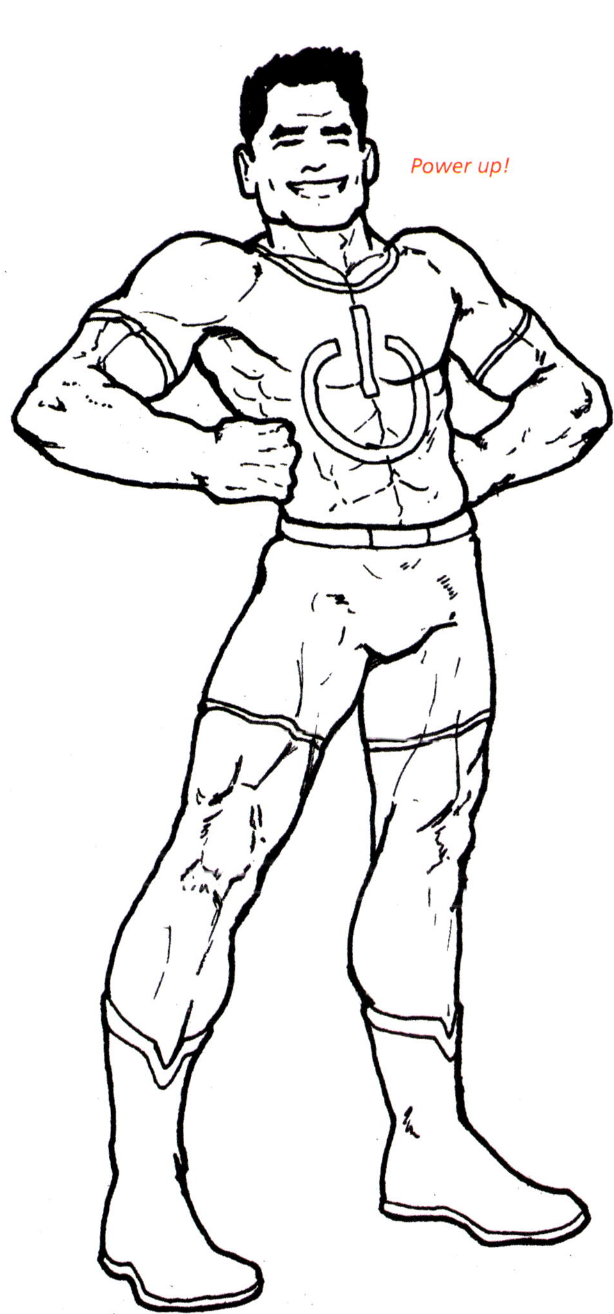

Power up!

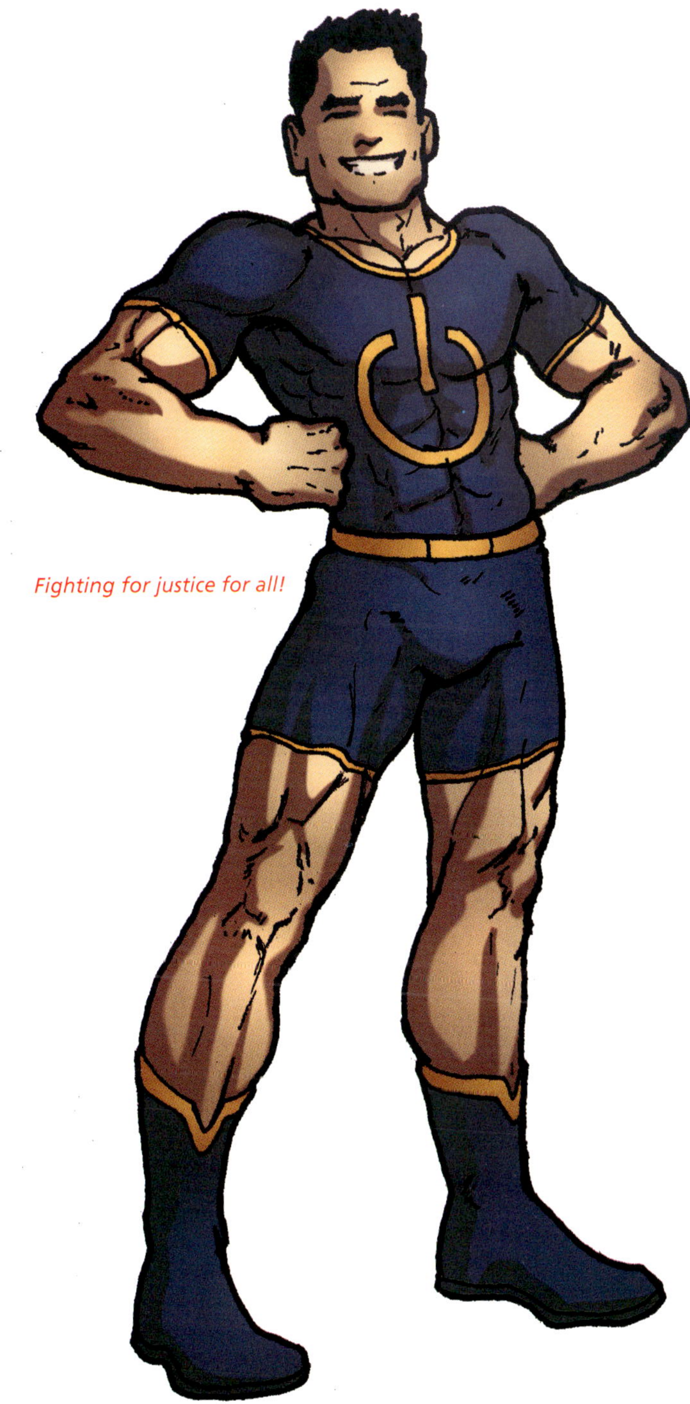

Fighting for justice for all!

5. Use bold inks around the character's perimeter and on his face and costume. Use lighter lines only for his musculature.

6. His outfit is blue with yellow piping, and his icon is yellow, too. Use shading on his skin and costume to show the position of the light (to the artist's upper right in this case). His teeth are pure white.

THE CHAMP

The Champ trained as an Olympic athlete for many years, unaware that she had superpowers. Only after she had shattered every track-and-field record did the Olympics test her for genetic alteration, and they discovered the secret even she didn't know. After she was banned from further competition, she decided to push herself to the next level. Now she competes against the top superpowers in the world, always pushing herself to do better.

She's ready for the sky.

Yair changed her outstretched hand from a plane to a fist.

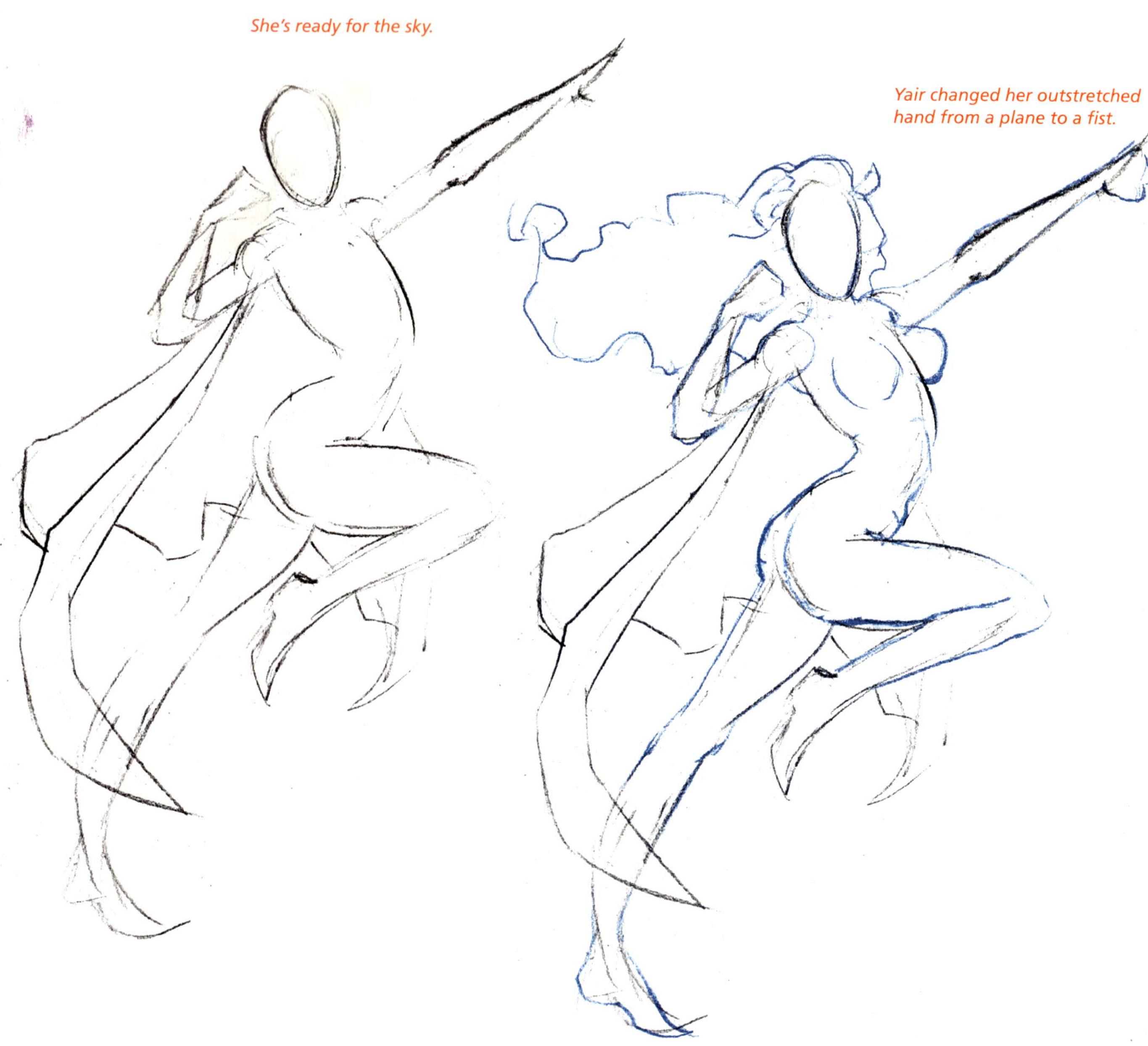

1. In addition to her athletic prowess, the Champ can fly. Yair poses her taking off into the sky. Use rough shapes to do the same. Don't forget to include her cape, which flutters behind her in the wind.

2. Refine the Champ's stance. Add long, flowing hair behind her. Place breasts on the figure.

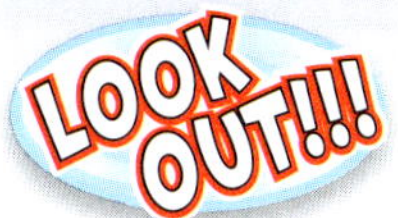

While it's important to know where your light sources are for any drawing, it's also good to know which direction the wind blows. Figure that out and apply the effects to any loose bits on the figure, including hair and clothing. This is especially true with a cape. Seeing the Champ's hair go one way and her cape another would be ridiculous.

Yair adds a laurel wreath—the ancient symbol of winners—to her hair.

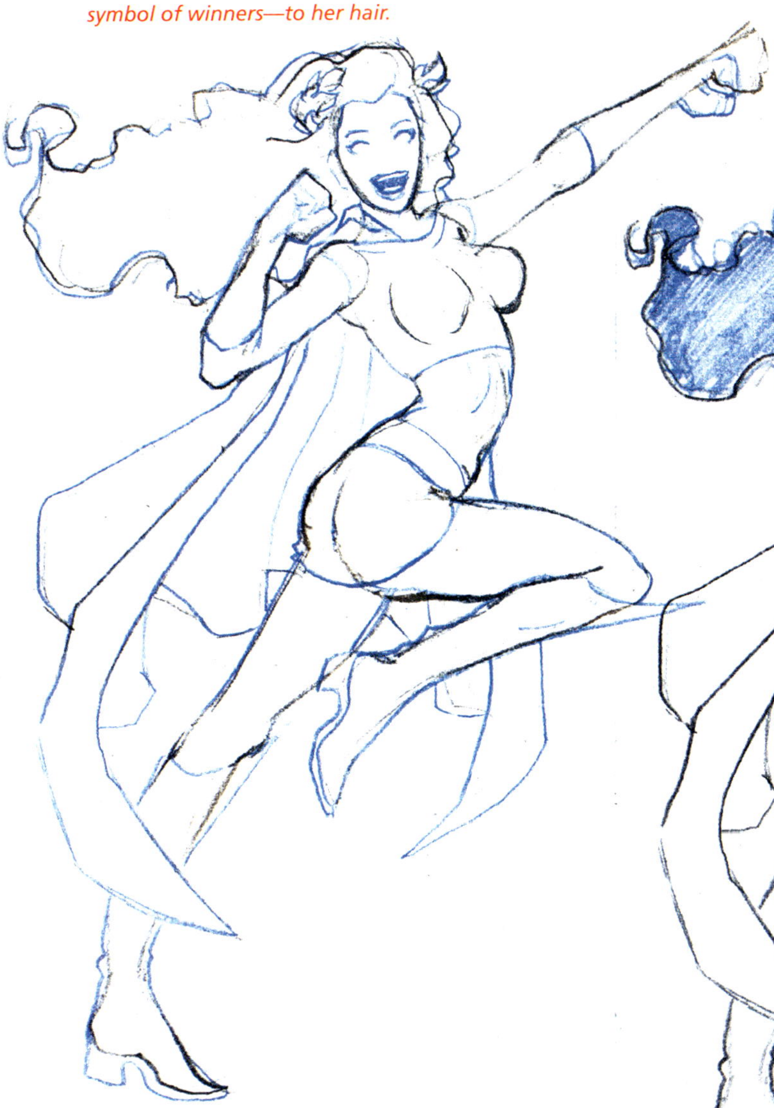

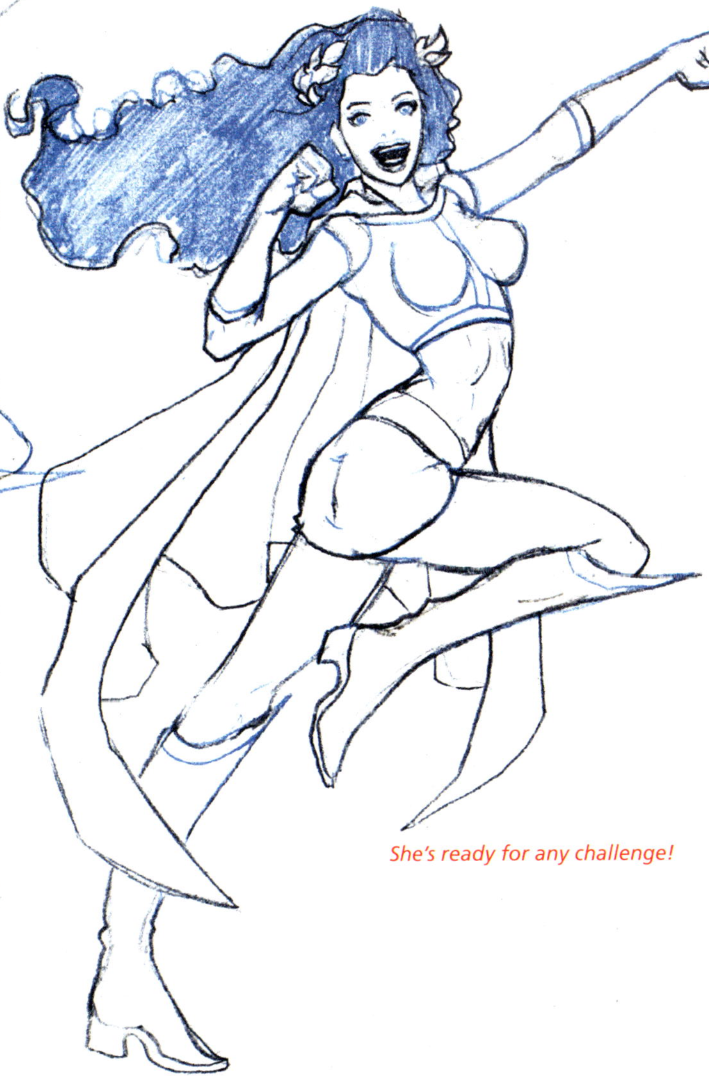

She's ready for any challenge!

3. Put some clothes on her, a short skirt and a bare-midriff top. Put long gloves on her arms. Add some folds to her cape and put heels on her boots. Give her a happy, triumphant face.

4. Darken her hair. Add pupils to her eyes. Put piping on the edges of her gloves, boots, and shirt, plus a seam down the middle of her shirt, too.

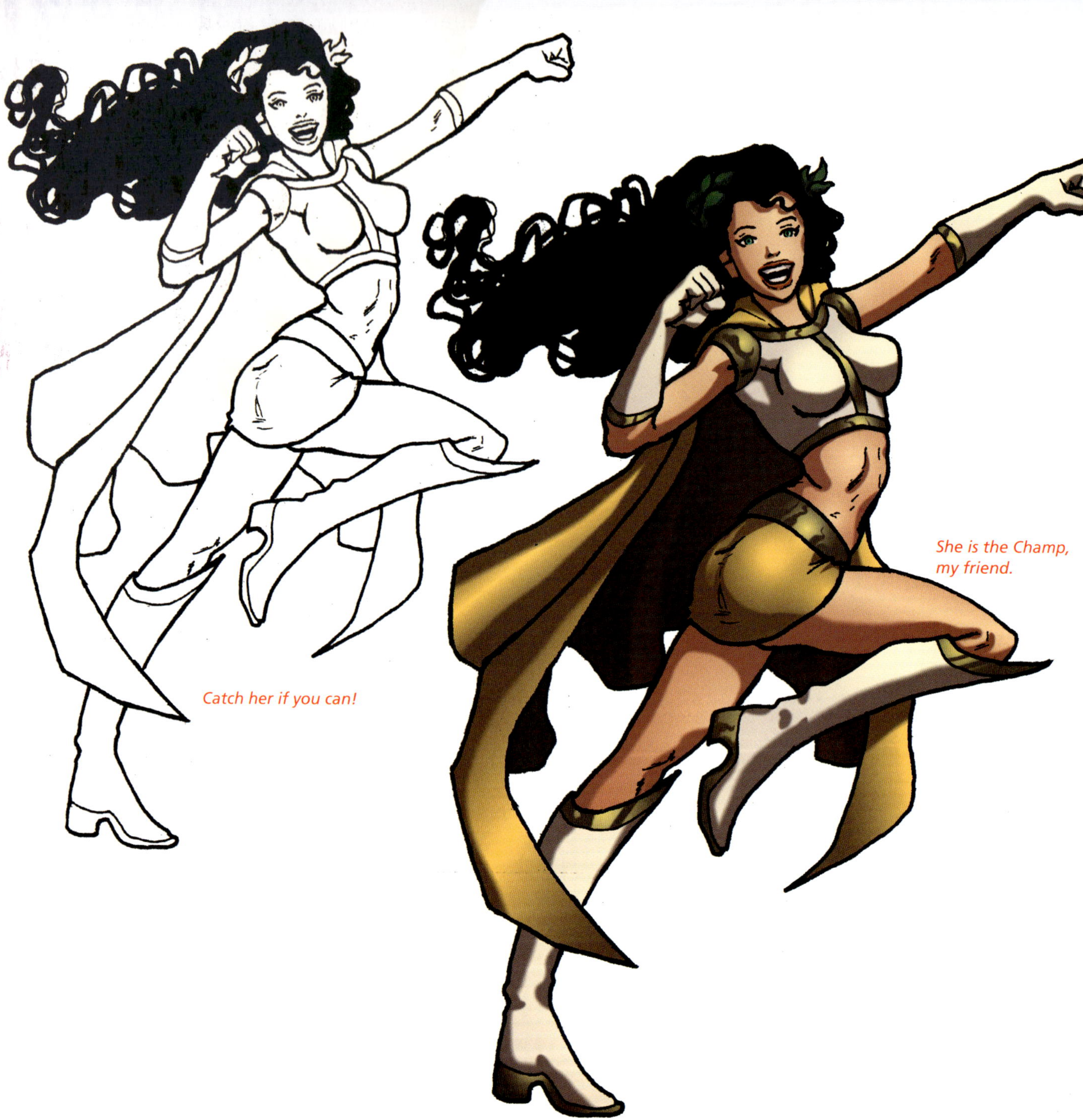

5. Use thick lines for most of the Champ, with the exception of the few wrinkles in her skirt or on her limbs. Use a marker for most of her hair, and add some smaller lines with your regular inking tool to give it more variety.

6. Her cape and skirt are colored gold. Her belt and the piping on her gloves and boots are just slightly darker to provide a hint of contrast. The rest of her clothes are white. The laurel wreath is green.

THE PUNCH

Born without a right arm from the elbow down, Punch dedicated his life to the pursuit of a cybernetic prosthetic that would not only replace the missing limb but exceed it. He tried genetic manipulation, but it only made him stronger and tougher. After several long years, he stumbled upon alien technology that bonded to him instantly. If not for his super-toughness, his body would have rejected the new, oversized limb, but he is not only able to accept it but wield it as if he'd been born with it.

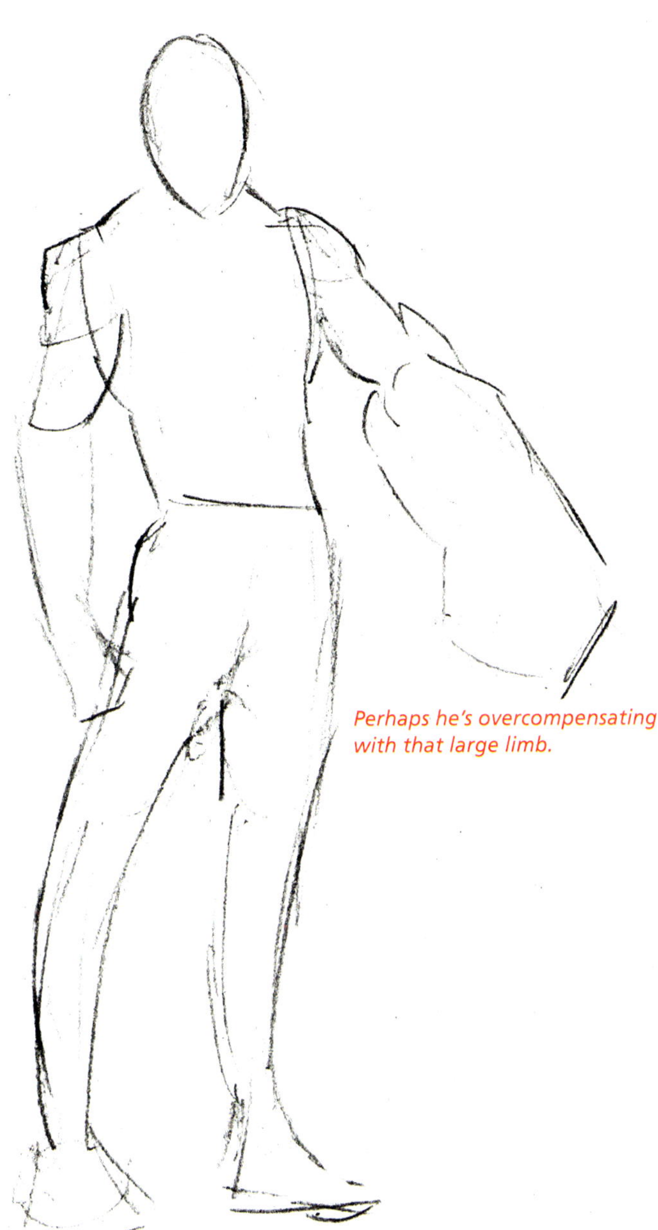

Perhaps he's overcompensating with that large limb.

He's starting to come into focus.

1. Punch is tough and doesn't need to show off. He's proud of his steel fist, though, and puts that forward on display. Pose him naturally, but amplify his replacement arm.

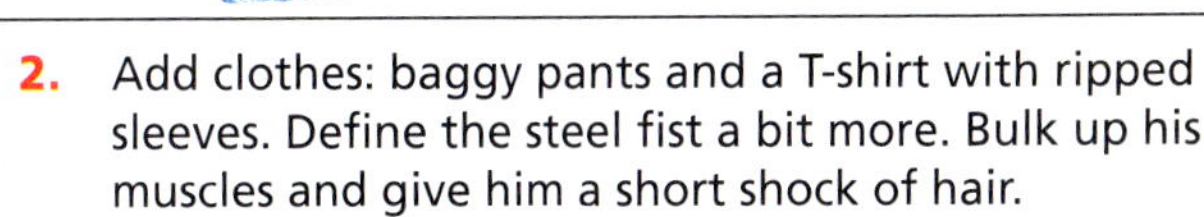

2. Add clothes: baggy pants and a T-shirt with ripped sleeves. Define the steel fist a bit more. Bulk up his muscles and give him a short shock of hair.

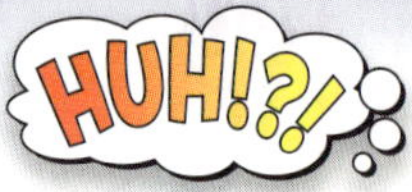

Alien technology is another good source of powers. While some creators prefer to have their characters' powers all emerge in a single way, others like a grab-bag approach, coming up with new kinds of origins for all sorts of different powers.

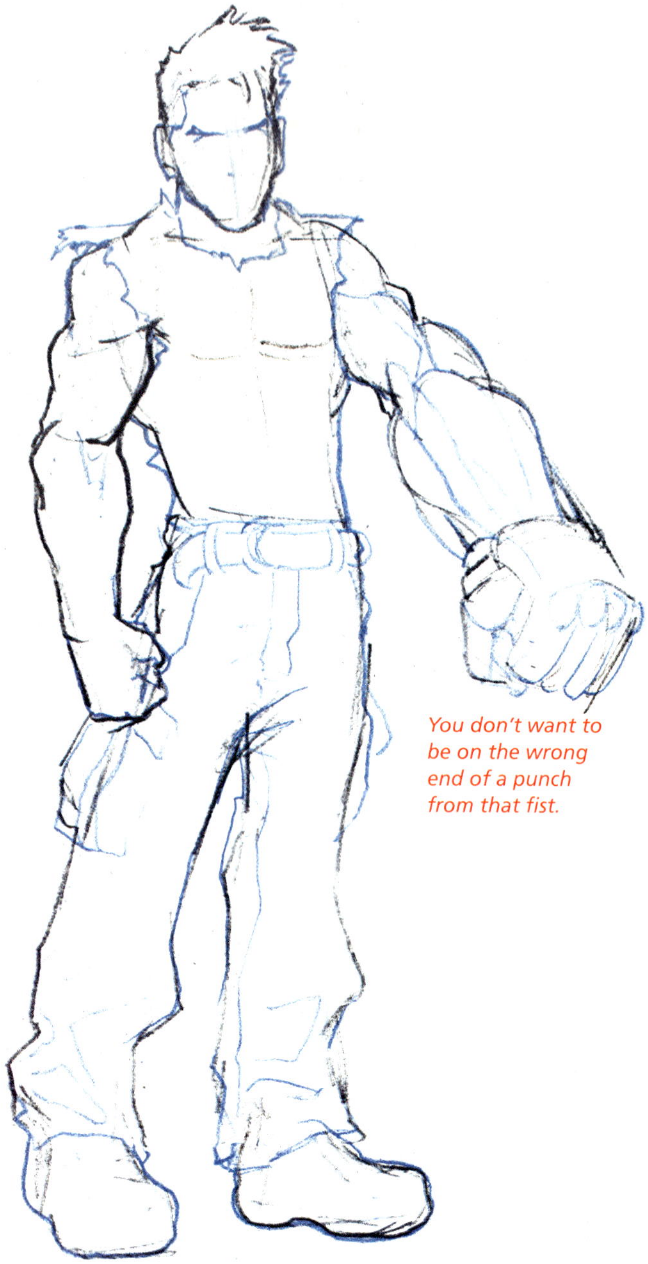

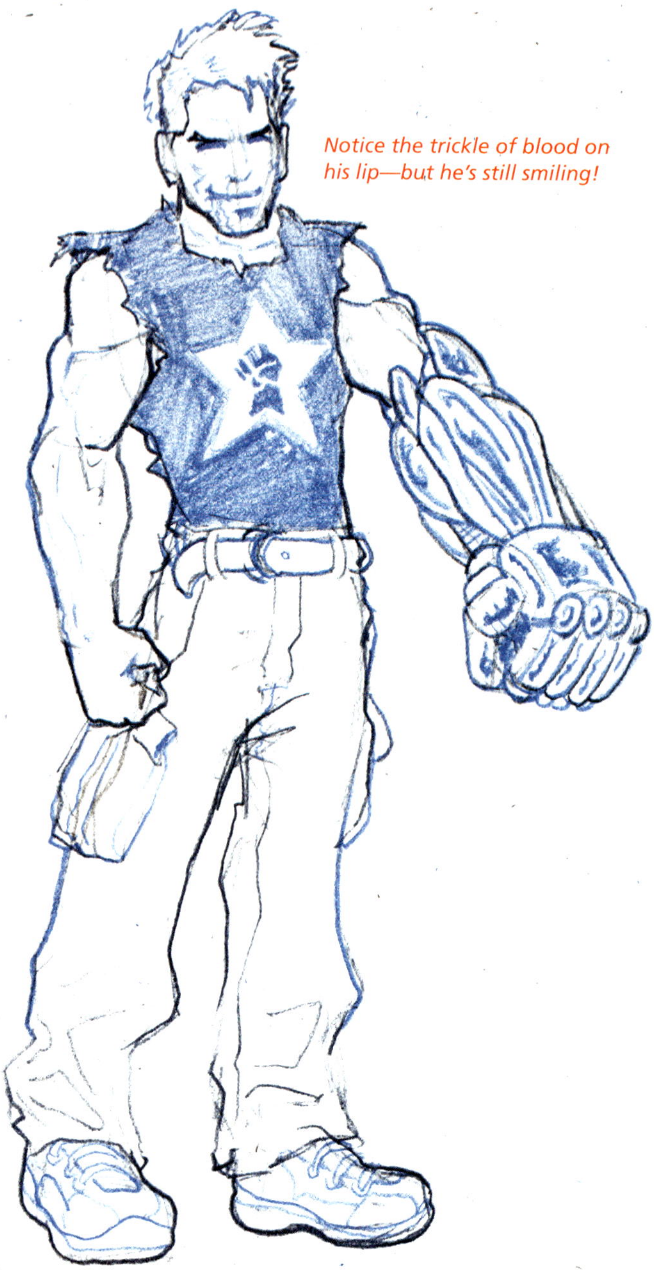

Notice the trickle of blood on his lip—but he's still smiling!

You don't want to be on the wrong end of a punch from that fist.

3. Add wrinkles to the pants, and slap a belt around his waist. Put some cargo pockets on his legs. Tatter the edges of his torn-off sleeves. Give him some low-arched eyebrows, too.

4. Darken Punch's shirt and add his icon: a clenched fist in a five-pointed star. Add chroming to his metallic fist, and flesh out his face. Finish off with details all around, from enhancing his muscles to putting laces on his shoes.

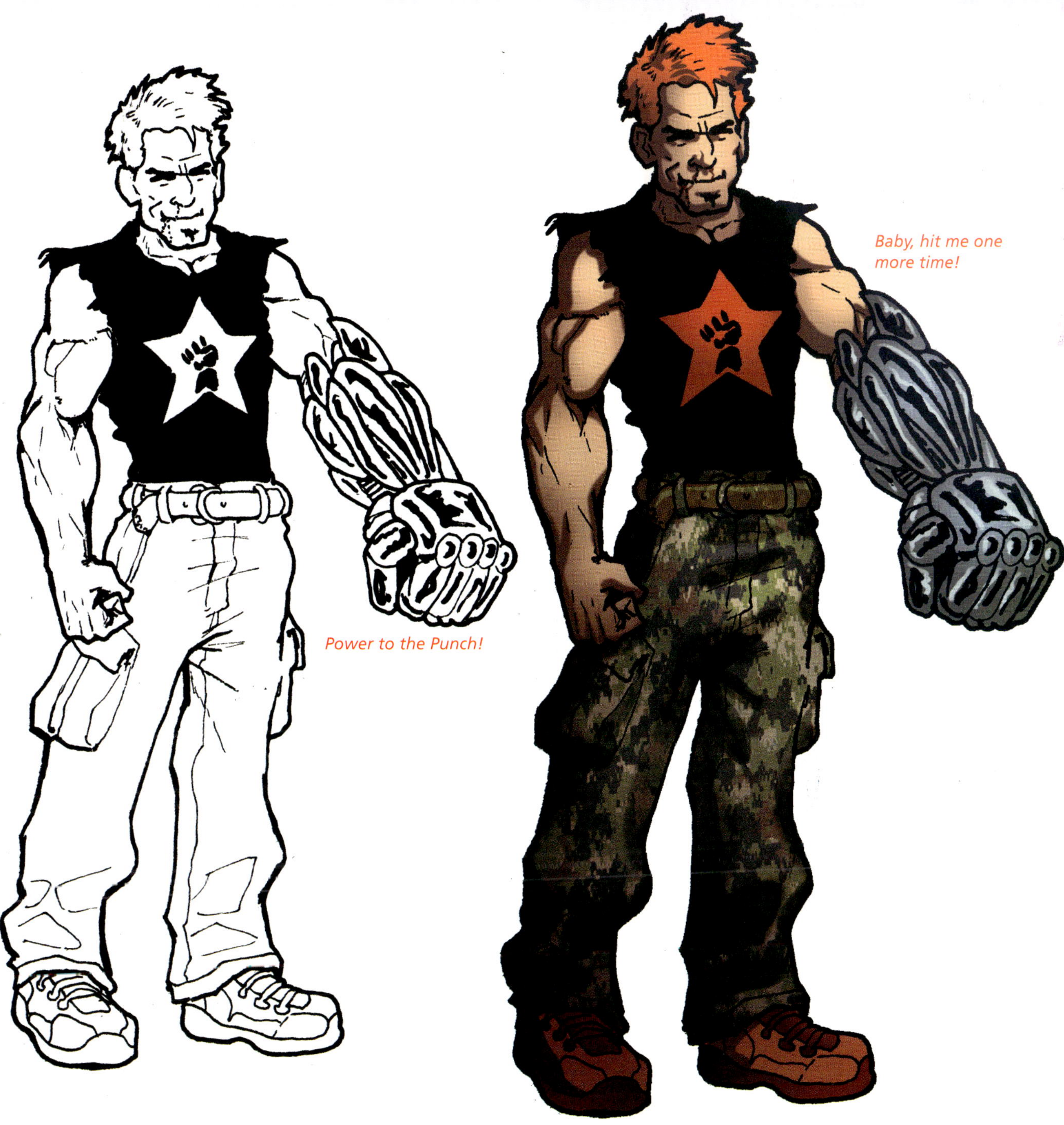

5. Use thick lines on Punch's perimeter and on his fist. Use lighter ones on his arms, pants, shoes, and hair. The contrast emphasizes the strength of his alien arm.

6. Give Punch red hair, brown shoes, and a metallic-blue arm. Pick up on the red hair with the star on the center of his shirt. Apply a digital camouflage texture to his pants for an easy, realistic, and grungy look.

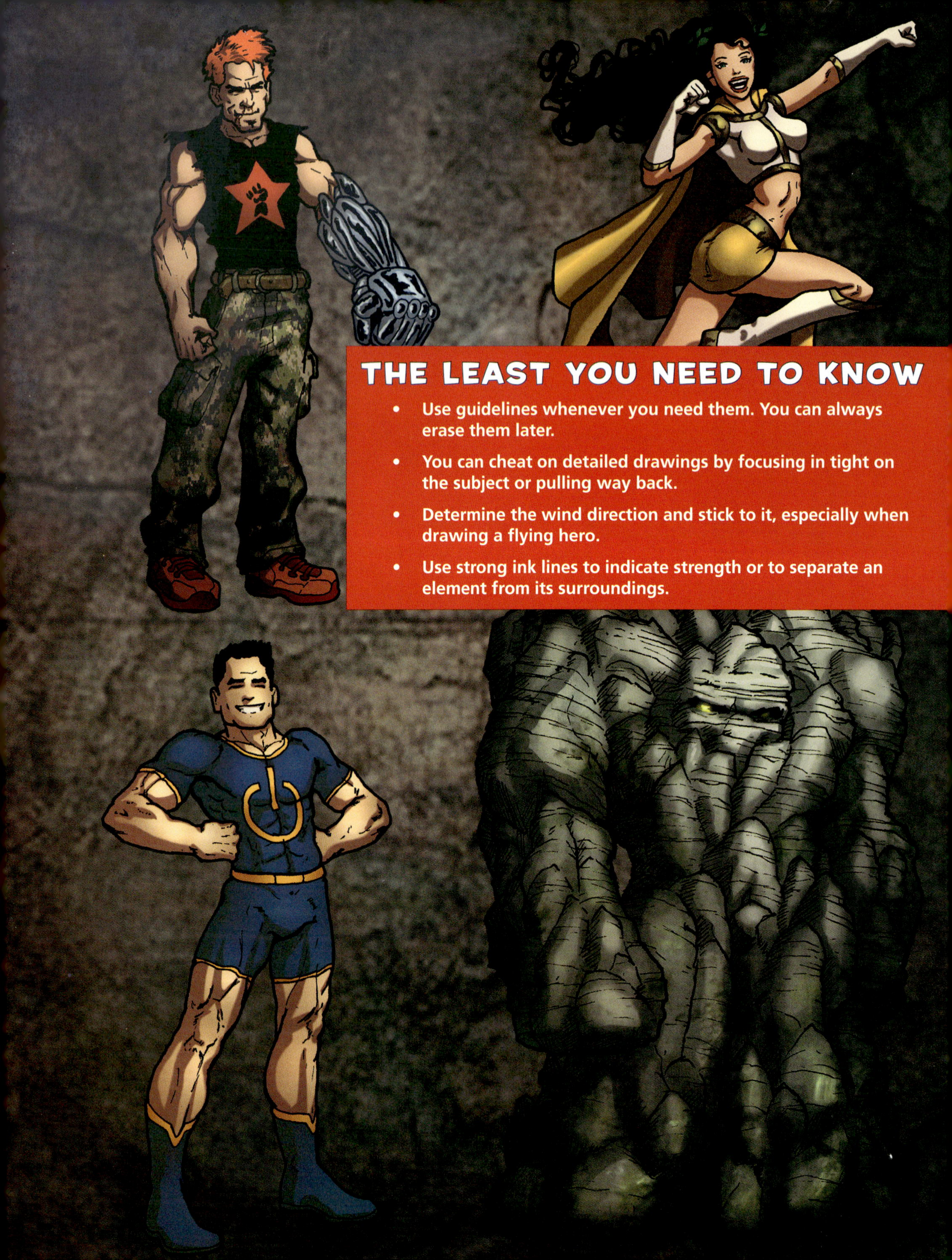

THE LEAST YOU NEED TO KNOW

- Use guidelines whenever you need them. You can always erase them later.
- You can cheat on detailed drawings by focusing in tight on the subject or pulling way back.
- Determine the wind direction and stick to it, especially when drawing a flying hero.
- Use strong ink lines to indicate strength or to separate an element from its surroundings.

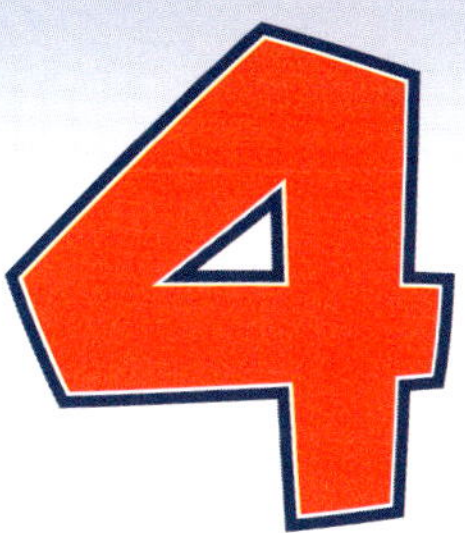

Shooters: Pull!

In This Chapter

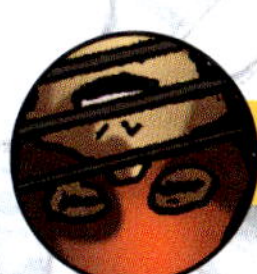

- An amazing archer

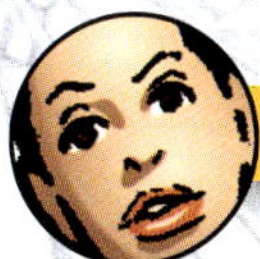

- A gunslinger for hire

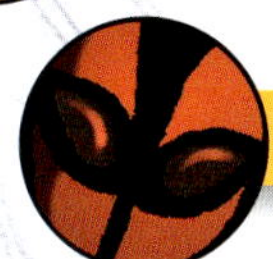

- A wily webslinger

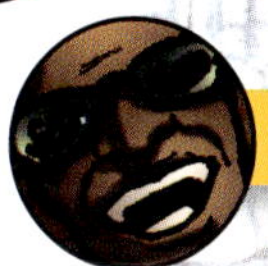

- A blaster with a point

There's another class of combatant outside of the zappers and the bruisers: the shooters. These people rely on tools rather than powers to pepper their foes with ranged attacks, blasting them with bullets and arrows rather than lasers or electricity. Their power isn't in what they're shooting but how well they shoot it.

The Bowman is a classic example of this sort of hero. He shoots arrows, which don't amount to much in most gunfights. He's so good at it, though, that any punk with a pistol is bound to lose to him.

The Pistoleer is similar to the Bowman, but for the fact that she uses a gun (or guns) as her tools of destruction. She can plant a bullet straight between any two keys on the cell phone of the man chatting down the street. Or she can bounce a bullet off a wall or even around a corner.

The Webber fires something unique (for most people): sticky webs that entrap his foes. While being able to so do at all is certainly a power, the fact that he can net up a handful of thugs at once with a pair of carefully aimed shots is the amazing part.

Ray-Man's another sort of crossover hero. Because he shoots rays from his fingers, you might call him a zapper, but he's so good at it he counts as a shooter, too. The fact that he fires the rays by forming his hands into guns clinches the shooter tag for him.

THE BOWMAN

The Bowman used to bow-hunt in his native Colombia. As he came of age, he realized that he could outshoot anyone around and even fire arrows faster than a pistol could blast bullets. He donned a red and blue costume and his trademark red mask and dedicated himself to ridding his native land of the drug lords who control it in their collective iron grasp.

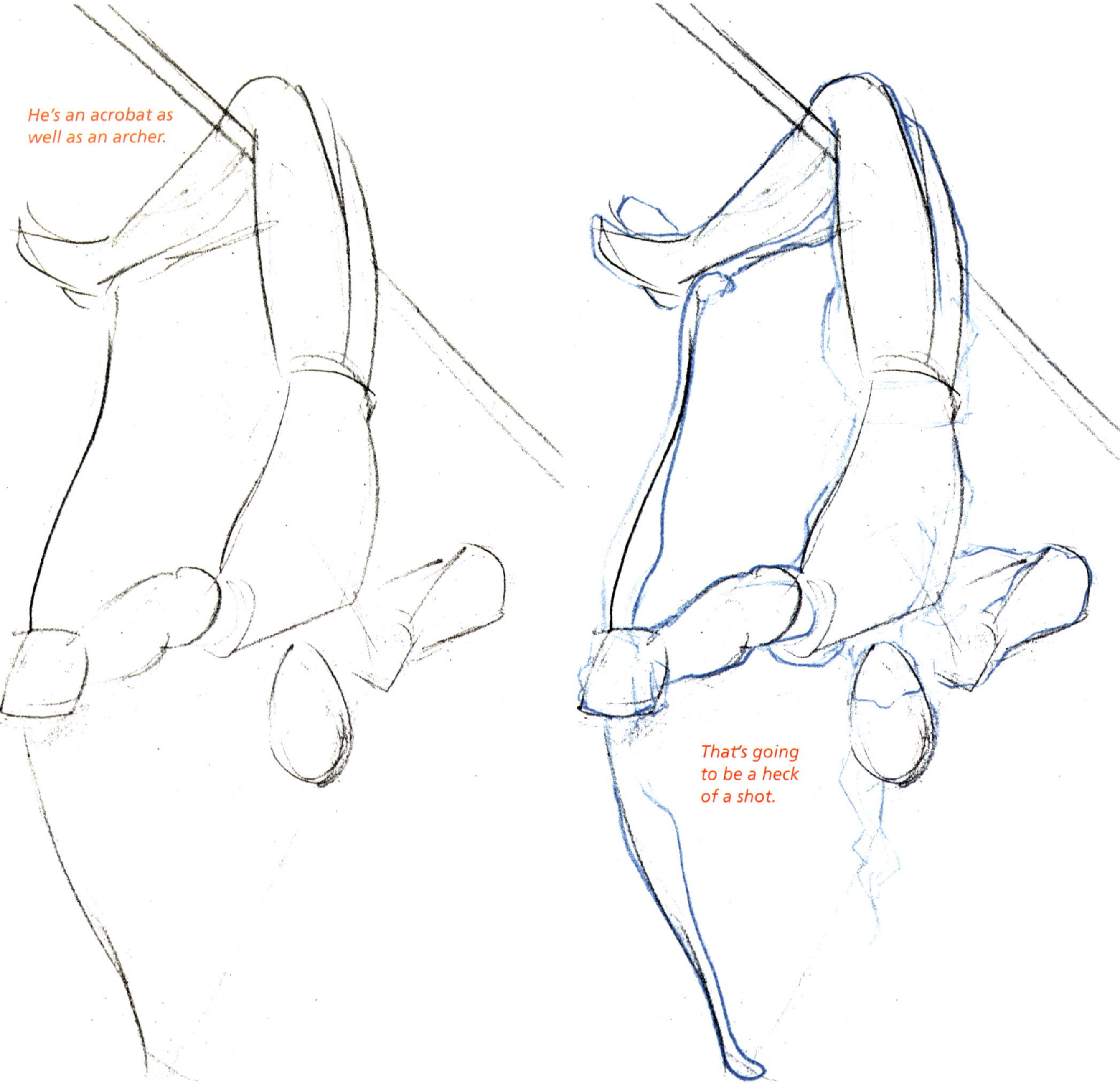

1. Block out the figure using simple shapes. Yair puts him in a daring pose, hanging upside down from a metal pole. Don't forget to include the bow, as using it defines much about how the character should be posed.

2. Add clothing, including baggy pants and a sleeveless shirt. Form the shape of the bow. Be sure to take gravity into account, especially for the tail on his mask.

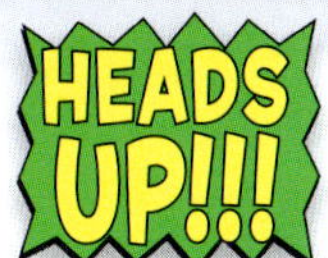

If drawing a figure upside down throws off your sense of perspective, just turn your paper 180° and work on the figure from that angle. When you're done, turn it back right side up, and you're all set.

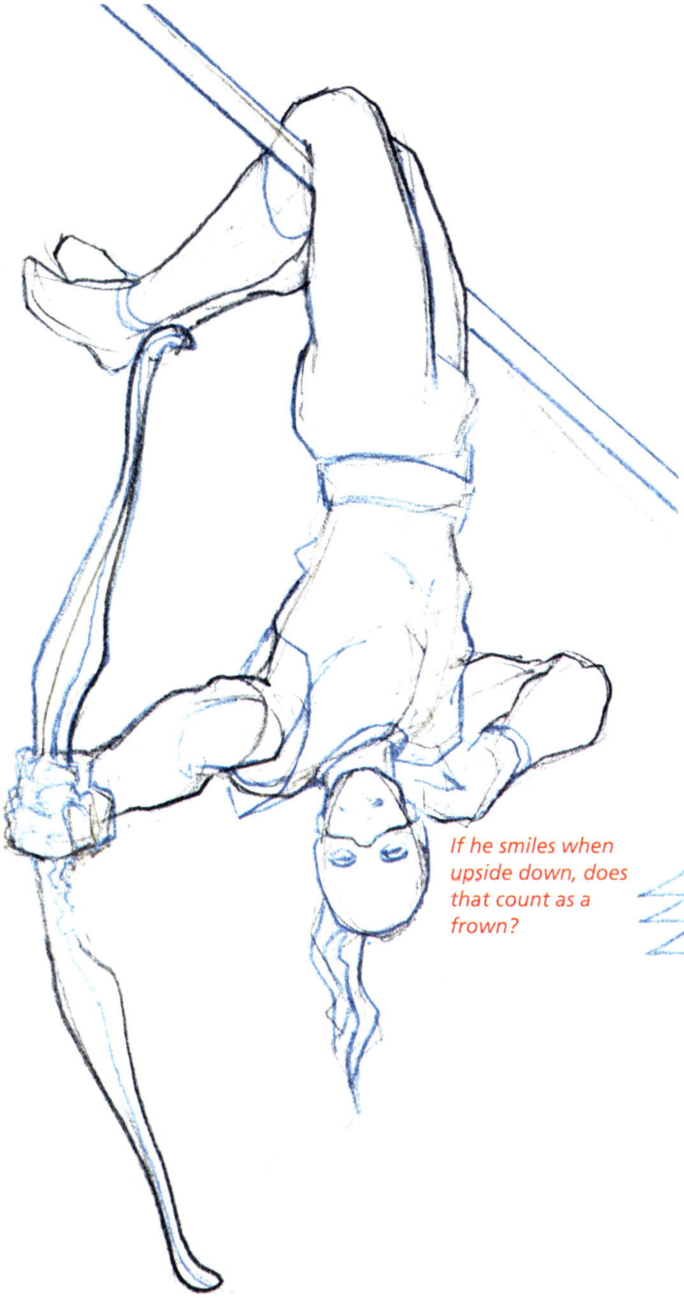

If he smiles when upside down, does that count as a frown?

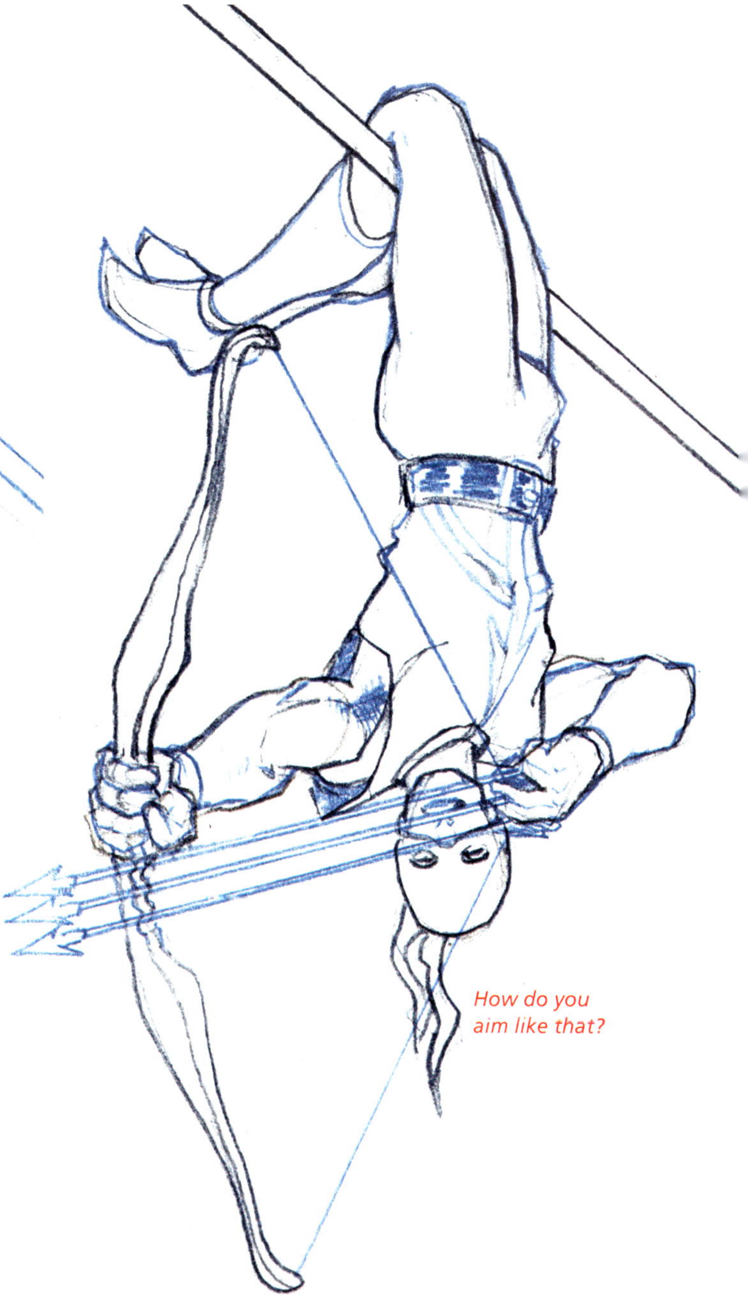

How do you aim like that?

3. Give the bow some depth and put some eyes in that mask. Work in details on the costume, from the boots all the way to the tail of the mask.

4. Add three arrows to the bow and finish off the mouth. Place his nocked arrow icon on his chest. Black out his belt and the inside of his shirt (which shows around his left arm), but leave some white space on the belt for highlights.

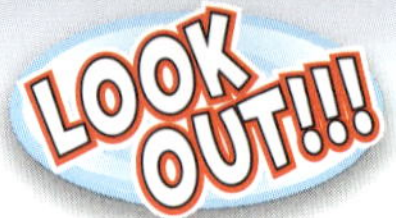

Accuracy of details matters. If you don't know exactly what a particular object (like, say, a bow) looks like, find out. Grab a photo reference or search for it on the Internet. Make it look real.

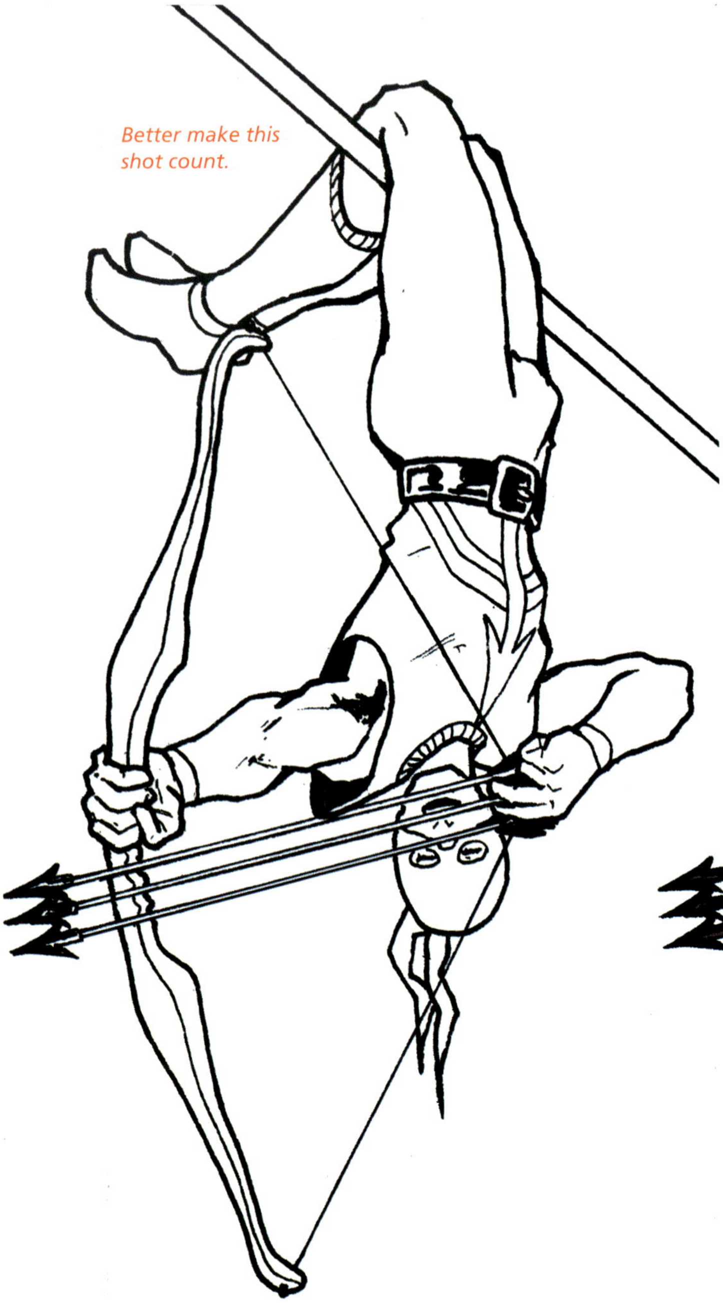

Better make this shot count.

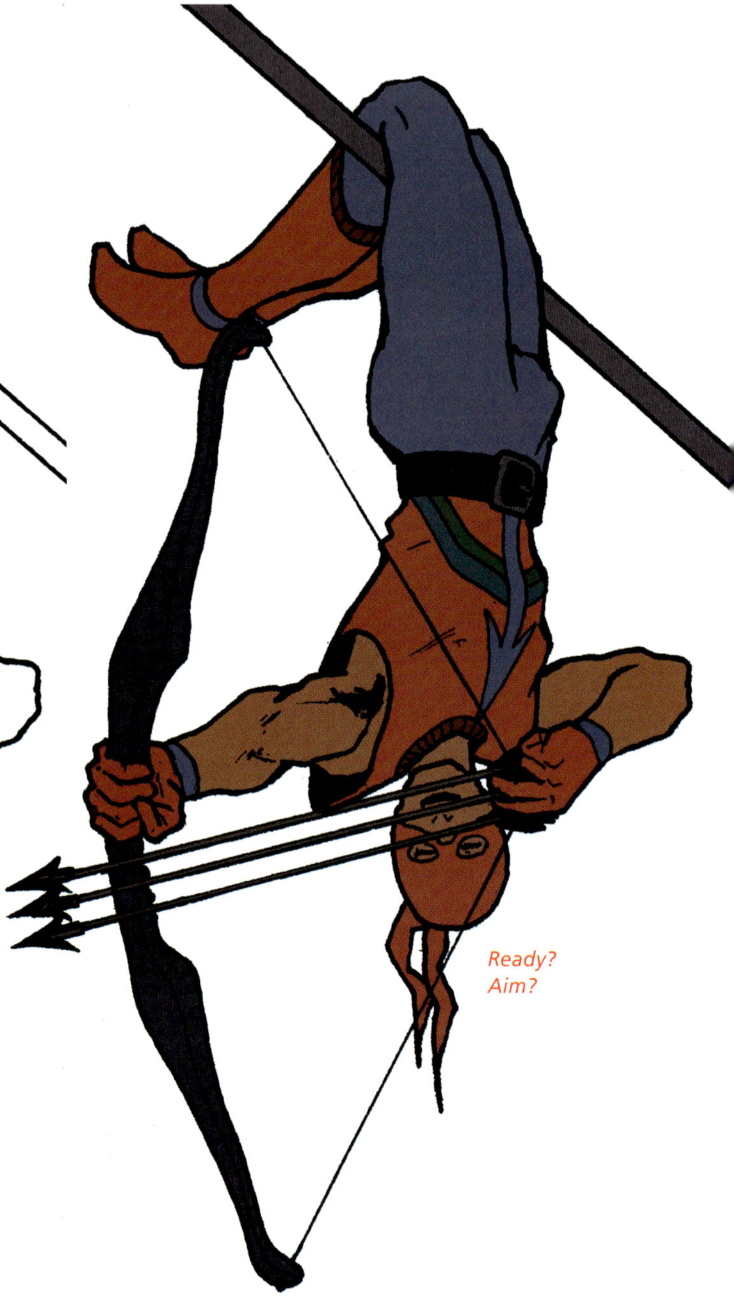

Ready? Aim?

5. Use a consistent inking line throughout. The only exceptions are slightly lighter lines for the icon, the arrow shafts, and the corner of the bow.

6. Go with blue for the pants and icon, red for the shirt, boots, and mask. Gray works well for the arrows, bow, and pole.

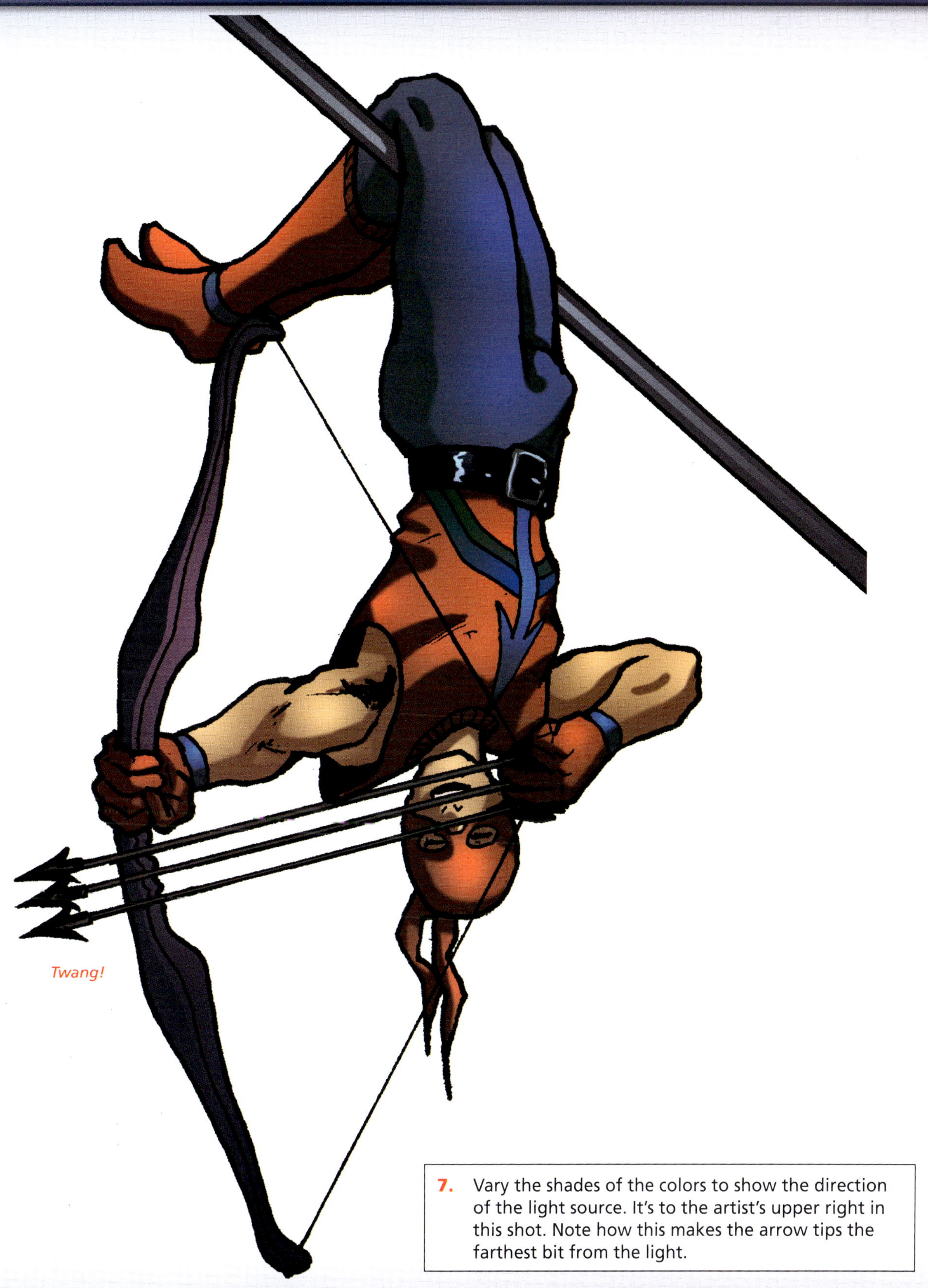

7. Vary the shades of the colors to show the direction of the light source. It's to the artist's upper right in this shot. Note how this makes the arrow tips the farthest bit from the light.

THE PISTOLEER

The Pistoleer always liked to play with guns, even as a young girl. She somehow managed to modify her cap gun to fire pebbles, and she killed her first bird at the age of three. As she grew older, she realized that guns are only really good for one thing—killing—so that's what she took up as her career.

She's got you in her sights. (Okay, she's actually got the guy looking over your left shoulder.)

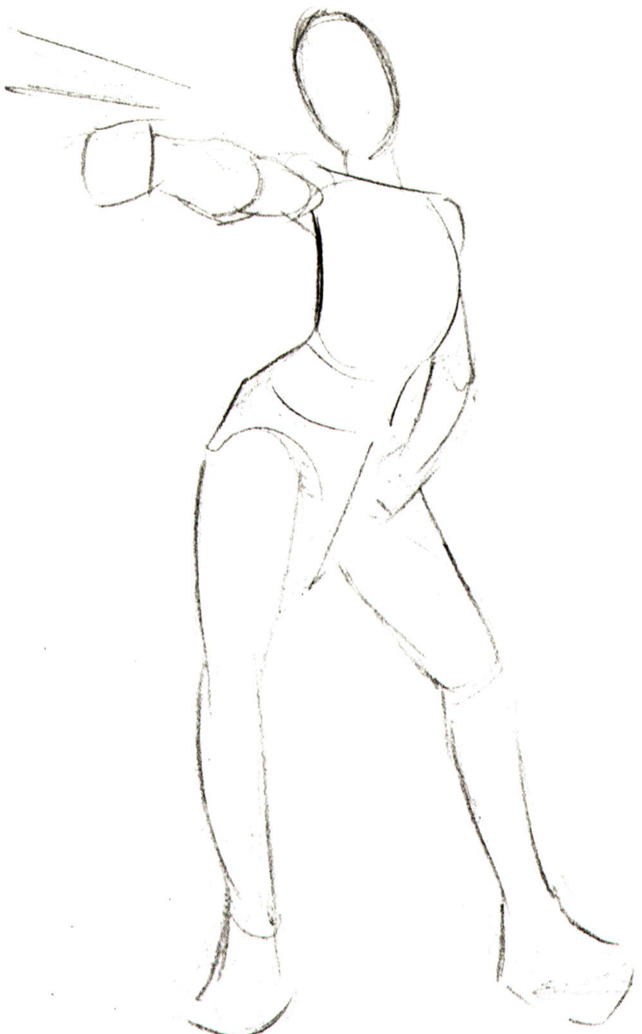

Lock and load!

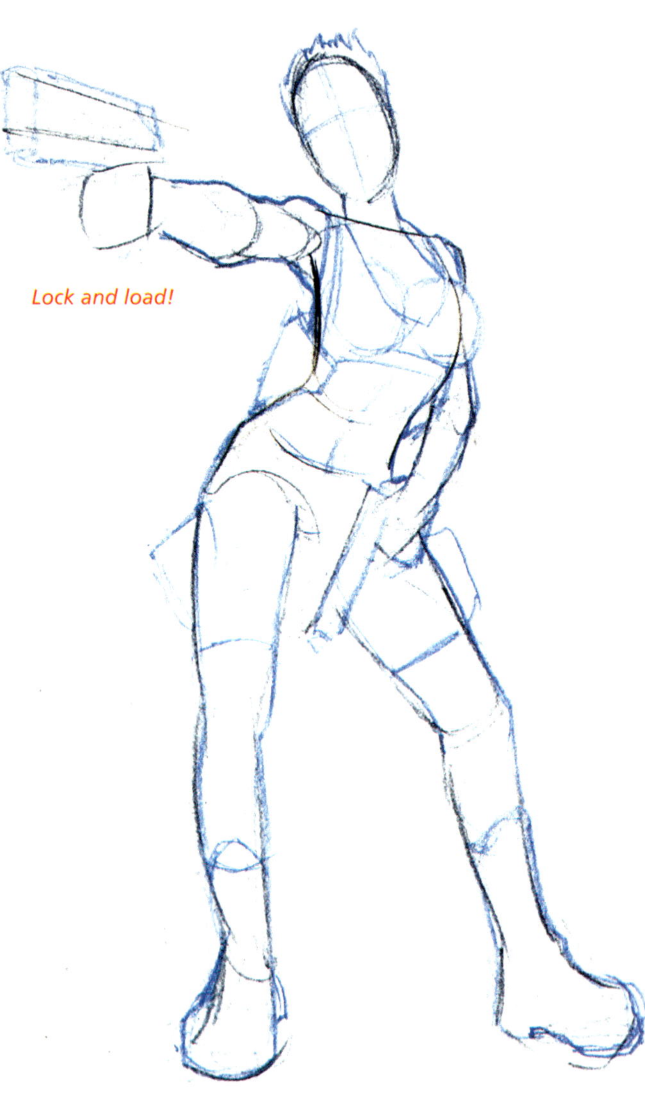

1. Break down the Pistoleer's form. She stands with her hips at an angle as she stares down the sights of her gun. Note the foreshortening of the arm and how the forced perspective makes the gun seem bigger at its muzzle.

2. Add in the Pistoleer's breasts, clothing, hair, and guns. Note the guidelines on the face and belly that help keep track of the woman's center. The guns are just rectangles now, but that's going to change soon.

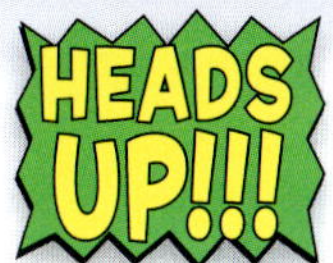

When breaking down the pose of a woman, you can leave off the breasts and worry about them later. The shape of the hips and the bend of the back still mark even this basic shape in this section as a woman. Secondary sexual characteristics you can worry about later.

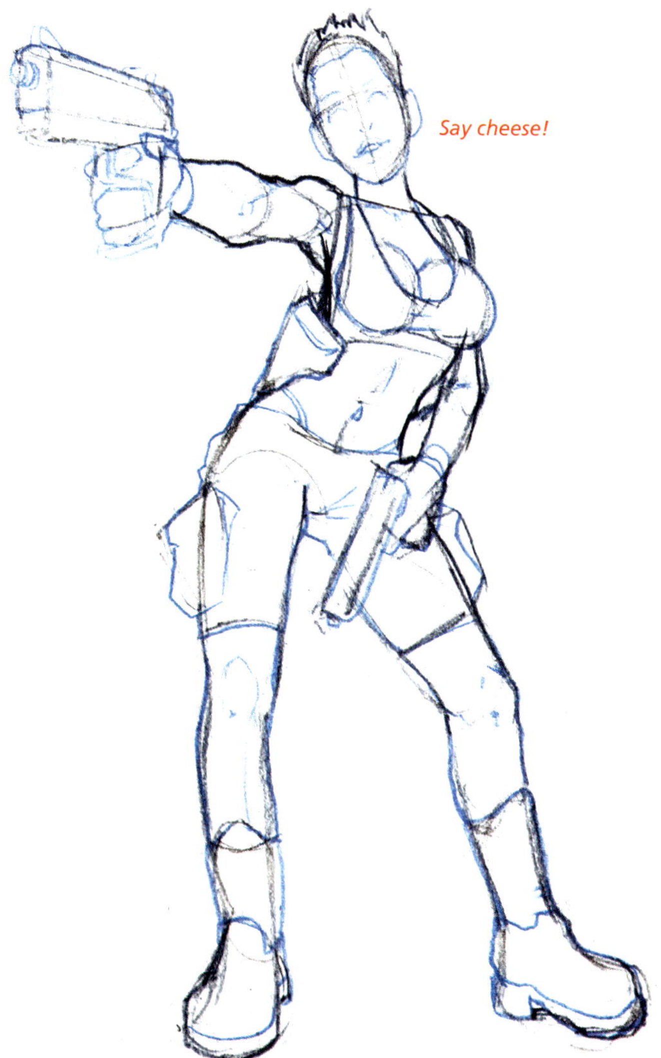

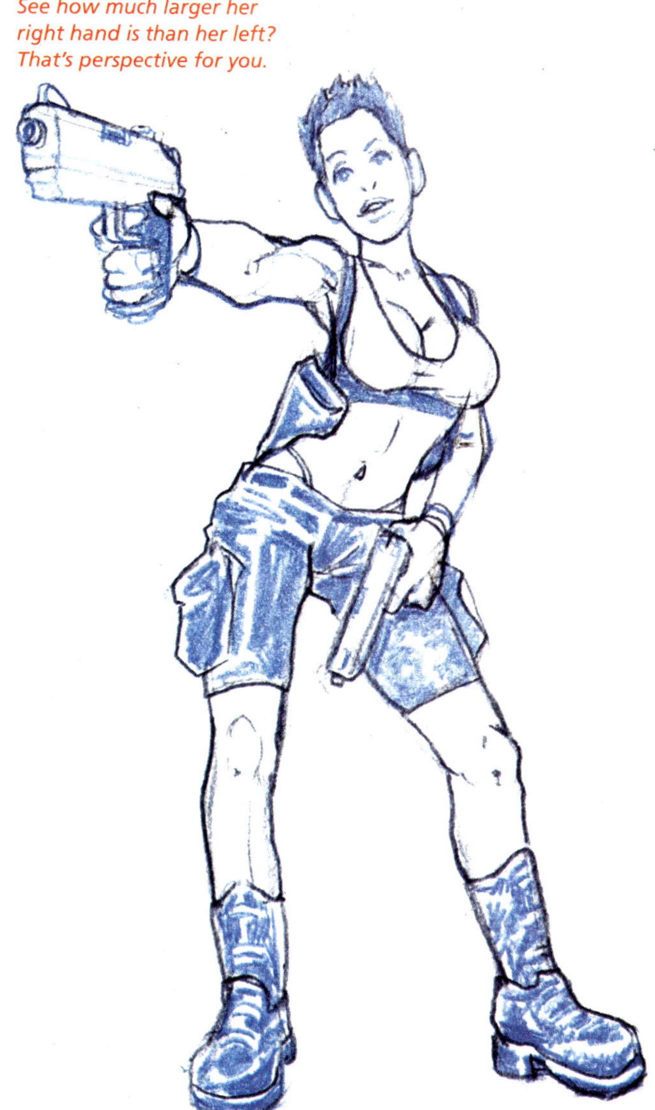

3. Work the details onto the guns. Clarify the Pistoleer's fingers. Add some baggy pockets to her shorts, large enough to carry lots of ammo. Sketch in her face and her ears.

4. Black out her shorts and boots, as well as the harness that carries her double holsters for her guns. Use white space to show the wrinkles and highlights. Black out her hair as well. Refine the face, concentrating on the eyes.

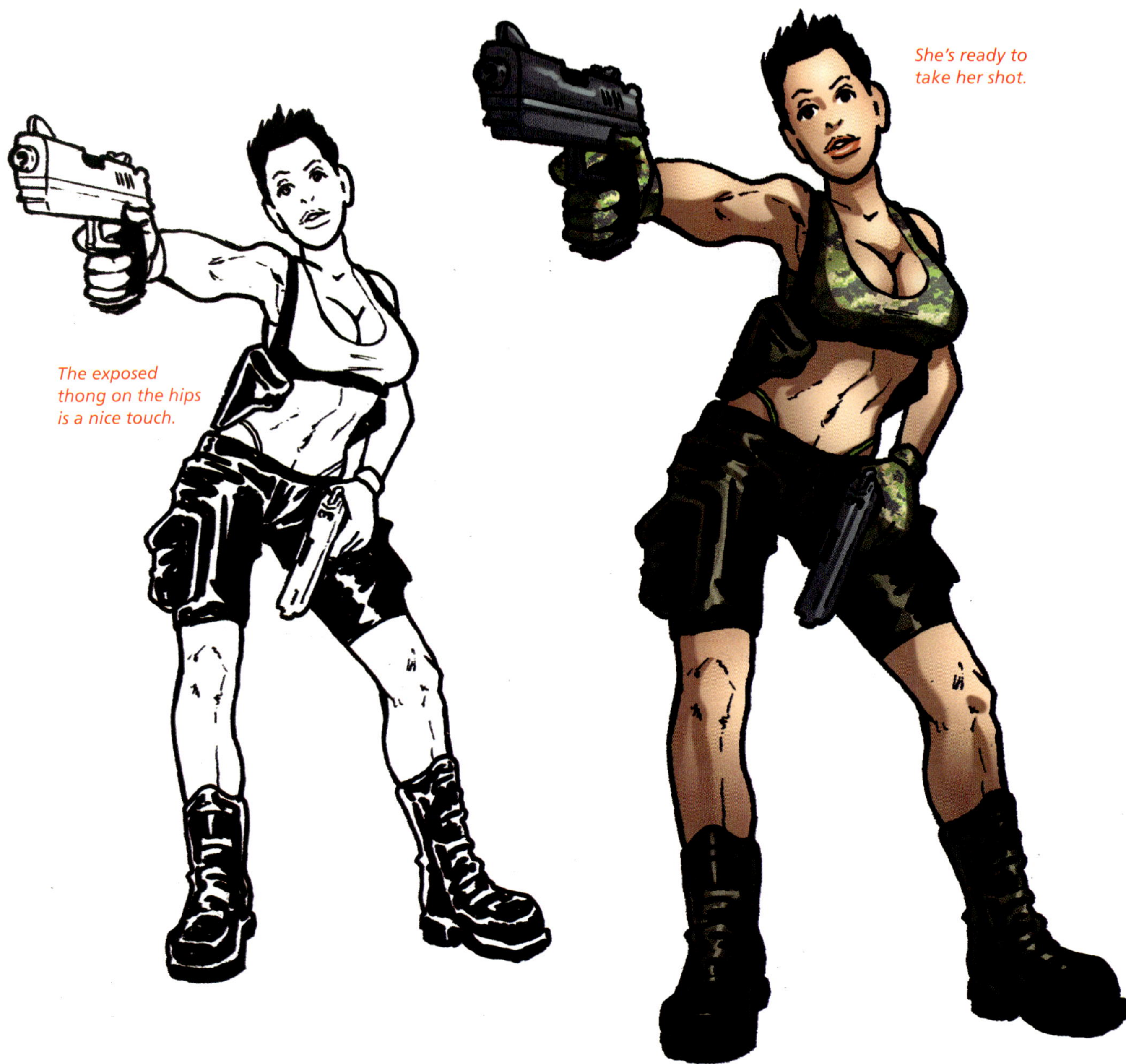

5. Use varied weights for your lines. While heavy inks work for the exterior lines, use lighter ones for the interior bits.

6. Go with camouflage or army green for every bit of clothing. Even the pants and boots, which are mostly black, show olive drab highlights. Subdued bluing on the guns works well here and contrasts well with the green.

THE WEBBER

The Webber was once a not-so-mild-mannered research scientist working in the field of nanotechnology. He developed a strange series of nanites based upon proteins found in his blood and then injected himself with them in order to smuggle them out of his place of work after his villainous employer tried to steal credit for his discoveries. The nanites transformed the man into the Webber, an incredibly agile man who can fire sticky webs of nanites from the backs of his hands.

The clean line of the webbing under his right arm makes it seem like he's swooping straight at you.

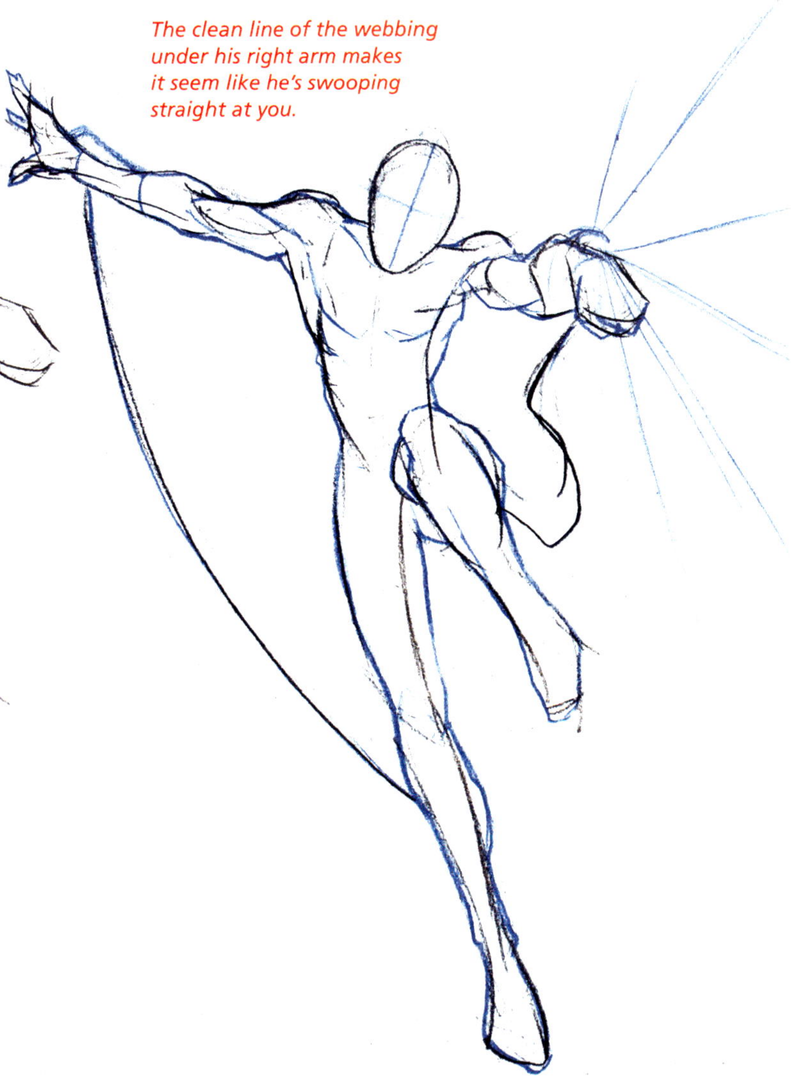

Notice how foreshortening makes his left thigh disappear.

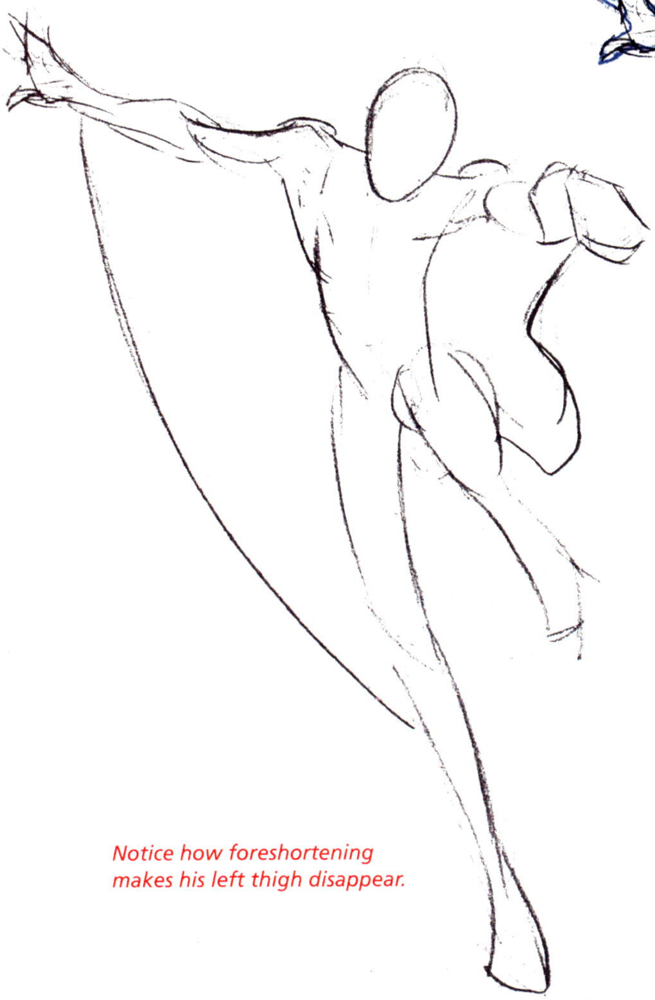

1. Break down the Webber, showing him swinging through the air. He wears nanites webbing under his arms, too, stretching it from his wrists to his ankles. This allows him to glide for short periods.

2. Add guidelines on the face and chest to help you keep things centered. Buff up his muscles a bit. Add housings for his web blasters on the backs of his hands. Show a spray of webbing coming out of his left wrist.

LOOK OUT!!!

Many of the characters in this book are clearly original approximations of already existing characters. It's fine to do that, especially for something like a drawing book, as long as you're aware of it. Copying someone else's work directly is a violation of their copyright. Coming up with your own version of it is fair play.

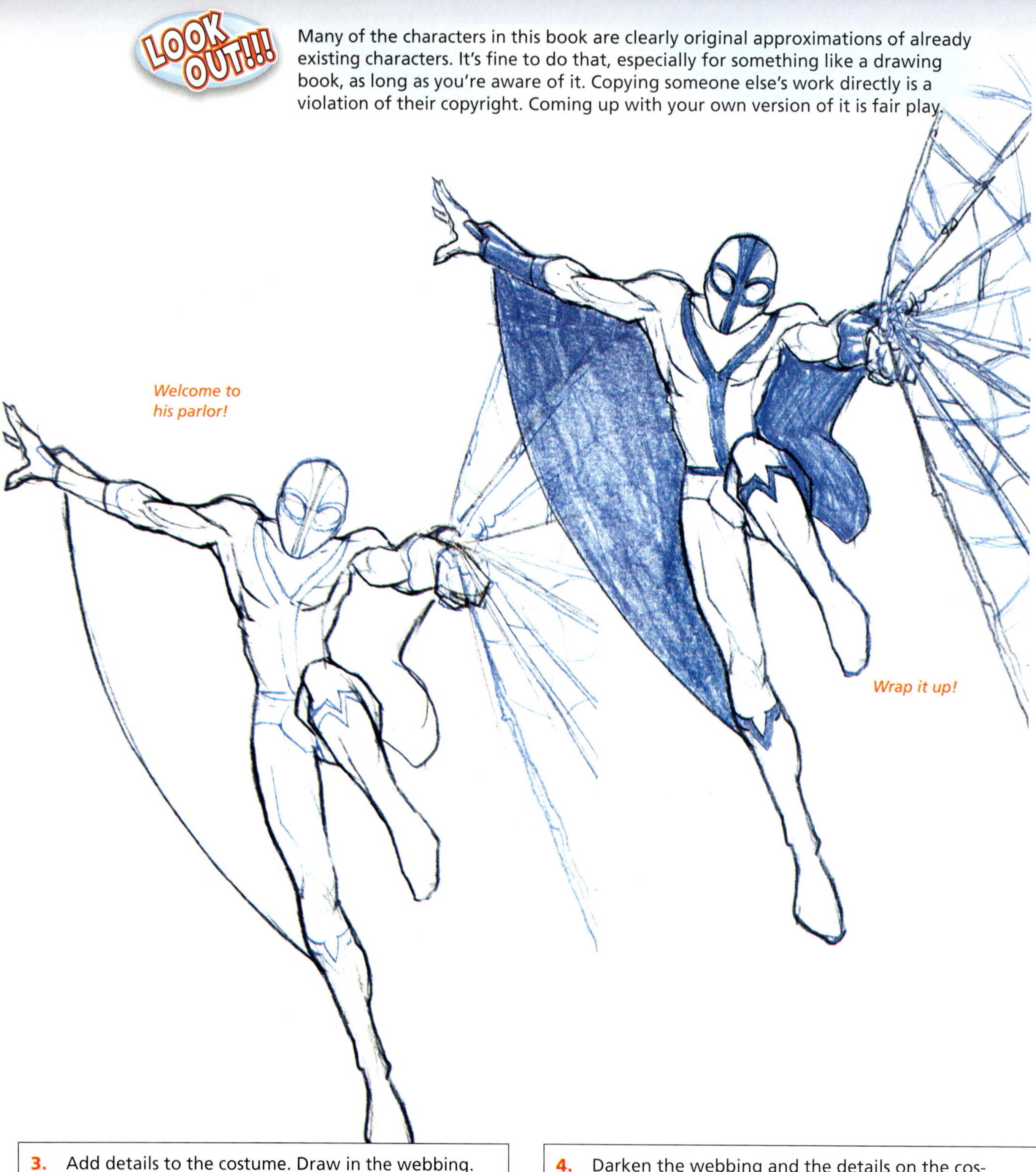

3. Add details to the costume. Draw in the webbing. To make it distinct from that of other webslingers, show it fanning out from the Webber's wrist.

4. Darken the webbing and the details on the costume. Leave the lenses covering his eyes wide and blank. Work more details into the webbing to make it look like it's spraying toward you and not directly to the viewer's right.

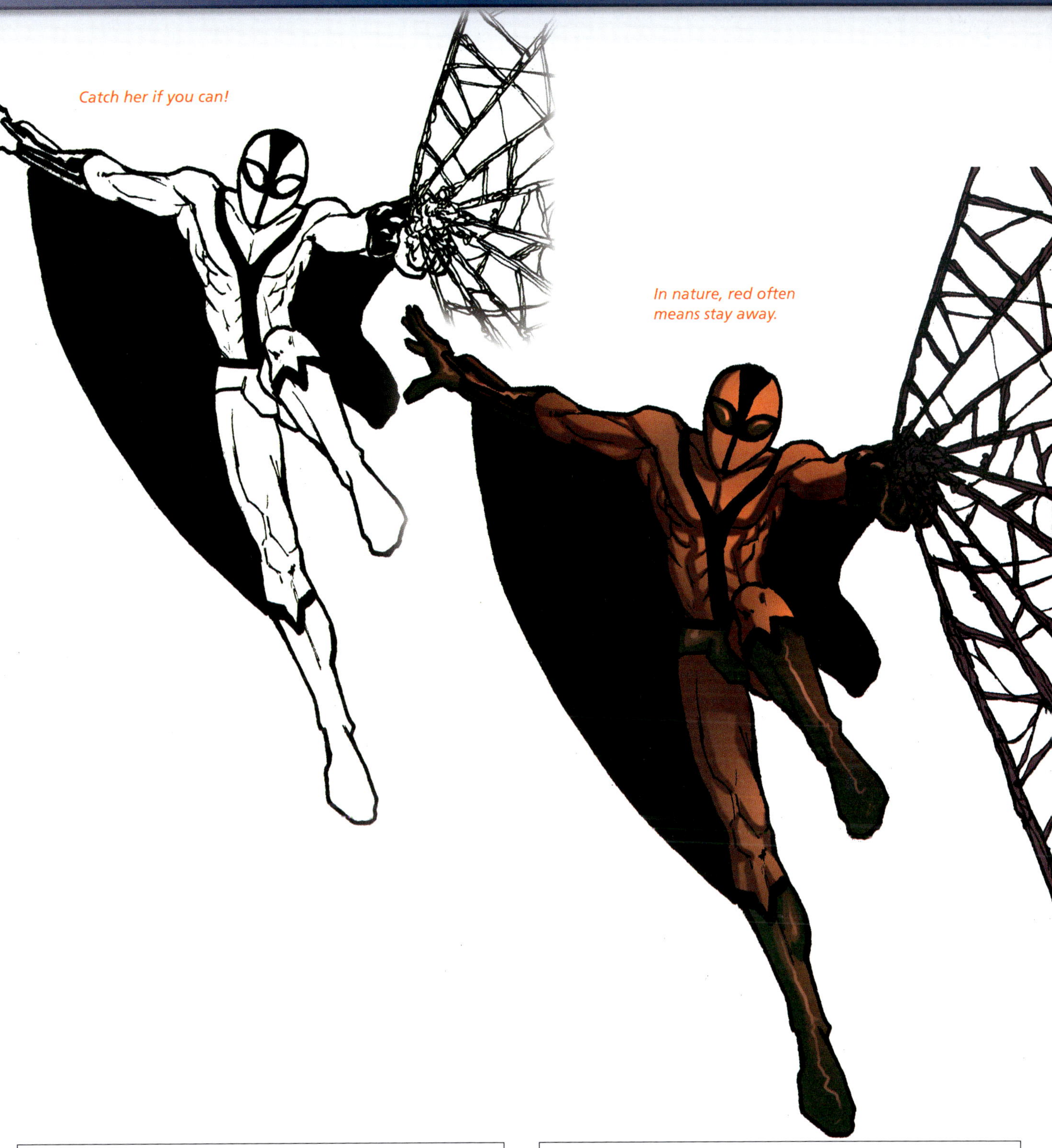

5. Use strong lines for the edges of the costume, and thinner lines for interior marks, like those that show his muscles. Make the webbing as intricate as you like.

6. Tint the whole hero a blood red, including his webbing. That's the source of his powers but also a warning to those who might try to mess with him.

THE RAY-MAN

Ray-Man was once a preacher in a Baptist church, but after he developed his powers, his parishioners tossed him out. It seemed only fair because he'd been the one who'd preached to them about the evils of superpowered folks. He's since seen the error of his ways and now fights against injustice more directly than he did in the past, although the past few years have shaken his faith to its core.

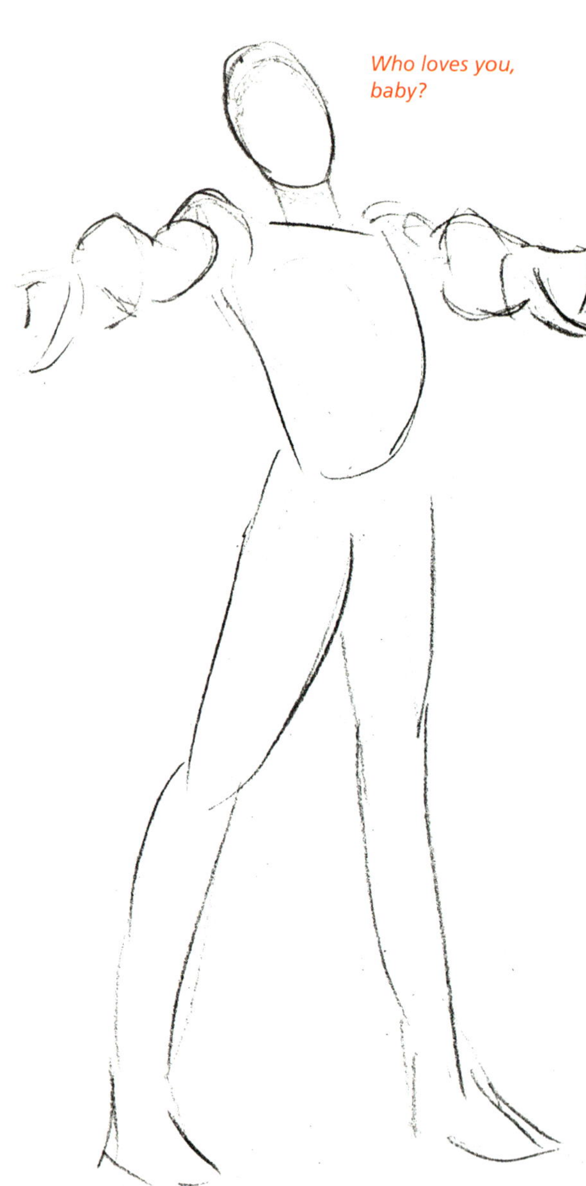

Who loves you, baby?

1. Break down Ray-Man's pose. He stands with his arms out, like a preacher about to bring down the thunder of God. This foreshortens both limbs about the same amount.

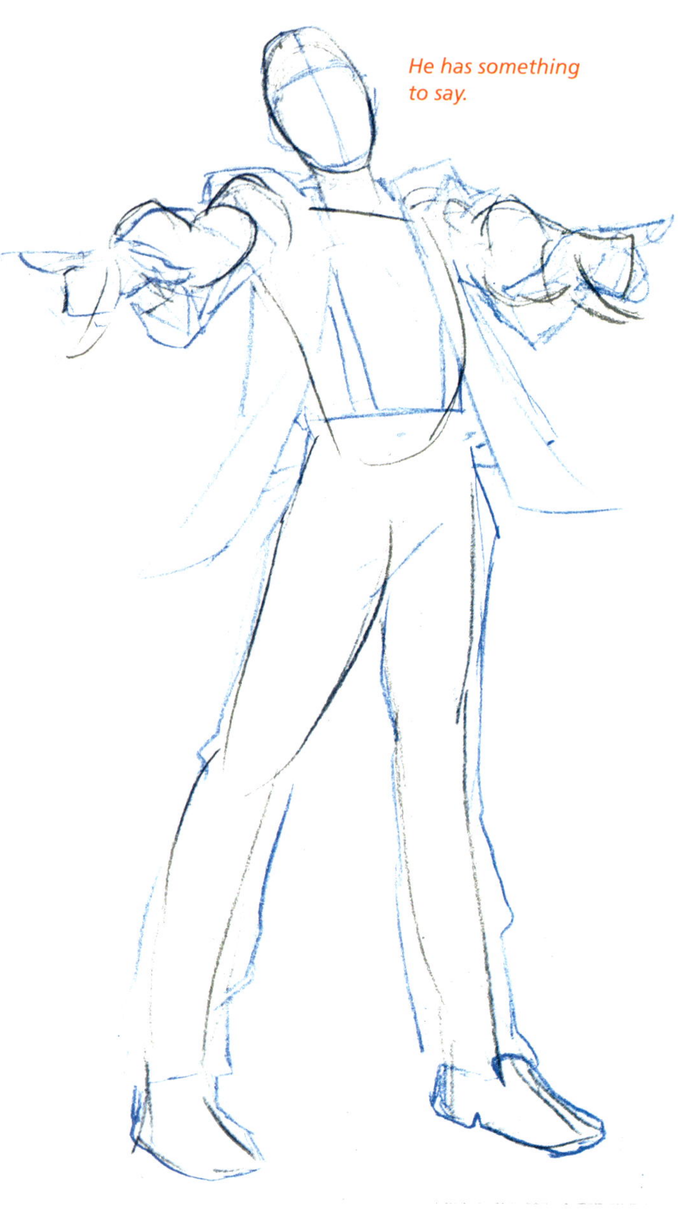

He has something to say.

2. Add his clothes. Flair out the jacket to give him a sense of action. Watch how the shoulders bunch up as he raises his arms.

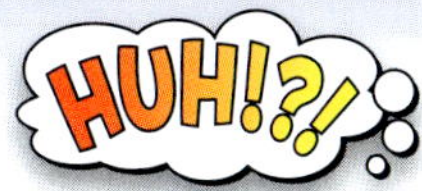

Ray-Man suspects his powers came to him from God, but he's not sure. That's alright. A little mystery about such things can add a layer of intrigue to the character and pull readers more firmly into his story. Even if he did believe that God gave him his powers, though, doesn't mean he'd be right.

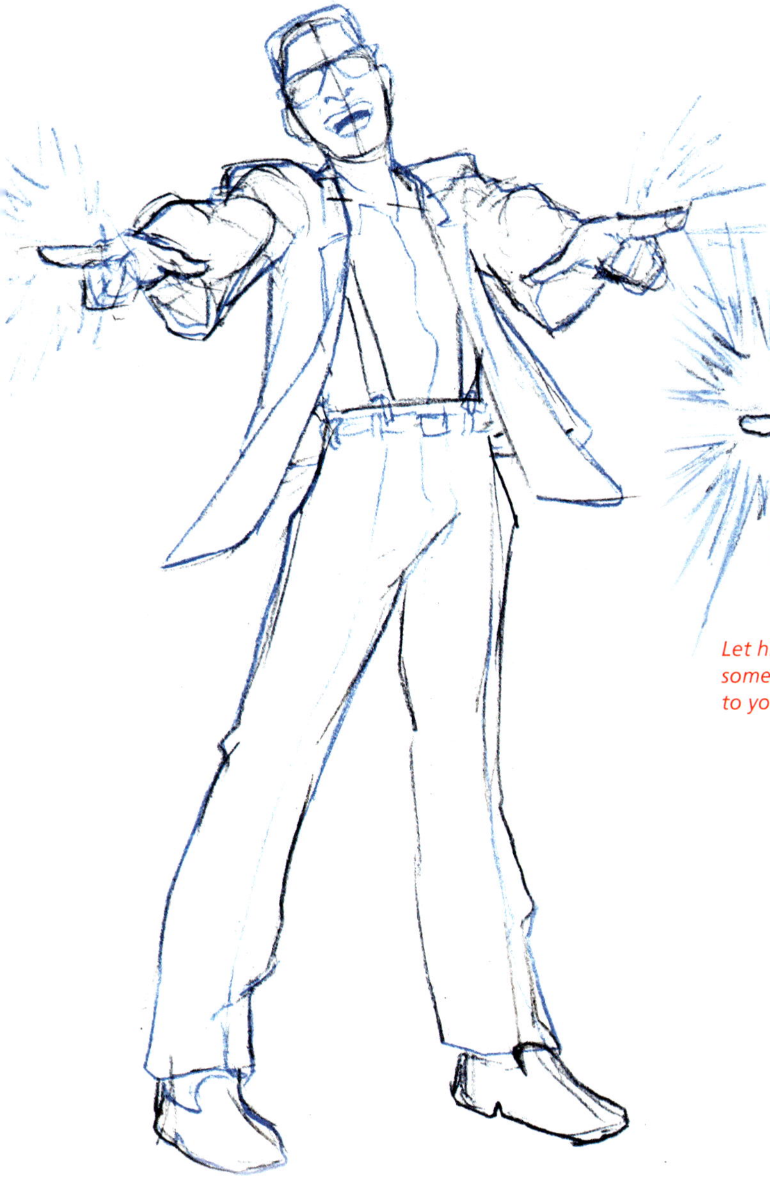

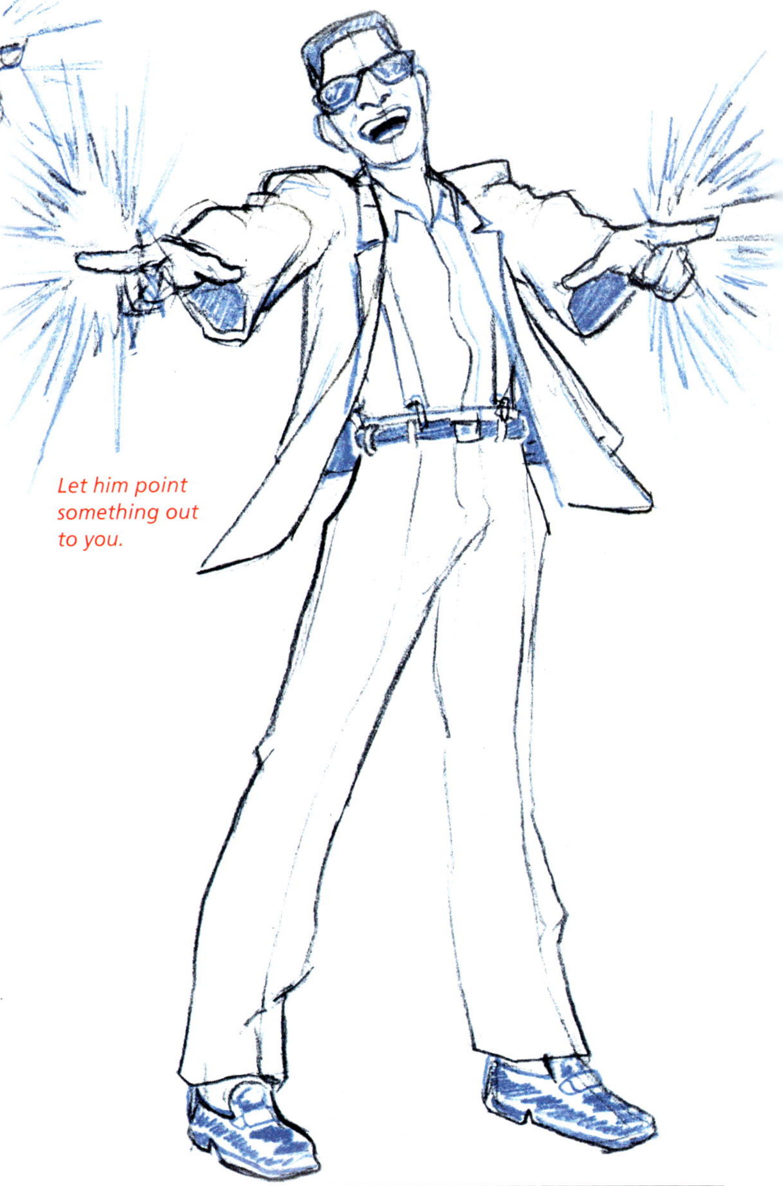

Let him point something out to you.

Ray is one of the better-dressed heroes. No Spandex here.

3. Define the hands, and show power glowing from their index fingers. Slap a pair of shades over his eyes, and a wide smile on his mouth. The suspenders give him an old-timey feel, too, a nice touch.

4. Blacken his shoes and belt and the interior of his coat and sleeves. Sharpen up the other details.

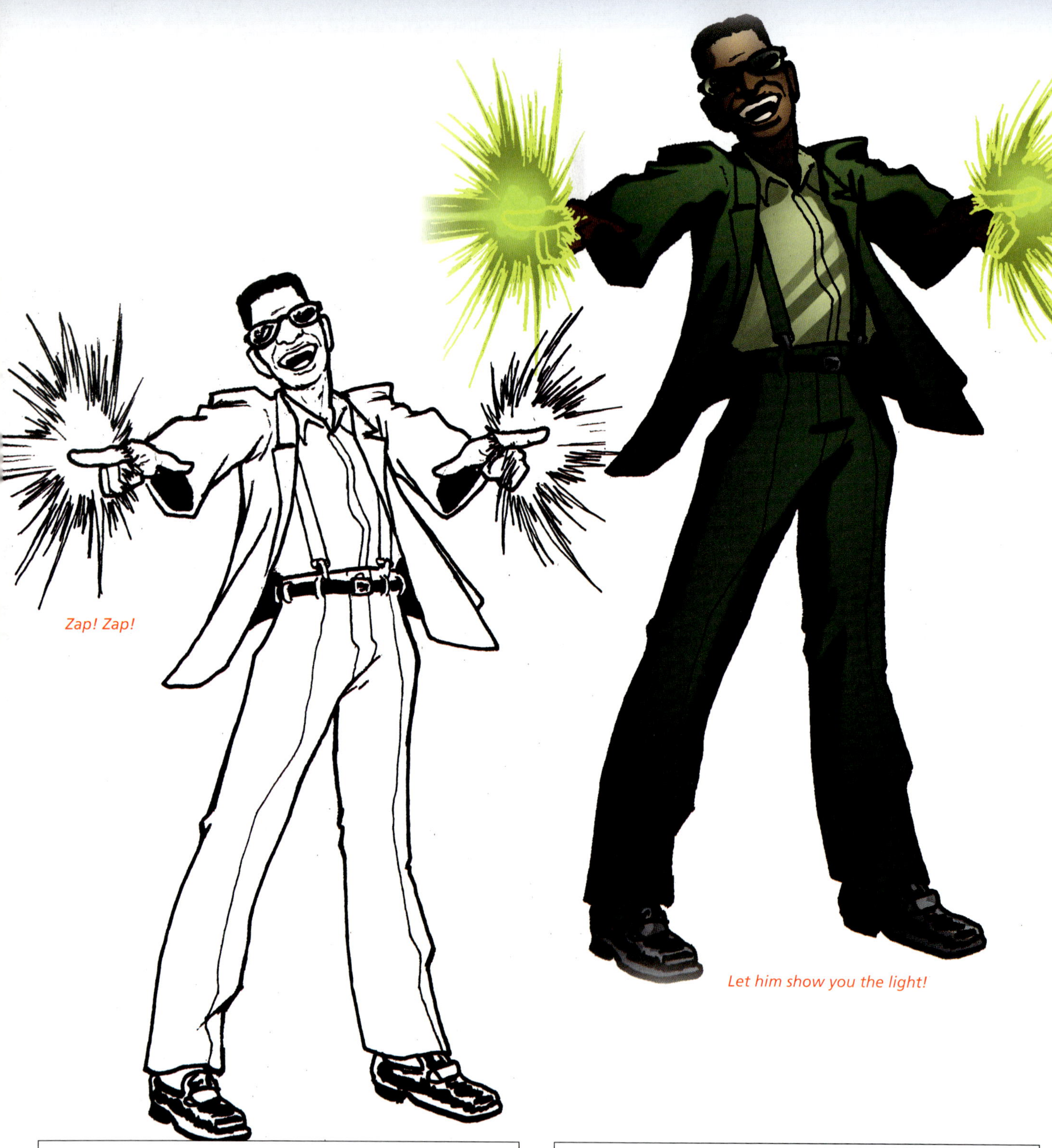

5. Ink Ray-Man with standard lines. For the creases on his pants and the stubble on his chin use the lighter-weight lines, leaving the rest of it to heavier inks.

6. Ray-Man looks like he loves everyone, but he stands ready to put sinners back in their places—by any means necessary. Choose greens or variants on it to show colors like those his powers manifest.

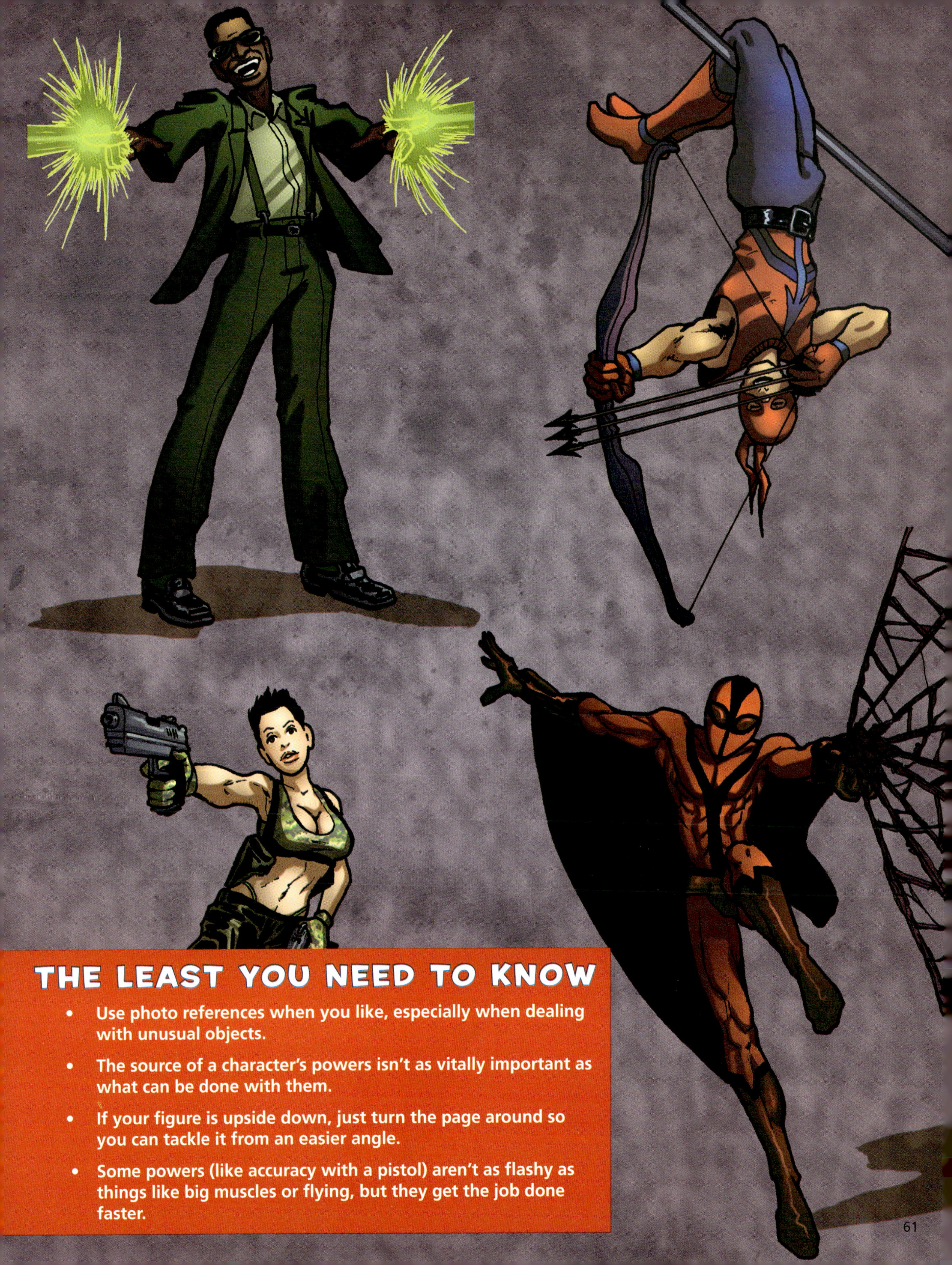

THE LEAST YOU NEED TO KNOW

- Use photo references when you like, especially when dealing with unusual objects.
- The source of a character's powers isn't as vitally important as what can be done with them.
- If your figure is upside down, just turn the page around so you can tackle it from an easier angle.
- Some powers (like accuracy with a pistol) aren't as flashy as things like big muscles or flying, but they get the job done faster.

PART 2

BRAINS

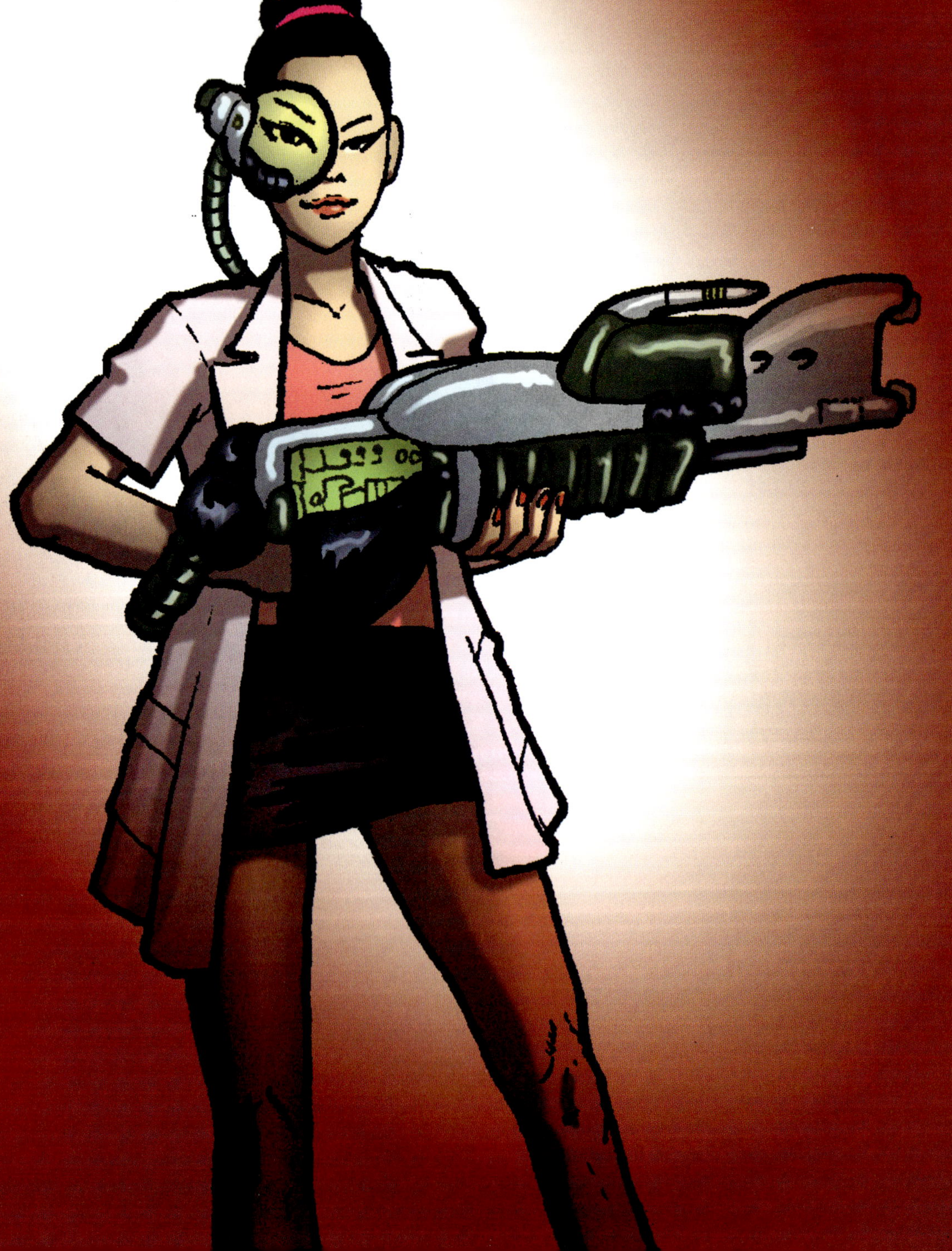

IN THIS PART

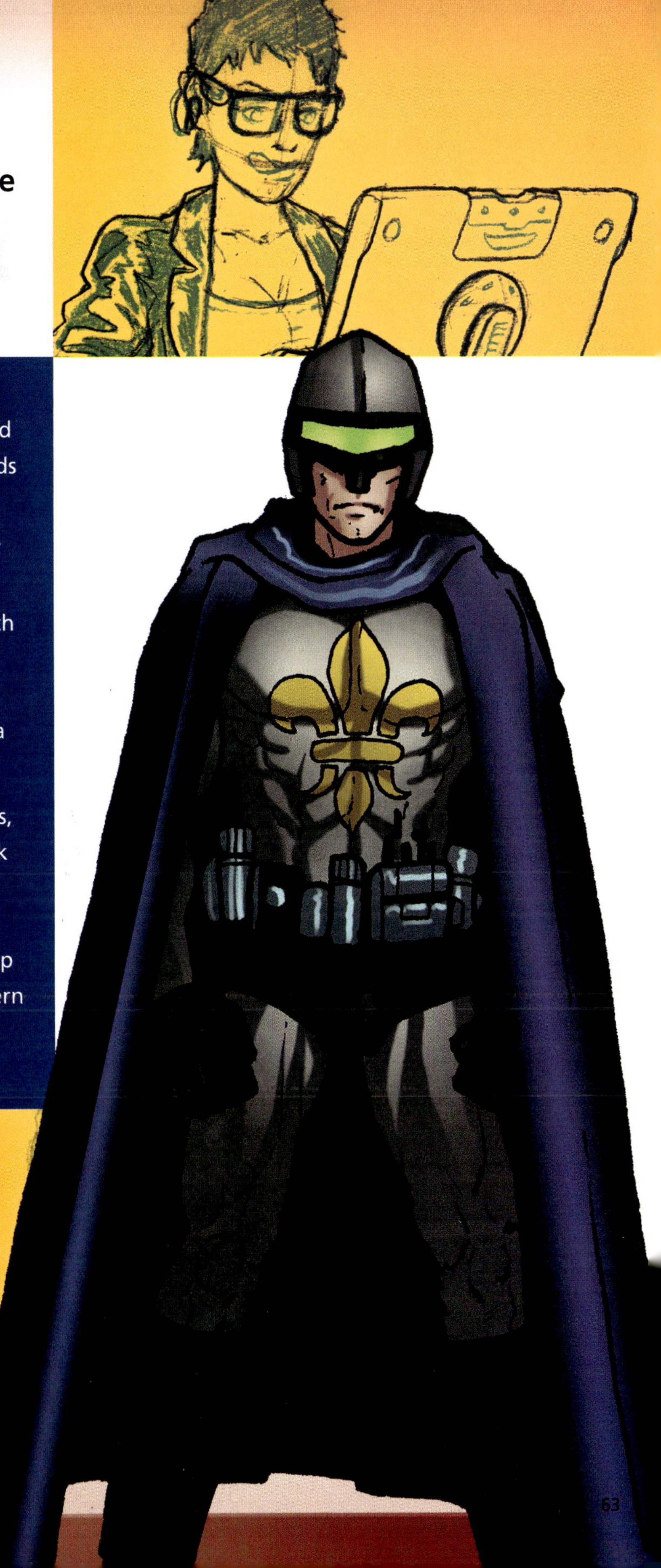

Even in comic books, it's not all about brawling. Sometimes the heroes—and even the villains—need to put a little mental sweat into their jobs. This adds an element of sophistication to the stories, too, that's hard to find with simple toe-to-toe beatings.

Smart folks come in a variety of styles, of course. There are many ways to be smart, from the research scientist to the detective to the master of the mystic arts. Each of these types of people can come in handy in a comic-book tale, and it's good to have a command of each type in your arsenal.

In this part, we begin with the straight-up geniuses, the characters who'd make Einstein wish he'd stuck to remedial math. Then we meet the gadgeteers, the characters who create and use amazing bits of technology to aid them in their efforts. We wind up with the mystics, the people who go beyond modern science into the world of the weird.

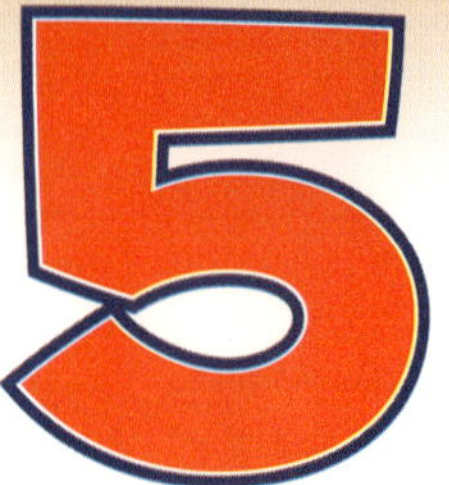

5 Geniuses: That Smarts!

In This Chapter

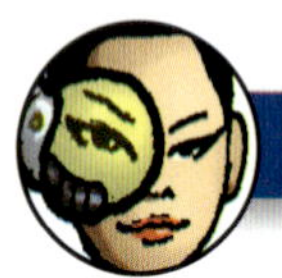

- A knowledgeable woman

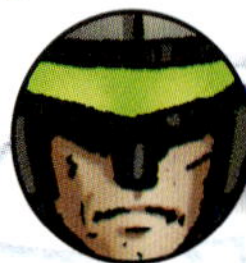

- A dark detective

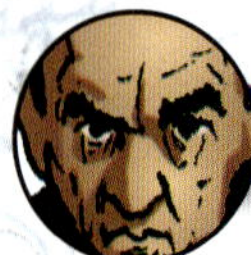

- A master of young minds

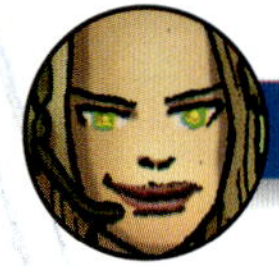

- The brains behind it all

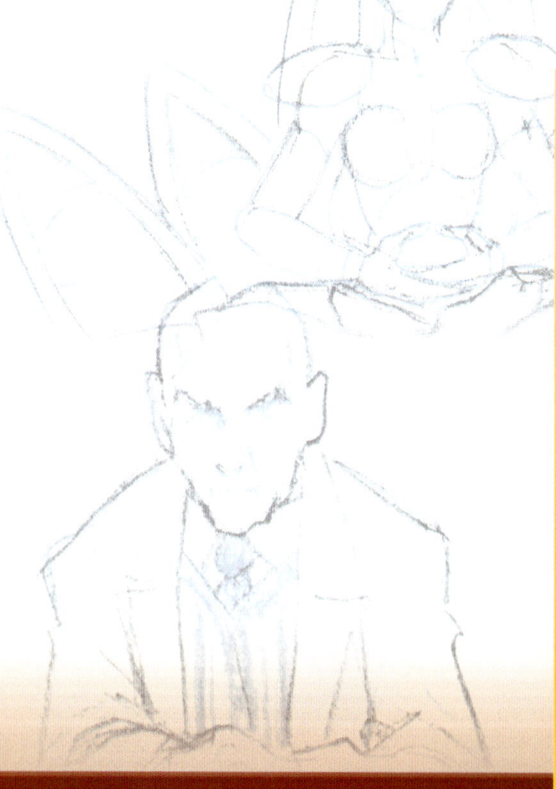

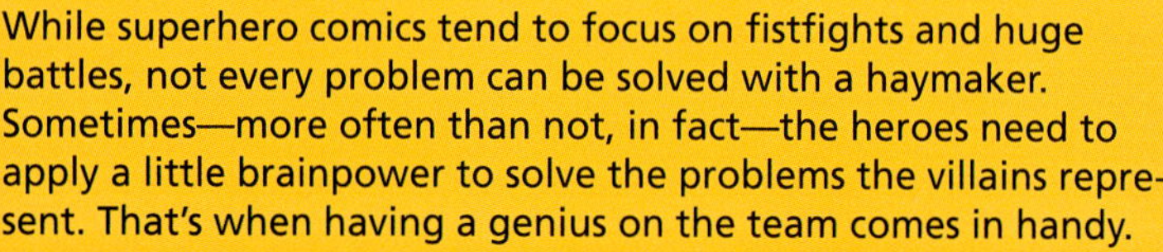

While superhero comics tend to focus on fistfights and huge battles, not every problem can be solved with a haymaker. Sometimes—more often than not, in fact—the heroes need to apply a little brainpower to solve the problems the villains represent. That's when having a genius on the team comes in handy.

First up, we have Encyclopedic, a woman who knows a bit about everything and can access information faster than Google. If you want to know about anything, she's the person to ask. If she doesn't know it off the top of her head, she'll figure it out in seconds.

Next we have the Accuser, a detective who makes your favorite CSI team look like the Keystone Kops. Investigating crimes is his game, and there's no mystery he can't solve.

Enter the Headmaster, a brilliant sociologist with fascist aspirations. He works mostly behind the scenes, engineering discontent within societies, luring them closer and closer to following his plans to bring them all under his iron control.

We wrap up the chapter with Brains, a brilliant strategist who orchestrates the criminal activities of the Green Lotus. Her international organized crime outfit may have aspirations, but all such motivations spring from her and her carefully laid schemes.

ENCYCLOPEDIC

Encyclopedic grew up in Seattle, the child of a pair of computer programmers who specialized in search engines. As she grew older, her parents experimented on her with special mnemonic-building lessons, and she took to them like a guitar takes to music. As an adult, she uses her knowledge to help humanity—mostly by protecting everyone from less well-informed villains.

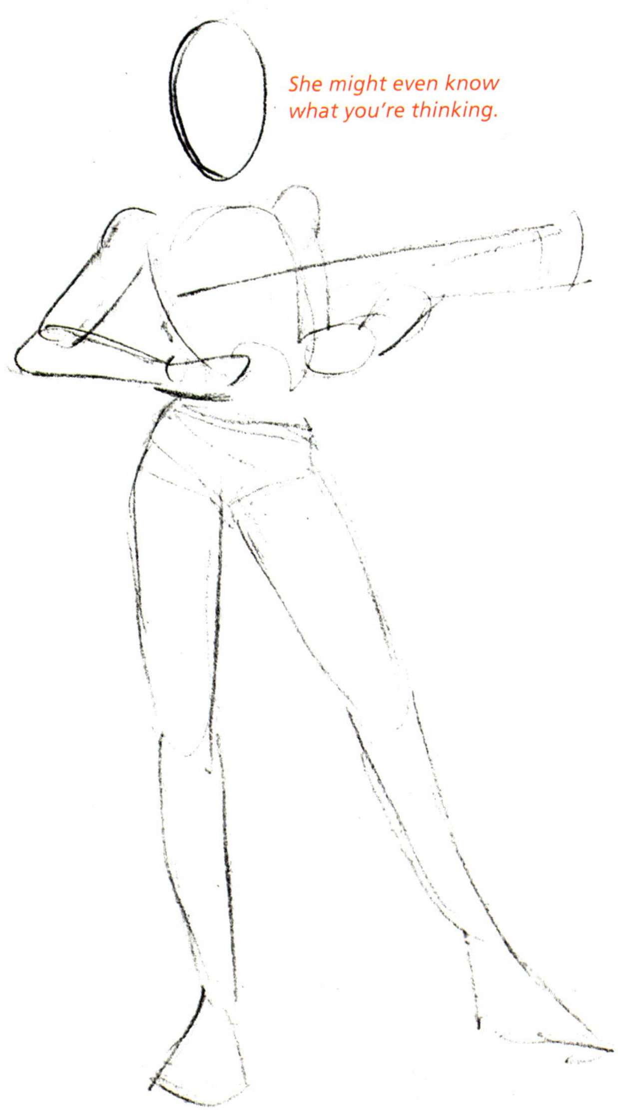

She might even know what you're thinking.

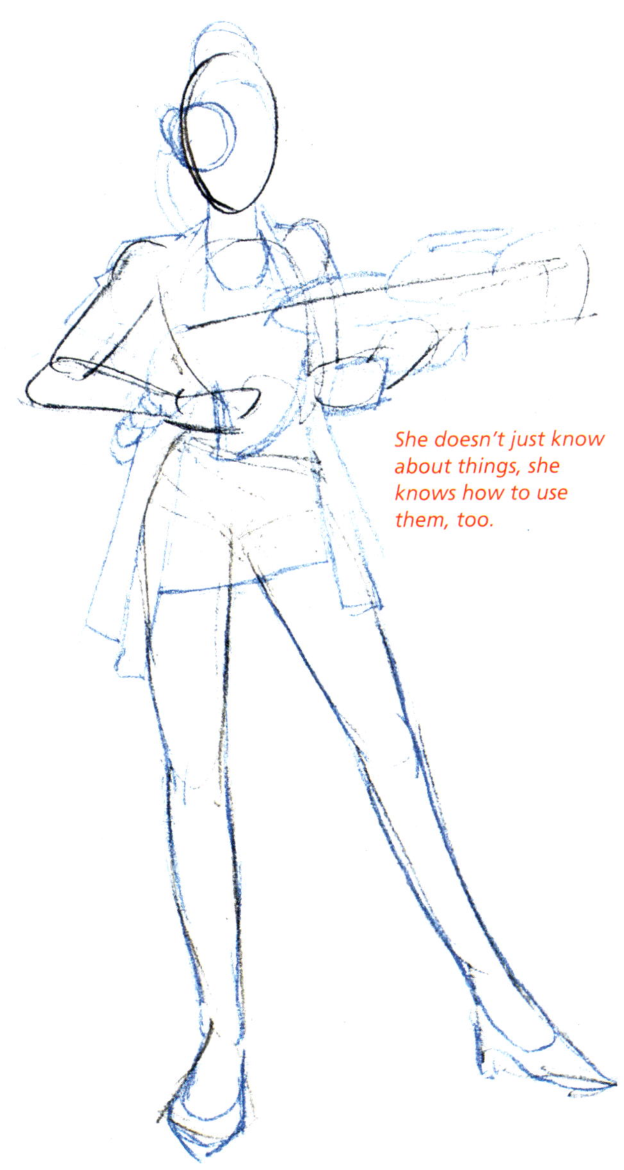

She doesn't just know about things, she knows how to use them, too.

1. Block out Encyclopedic's form. She's a petite Asian American, and she's carrying a weapon of her own design. She stands confidently, ready but not aggressive.

2. Put some clothes on her: a short skirt and a fashionable blouse under her lab coat. Put her hair up in a stylish bun and slap a targeting lens over her right eye.

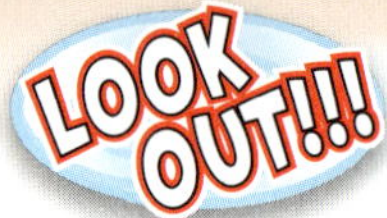

It's easy to just put all your brains (your smart characters, not the ones in your head) in lab coats and thick glasses. That's what people expect, so resist it. Encyclopedic is the closest we'll get to that in this book, and she still stands outside that mold.

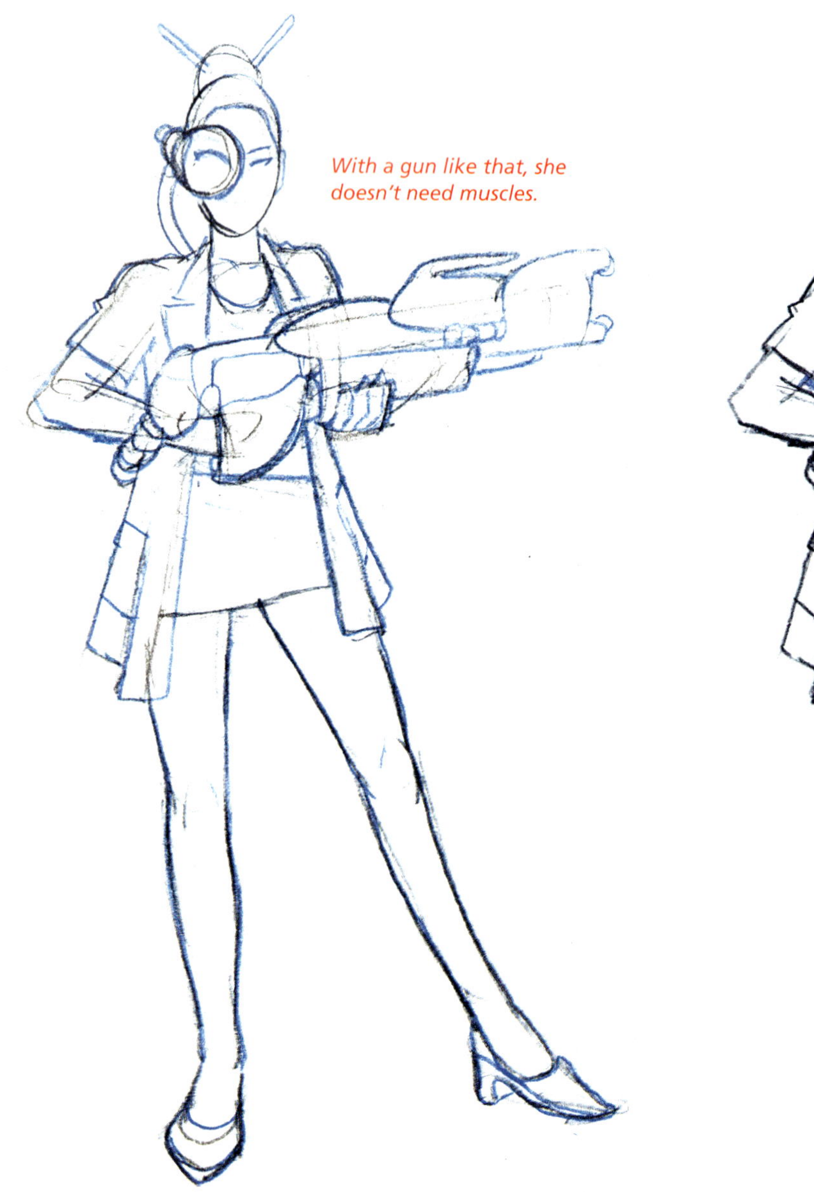

With a gun like that, she doesn't need muscles.

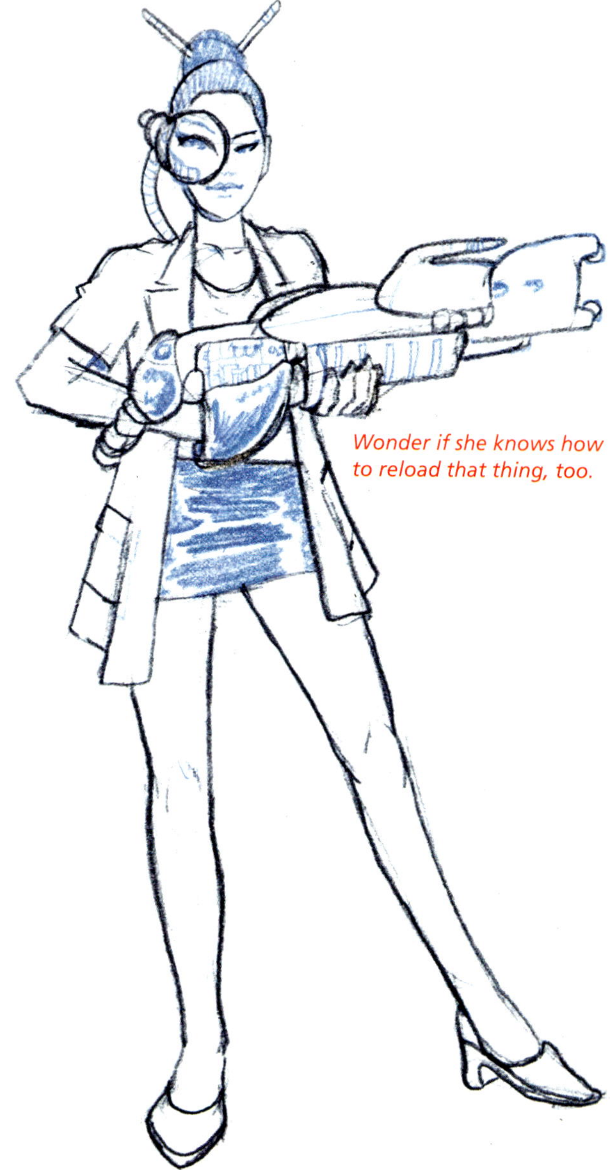

Wonder if she knows how to reload that thing, too.

3. Put hair sticks in her bun. Add lapels and pockets to her lab coat. Define her shoes as pumps, not the boots or heels most of the brawny characters wore. Add some high-tech details to the gun and the targeting lens.

4. Black out her skirt, leaving white space for wrinkles. Black out her hair, too. Add in her mouth, nose, and eyes. Make the right eye larger to show that it's behind the magnifying effects of the targeting lens. Add more details to the gun and sketch out her kneecaps with a couple subtle lines.

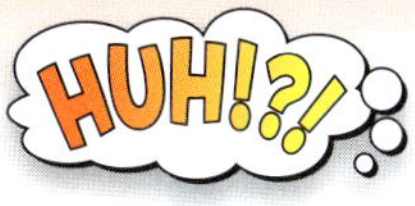

Most brains look just like regular people. To make them stand out, concentrate on their trappings or accessories. Without the space-age weapon and targeting lens, Encyclopedic might look much like a modern research scientist. The extras notify the viewer that she's much more.

Know something? She does.

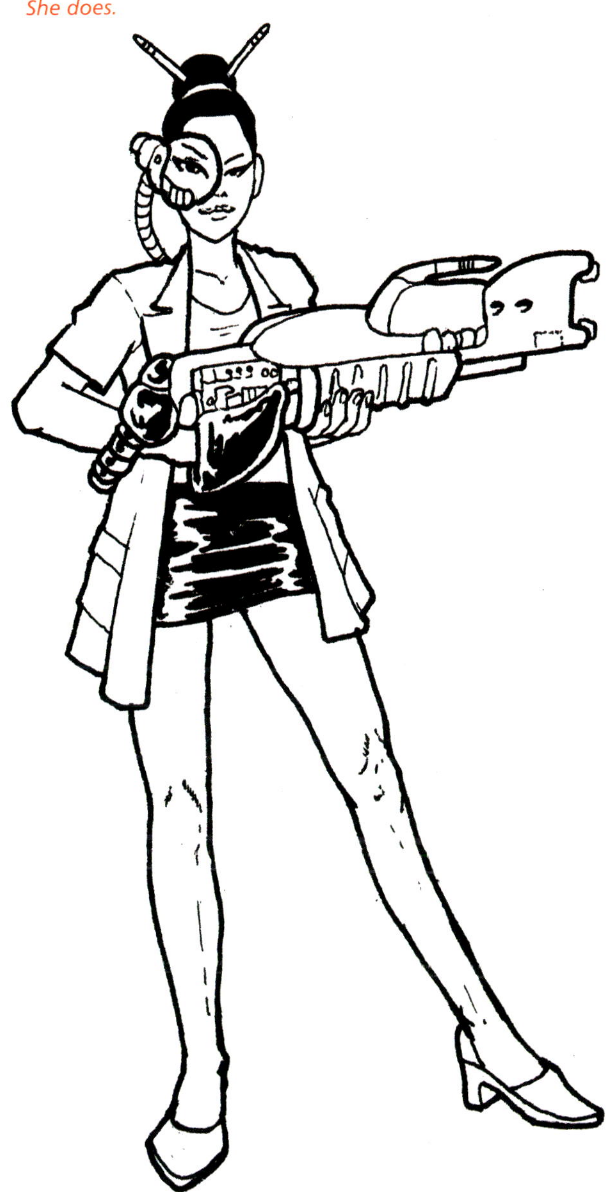

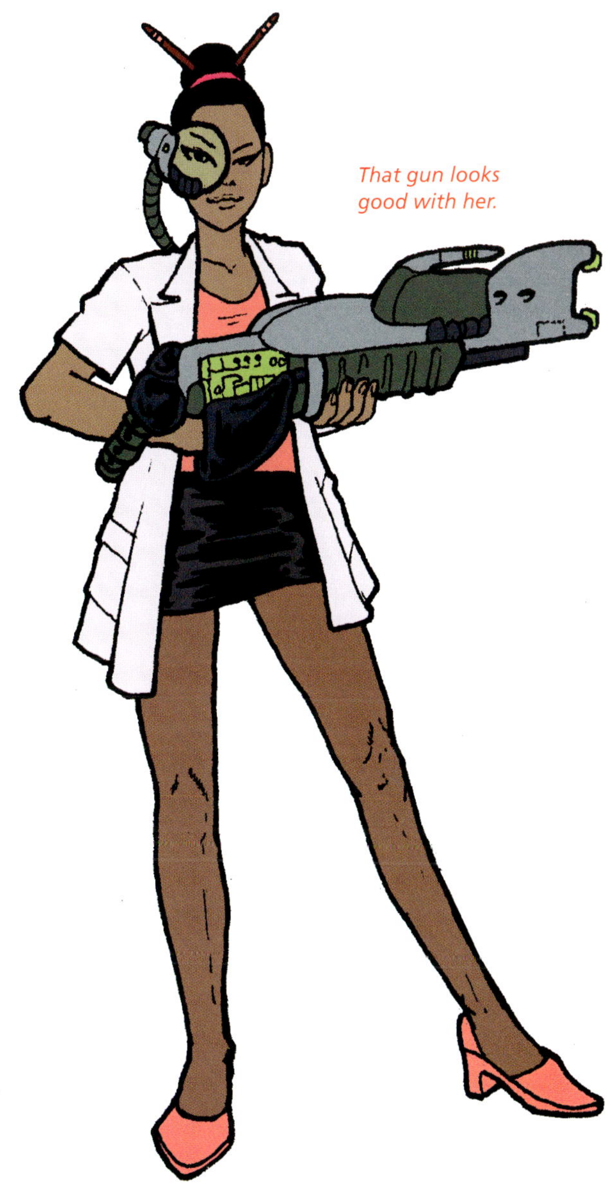

That gun looks good with her.

5. Use regular lines on Encyclopedic's limbs and clothes and on the weapon, too. More subtle lines on the knees, lower legs, and collarbone soften her just a bit, as does the seam on the shoulder of her coat.

6. Give her a lavender shirt and pink shoes and blouse. Her hair band is red as are the sticks in her bun. Make the gun and lens shades of military gray and green. This causes them to contrast with her, but the similarity of the subtleness of the colors helps them still complement each other.

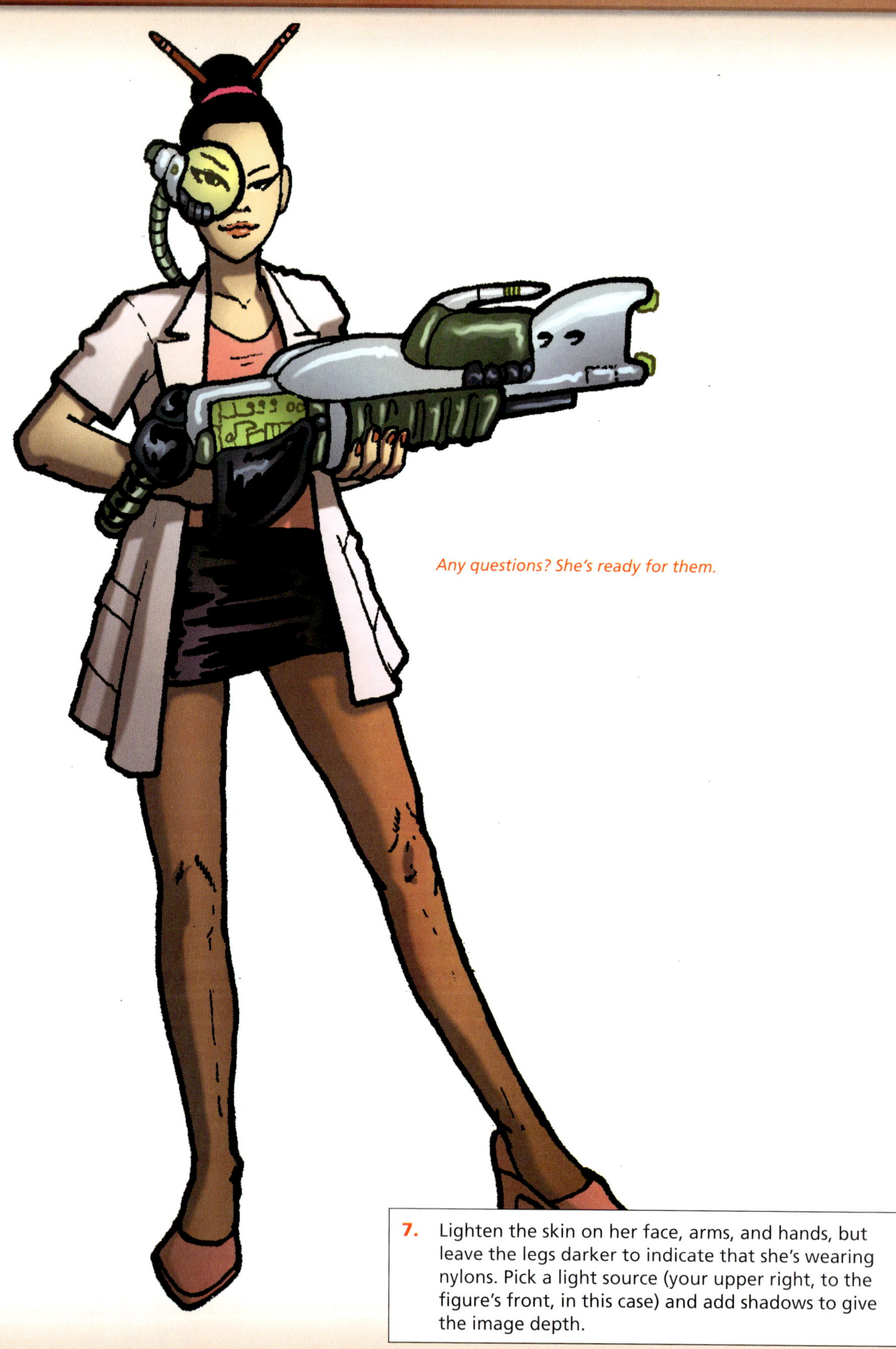

Any questions? She's ready for them.

7. Lighten the skin on her face, arms, and hands, but leave the legs darker to indicate that she's wearing nylons. Pick a light source (your upper right, to the figure's front, in this case) and add shadows to give the image depth.

THE ACCUSER

The Accuser is the direct descendent of Eugéne François Vidocq, the Frenchman who was arguably the first private investigator. He works in the same line as his famous ancestor, using the latest in high-tech tools, along with his own laser-sharp intelligence, to solve every mystery he comes across. A master of disguise and of the martial arts, he also has worked as one of the greatest spies in history.

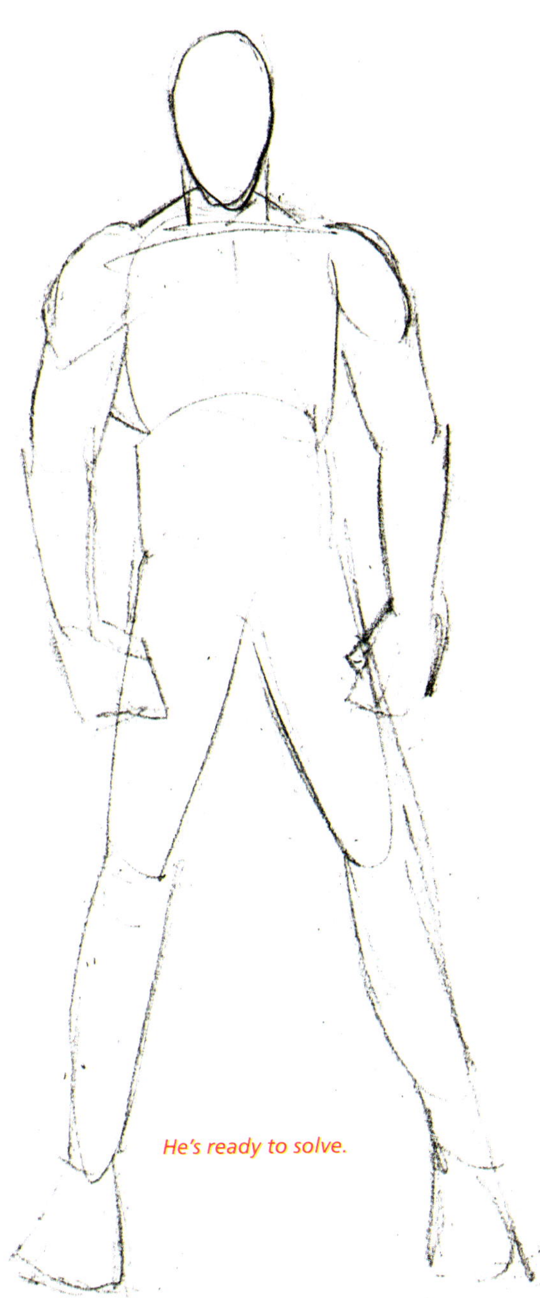

He's ready to solve.

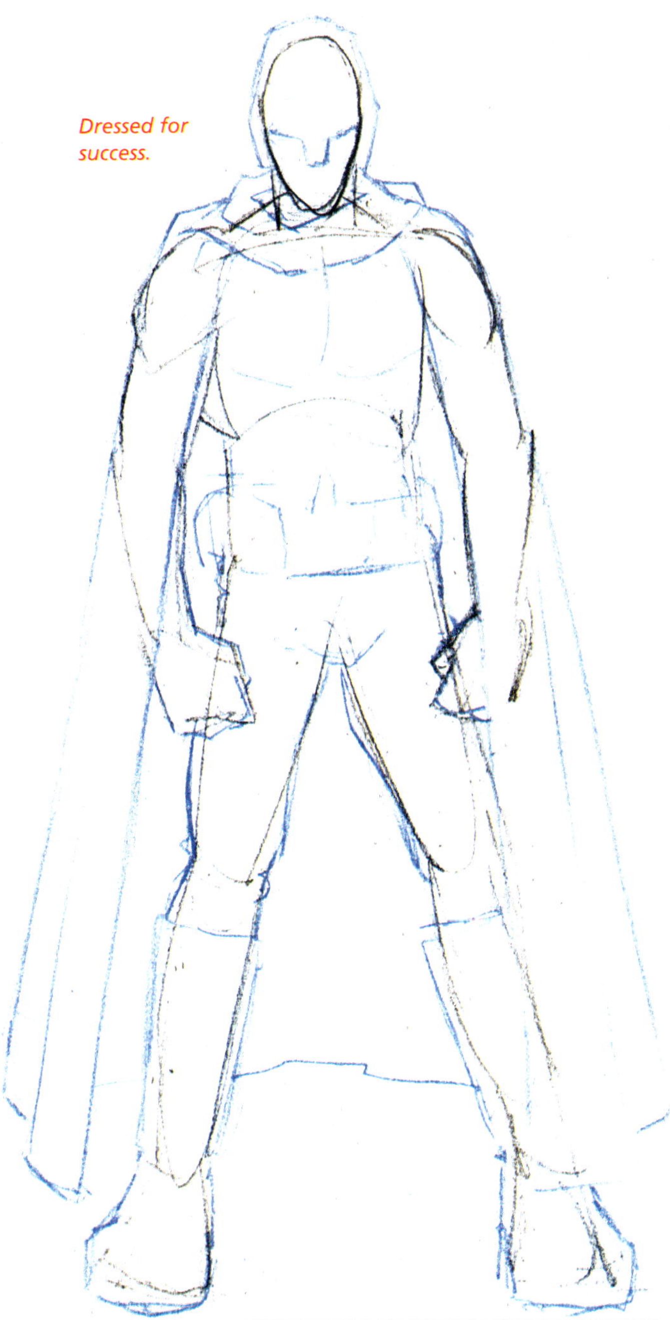

Dressed for success.

1. Break down the Accuser's stance. He stands ready for anything, a coiled spring about to burst forth at a moment's notice. He takes in everything around him with all his senses, and nothing—and no one—escapes him.

2. Dress the Accuser in a shirt, pants, knee-high boots, a utility belt, and a cape. Add a mask/helmet with multipurpose goggles (night vision, infrared, etc.) over the eyes. And don't forget the cape.

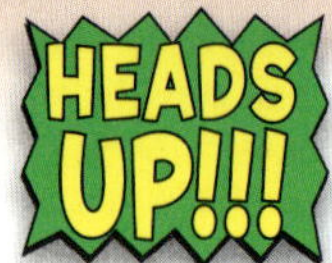

A character's body language—the way he holds himself—tells you much about him. Crossed limbs means he has something to hide. An open stance indicates readiness. Showing the backs of his hands (as the Accuser does here) is a declaration of dominance.

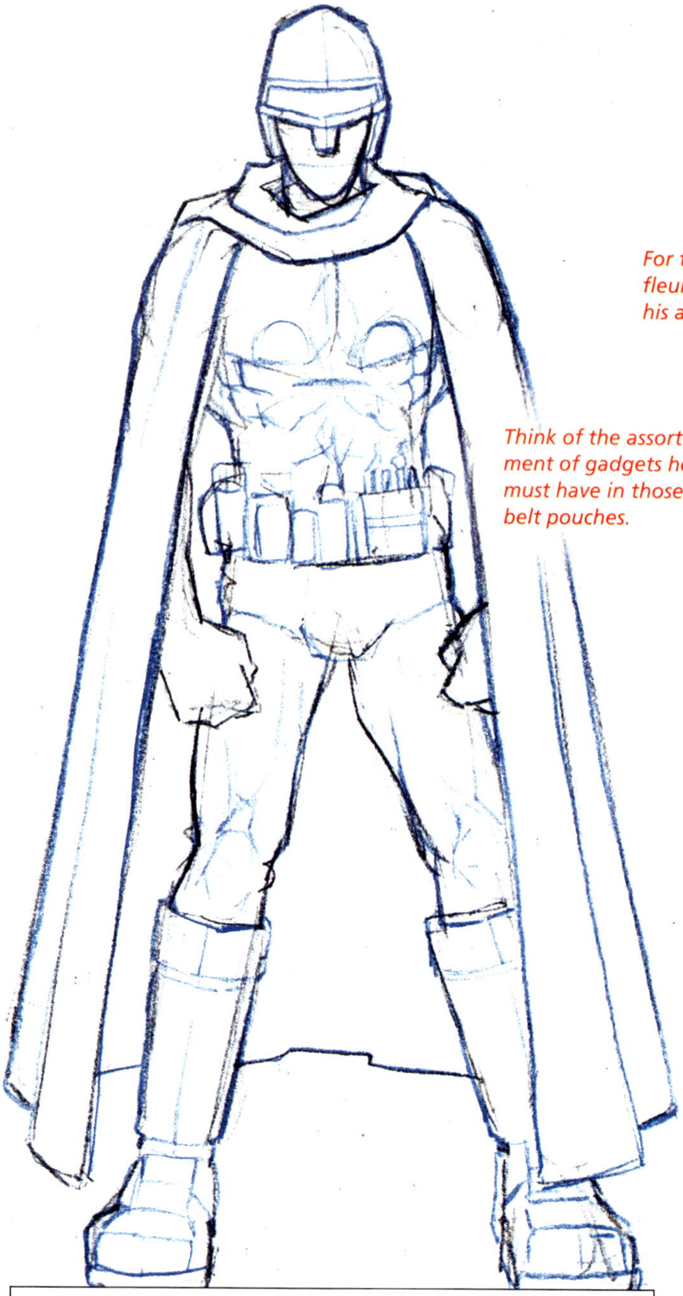

For the Accuser, the fleur-de-lis represents his ancestral homeland.

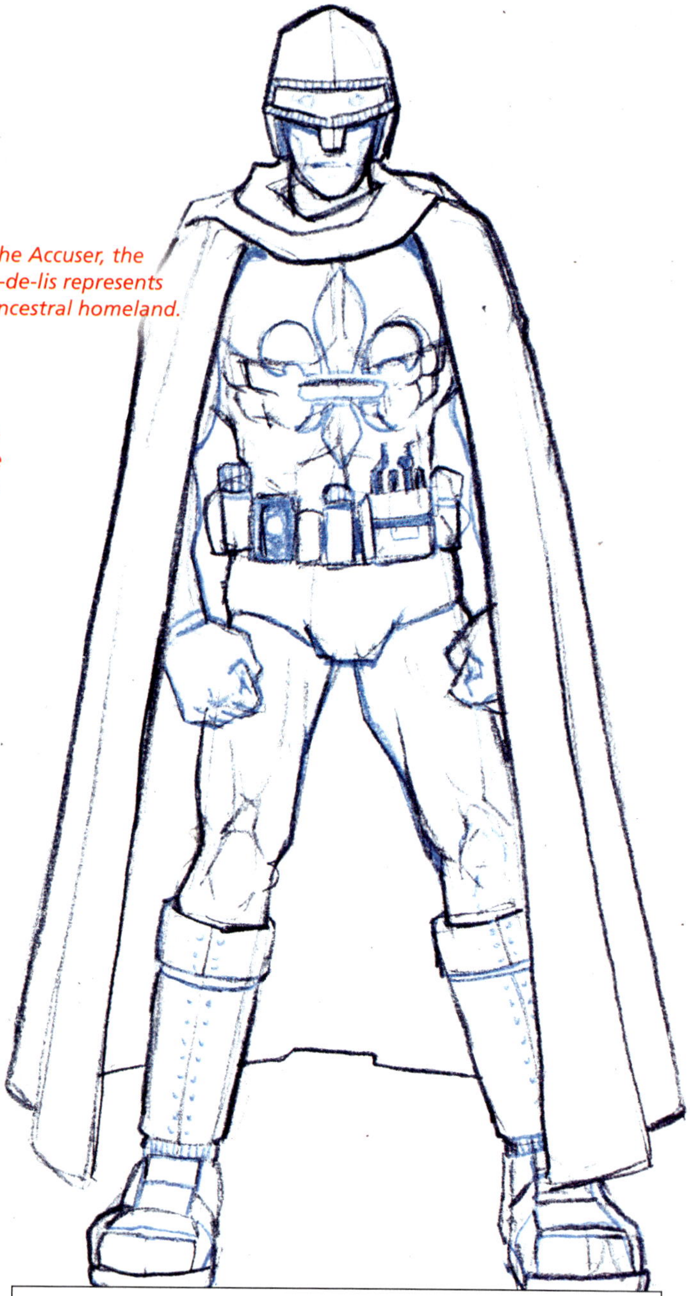

Think of the assortment of gadgets he must have in those belt pouches.

3. Work on the Accuser's muscle tone. He's a man who knows the value of exercise. Add some folds to his cape and details to his boots and helmet. Have fun with putting pouches and other bits on his belt.

4. Place the fleur-de-lis icon on his chest, establishing his connection to France. Give him a determined slit for a mouth. Make his hands into fists, and add rivets to his leg armor.

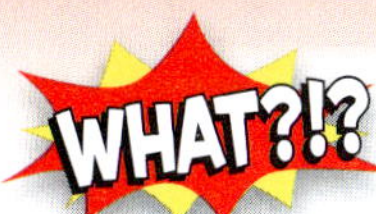

The **fleur-de-lis** symbol has many meanings. Its name translates from French as "flower of lily," and French royalty used to use it in their heraldry. Today, organizations ranging from the Boy Scouts to the New Orleans Saints employ it for various reasons. It can represent the Holy Trinity, the direction north, and many other things, depending on who uses it.

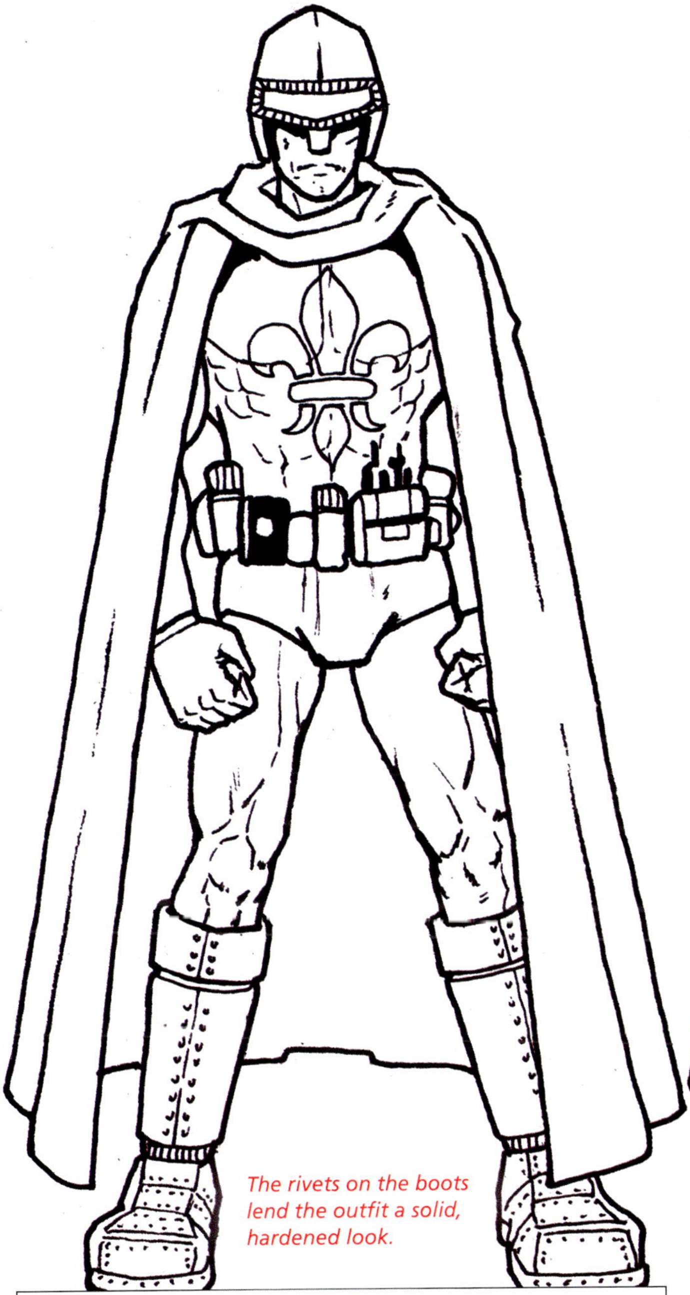

The Accuser is always right!

The rivets on the boots lend the outfit a solid, hardened look.

5. Use strong inks throughout. The contrast of the musculature lines on the Accuser's chest against the clean lines of his icon play well against each other: the organic versus the iconic.

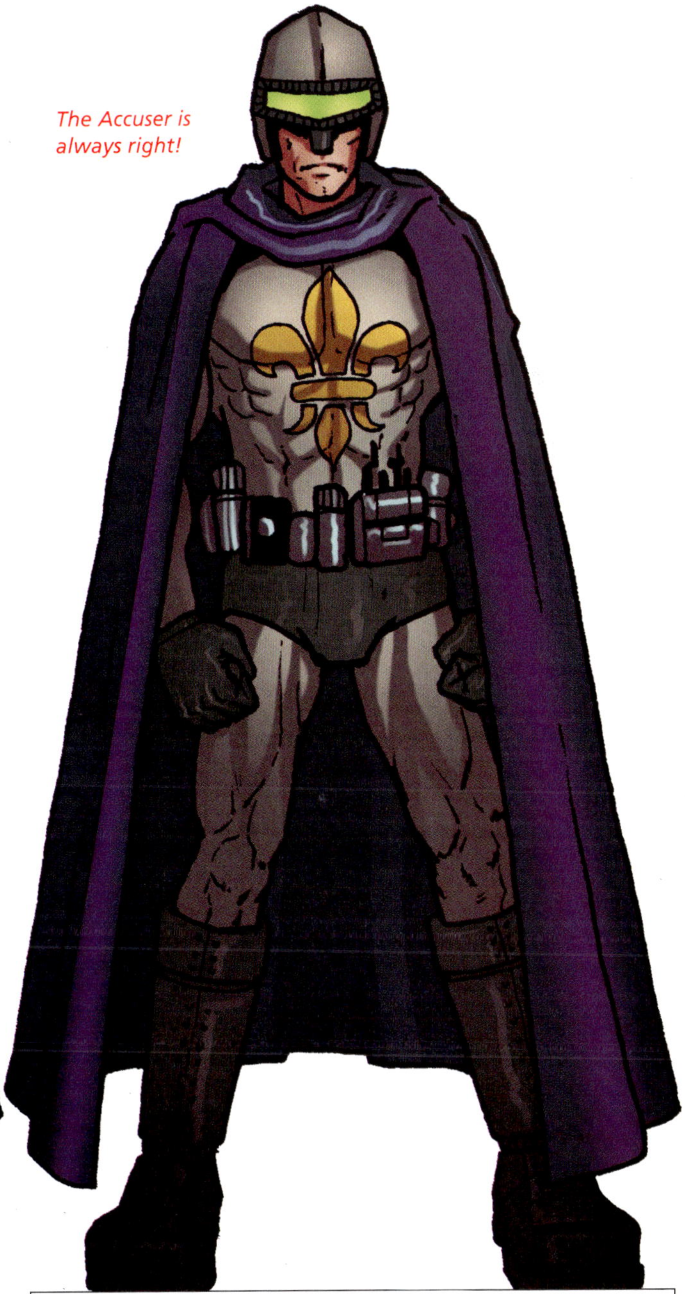

6. Use various shades of steel gray for the costume. They make the Accuser seem like a weapon rather than a man. The glowing green eyes add to the idea that he's something other than human. The dark blue cape cools the image further, while the yellow of his icon is the only splash of brightness in the whole ensemble.

THE HEADMASTER

The Headmaster runs a private prep school for superpowered teens. He's supposedly training them to integrate well into society, but he's really indoctrinating them into his fascist philosophies. With so many superpowered people loyal to him and his goals, it's only a matter of time before he achieves his aim: the domination of the entire planet.

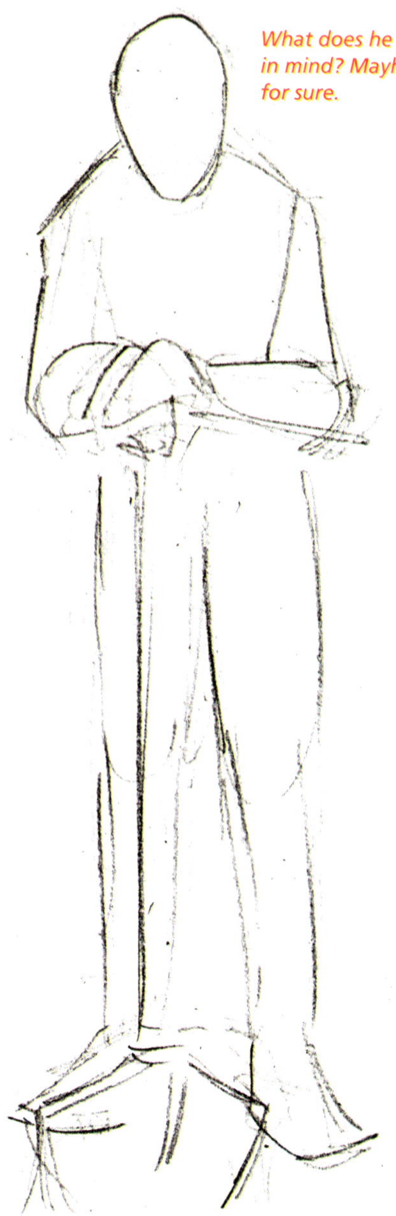

What does he have in mind? Mayhem for sure.

Subtle as it is, you can already sense the menace in the man.

1. Break down the Headmaster's pose. He's an older man, and he walks with a special cane with three articulated legs. Hunch his shoulders a bit to indicate his age, and place his hands atop the cane to show that he's a plotter holding secrets.

2. Drape a suit over the Headmaster's scrawny frame. Put a vest and tie on under that jacket. Show the articulated legs on the cane, establishing that he is more than just an old man hobbling about.

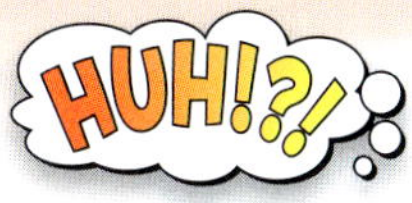

One way to come up with new characters is to take a popular archetype (like, say, the benevolent head of a school for mutants) and turn it around. Make the hero into a villain or vice versa. This can give tired or overused concepts a fresh spin.

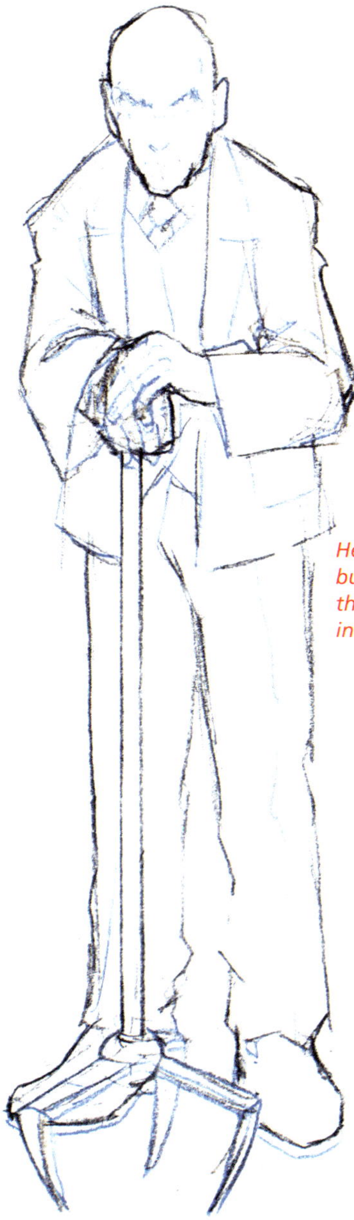

He seems reserved, but that's a façade for the horrible schemes in his head.

There's something you don't see on characters with hair: dimples on the sides of the skull.

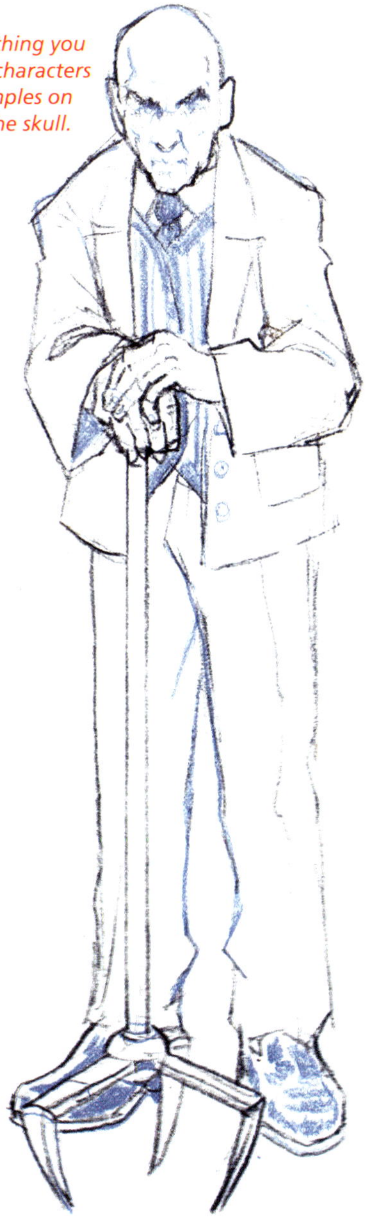

3. Toss a pair of arched eyebrows on the man and rough out the features on his face. Put lapels and pockets on the jacket and place creases on the legs of his pants.

4. Put stripes on the vest. Add wrinkles to the suit. Blacken the shoes and the tie. Finish the features on his face.

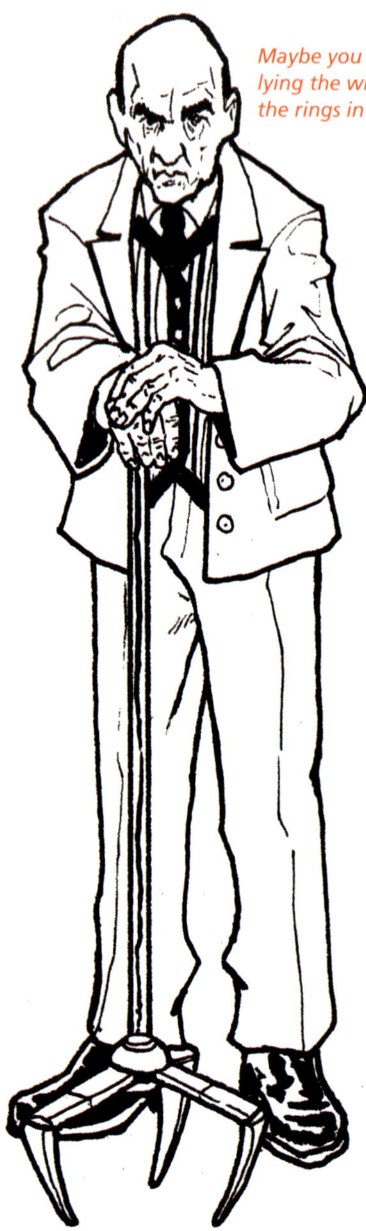

Maybe you can guess his age by tallying the wrinkles, just like counting the rings in the trunk of a fallen tree.

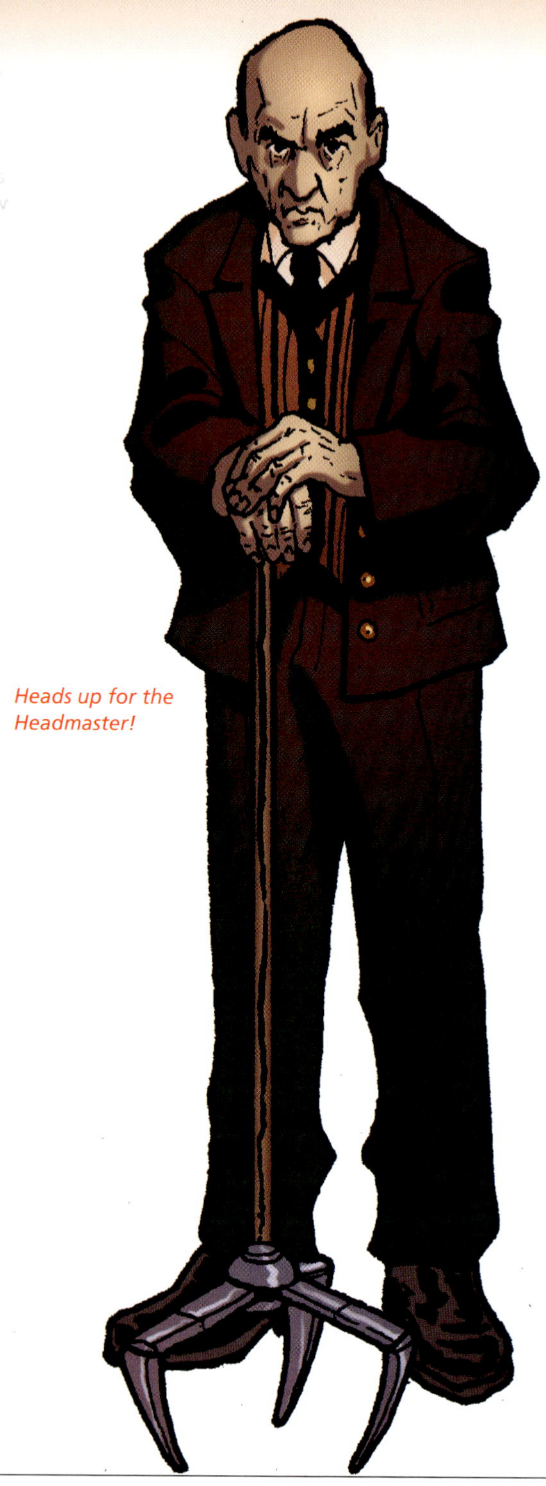

Heads up for the Headmaster!

5. Use heavier lines on the perimeter of the figure and its clothing. Use more light lines on the exposed skin and the wrinkles of the suit. These communicate the age of the character. Young figures have smooth features, while older ones have many more wrinkles, even on their clothing.

6. Make the suit burgundy brown. It's an unstylish color that speaks of old wealth and musty money. Make sure you add even a subtle tint to his shirt. Nothing about the Headmaster should seem pure. The metallic look of the claw at the end of his cane betrays his scheming nature.

THE BRAINS

The Brains was once a shy and reclusive girl who studied at the most exclusive private schools in Europe and Asia. Under the tutelage of her ambassadorial parents, she learned the ways of *realpolitik* and turned her attention to the study of the rise and fall of civilizations so that she might someday control their courses. Years ago, she wrested control of the infamous Green Lotus gang from its mundane masters and transformed it from a criminal organization to one obsessed with altering the course of history and placing the world's governments firmly in her pocket.

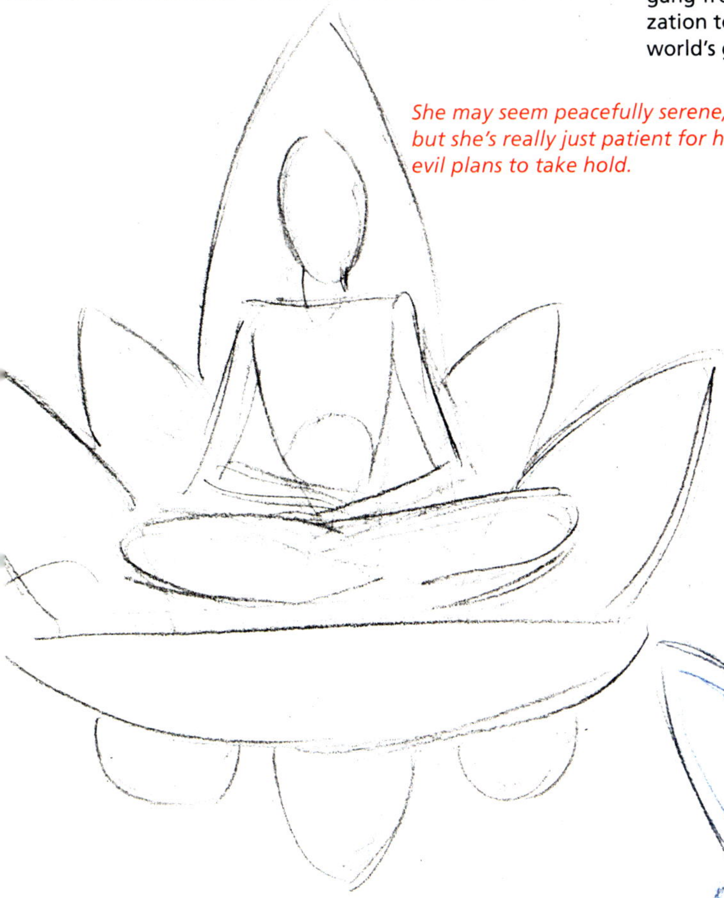

She may seem peacefully serene, but she's really just patient for her evil plans to take hold.

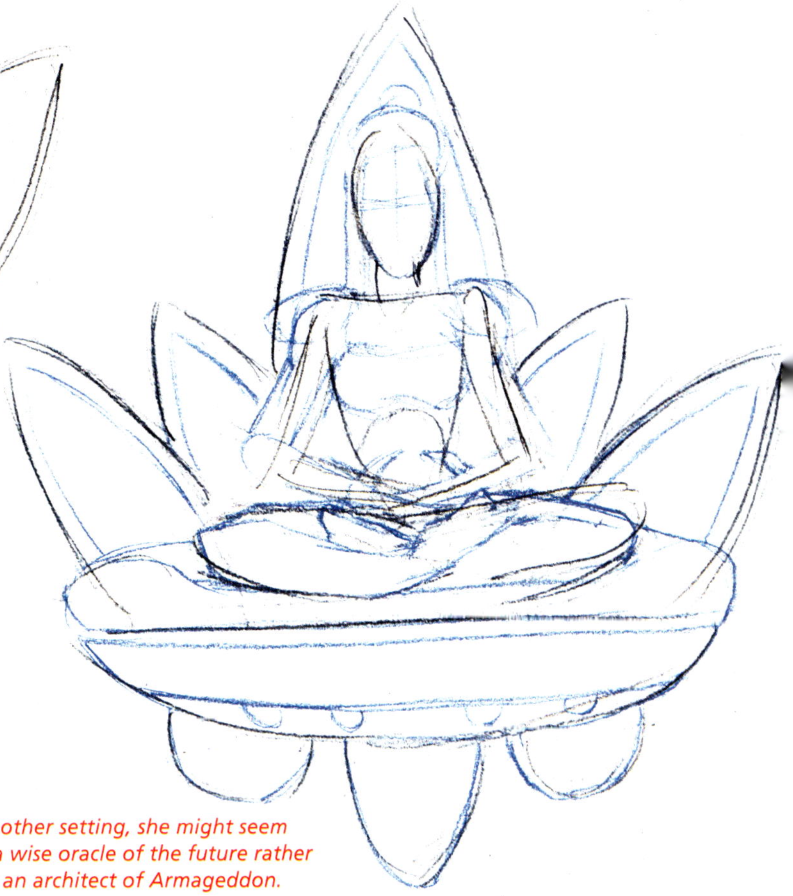

In another setting, she might seem like a wise oracle of the future rather than an architect of Armageddon.

1. Brains sits lotus style in a hovering chair built to resemble a giant lotus blossom. Pose her in this traditionally thoughtful way.

2. Add hair and armor plating to the figure. Place piping around the petals that frame her. Use guidelines to keep her face centered.

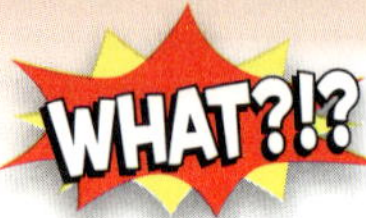

Realpolitik is a political viewpoint based on practical analysis of reality rather than on ideals. Those who practice it often care only for their own direct benefits rather than the greater good or any other loftier goals.

She may seem to have the asceticism of a monk, but the boom-mike betrays how connected she is to the modern world.

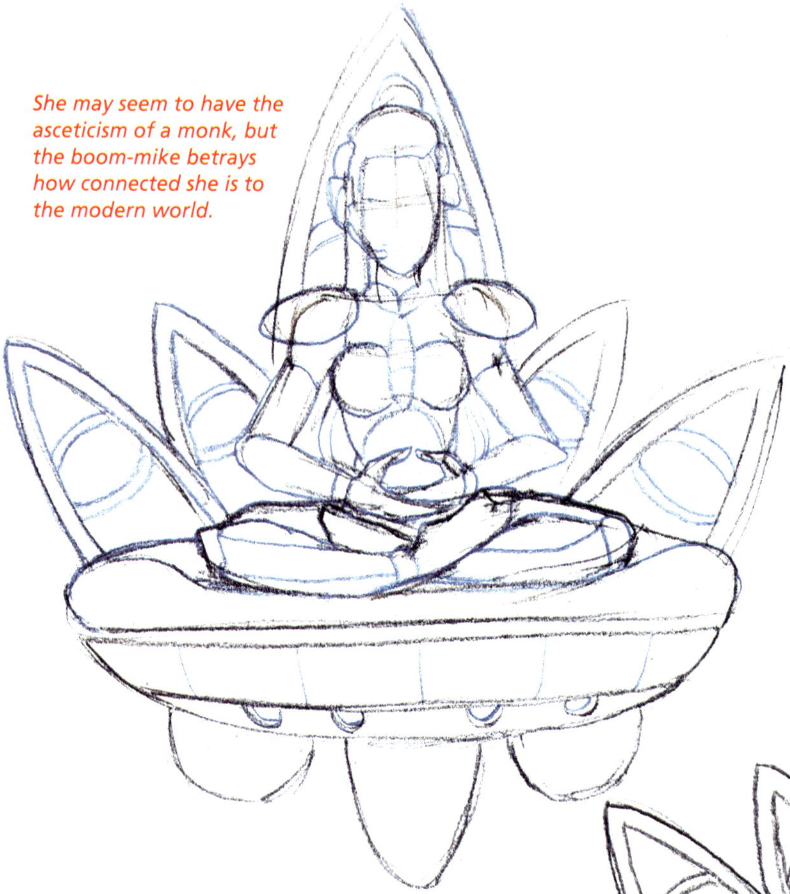

She cradles her hands as if she might someday clutch the world between them.

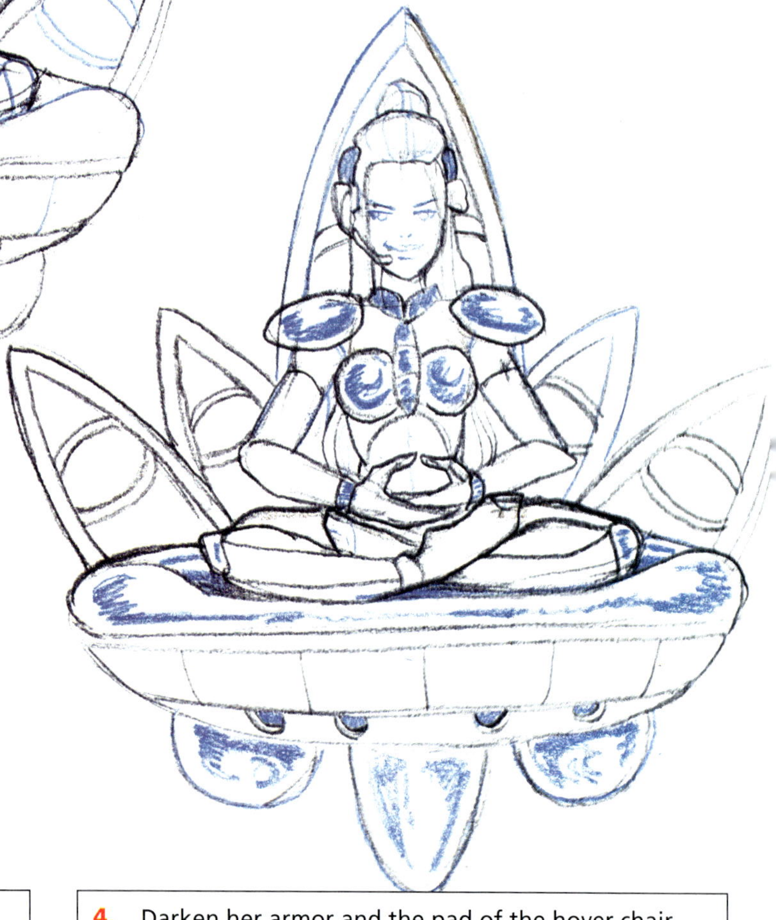

3. Add details to the hover chair and to her costume and hair. The designs on the petals look like open eyes, as if the Brains has many ways to see everything around her. Notice the mini-boom mike stretching down from her right ear.

4. Darken her armor and the pad of the hover chair. Do the same for the metallic jets beneath her. Give her a pleasant yet scheming expression.

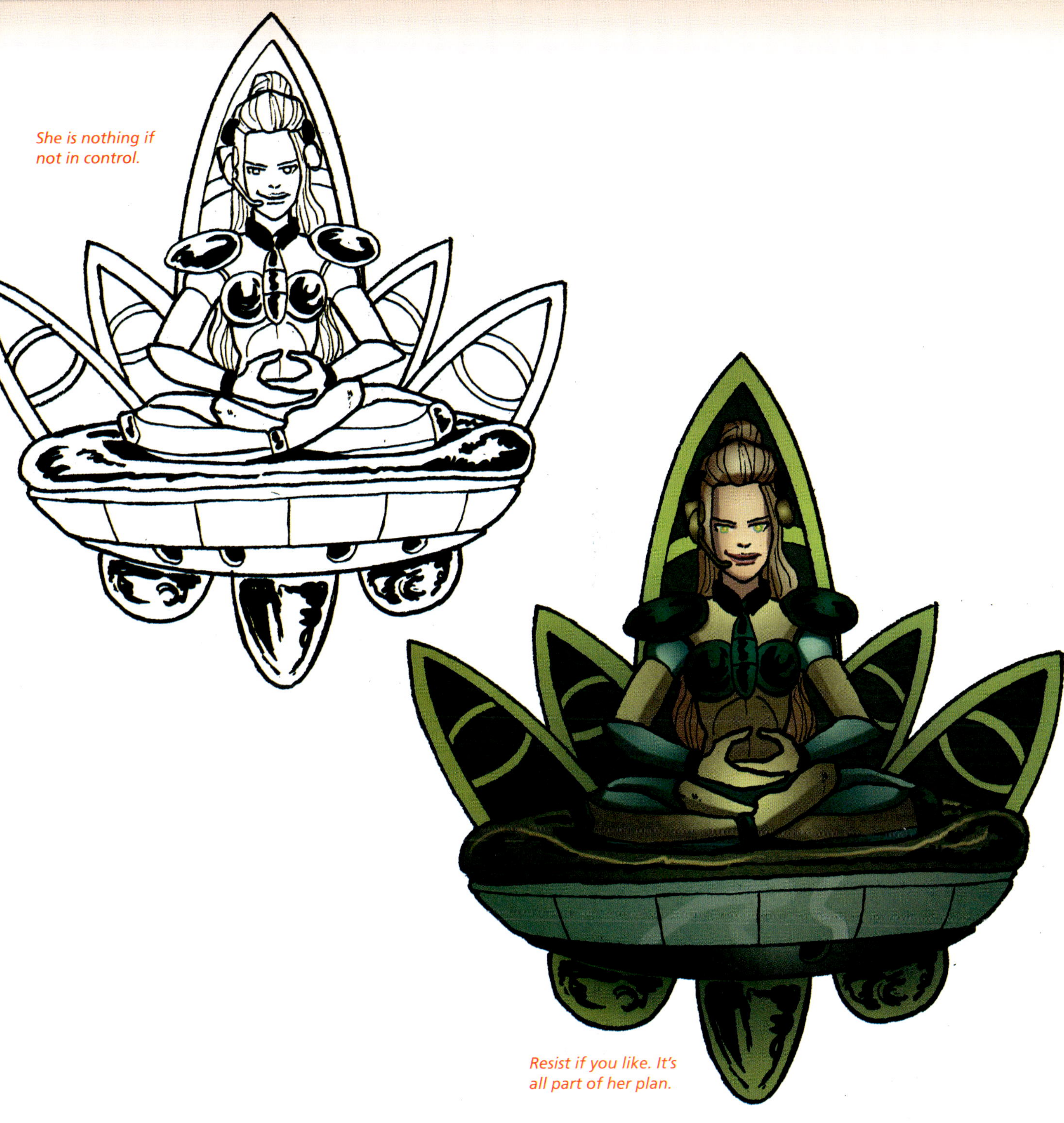

She is nothing if not in control.

Resist if you like. It's all part of her plan.

5. Use strong, clean lines throughout the figure. The only nod to her humanity is her long hair, which she wears tied up and back with trails of it held behind her.

6. Color her in various shades of green. This represents her true feeling toward the world—jealousy—as well as the lizardlike attitude she takes toward those around her. If they aren't useful, they are either obstacles or something to be devoured.

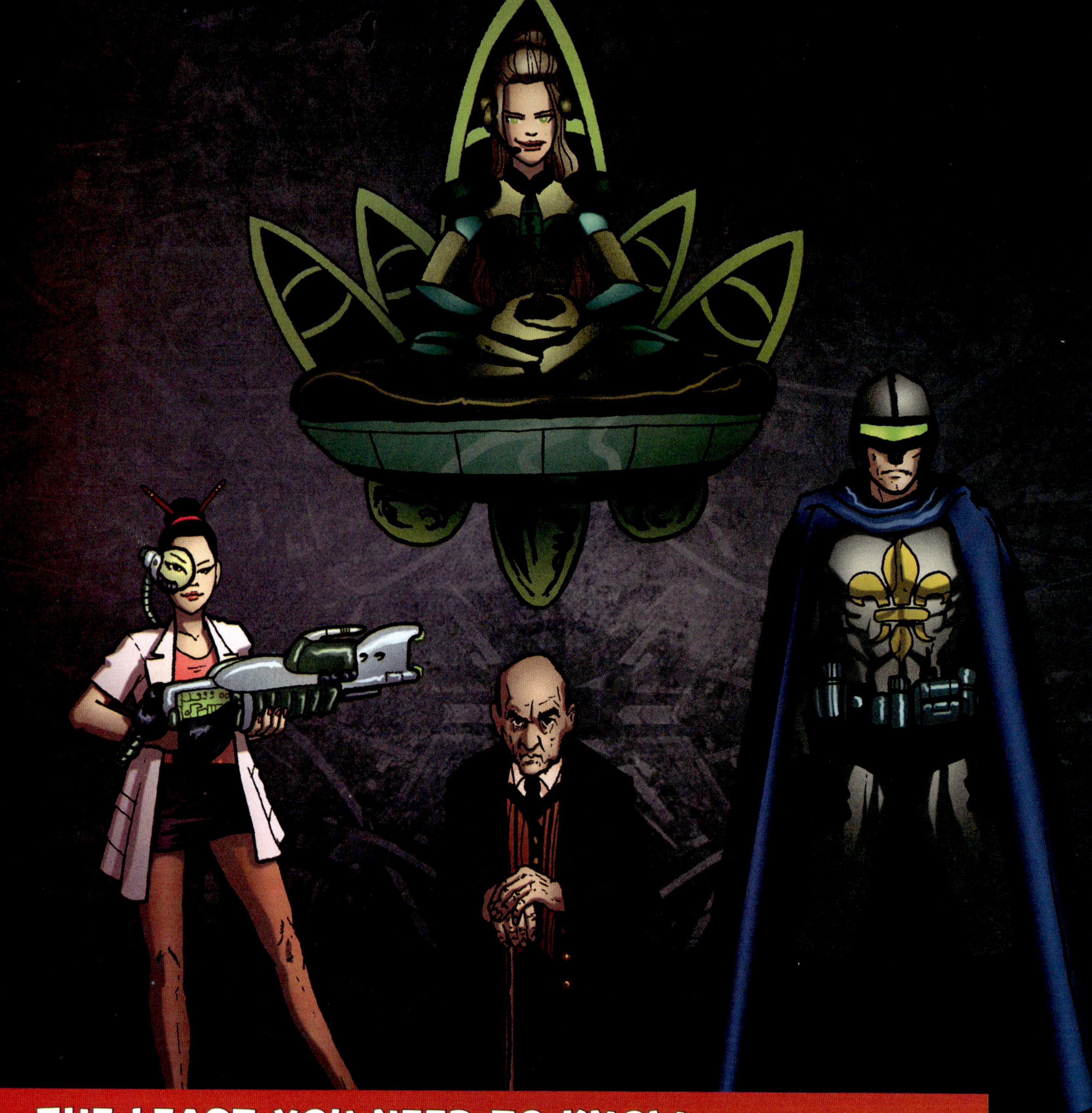

THE LEAST YOU NEED TO KNOW

- The powers of geniuses aren't often as obvious as they are in combat-oriented characters, so you need to add trappings to indicate their powers and goals.
- Your character's pose has body language, just like that of real people. Be aware of what each pose communicates, and make sure you're using it properly.
- You can make fresh versions of old characters by having them work on the other side (good vs. evil). Play with your audience's expectations.
- Not all geniuses think in terms of high-tech devices. Exploit other sciences as well.

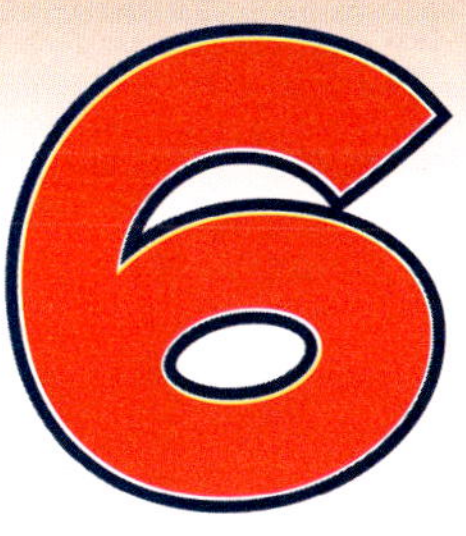

Gadgeteers: Dancing on the Bleeding Edge

In This Chapter

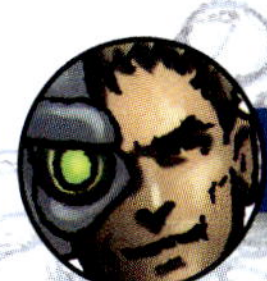

- Man as meat and machine

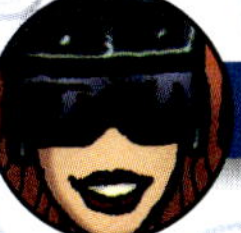

- Working with miniature machines

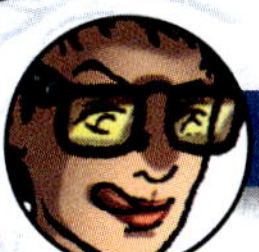

- The computer whisperer

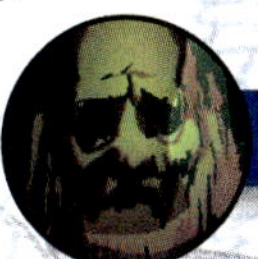

- The high-tech knight

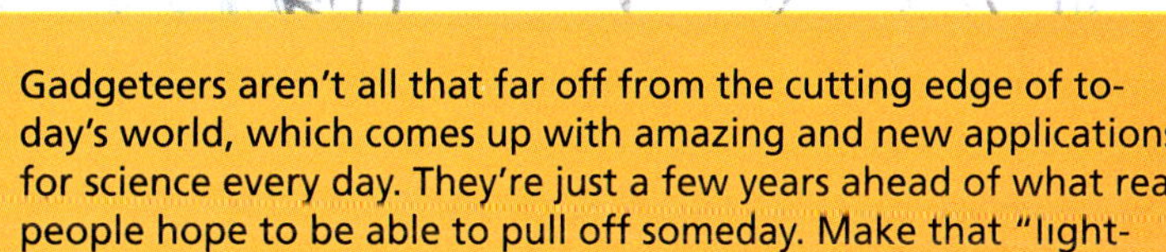

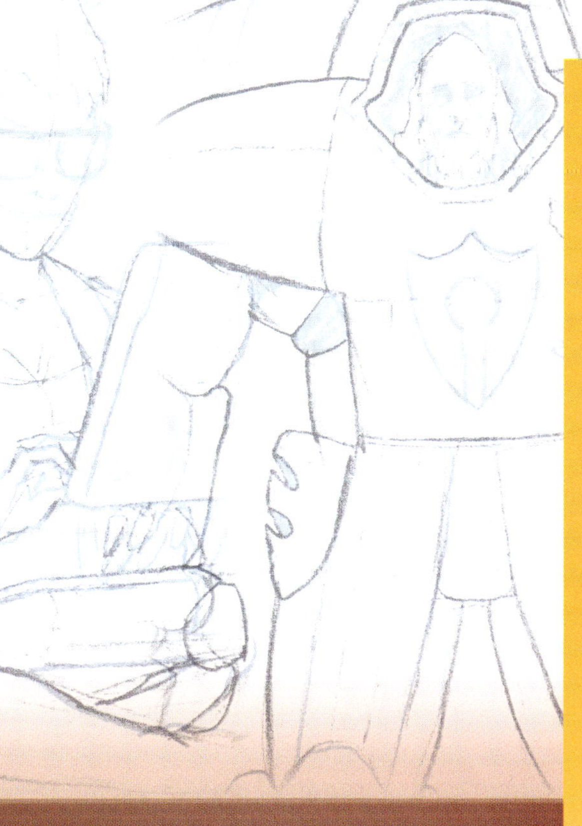

Gadgeteers aren't all that far off from the cutting edge of today's world, which comes up with amazing and new applications for science every day. They're just a few years ahead of what real people hope to be able to pull off someday. Make that "light-years."

We crash into a most modern bionic man. While bionic heroes of previous generations were rebuilt victims of horrible disasters, Bionic not only chose to replace his original parts, but he used devices of his own design. Think of him as Humanity 2.0, based in oil rather than blood.

The Nanotechnician uses machines of a different scale in her villainous plans. They're small enough to be hard to see with the naked eye—at least one at a time. She's built millions of them, though, and in the aggregate they're a formidable threat.

Hackette can't quite talk directly to computers, but she can make them sing and dance whatever tune she calls. There's no security system she can't crack. With so much of the world dependent on computers, we all have her to thank for when they work well.

The Armorer created a suit of armor that works more like a weapon of mass destruction than a set of steel plates. He built and maintains the thing himself, riding it into action whenever the world demands it.

BIONIC

Bionic used to be short, awkward, and shy. As a scientist specializing in bionic prosthetics, he knew that not only could he replace body parts but also improve upon them. Using himself as the first test subject seemed like a natural choice.

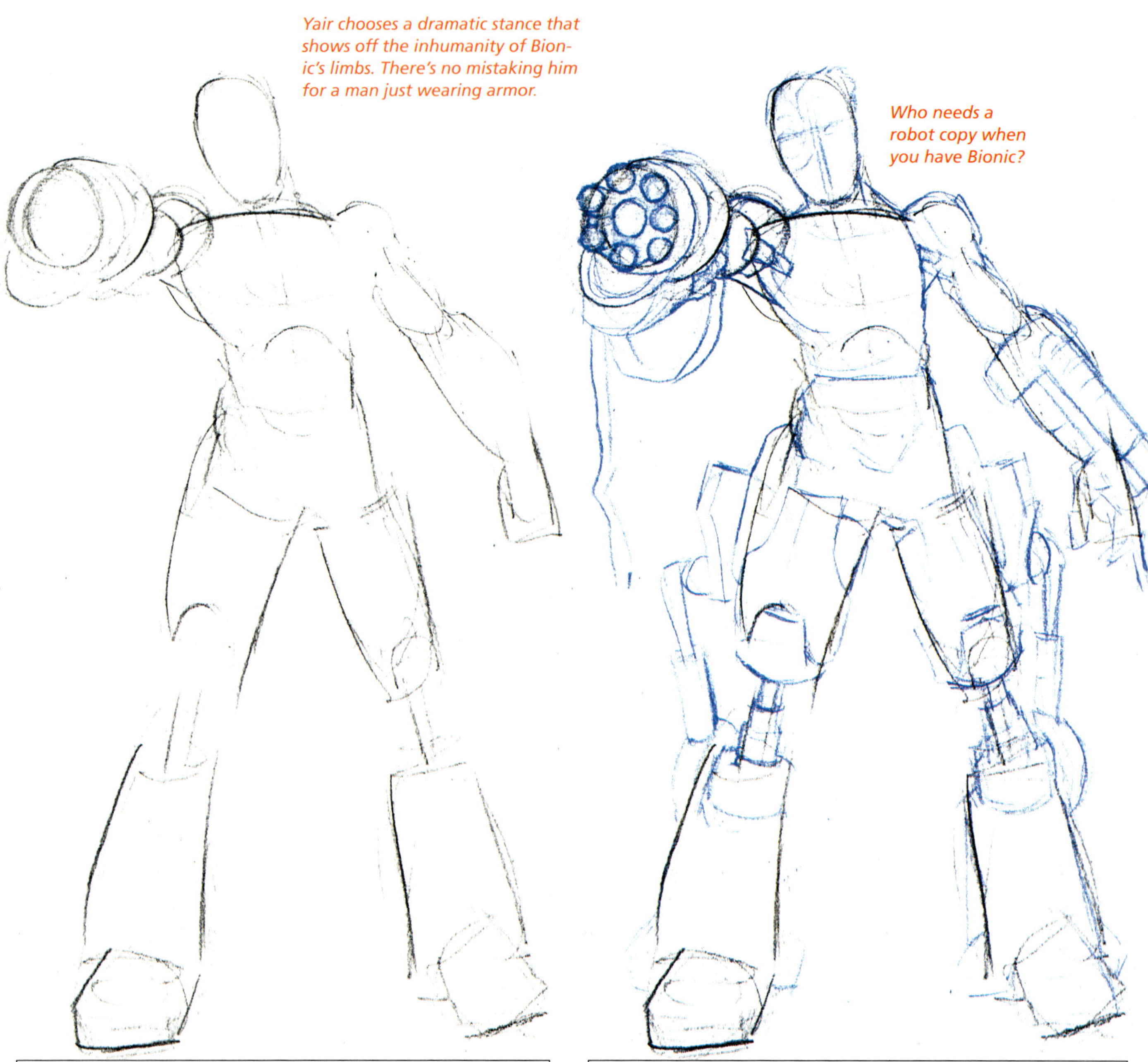

Yair chooses a dramatic stance that shows off the inhumanity of Bionic's limbs. There's no mistaking him for a man just wearing armor.

Who needs a robot copy when you have Bionic?

1. Break down Bionic's form. You can play a little loose with the anatomy here, as much of his is artificial. Notice the foreshortening of his arm-cannon as he points it toward you.

2. Rough in some more details. Add all sorts of techy gear to the figure. Concentrate on the barrels of the mini-gun on the end of the arm. Getting the perspective right there can be tricky.

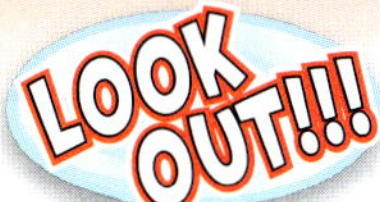

While it's okay to play loose with Bionic's anatomy—or that of many superheroes and villains—you still have to be consistent and respect the laws of perspective. Otherwise, you'll just end up with a big mess. Just because you're drawing superheroes doesn't mean you can be lazy about it.

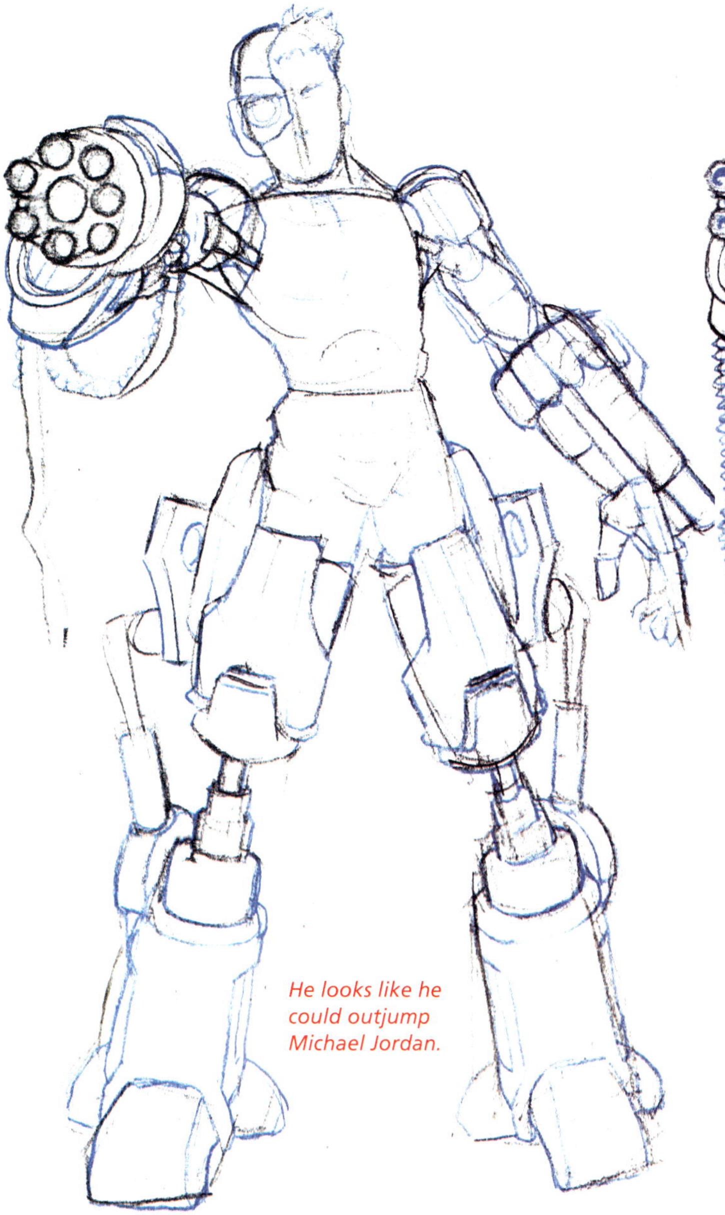

He looks like he could outjump Michael Jordan.

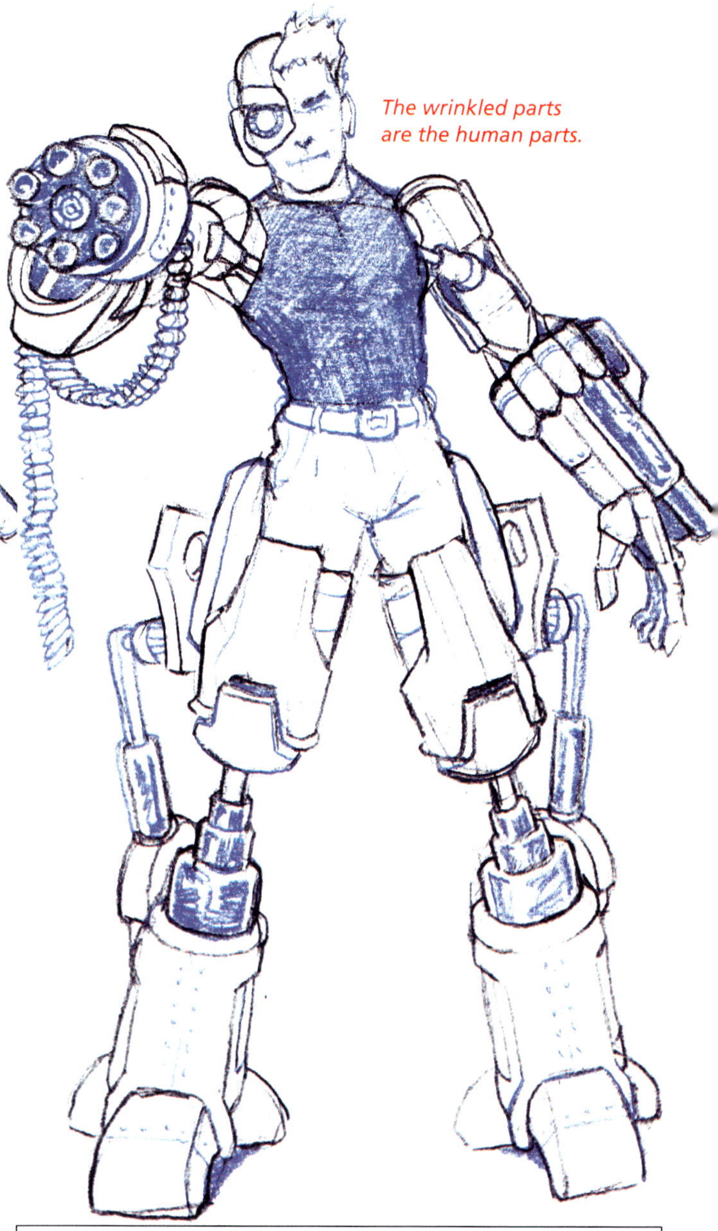

The wrinkled parts are the human parts.

3. Add in more details. Make the lines harder and more solid, particularly for the inhuman materials. Add ammo to the belt hanging from the mini-gun. Add hydraulic amplifiers to the leg joints.

4. Black out the T-shirt and add darkness to other areas. Place lines of rivets along the seams of the mechanical parts. Liberally use wrinkles on the fleshy parts.

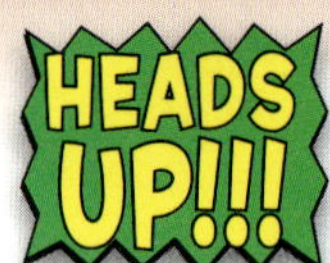

It's easy to make comic-book artificial limbs look just like real ones, only steel-colored. Instead, use straighter lines to give the limbs an unnatural feel. Flesh has curves and ripples, while steel does not.

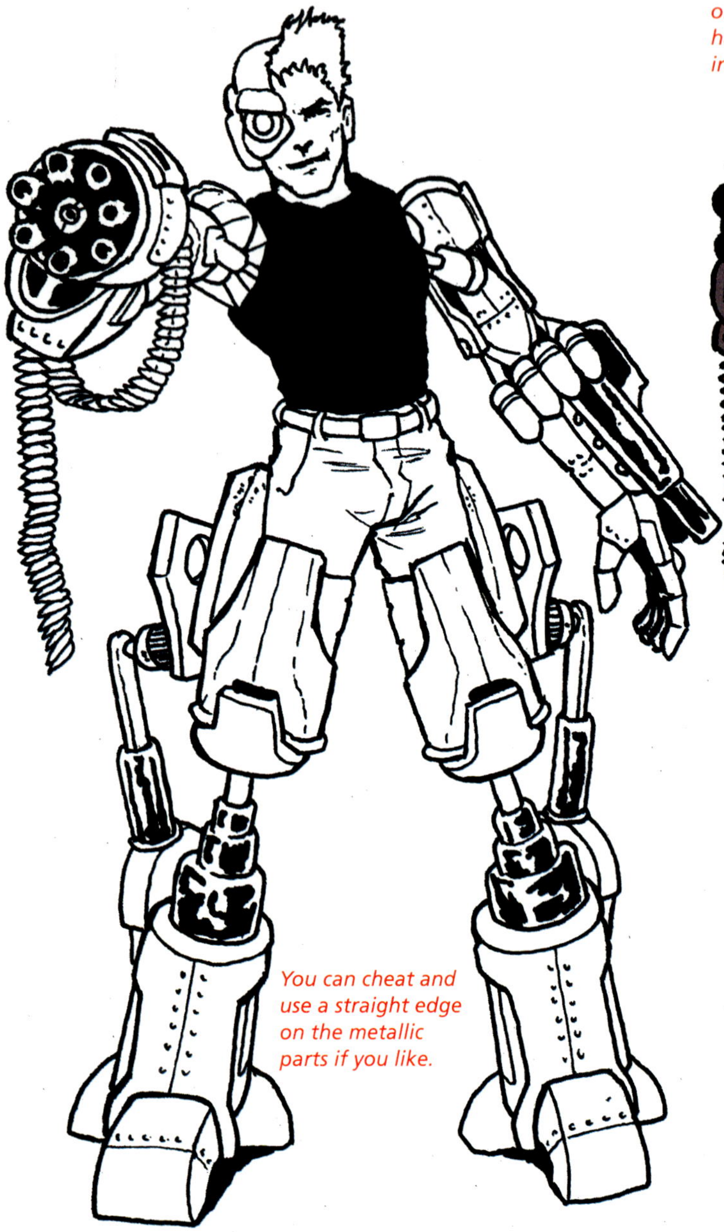

Note that the brightest thing on the figure is his yellow hair, which symbolizes his irrepressible humanity.

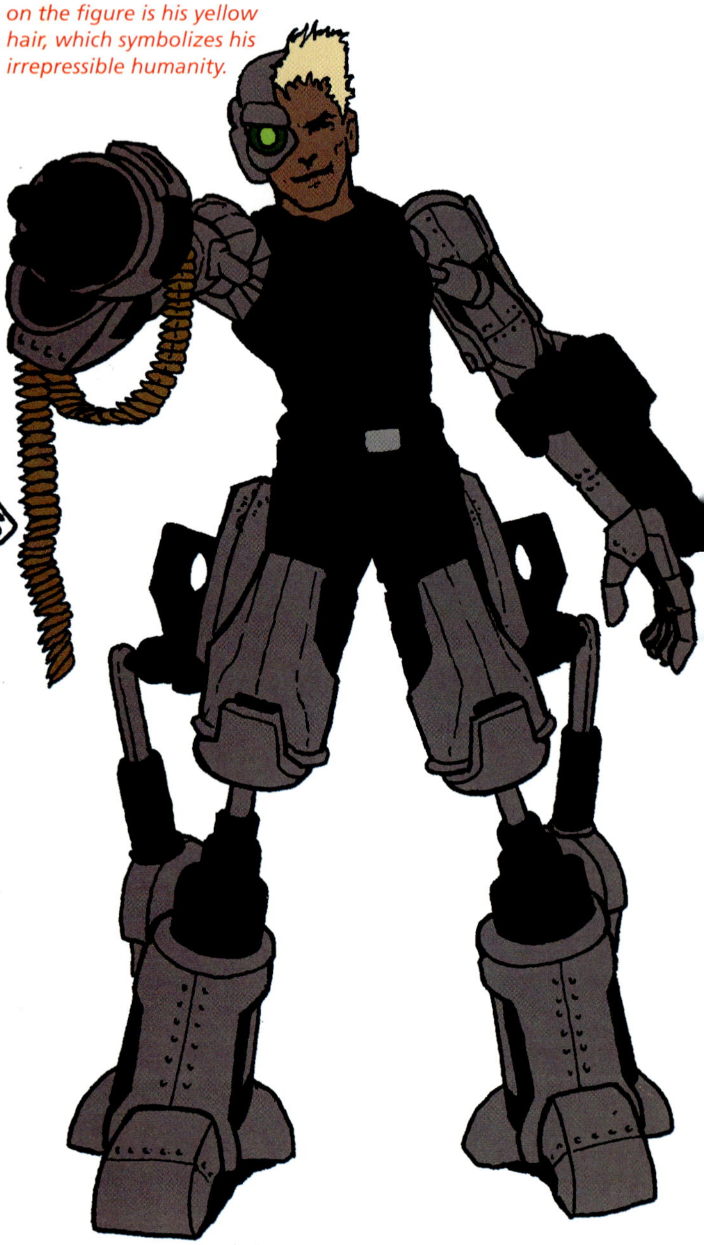

You can cheat and use a straight edge on the metallic parts if you like.

5. Use solid inks on the metal parts: heavy lines around the outside and thinner ones for the bends in the metal. By sticking with a uniform line throughout, Yair emphasizes how integrated Bionic is with his new form, although you could use thinner lines for the human parts to call out the differences instead.

6. Go with drab colors here: gray for most of the metallic bits, except when they're dark gray. Try olive pants and a black shirt, too. The gold of the bullets and the green of the bionic eye pull your eyes to those positions.

See how the darkest parts of the figure are the barrels of the mini-gun.

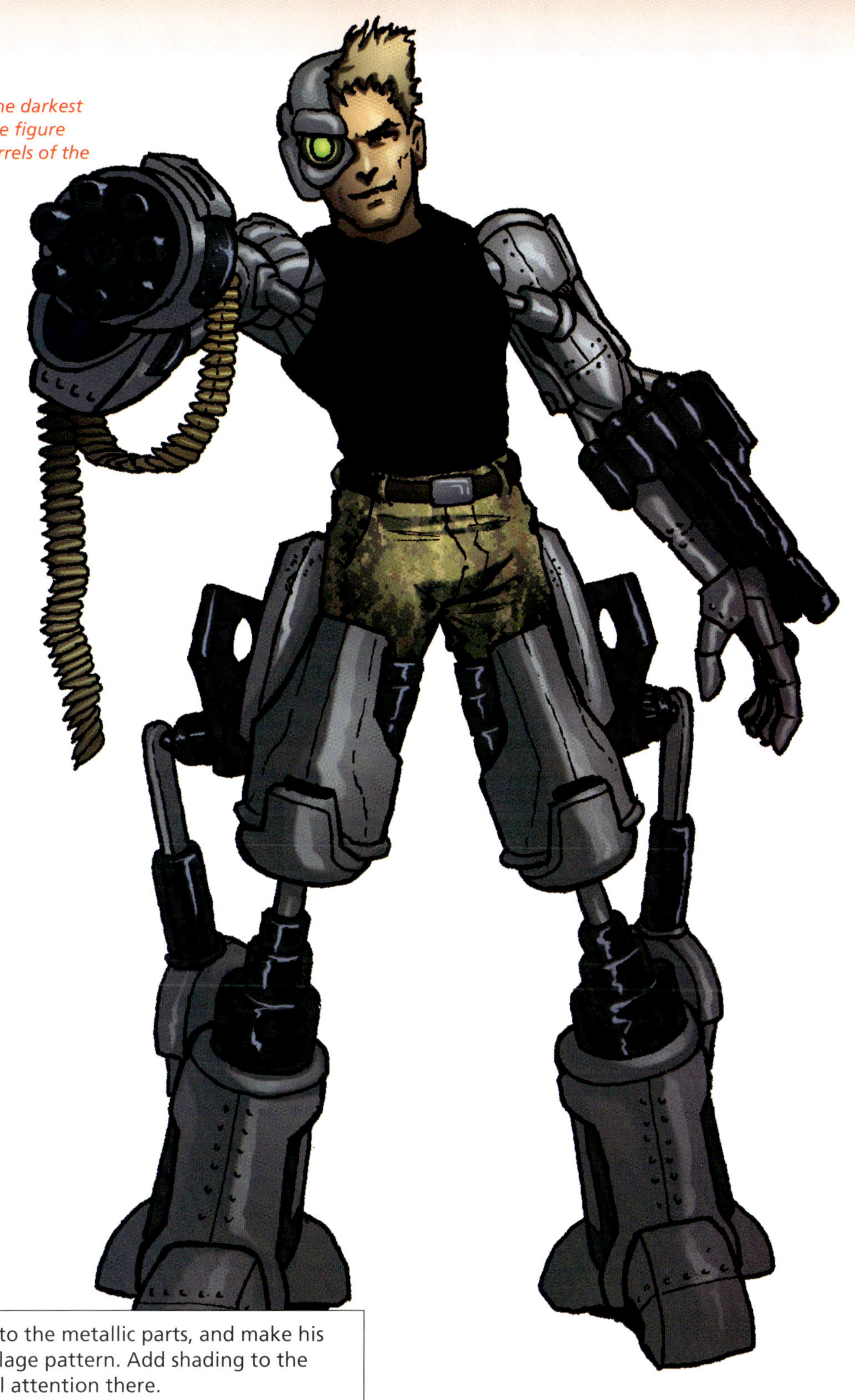

7. Add highlights to the metallic parts, and make his pants a camouflage pattern. Add shading to the face, too, to call attention there.

THE NANOTECHNICIAN

The Nanotechnician works with robots so tiny that they're barely visible to the naked eye, except when you gather them into large groups. Yair takes some license here and shows some of her larger, though no less deadly, inventions as well. She controls them via the virtual reality rig formed by her goggles and gloves.

You could use this stance for a zombie, too.

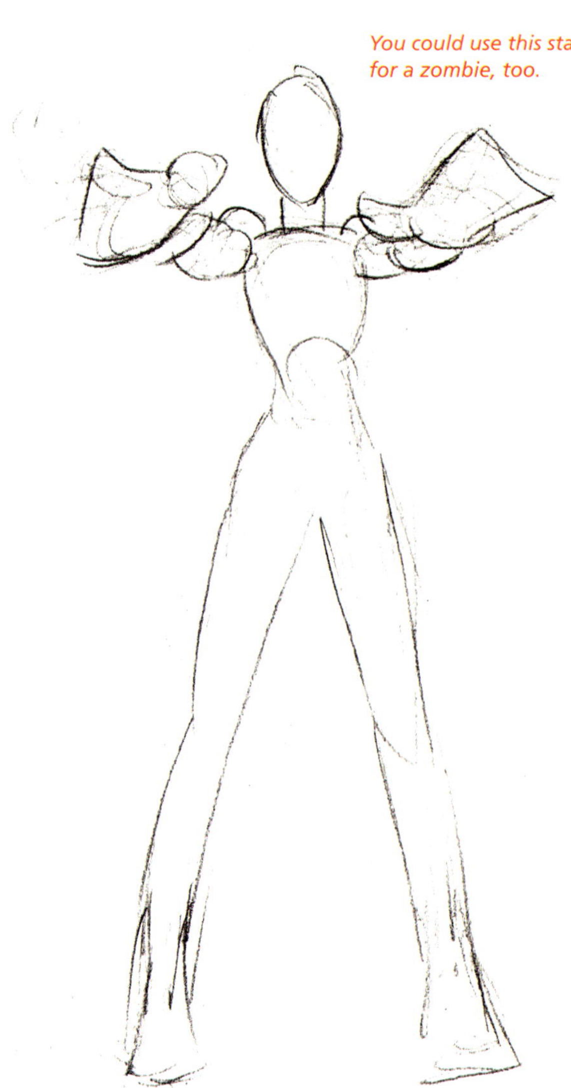

The curl of hair around her back helps frame her upper torso.

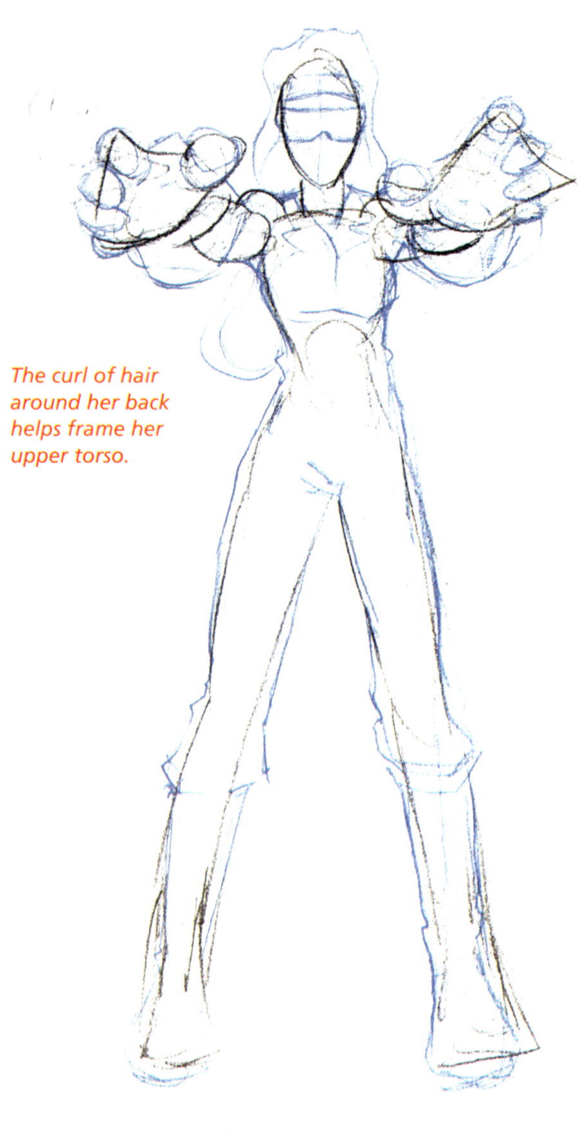

1. Break down the figure into simple shapes. She has an aggressive stance, with her arms pointed straight out at the viewer. Note how Yair uses *forced perspective* to make the hands huge.

2. Work out the edges of the hair and clothes. Refine the hands to show bent fingers coming at you, like claws. Give her a pair of shades for her virtual reality rig.

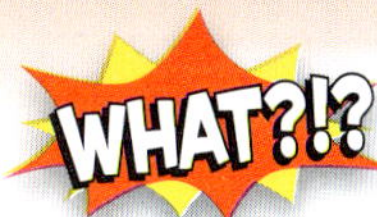

Forced perspective is the means by which you can show that something is closer to the viewer. Larger things seem to be closer, so you draw closer items larger. See how the Nanotechnician's hands are larger than her head? Combine this with foreshortening to add a dramatic energy even to static shots.

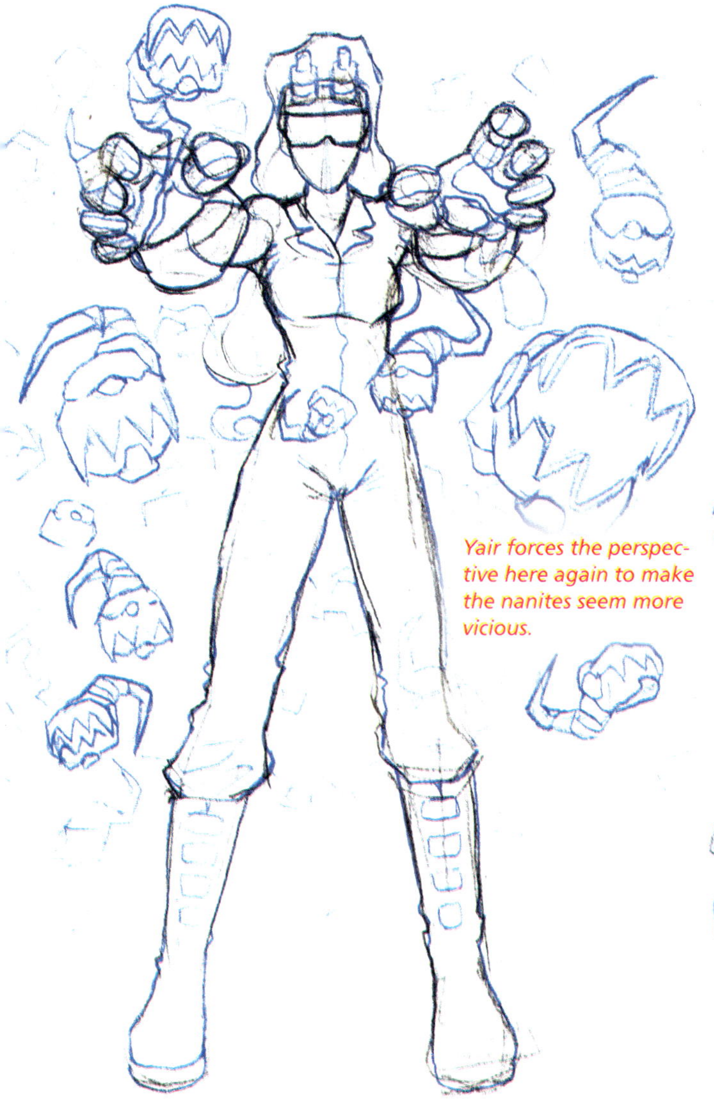

Yair forces the perspective here again to make the nanites seem more vicious.

Her icon shows a shrinking sphere, which makes sense given that she works with the very small.

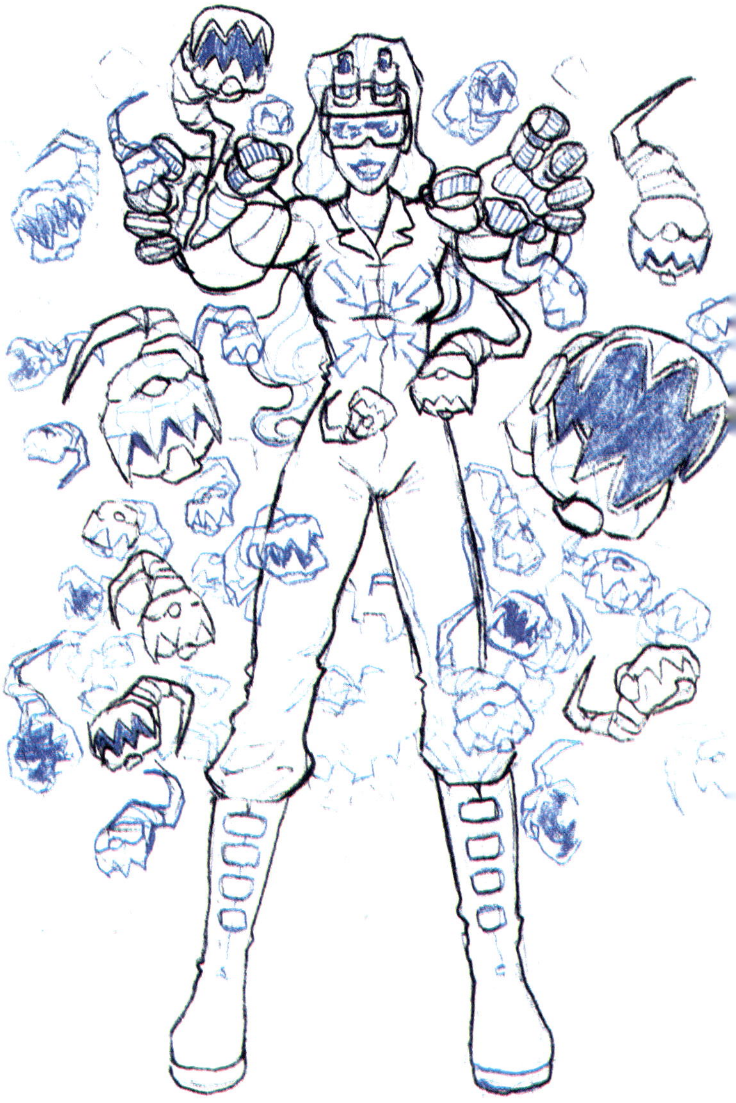

3. Add details to the costume, like goggles atop her head and bindings to her boots. Add in a number of her nanites (tiny machines) to show what she's controlling.

4. Black in the mouths of the nanites. Add an icon to the Nanotechnician's chest. Draw in a lot more nanites, including a mass of them coalescing behind her.

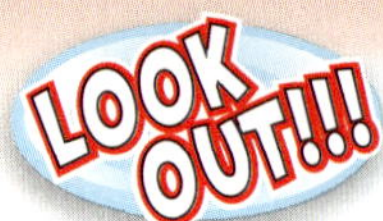

Without the mass in the background, the Nanotechnician would seem like she was floating in midair. The addition of the mass of creatures gives the entire drawing more weight.

She looks like she enjoys being in control.

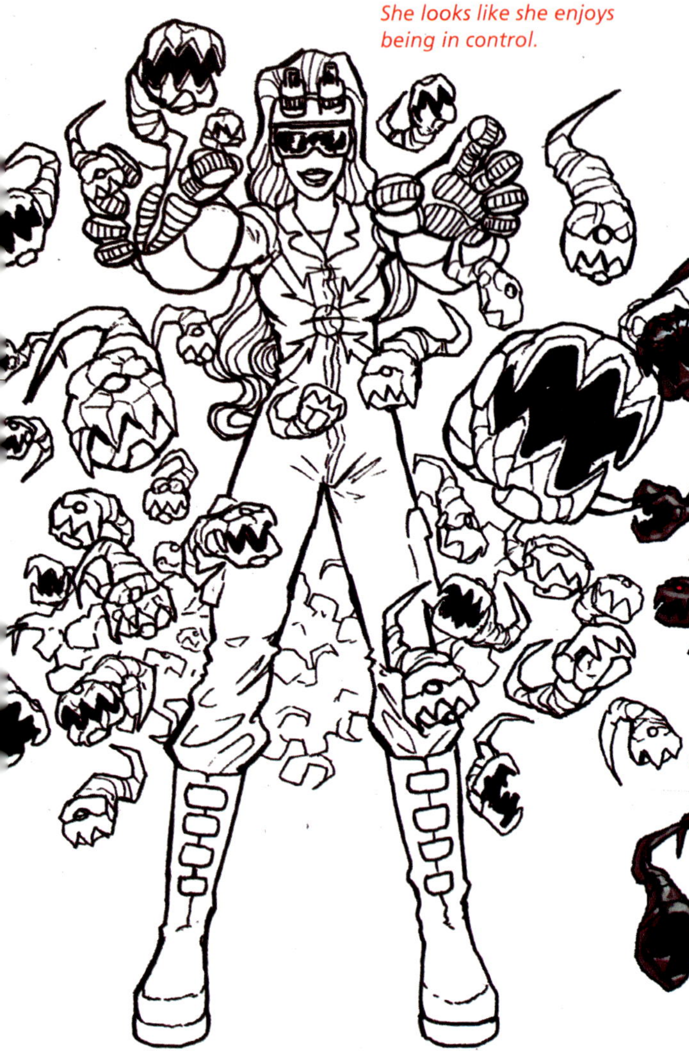

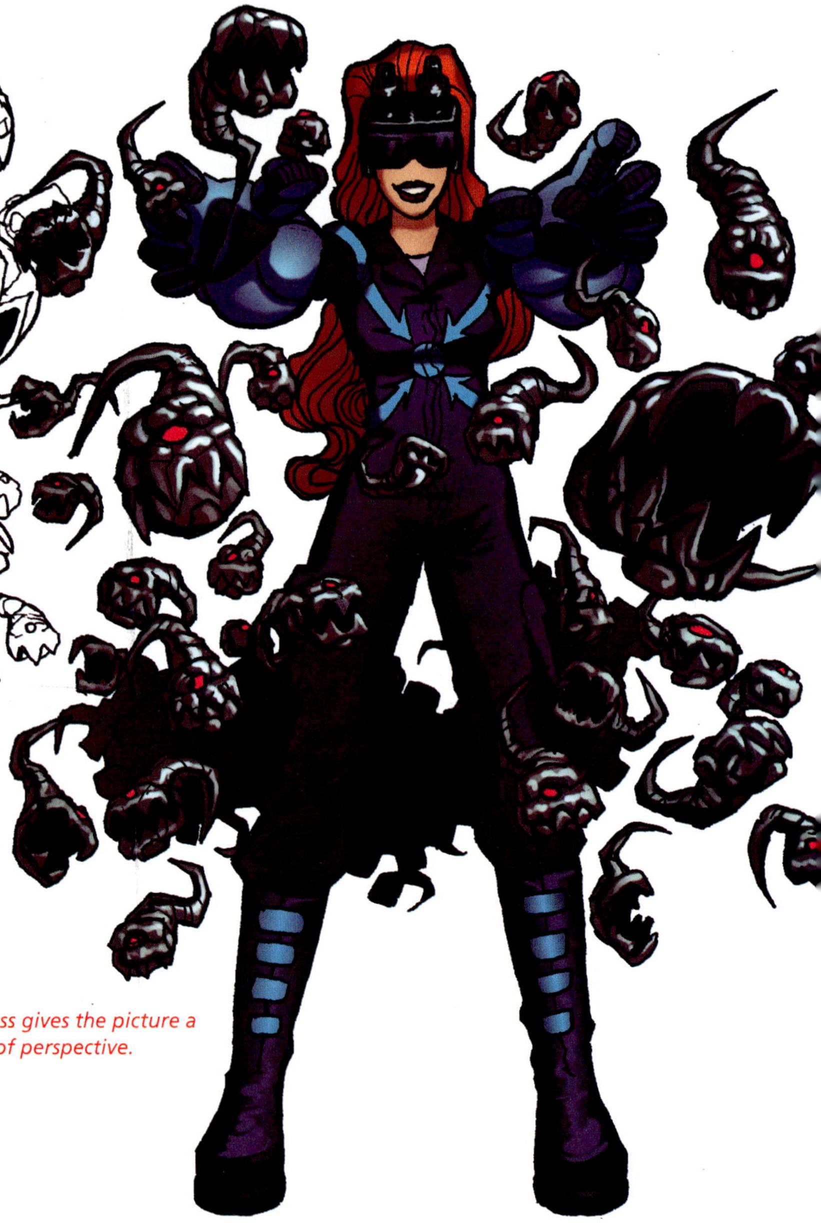

The gray mass gives the picture a good sense of perspective.

5. Use a good variety of lines for your inks here. Stick with strong lines for the borders, but use medium lines for the lines around the nanites' eyes and the icon on the woman's chest. Use light lines for wrinkles on her clothes and on the nanites.

6. Try grays and silvers for the nanites, with a single red eye for each. For her, go with indigo with sky blue highlights. Her red hair and lips draw your eyes to the center of the drawing, too.

HACKETTE

Hackette always had a flair for working with computers. Her parents say she seems like she was born with a laser mouse in one hand and a keyboard in the other. Over the years, she's honed her skills to an almost supernatural level. It's said there is no system she can't crack, which is what makes her such a great protector instead.

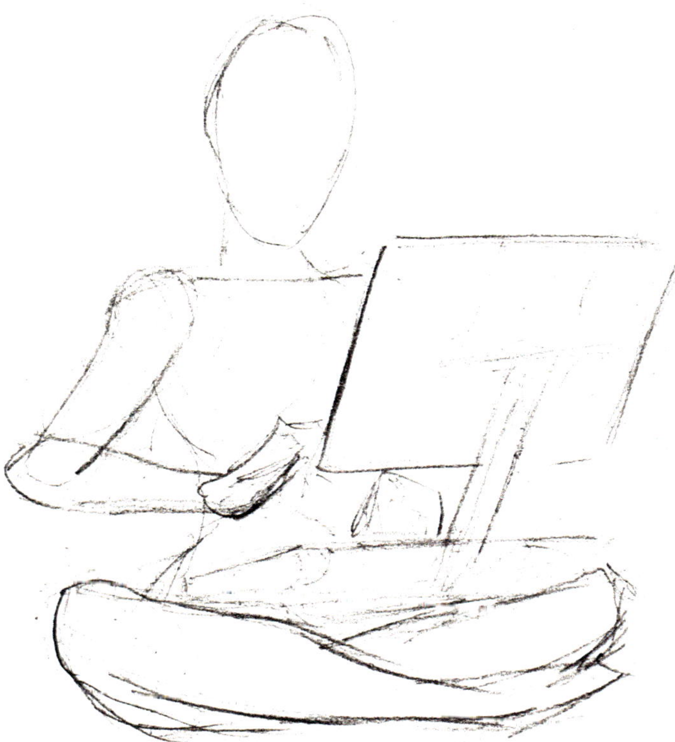

Other characters in this chapter hide within their tech, but none of them has as much control over it as Hackette.

Notice the guidelines Yair draws on Hackette's face to make sure he gets all the details right.

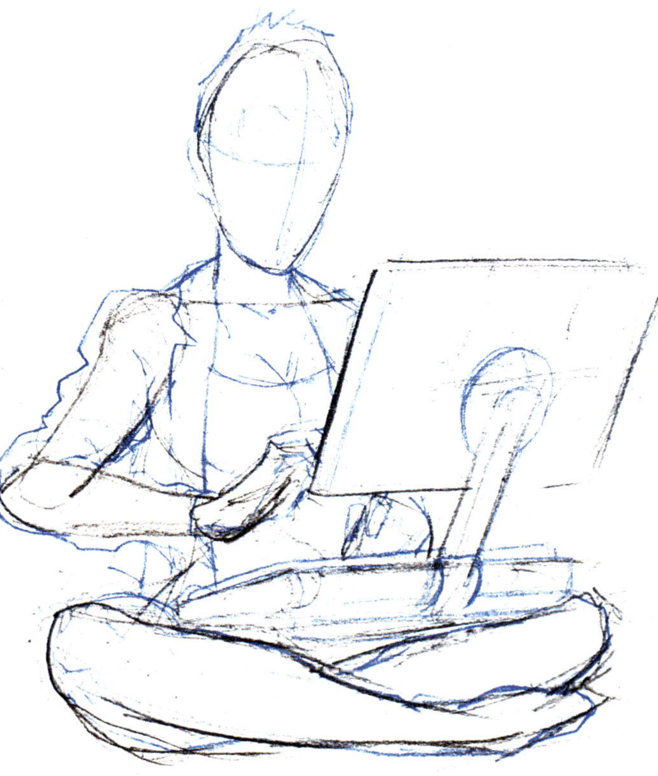

1. Rough out Hackette's basic shape. She's seated, working on a high-end laptop. Note the fold of the legs. Getting the anatomy right is vital, since she has so little to hide behind.

2. Add a jacket and pants to the girl, and rough out the edges of her hair and her breasts. Work up the details on the laptop a bit, too.

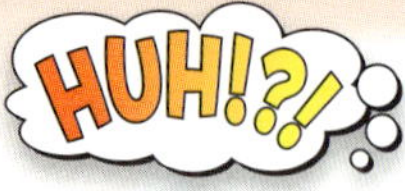

We could just draw a girl working on a standard laptop here, but the world of superheroes is always assumed to be a bit more technologically advanced than ours. That's why it's worth taking the time to come up with a different look for something as simple as a laptop. It reminds the viewer that this isn't their world—it's much cooler.

She looks sharp and serious.

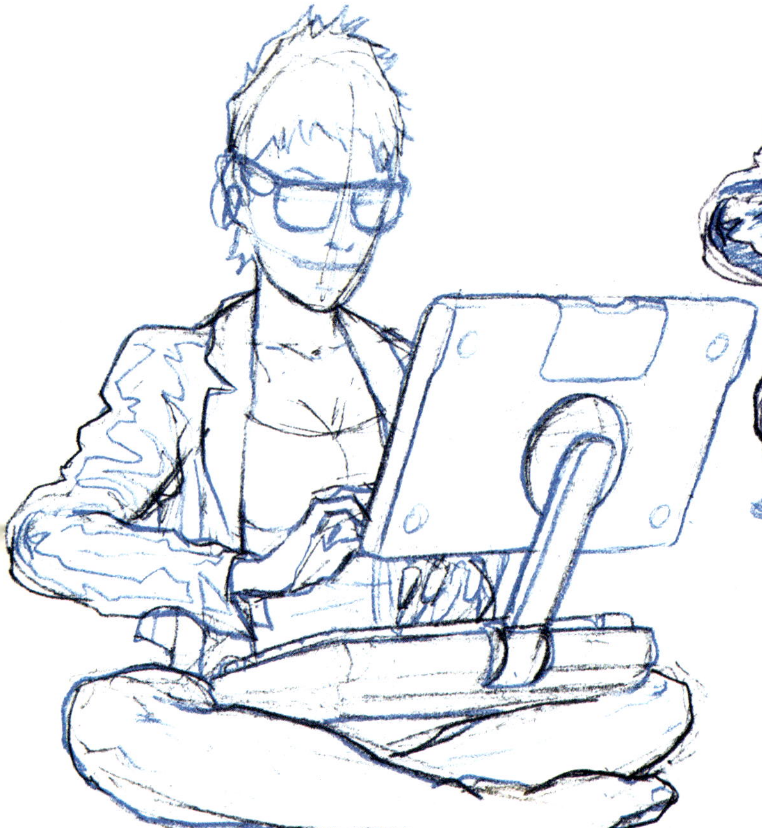

Wonder what she's playing on that computer?

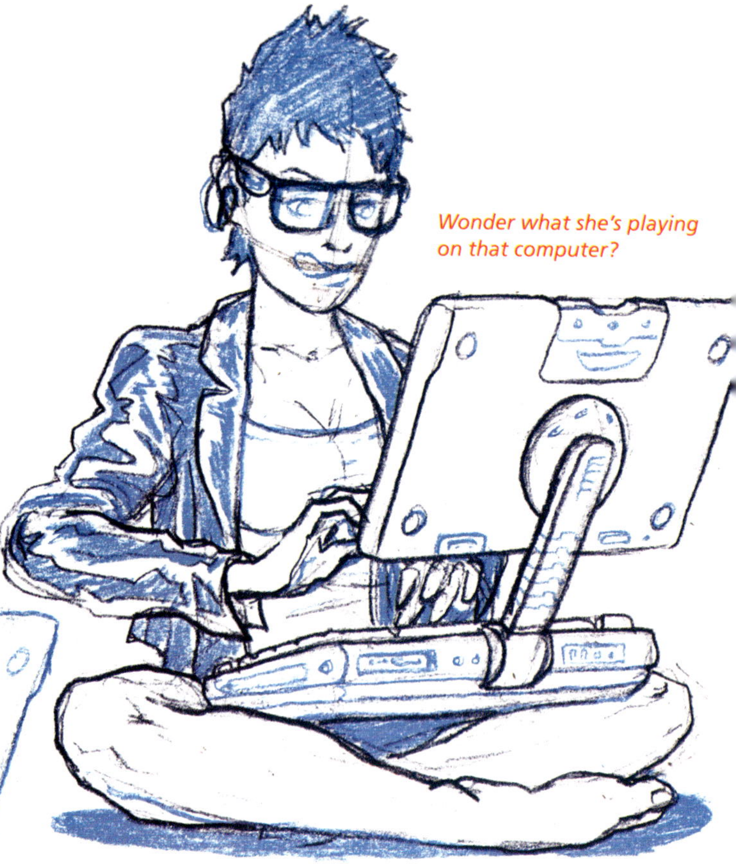

3. Work in lots more details to the computer and the woman. Hackette wears shades with built-in headphones, for instance. Finish the fingers, and add some wrinkling detail to the jacket to see how it looks. Rough in the mouth and eyebrows.

4. Black out large parts of the jacket. Add more details to the laptop. Give her some eyes and stick her tongue out of her mouth to show she's concentrating.

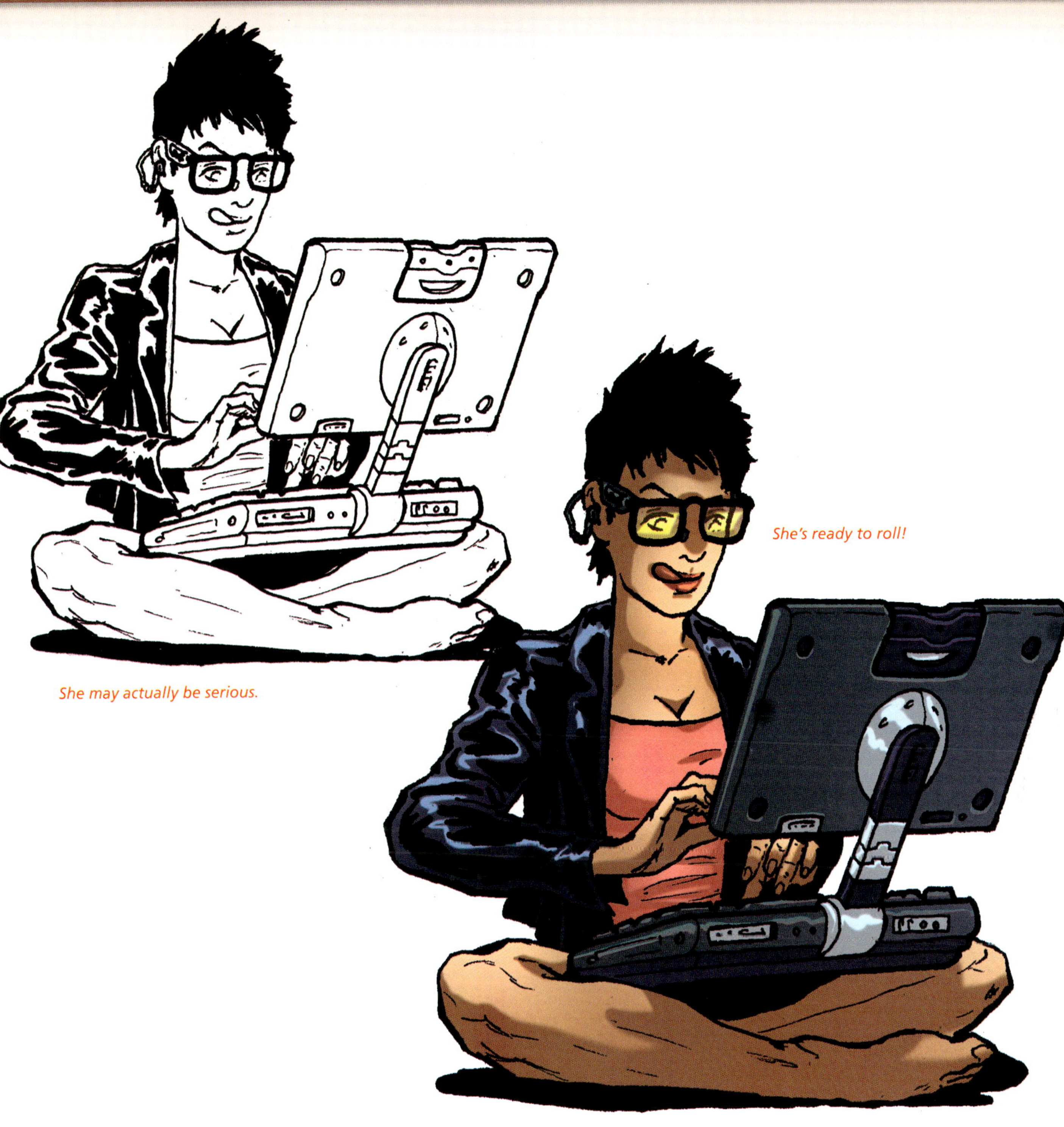

She's ready to roll!

She may actually be serious.

5. Use heavy inks throughout most of the illustration. Pay special attention to how Yair uses white space to create the effect of shiny leather on the Hackette's jacket.

6. Go mostly with flesh tones. Use a black jacket and a pink skirt. Tint the lenses yellow. Keep in mind the odd lighting properties of a laptop and be sure to depict them accurately.

THE ARMORER

This scientist contracted ALS (Lou Gehrig's disease), a horrible illness that slowly but surely destroyed his nervous system. Determined to fight against his fate, he constructed a suit of armor that reacted as fast as his thoughts and made him stronger than ever. Outside of it he's as feeble as a kitten, but inside he's a hero unparalleled.

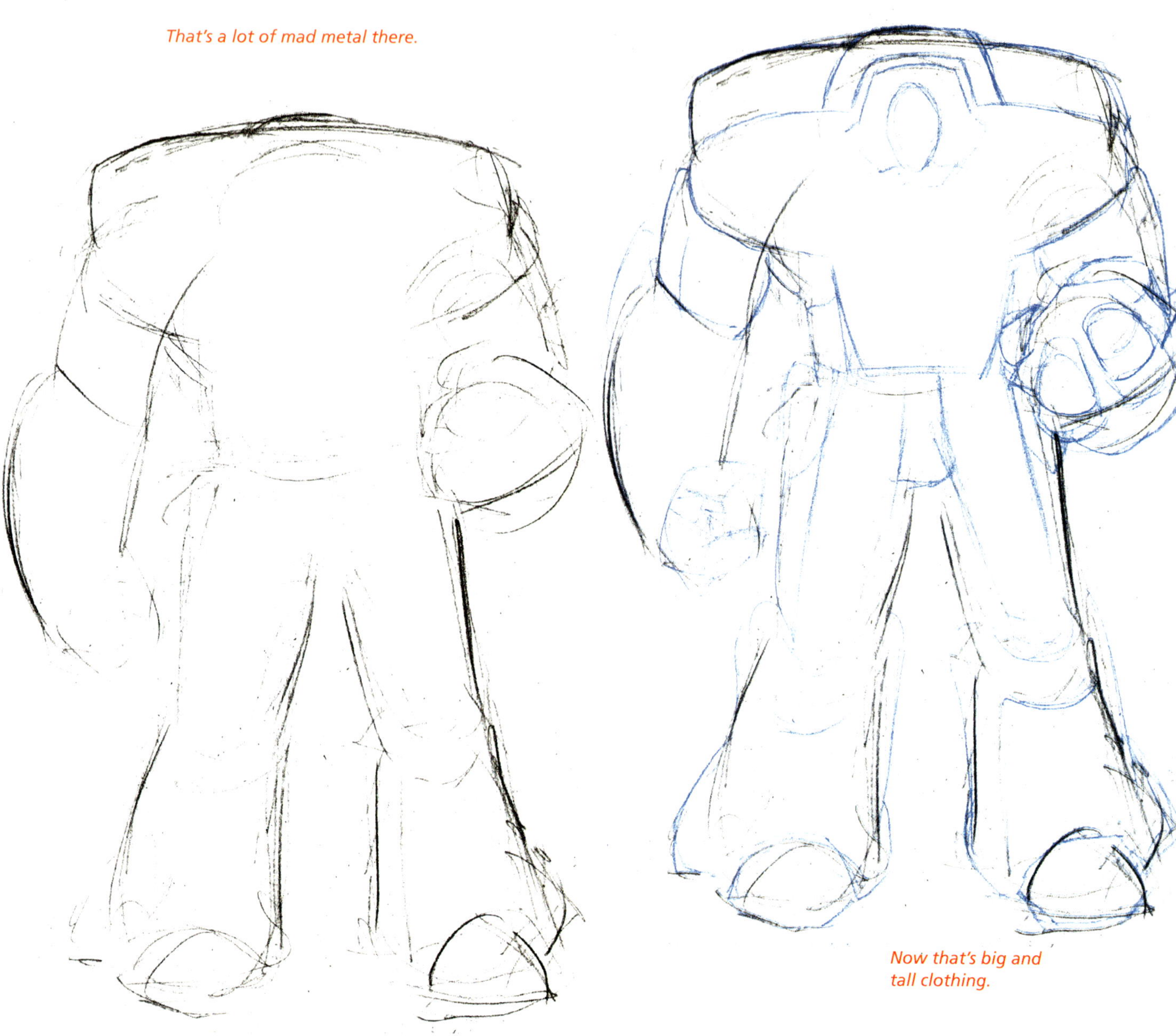

That's a lot of mad metal there.

Now that's big and tall clothing.

1. Rough out the Armorer's shape. He's huge, so much so that his shoulders stand taller than his head. Think of him as a walking tank.

2. Work in more details. Show the thickness of the armor by curving it at certain points. Add a viewpoint for the driver.

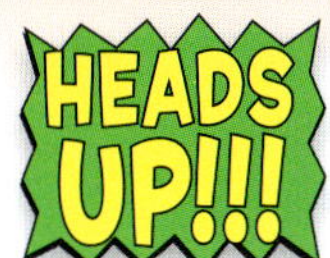

It's possible to overdo armor—or any costume—and the Armorer certainly pushes that boundary. The suit is recognizably human in shape, but it wouldn't take too much more exaggeration for it to lose that as well.

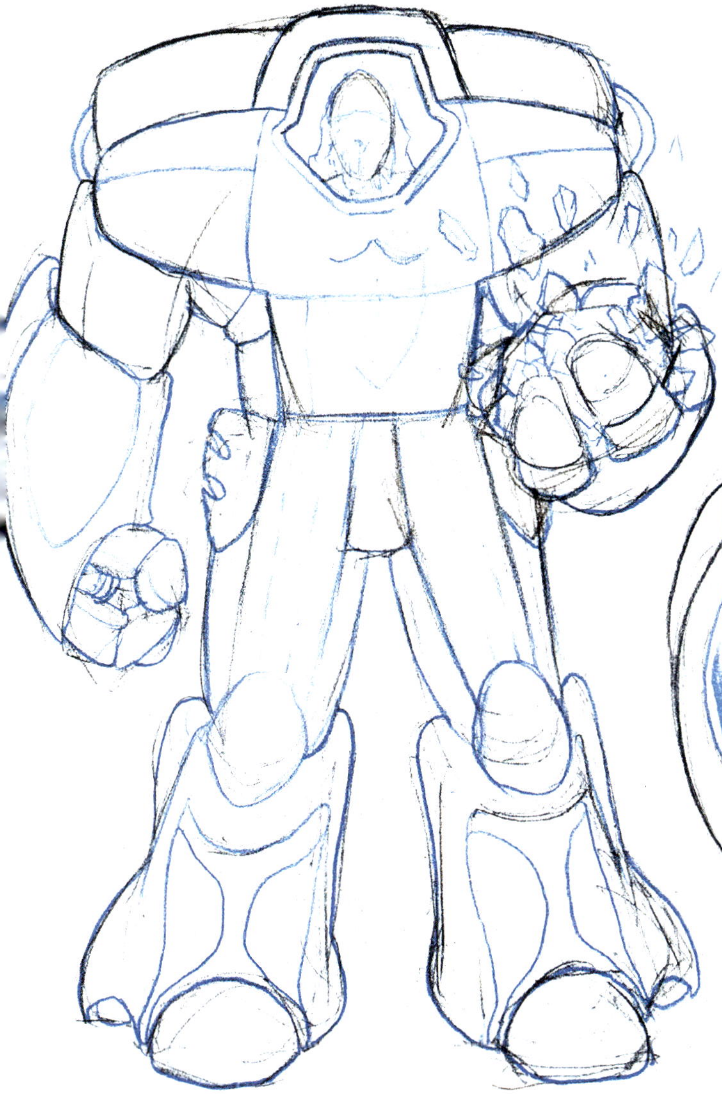

You'd almost think he was a robot if not for the face.

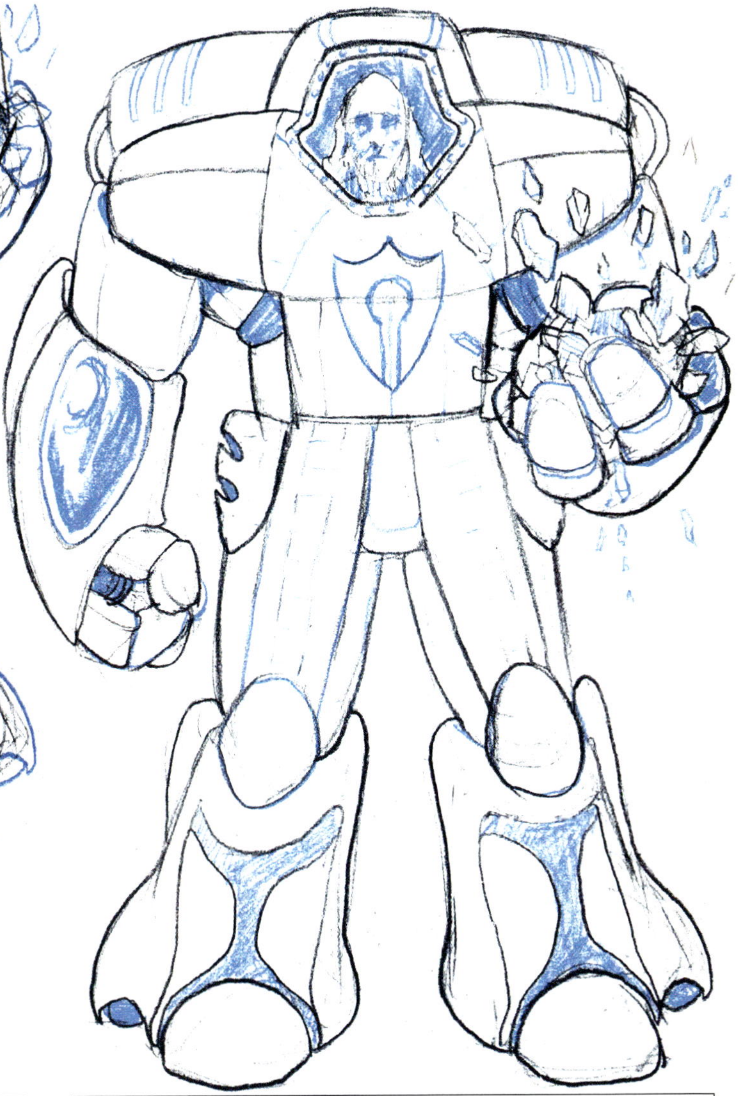

The man inside isn't even half the size of his suit.

3. Work on the armor's trim. Give it rounded edges for a modern look. Show a crushed boulder in one hand to emphasize the suit's strength.

4. Black out parts of the armor that might look like rubberized metal. Put an icon on his chest (a shield). Add lots more trim to the legs and the rest of the armor.

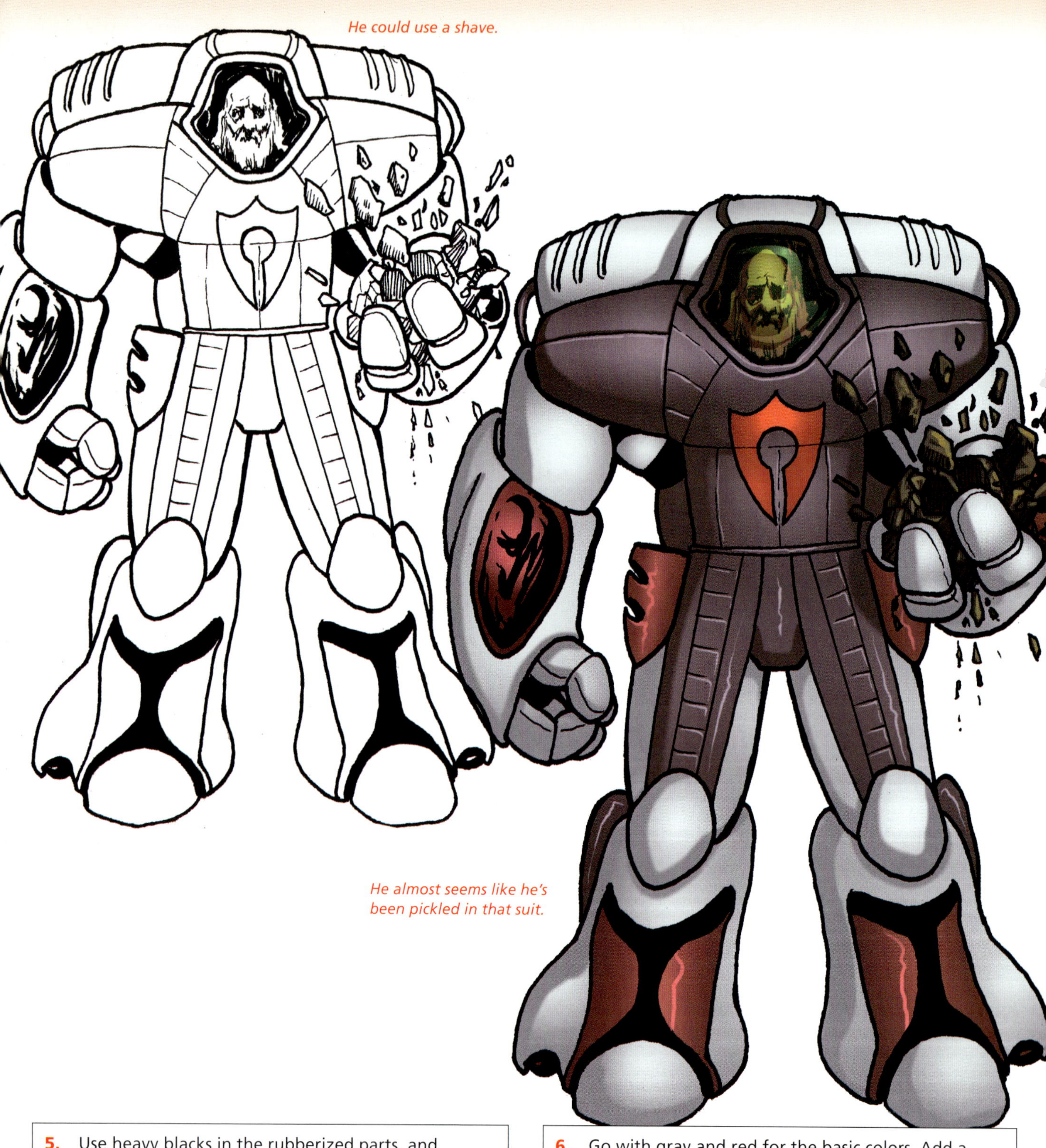

He could use a shave.

He almost seems like he's been pickled in that suit.

5. Use heavy blacks in the rubberized parts, and thicker lines around the edges. Use thinner lines on the interior of the suit, which essentially shows where the driver's body is as he uses the suit.

6. Go with gray and red for the basic colors. Add a green lens over the man's face.

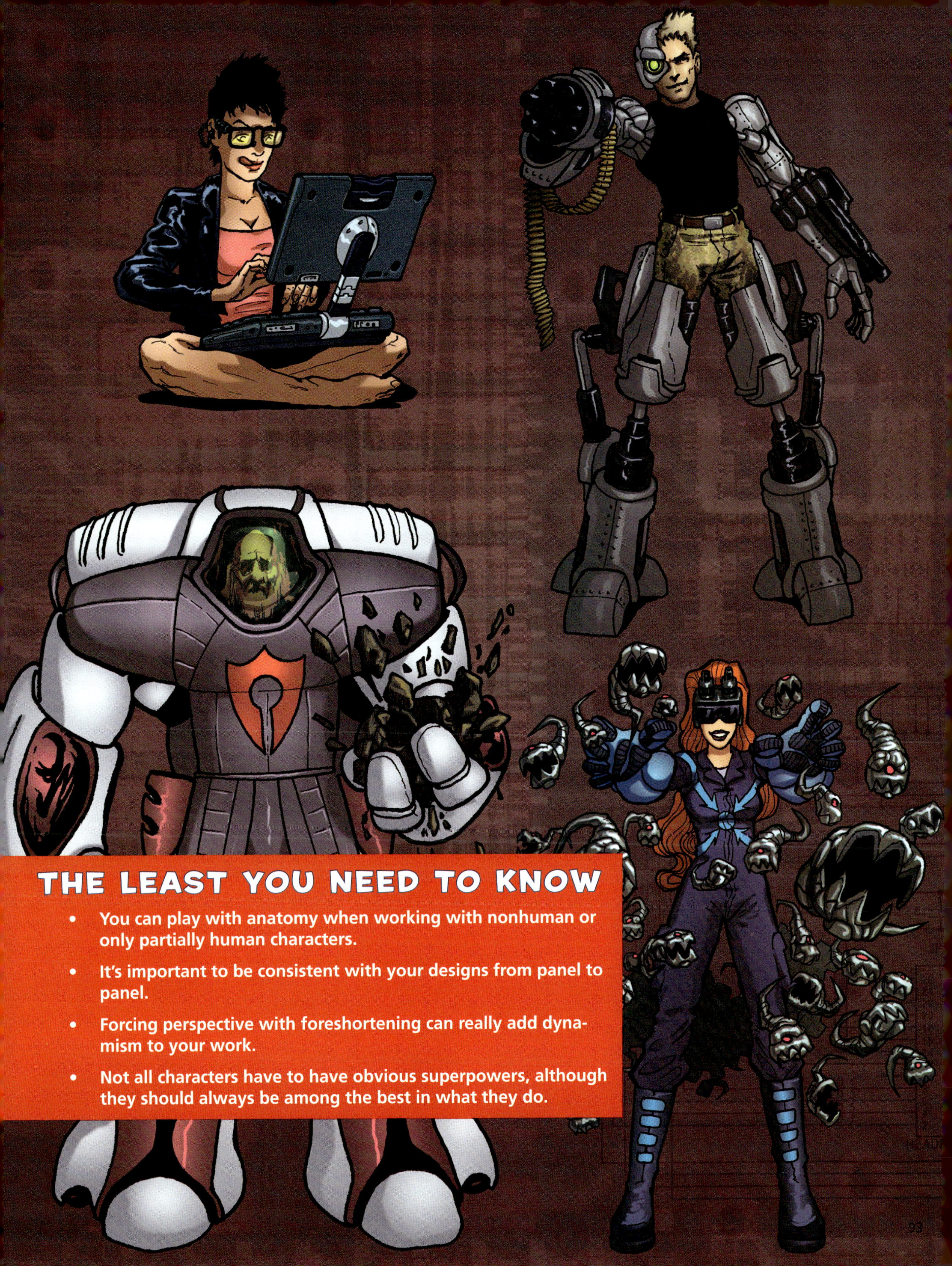

THE LEAST YOU NEED TO KNOW

- You can play with anatomy when working with nonhuman or only partially human characters.
- It's important to be consistent with your designs from panel to panel.
- Forcing perspective with foreshortening can really add dynamism to your work.
- Not all characters have to have obvious superpowers, although they should always be among the best in what they do.

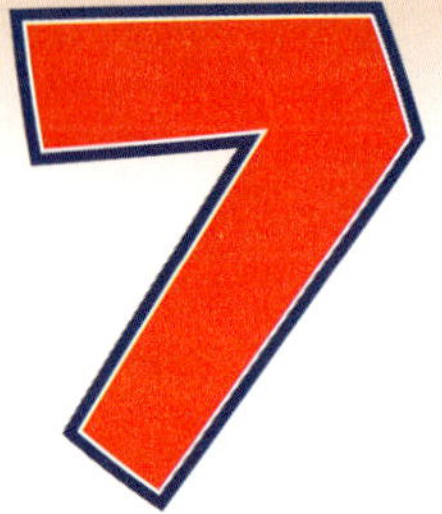

Mystics: Beyond the Brain

In This Chapter

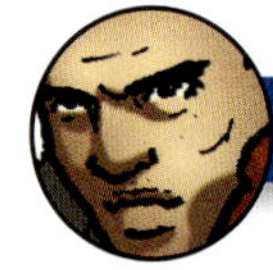

- Beatings brought by brain

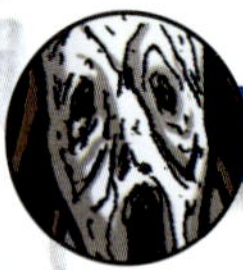

- Terror in a tuxedo

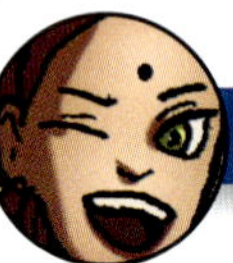

- A genetic genie

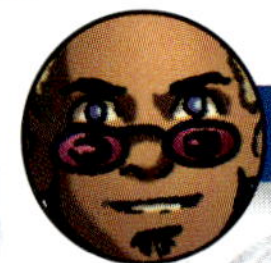

- The master mystic

Mystics use brains over brawn, but they employ weird science or even magic to pull off their amazing feats. The things they do shouldn't work by any scientific measure, but somehow they do. Whether they use hyper-advanced technology or mystical energies, some of the most offbeat characters can be called mystics.

TKO leads off our ticket. He once had dreams of being a boxer but gave them up as he got older. Then he developed the ability to fashion ectoplasmic fists with his mind, and the starting bell rang again.

The Frightener has a horrifying power. Just looking at him can turn a hero's heart to jelly. His favorite word? "Boo!" He also loves watching people run away.

Gene-E used to dabble in ritual magic, and one day she created a miniature black hole that sucked her right in. When she squeezed out the other side, she realized she had the power to alter her DNA with her thoughts and alter and stretch her body in inhuman ways.

The Mystic has dedicated his life to mastering the magical arts. Few know as much about the ways of magic as him. Luckily, he uses this knowledge to help others, battling back the darkness that threatens to consume us all.

TKO

TKO trained his mind like a boxer trains his body, until he learned how to generate telekinetic force that he could manipulate like fists. He now packs a harder punch than Muhammad Ali, but he can hit you from across the room. He might be able to use the telekinetic hands to grab or push things, too, but where's the fun in that?

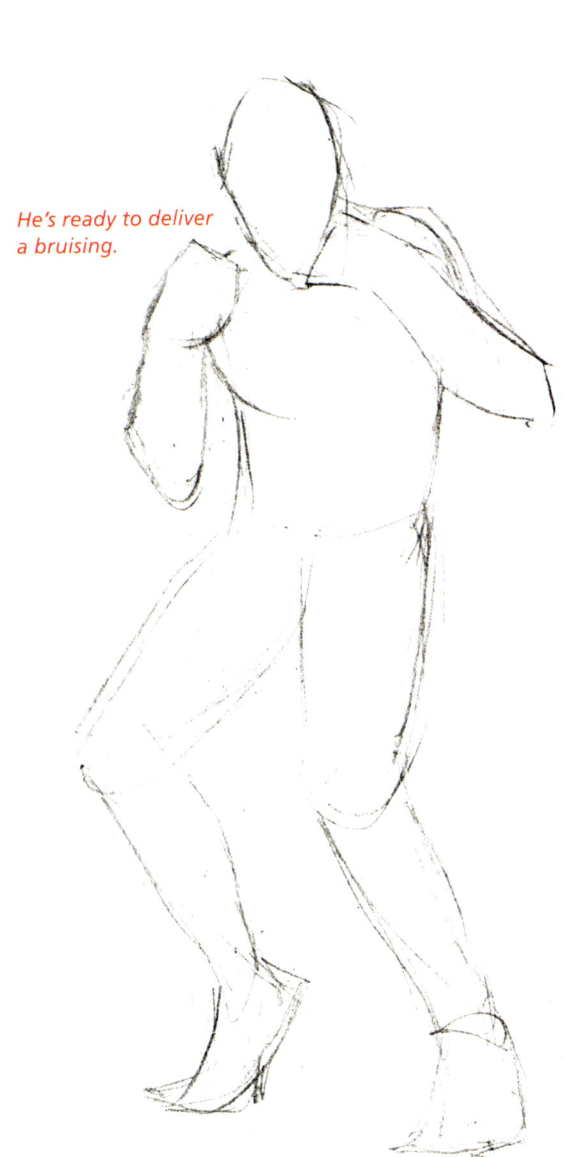

He's ready to deliver a bruising.

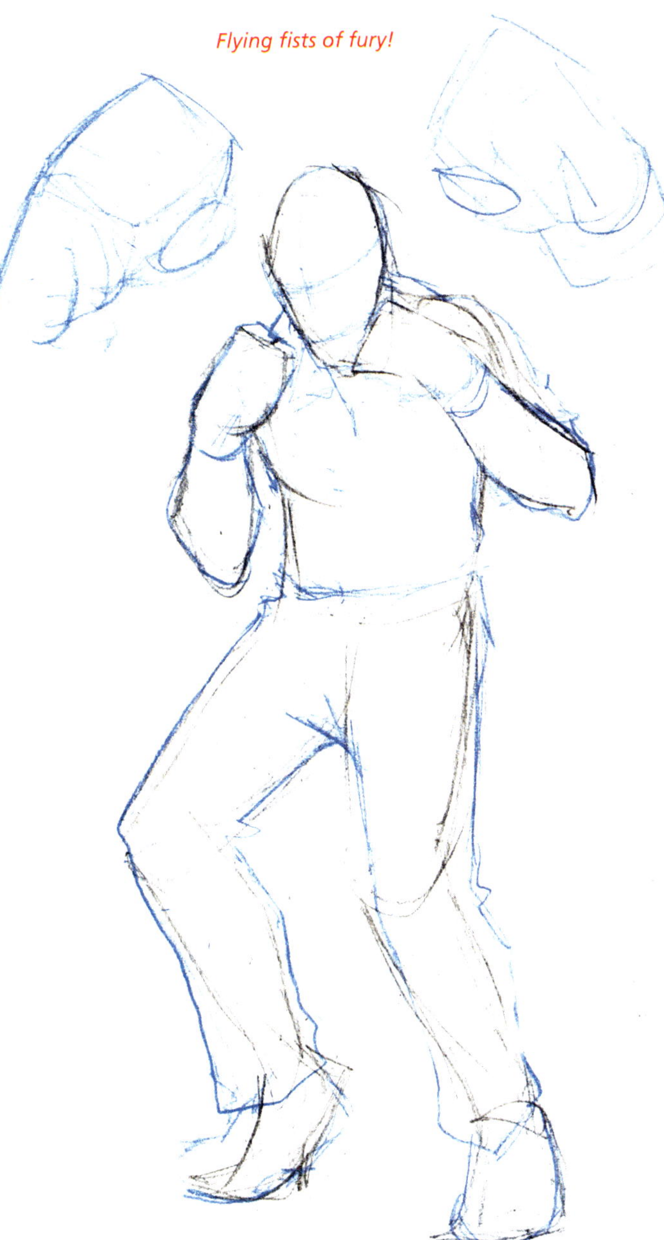

Flying fists of fury!

1. Break down TKO's rough form here. He's a boxer, so put him in a fighting stance, his fists held high. Notice how the right forearm entirely *masks* his upper arm. The image still works because Yair gets the anatomy right.

2. Add some clothes to TKO's frame. He's in business casual today—slacks and a polo rather than boxing shorts. Place his telekinetic fists above him, and make sure they mimic the placement of his real fists.

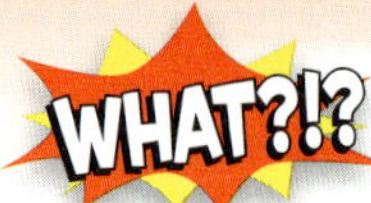

When people stand in many poses, parts of their bodies **mask** (or obscure) other parts. This can make it seem like the part in the foreground is floating without any support. However, if you get your anatomy right, it allows you to use more dynamic poses and still look correct. Use guidelines to show where the masked parts are if you like. You can always erase them later.

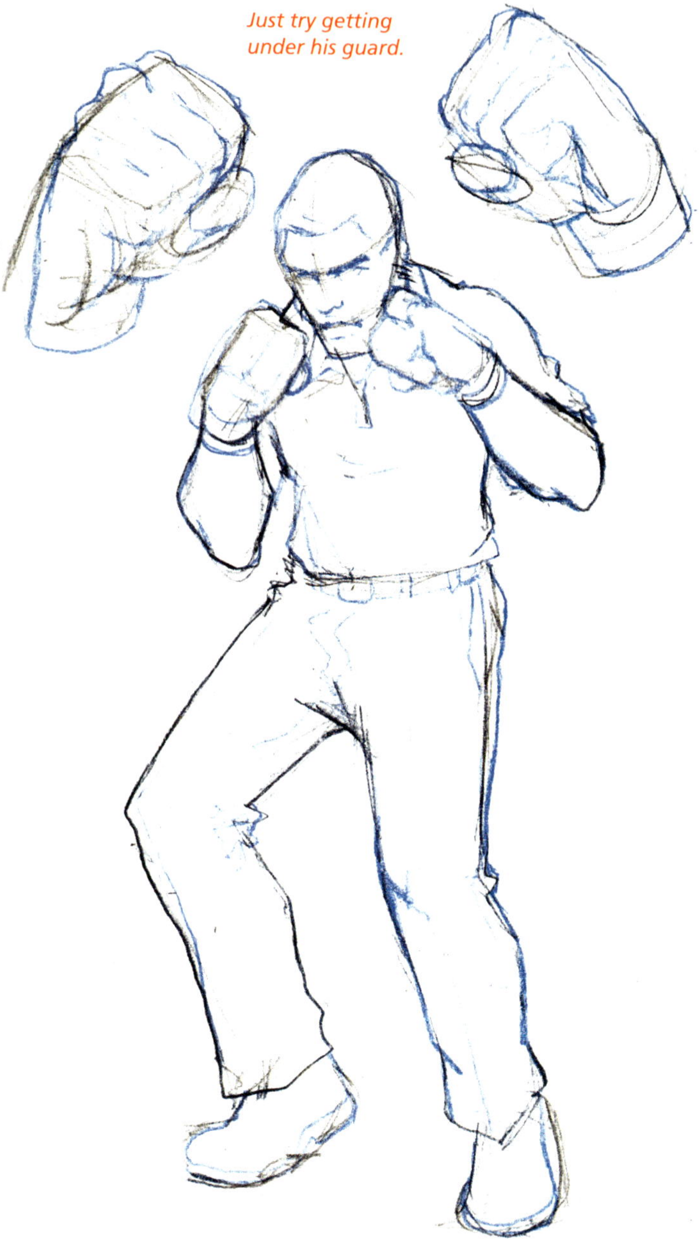

Just try getting under his guard.

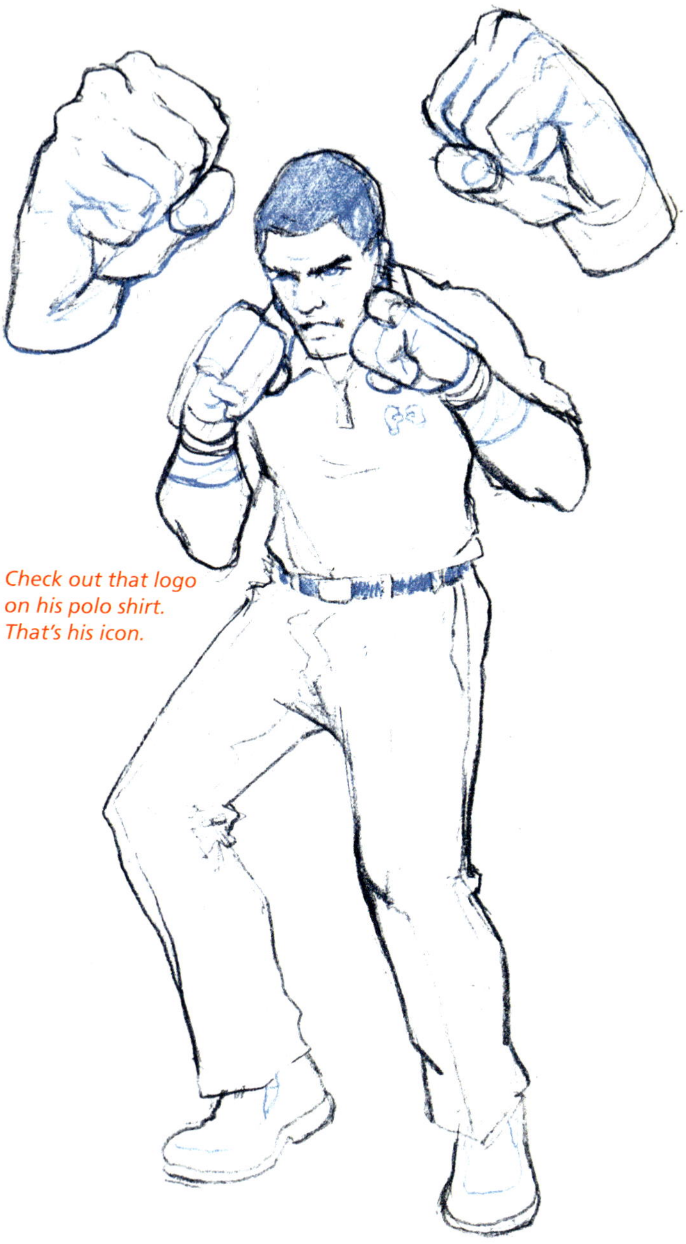

Check out that logo on his polo shirt. That's his icon.

3. Work in the details on the clothes: his belt, the wrinkles in his shirt and pants, the shoes. Also rough in his hair and facial features. Pay special attention to his boxing gloves and the telekinetic fists.

4. Black out TKO's hair and belt. Focus on those telekinetic hands. They're huge and will command a lot of attention, so it's important to get them right. Use your own for models if you like.

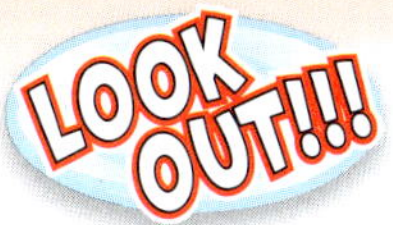

It would have been easy—too easy—to put TKO in a boxer's outfit or a spandex suit that resembled one. It's better to play with the reader's expectations and do something different than follow the easy way. Try surprising yourself and your readers by straying just a bit from the beaten path.

Looks like someone's got a beating coming.

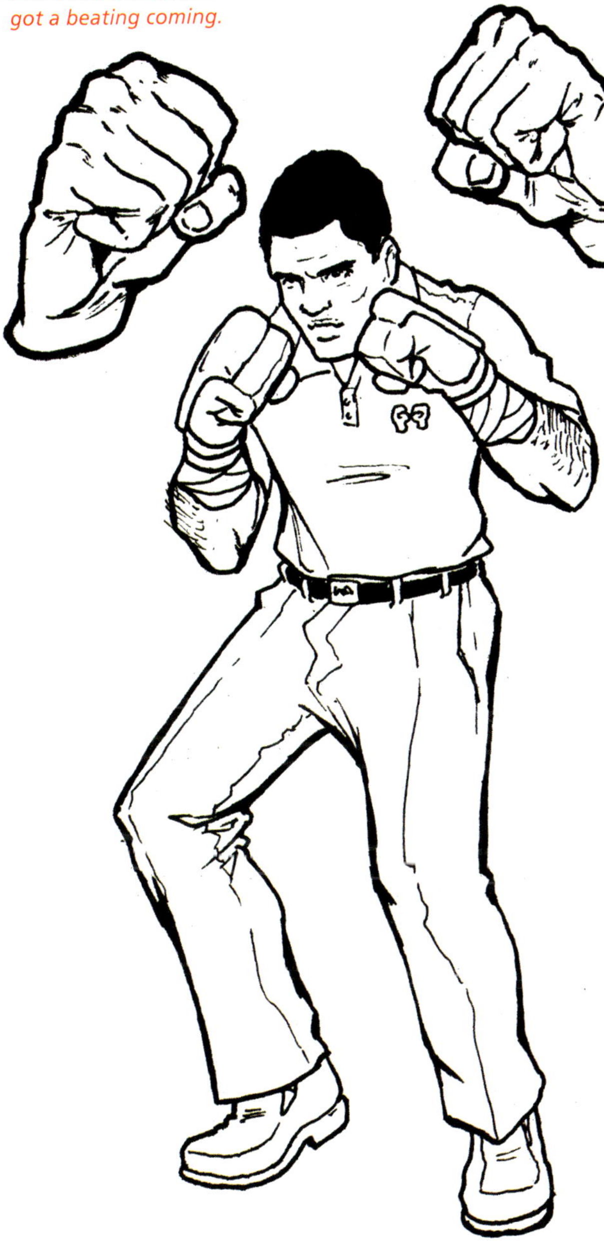

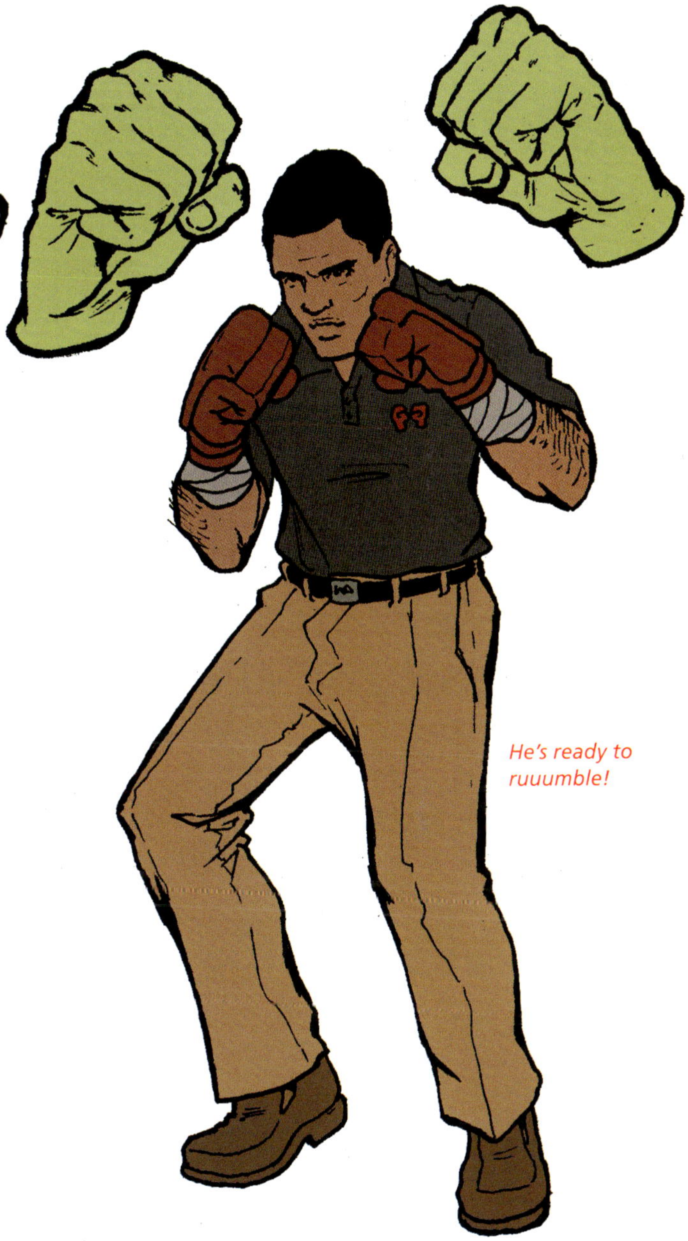

He's ready to ruuumble!

5. Use heavy inks on the outer edges and lighter ones for the wrinkles and for the hair on TKO's forearms. Go ultra heavy for the edges of the telekinetic fists. This should really make them pop.

6. Go with nondescript colors for TKO's clothing: a forest green shirt and khaki pants. The gloves should be red, and you should make the fists a glowing green. We'll pump up the brighter colors in the next step, but get your darker tones down first.

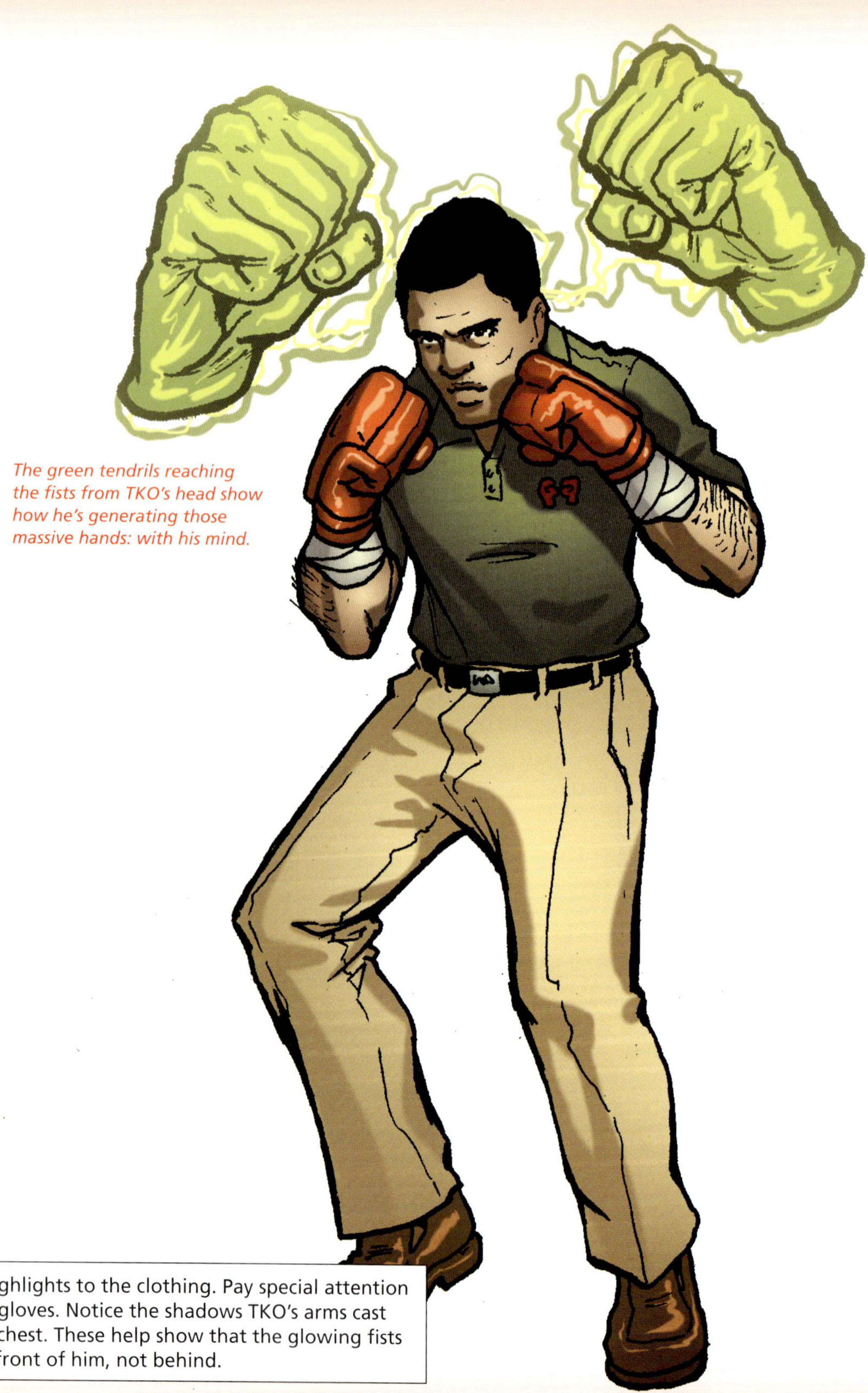

The green tendrils reaching the fists from TKO's head show how he's generating those massive hands: with his mind.

7. Add highlights to the clothing. Pay special attention to the gloves. Notice the shadows TKO's arms cast on his chest. These help show that the glowing fists are in front of him, not behind.

THE FRIGHTENER

The Frightener used to run the most popular haunted house around, but he had to shut it down when scores of people were hurt in a stampede from the place's most frightening exhibit: him. He now uses his powers to scare others away from him so he can do whatever he likes while they're gone. Only the bravest souls have a chance of meeting his gaze, and such people are rare, even among heroes.

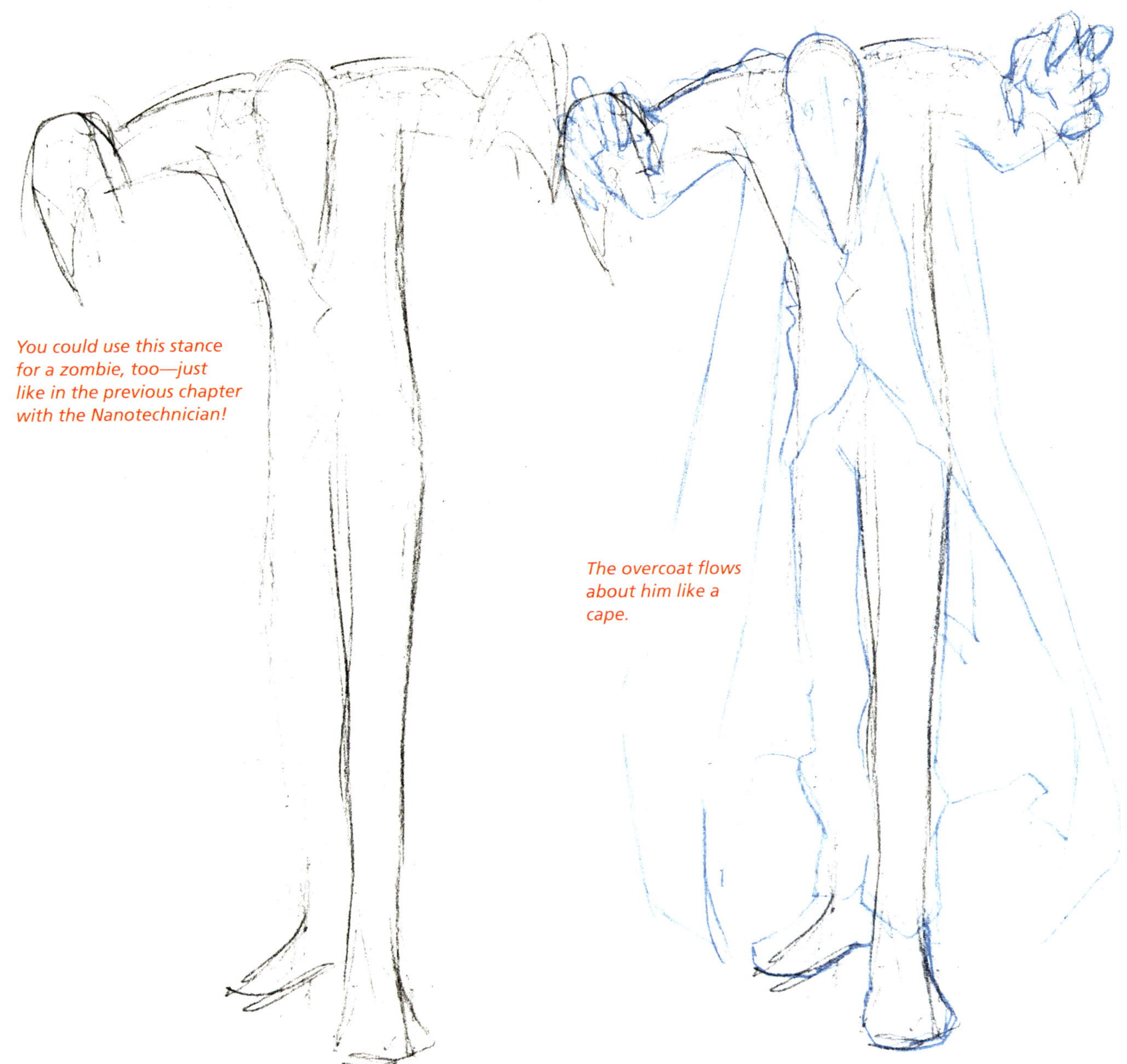

You could use this stance for a zombie, too—just like in the previous chapter with the Nanotechnician!

The overcoat flows about him like a cape.

1. Start with a scary stance. Make him tall and thin, and extend his arms, almost like he's a scarecrow. He should drip with menace.

2. Add a long overcoat to the Frightener and dress him in a tattered tuxedo. He wears a mask taken from Edvard Munch's *The Scream*. Form his fingers into claws reaching for you.

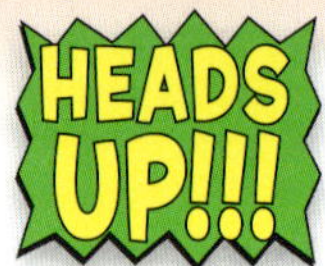

A character's body language says a lot about how it's feeling. The Frightener is aggressive, but in a different way than TKO, for instance. Study the way people move in real life to build a glossary of poses for your own work.

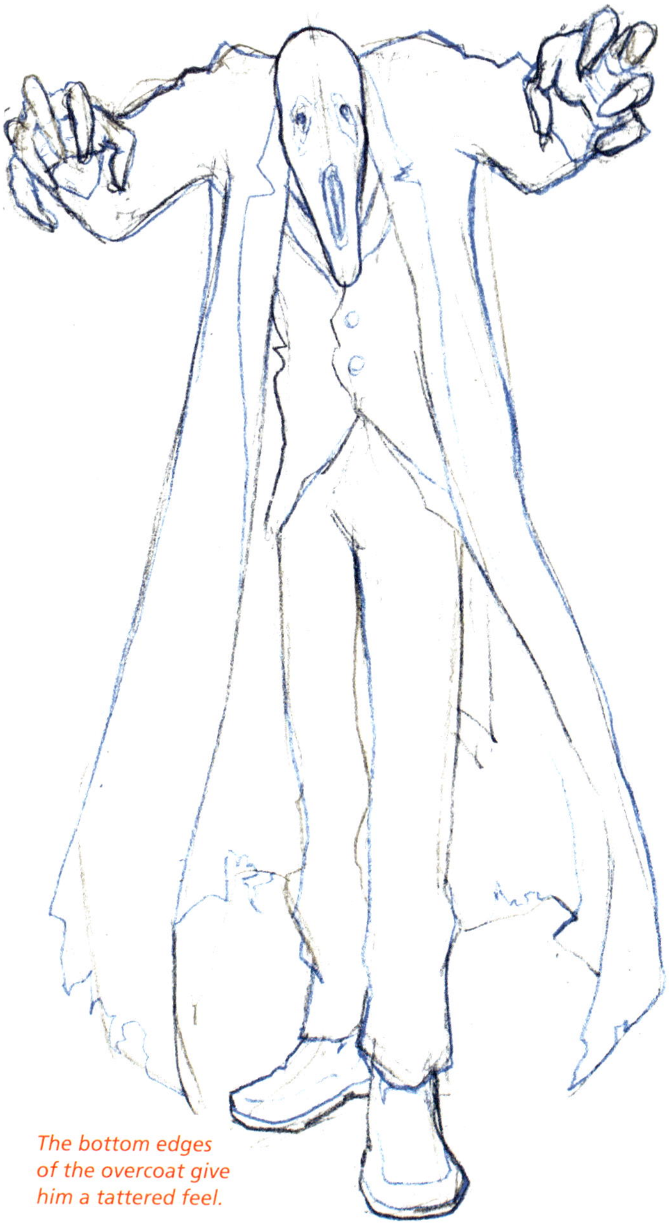

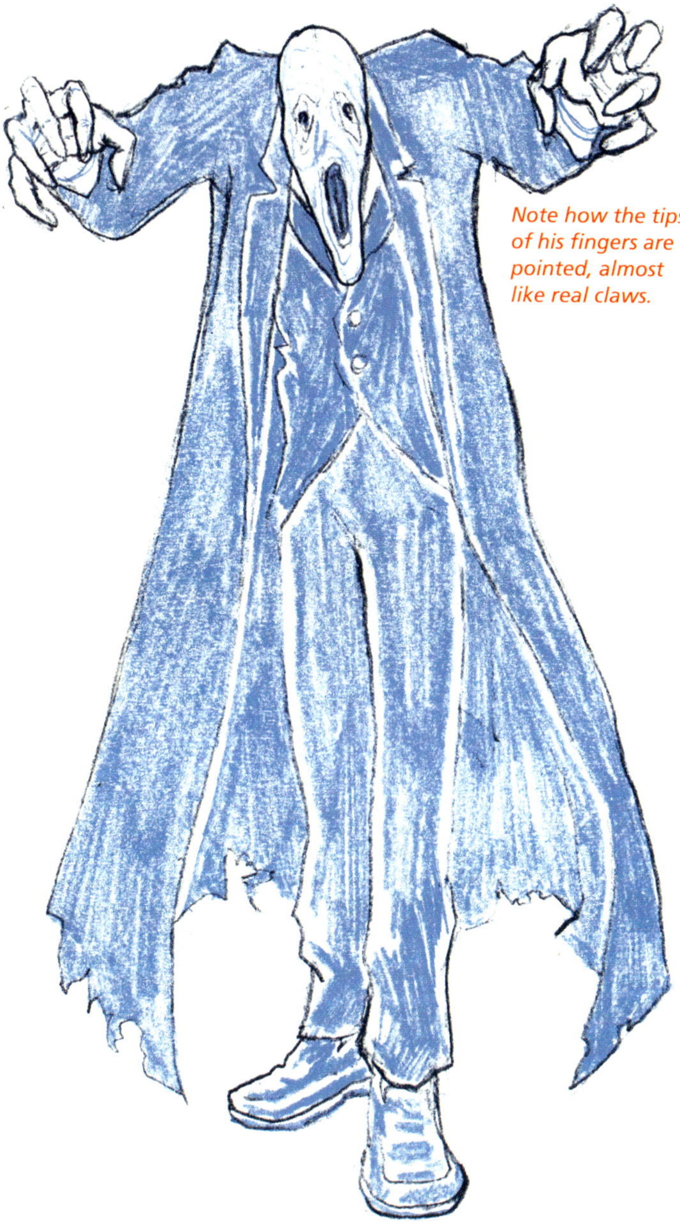

Note how the tips of his fingers are pointed, almost like real claws.

The bottom edges of the overcoat give him a tattered feel.

3. Add more details to the Frightener's clothes: a lapel to his overcoat, buttons on his vest. Work out the face on his mask. Take some liberties with Munch's original and give him long, gaping holes for his mouth and eyes.

4. Black out the coat and tuxedo. Leave the edges white to outline the edges of his clothes. Work the details on those fingers and on the mask.

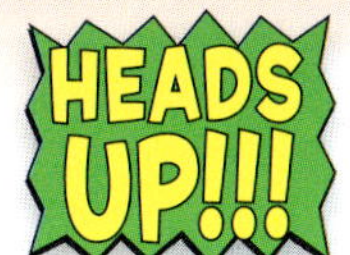

It's important to use either white or a lighter color to show the outlines of clothes when the figure wears all black. This may not be a strictly accurate capture of real colors, but if you don't use this trick the figure will look like a blob or silhouette. The contrasting color provides detail you can't easily get any other way.

The face leaps out of those blacks surrounding it.

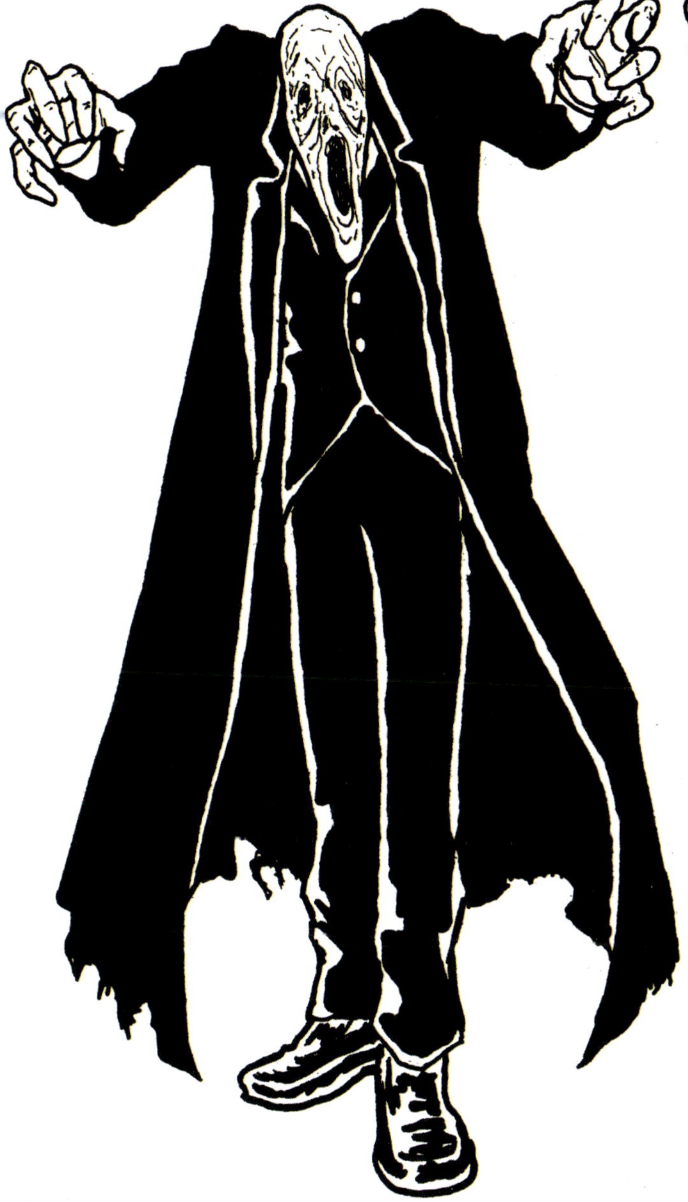

Chilling.

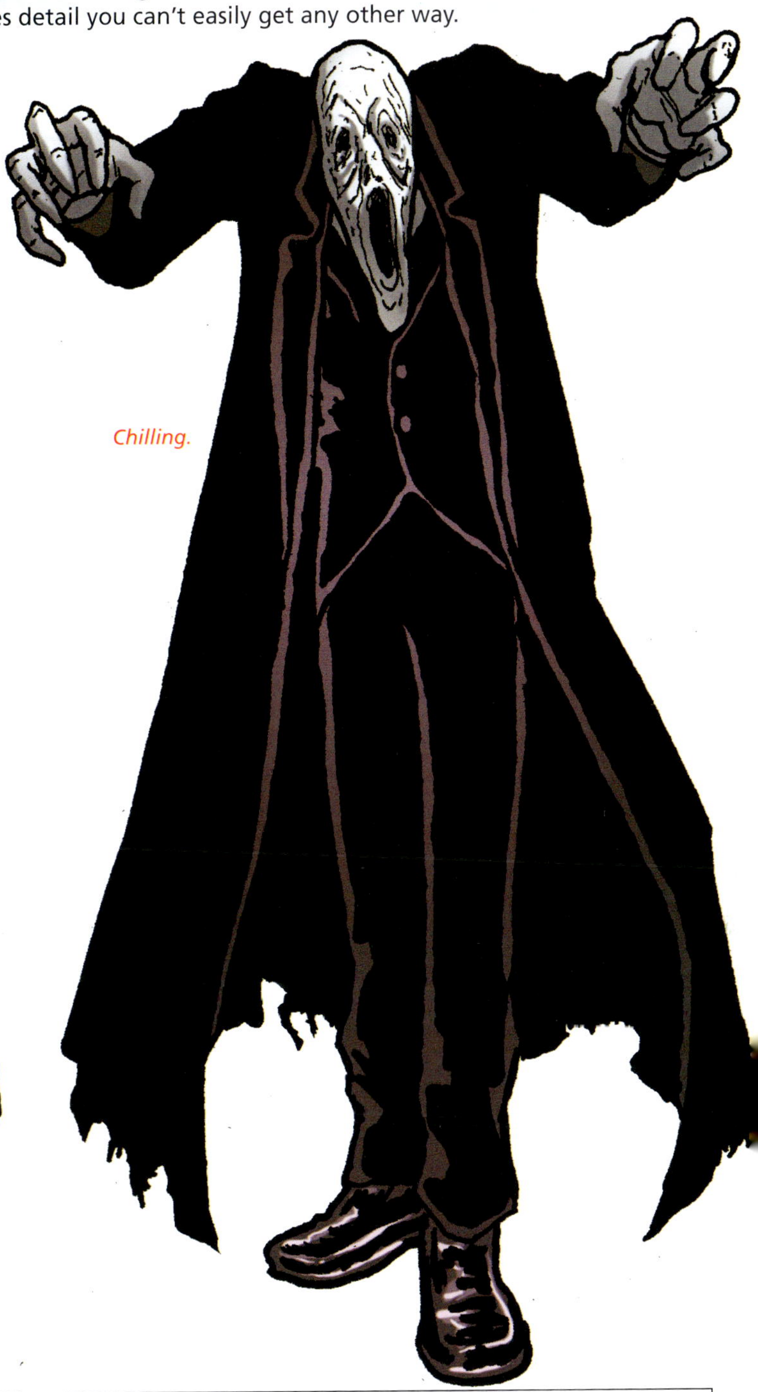

5. Use solid blacks on most of the figure, but again be careful to use white to outline the edges of his clothes. Use thinner lines on his face and fingers to give them a dirty, decaying feel.

6. Replace the white on the figure's clothes with a deep purple, like the color of the sky at dusk. Use gravestone gray for his mask and gloves. Use more highlights on the shoes to show that they're made of something shinier than his other clothes.

GENE-E

Gene-E stumbled into her powers while messing around with things she didn't really understand. She still doesn't have a strong command of just how amazing her powers really are, but that doesn't stop her from having fun with them. In a real sense, she's a self-made woman, fashioning herself in her own image.

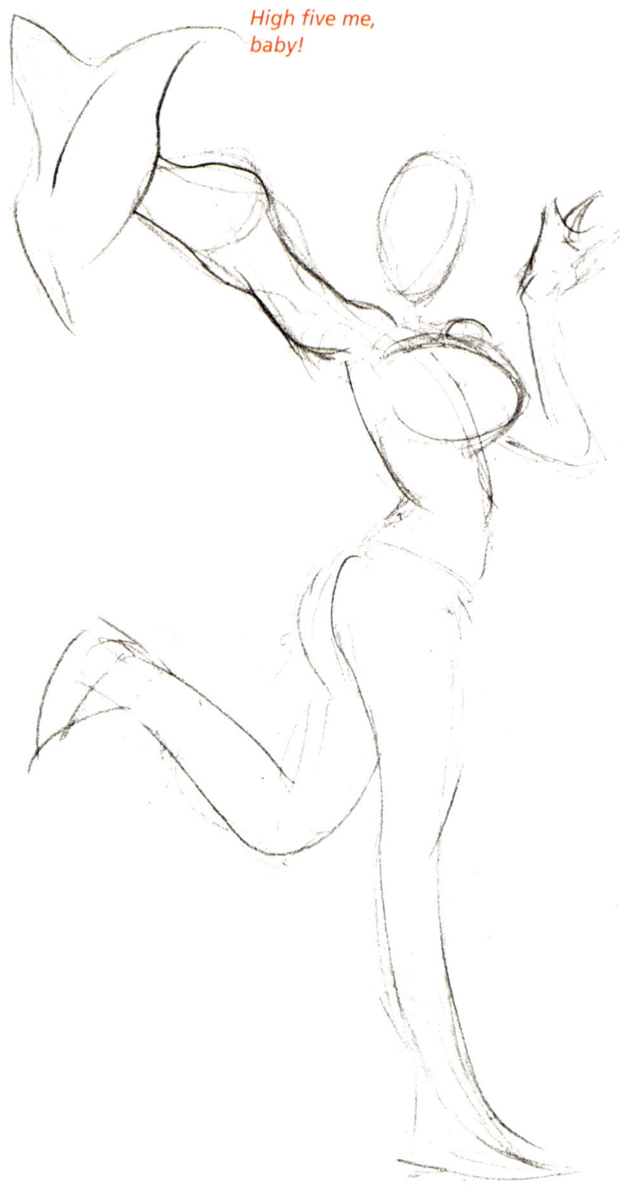

High five me, baby!

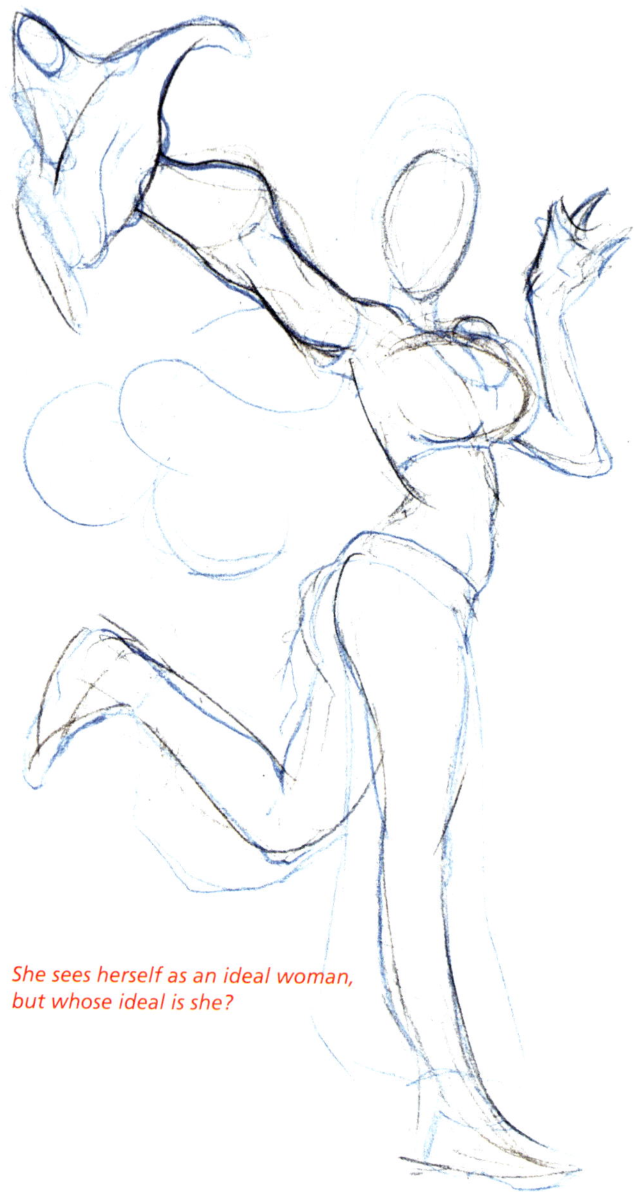

She sees herself as an ideal woman, but whose ideal is she?

1. Start with a wild, fun stance. Gene-E runs in one direction while reaching out in another. Her hand is huge, not because of forced perspective but because she's stretched it out with her powers.

2. Add hair and clothes. Gene-E sees herself as something of a genie in a bottle, so give her a halter top and silky leggings, as well as ridiculously large breasts. She has long, flowing hair that would be a royal pain to care for if she couldn't control every strand.

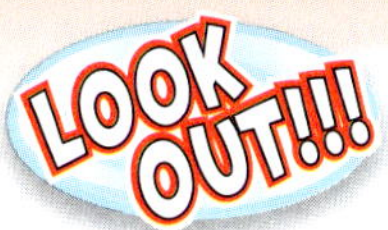

When working with a stretchable character like Gene-E, it's important to go a little wild with the poses. Otherwise, you run the risk that the viewer might think you're just not handling the anatomy well. Exaggerating the anatomy helps make sure there's no room for confusion.

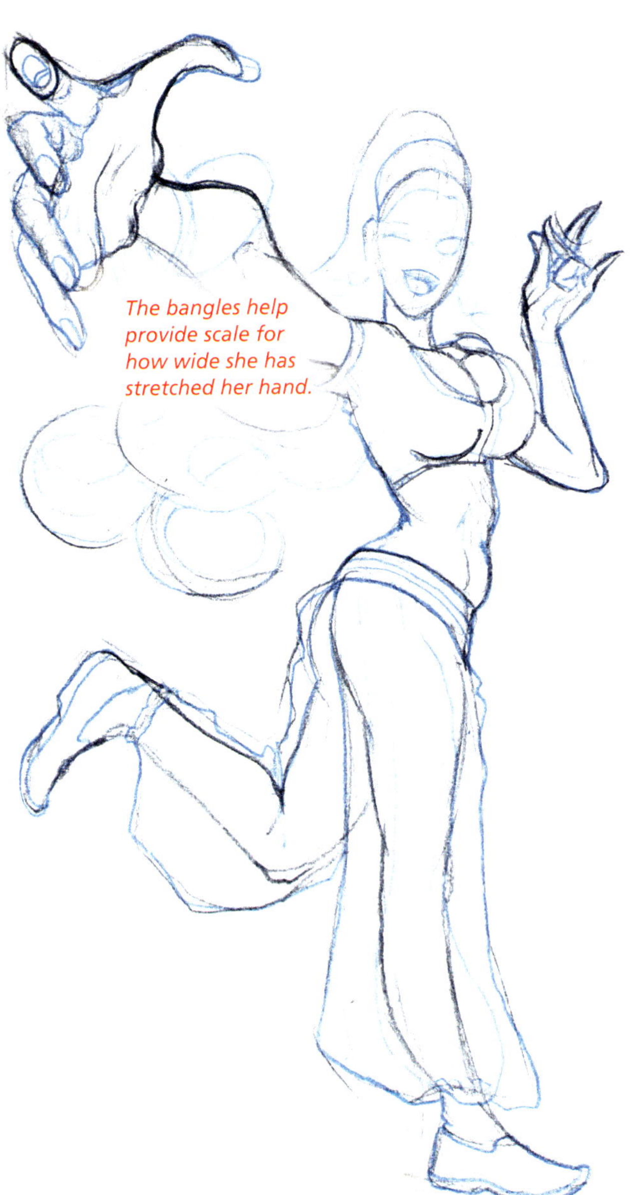

The bangles help provide scale for how wide she has stretched her hand.

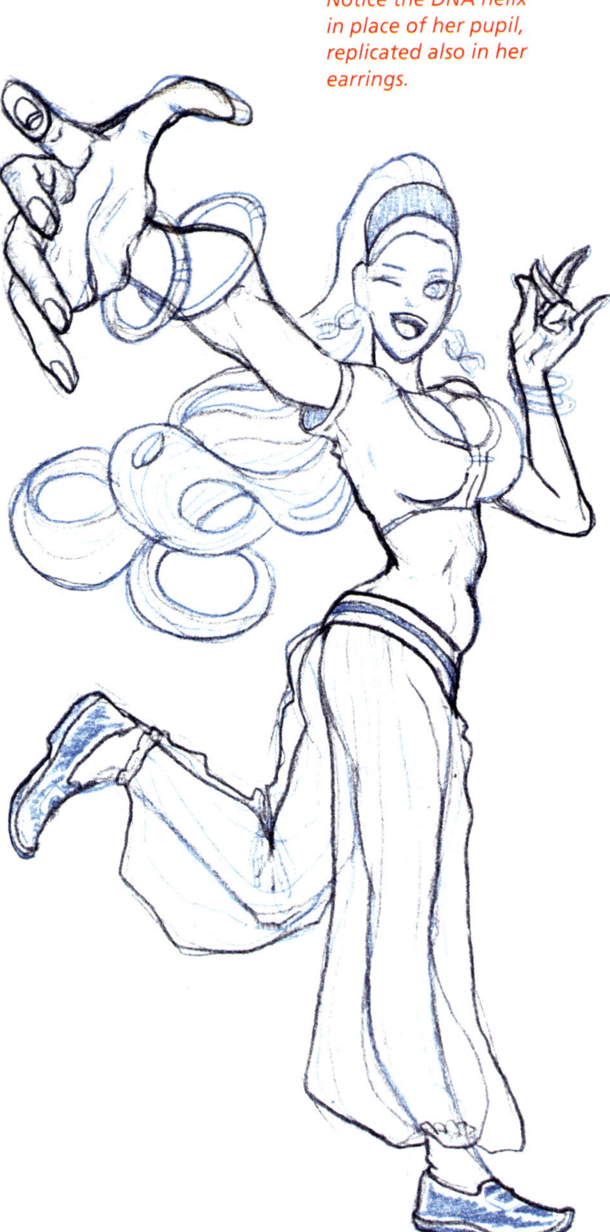

Notice the DNA helix in place of her pupil, replicated also in her earrings.

3. Work in more details. Give her a wink and show how that hair flounces about her, almost like a cape. Make those leggings even baggier, and add some edging to her belt and top. Add bangles around her arms and a band around her hair to top things off.

4. Finish off the details. Add more texture to her hair and add more details to the outstretched hand to show how nutty it really is. Black out her shoes and hair band, plus the trim on her belt. Also darken the edges under her top and the inside of her mouth.

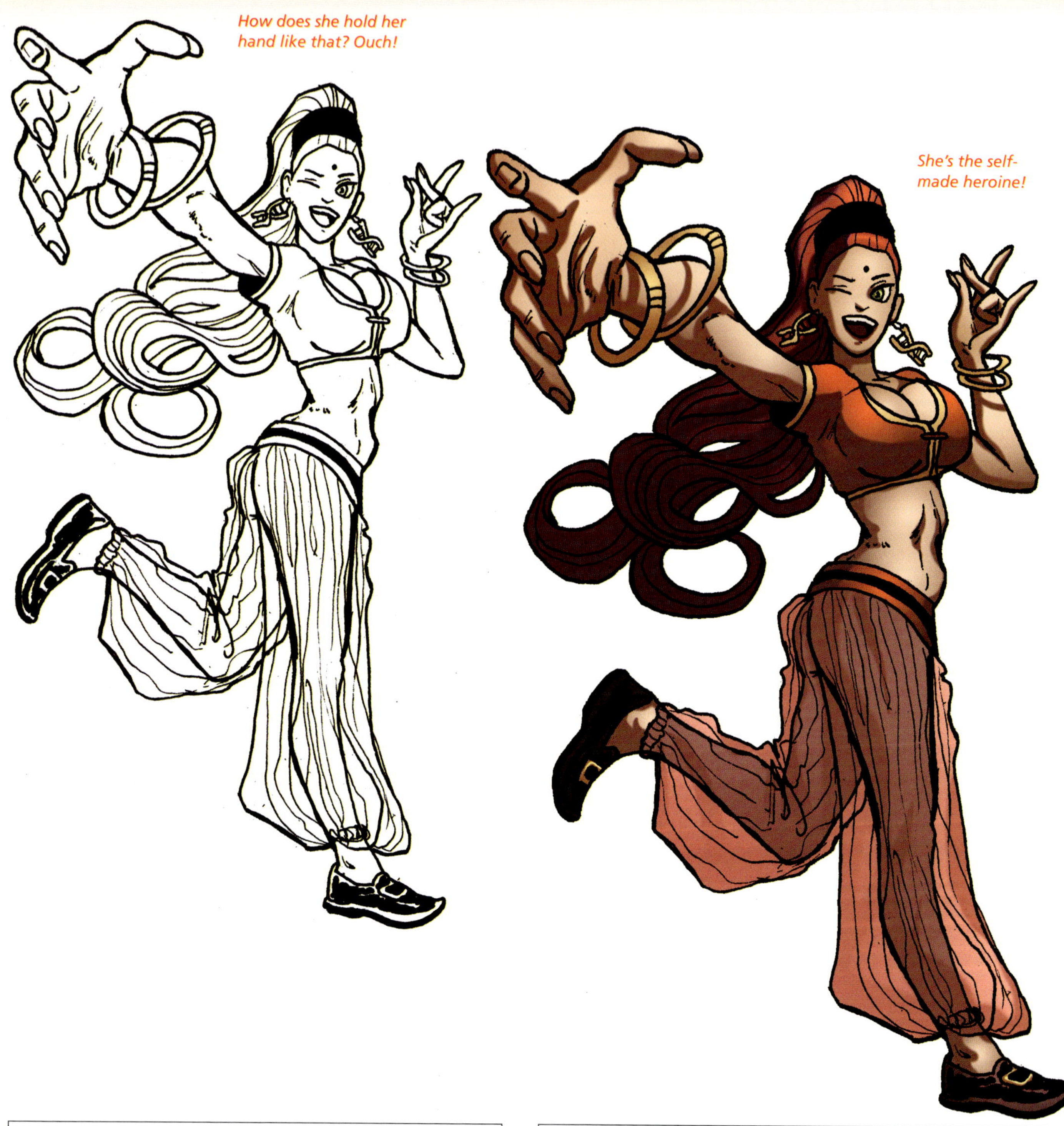

5. Use a wide variety of inks here. Save the lightest bits for the leggings. Note how the lines in the hair start out more varied at the top and become more uniform as they reach the ends.

6. Use reds throughout here, in various tones. For the leggings, overlay the standard skin tones with the pinks of the leggings to make them look transparent.

THE MYSTIC

The Mystic has studied since childhood to learn everything he could about the art of magic. He started out as a stage magician but gradually integrated himself into the subculture of true magic. Today, he stands as one of the premiere practitioners of the mystic arts, something that makes him both a hero and a target.

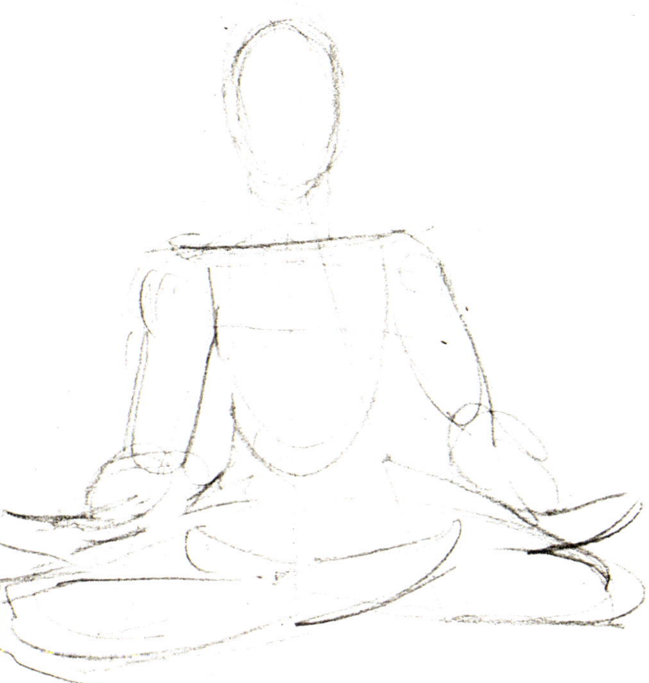

Note that Yair slips in a set of perspective lines there to help ground the image later.

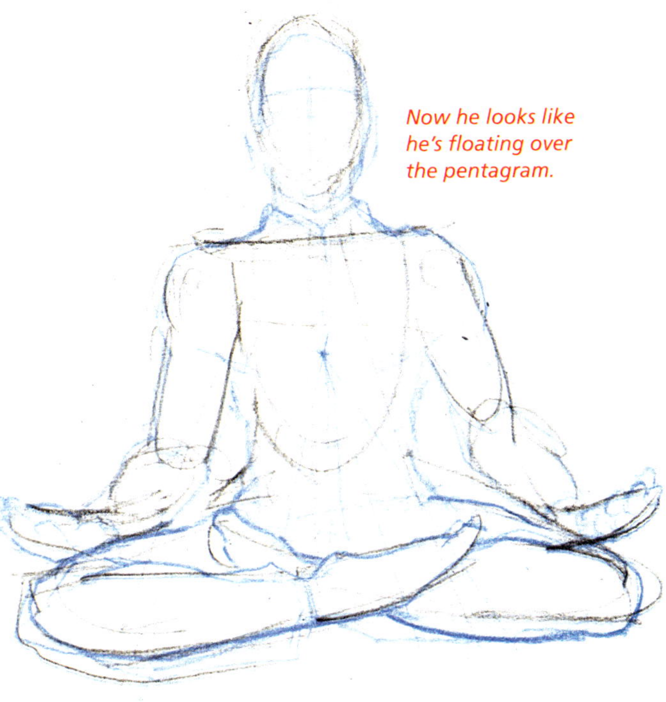

Now he looks like he's floating over the pentagram.

1. Break down the Mystic's pose. He sits in lotus position, his hands palms up, as if he's meditating. He radiates serenity and calm, confident power.

2. Add a pentagram below the Mystic, lined up on the perspective lines. By placing the perspective point in the Mystic's chest, you help draw the eye directly to him. Rough in his clothes while you're at it.

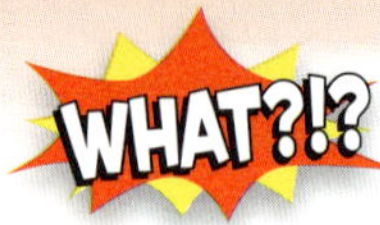

Perspective lines are guidelines that converge on a virtual vanishing point from the viewer's perspective. The default perspective point is in the center of the page, but by varying this or adding several points you can create dynamic, lifelike images.

Don't forget the candles and the flames riding from just over his palms.

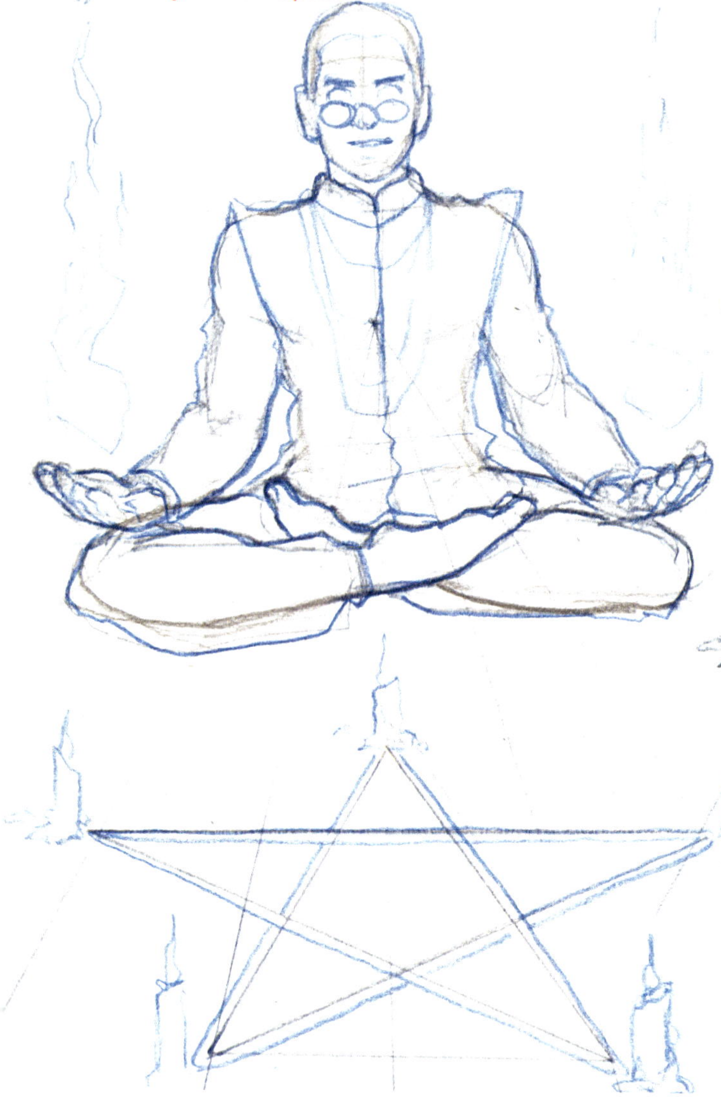

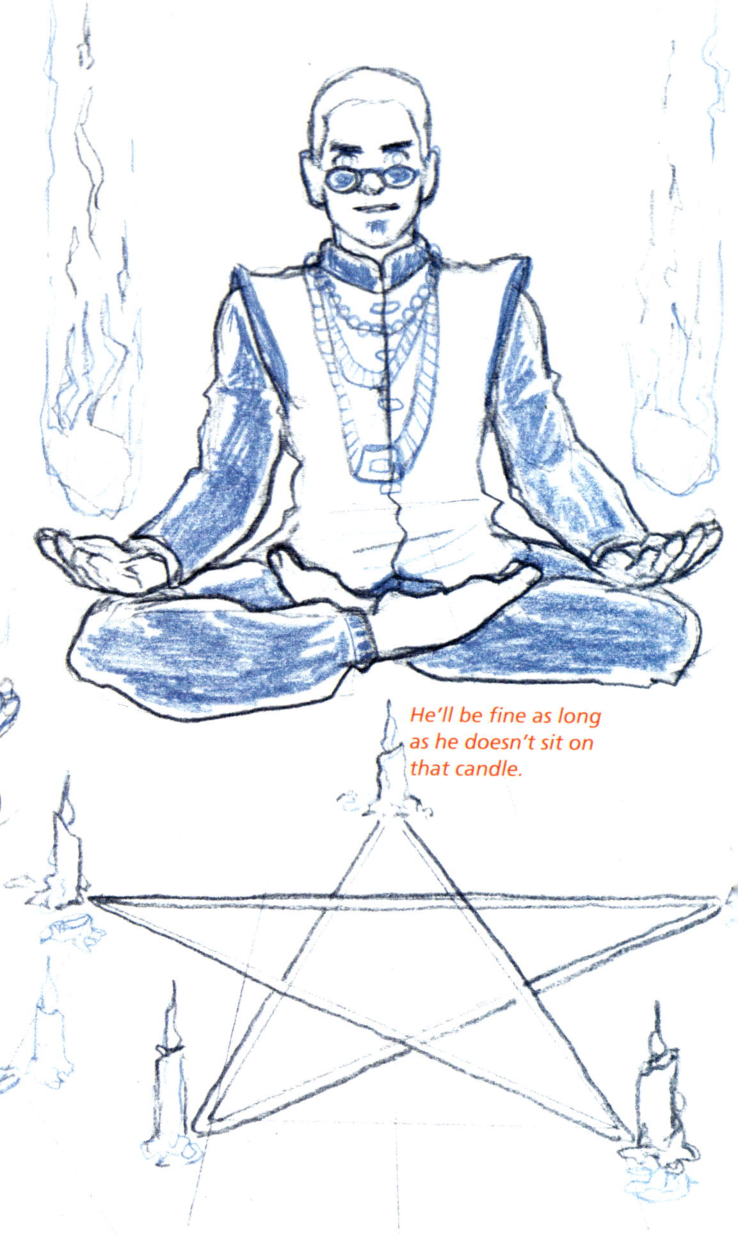

He'll be fine as long as he doesn't sit on that candle.

3. Dress the Mystic in a loose, long-sleeved bodysuit under a sleeveless Nehru jacket.

4. Black out much of his bodysuit, as well as his collar and the lenses of his glasses. Give him wide, curious, but confident eyes. Put a soul patch under his lip. Add details to the flames and scatter melted wax around the bases of the candles.

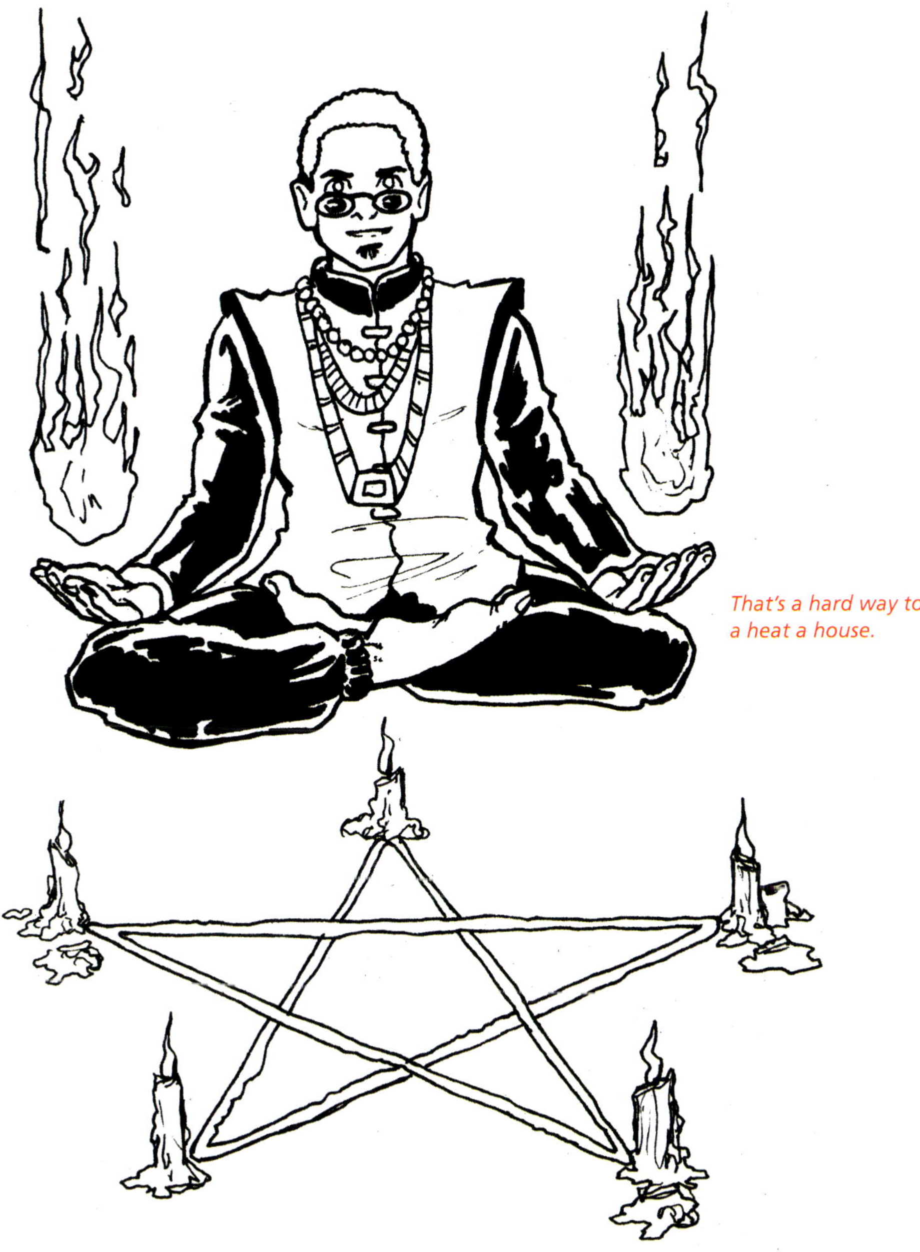

That's a hard way to a heat a house.

5. Use uniform inks throughout most of this image. It emphasizes the solidity and serenity of the scene. Use lighter lines only on the wrinkles on his jacket and on the melting candles.

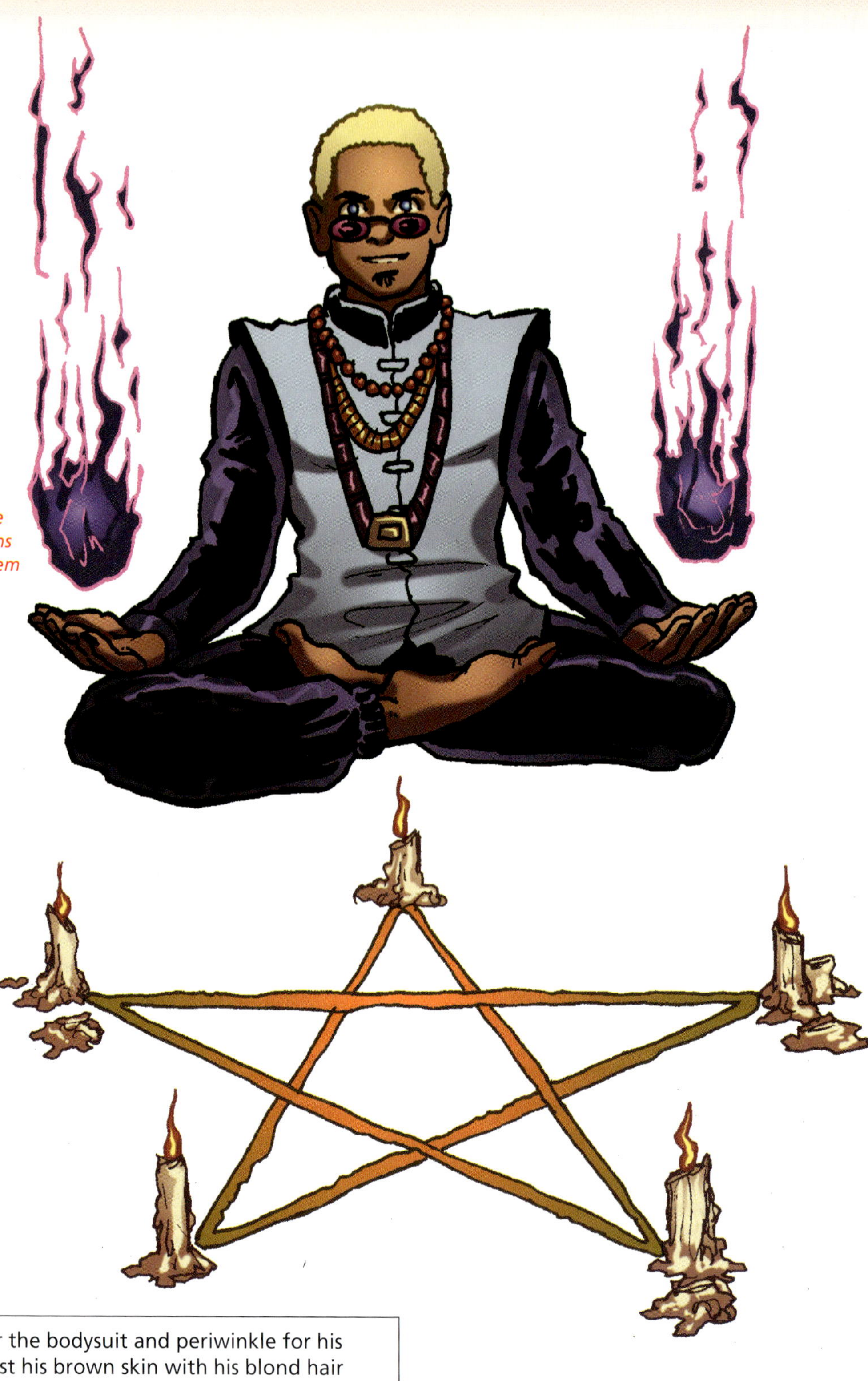

Yair turns the black lines of the flame illustrations violet to give them a glowing form.

6. Use purple for the bodysuit and periwinkle for his jacket. Contrast his brown skin with his blond hair and blue eyes. Use a blend of greens and oranges on the pentagram, and color the flames in his hands purple and violet to emphasize how unnatural they are.

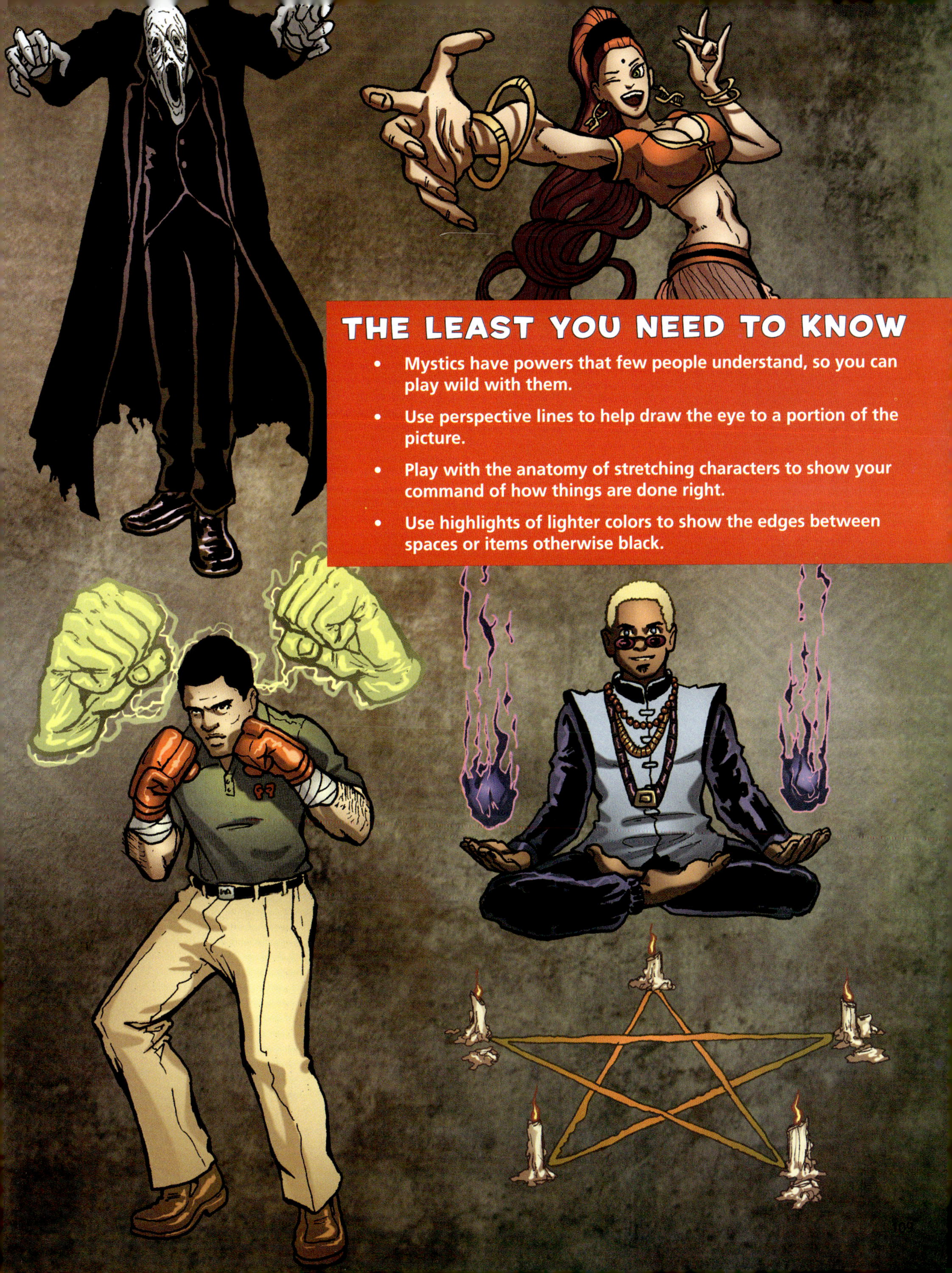

THE LEAST YOU NEED TO KNOW

- Mystics have powers that few people understand, so you can play wild with them.
- Use perspective lines to help draw the eye to a portion of the picture.
- Play with the anatomy of stretching characters to show your command of how things are done right.
- Use highlights of lighter colors to show the edges between spaces or items otherwise black.

PART 3
MISCELLANEOUS

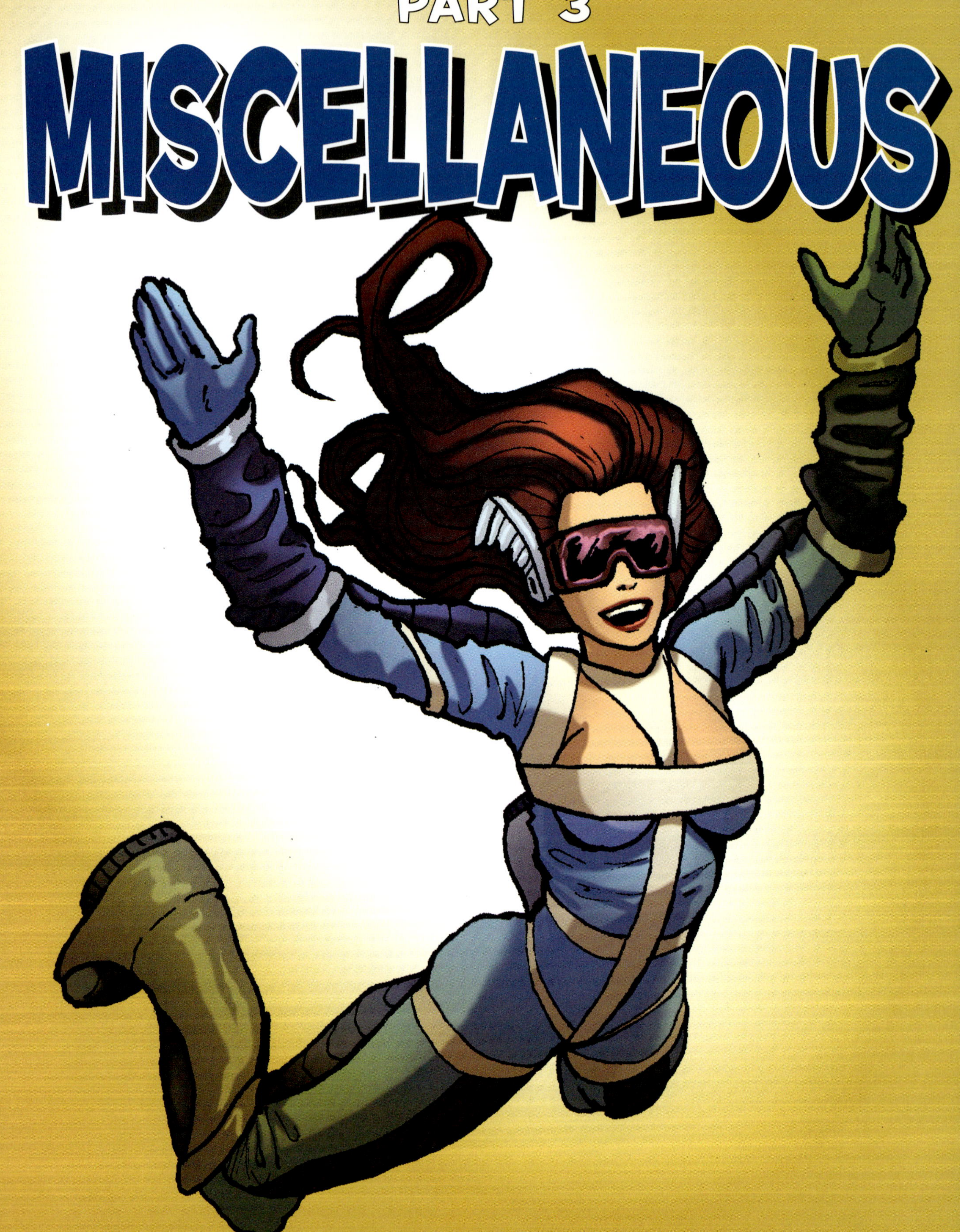

IN THIS PART

There are so many different types of superheroes and villains that it would take several books to cover them all. Rather than leave any of them out in the cold by means of classification, we've cast this part as a grab bag of superpowered characters of as many kinds as we could cram in.

Once you work your way through this, don't stop at the end of the book, of course. Come up with your own kinds of characters and stretch your skills far beyond these limits. The world is waiting to see what you and your pencil can conjure.

For now, we launch with a chapter on flyers, characters who take to the sky. We zoom over from there to fast ones, the speedsters who can pass by a jumbo jet like it was standing still. Then we change the topic to shapeshifters, people who can take the forms of animals, other people, or things even stranger. From there, we study national icons, characters who exemplify the best or worst of their chosen lands. We wrap it all up with a look at sidekicks, those heroes-in-training who stand ready to lend the heroes a hand.

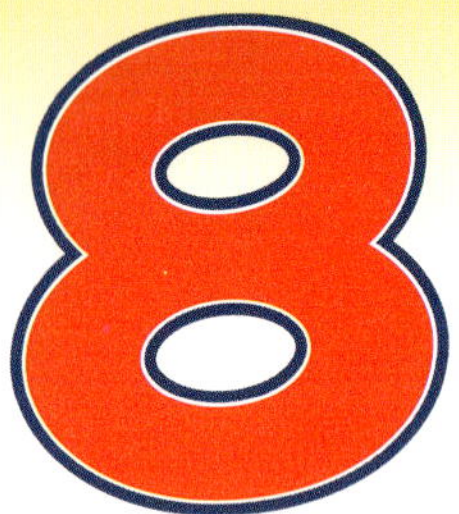

8 Flyers: High as Can Be

In This Chapter

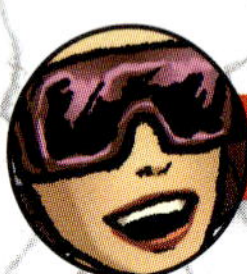

- Zooming along through the sky

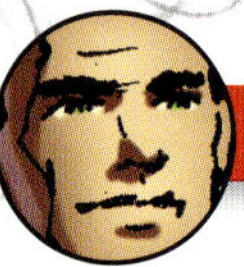

- Getting swept up in the wind

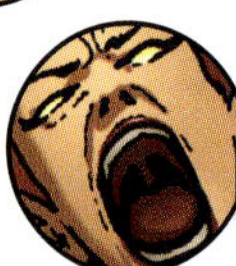

- Rocketing higher

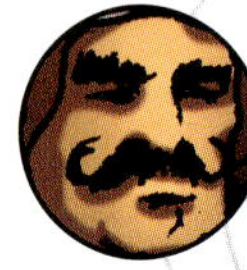

- Rider in the sky

One of the most common dreams is to be able to fly—without the use of a plane or helicopter, of course. It's a common superhero power, laced with sensations of freedom as it is. This chapter features four different ways for a character to get zipping along through the clouds.

We start with Zoom, the mistress of the power dive. She gets into the air fast enough, but it's when she joins her power to that of gravity that she really gets going. As a professional parachutist, she couldn't be happier.

Then we move on to Windswept, a man who rides hurricane-strength winds around the world. As a weather researcher, he was dragged into the sky by a weather balloon and nearly died. Instead, he discovered an uncanny control over the weather that he now masters with his will.

Rocket was the worst kind of daredevil: untrained, unprepared, and unsafe. After she lost her legs in a horrible stunt gone wrong, she had her lower body fitted with a jet on which she zooms from one bit of trouble to another. At that speed, who can stop her?

The Sky Pilot once flew jets for the Navy. When he got out, he built himself something more daring than any fighter plane: a rocket bike. Now this wild man patrols the skies, ever vigilant against danger.

ZOOM

Zoom is a professional skydiver who made the wrong kind of enemies, the kind who wouldn't mind slashing a chute to ribbons. The incident nearly killed her, but faced with her imminent death she pulled out a power she never knew she had and flew to safety. Now she always dives without a chute.

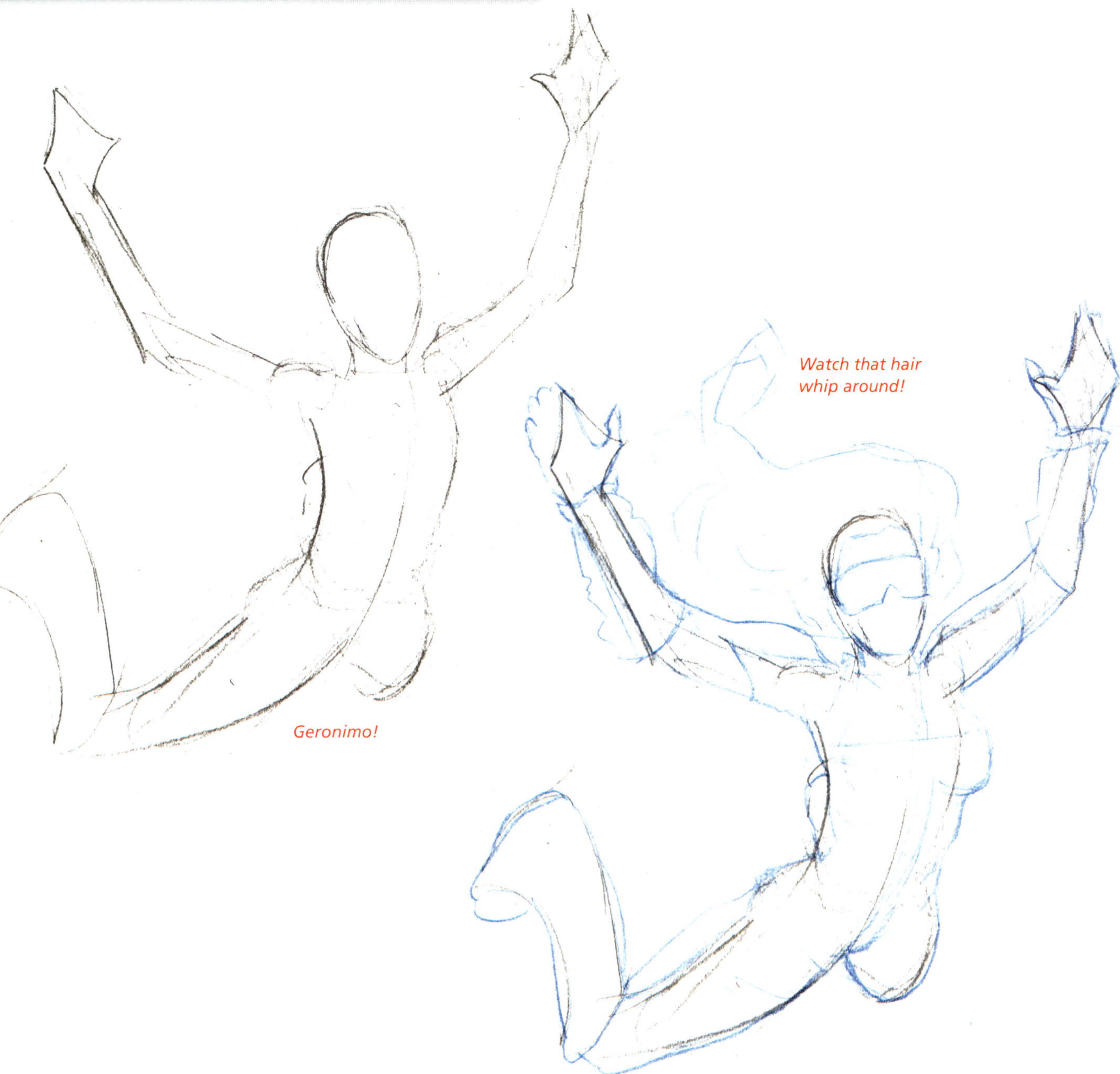

1. Break down Zoom's parachuting stance. This involves all of her limbs being bent backward in the wind as she dives through the air. This is one of the stranger body positions you may tackle. Just concentrate on getting your anatomy right and don't be afraid to mask her left leg.

2. Dress Zoom in a skydiver's outfit. Give her some gloves and a set of goggles, too.

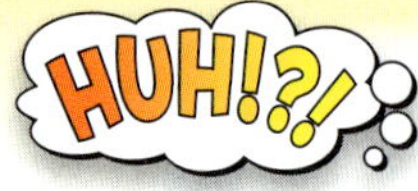

As shown, Zoom's in a standard skydiving position, which is designed to give the skydiver as much time in the air as possible. Were she to pull her legs together and bring her arms close to her sides, she could point her head down and enter an accelerated dive.

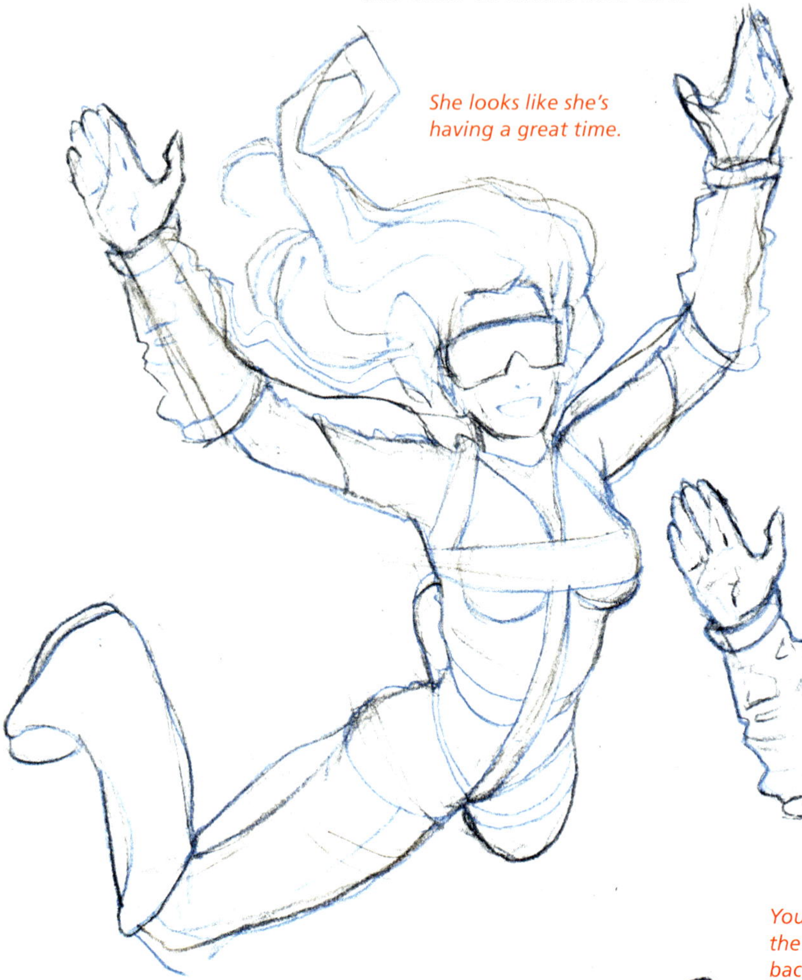

She looks like she's having a great time.

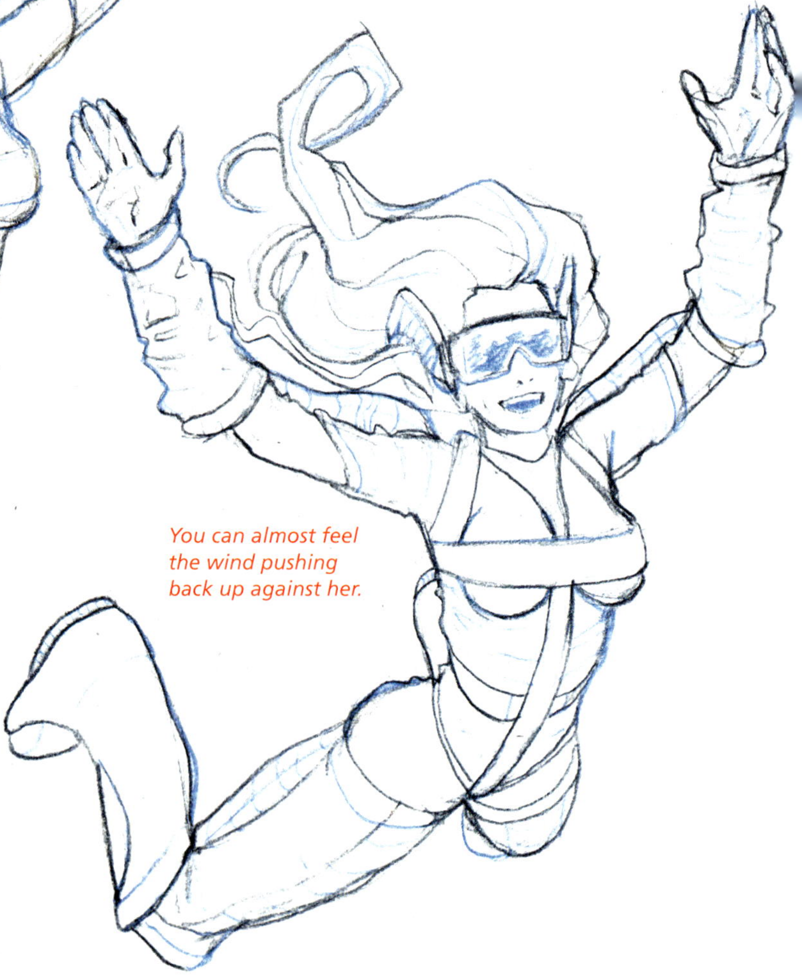

You can almost feel the wind pushing back up against her.

3. Add more details to the hair, face, and clothes. She wears thick boots designed to help her control her movements in the air. She also has a set of head wings that help her in the same way.

4. Add wrinkles and other details to her clothes. Black in her goggles and her mouth. Give her hair more texture, too.

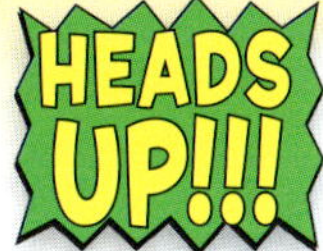

While it's easy to put every hero in skintight spandex, it's more fun to work with loose clothing, especially when dealing with flyers. Be sure to pick a direction for the wind and follow it for every element in the picture, though. Notice how Zoom's hair and the fabric of her costume all flap up behind her.

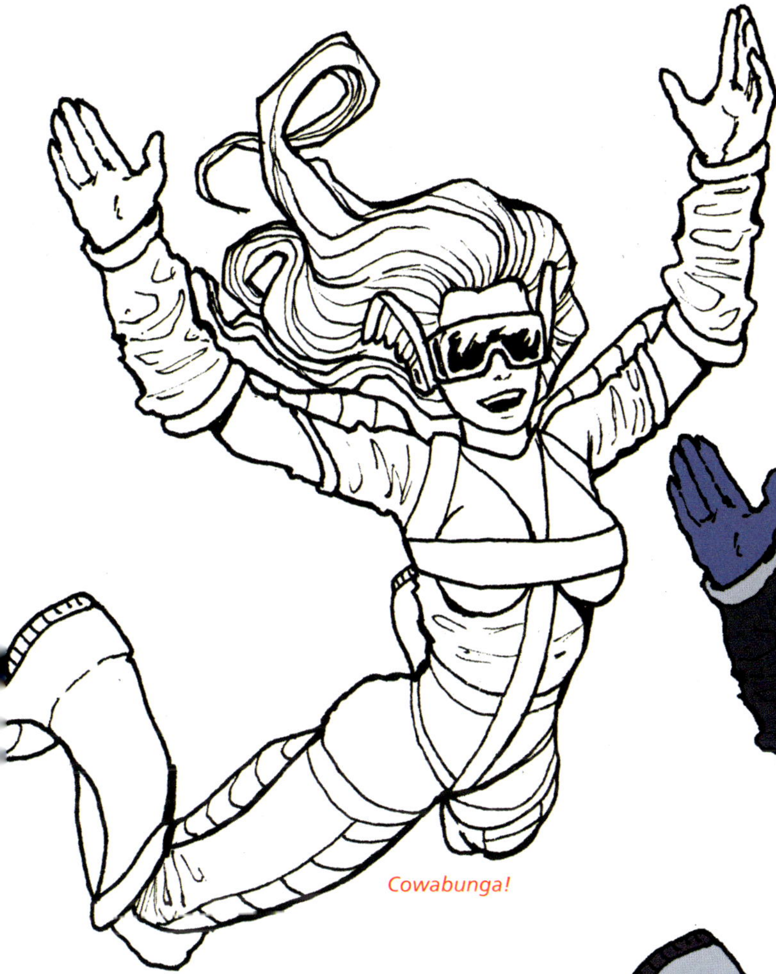

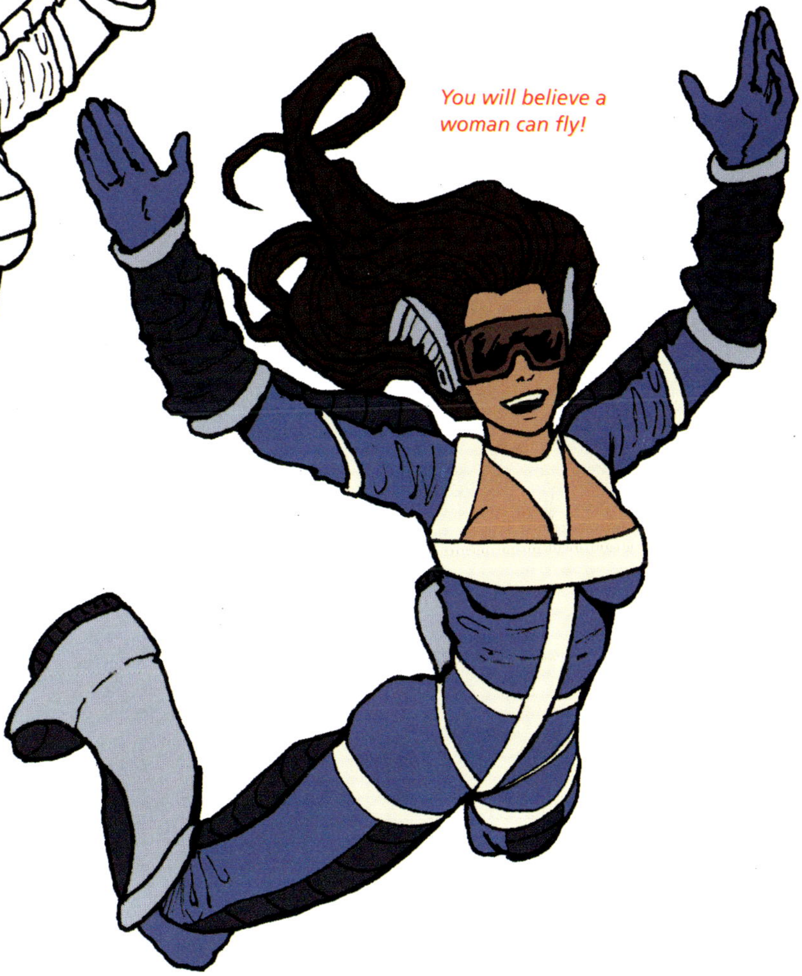

You will believe a woman can fly!

Cowabunga!

5. Use varied lines here. The wrinkles on the clothing and the texture in the hair should be lighter. Use thicker lines elsewhere.

6. Make her a brunette and use blue for her suit, with grays and cream for trim.

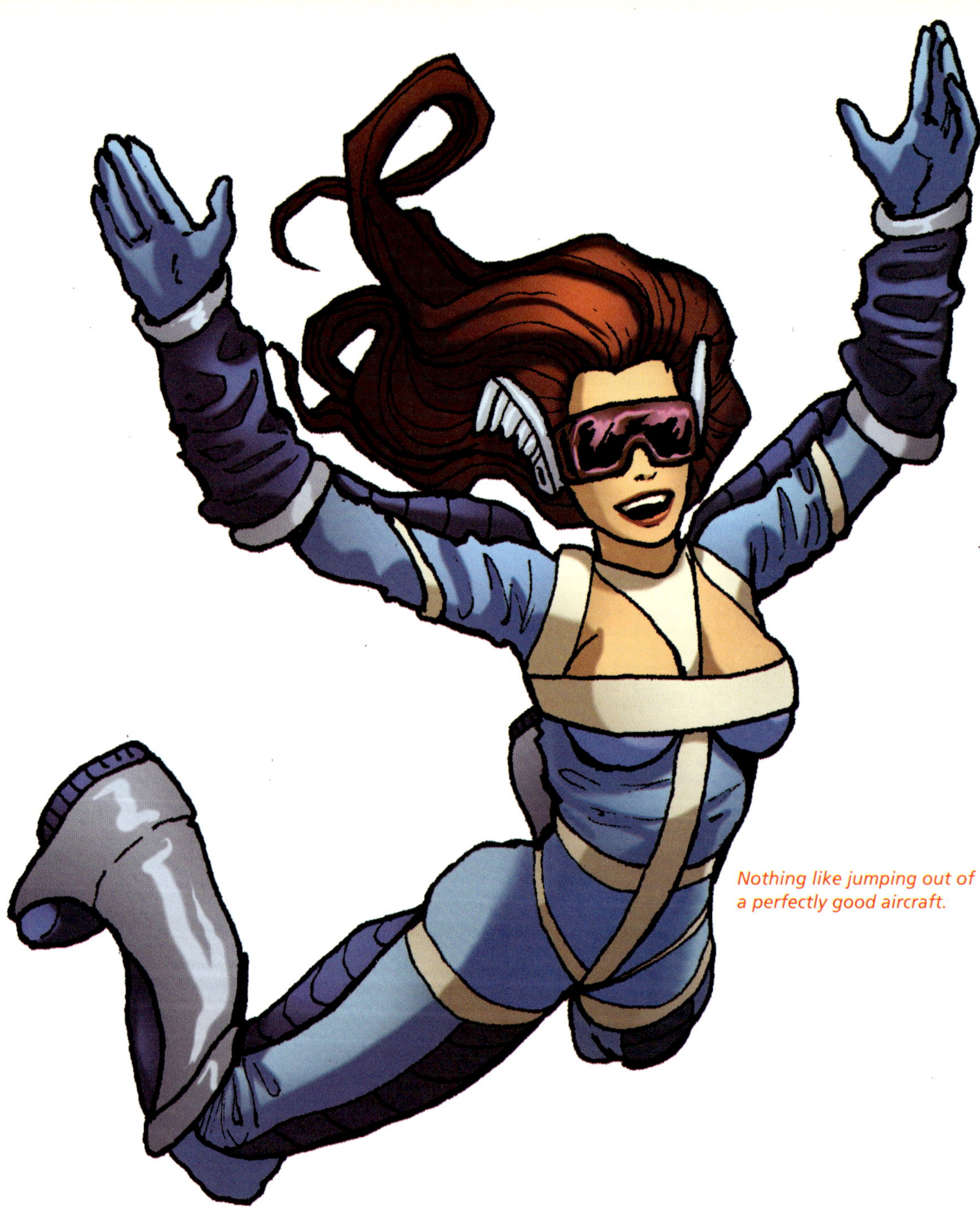

Nothing like jumping out of a perfectly good aircraft.

7. Add highlights. Take care to pick your light source and follow its placement for all shadows. In an unusual figure like this, it's easy to get lost.

WINDSWEPT

As a meteorologist, Windswept spent much of his time studying the weather. One day, he got tangled in a set of weather balloons, which hauled him high into the sky. Before he froze to death, he discovered something that had been causing his experiment to go awry for years. He could control the weather and had been doing so without even knowing it.

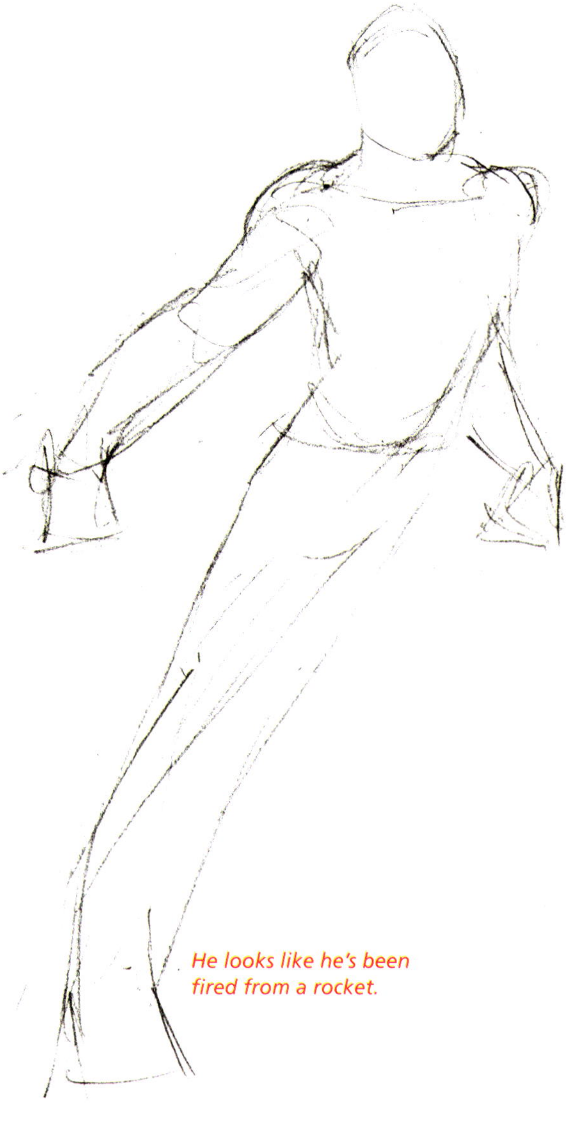

He looks like he's been fired from a rocket.

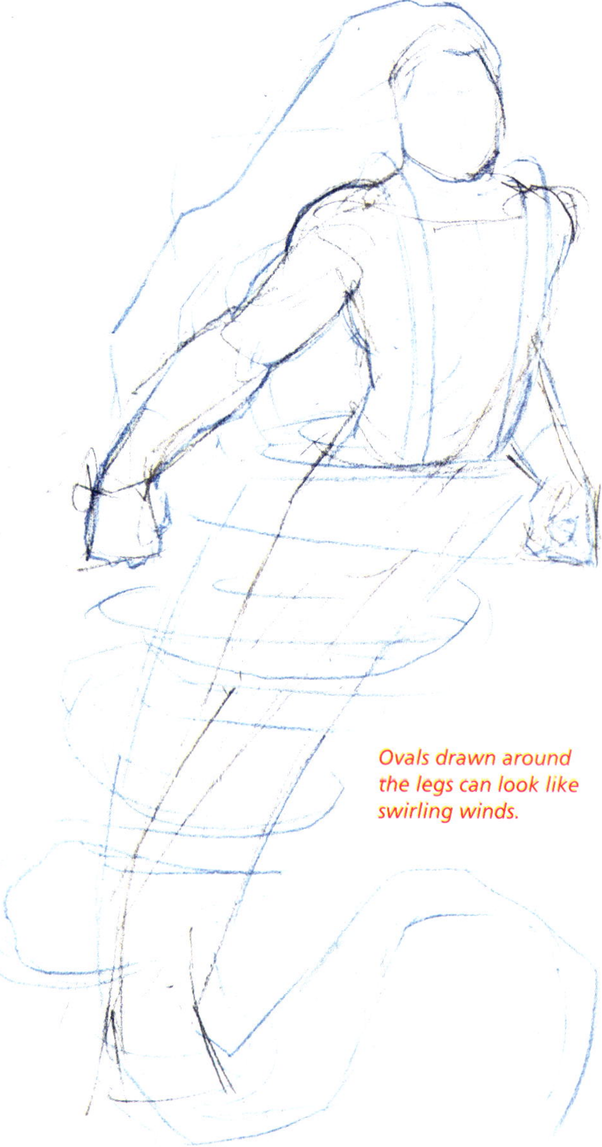

1. Break down Windswept's stance. Yair gives him a heroic pose that shows him rising into the air, his arms thrust back behind him and his chest pushed forward. The legs are less important, since we'll be covering them up soon.

2. Add hair to Windswept, and install a pair of perpendicular suspenders. (Really, they're fins used to guide Windswept through the air.) Surround his legs with a funnel cloud and give it an extended tail that whirls away from him.

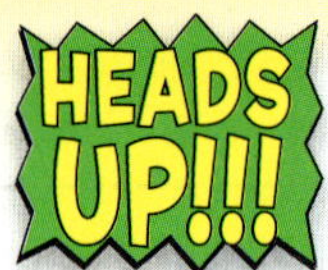

It's alright to exaggerate a character's physical features, especially when he's using his powers. Note, for instance, Windswept's impossibly long hair. On one level it's ridiculous, but on another it looks cool and fits with the character. When in doubt, go with what looks cool.

One of the tendrils of wind swirling about him is actually the end of his hair.

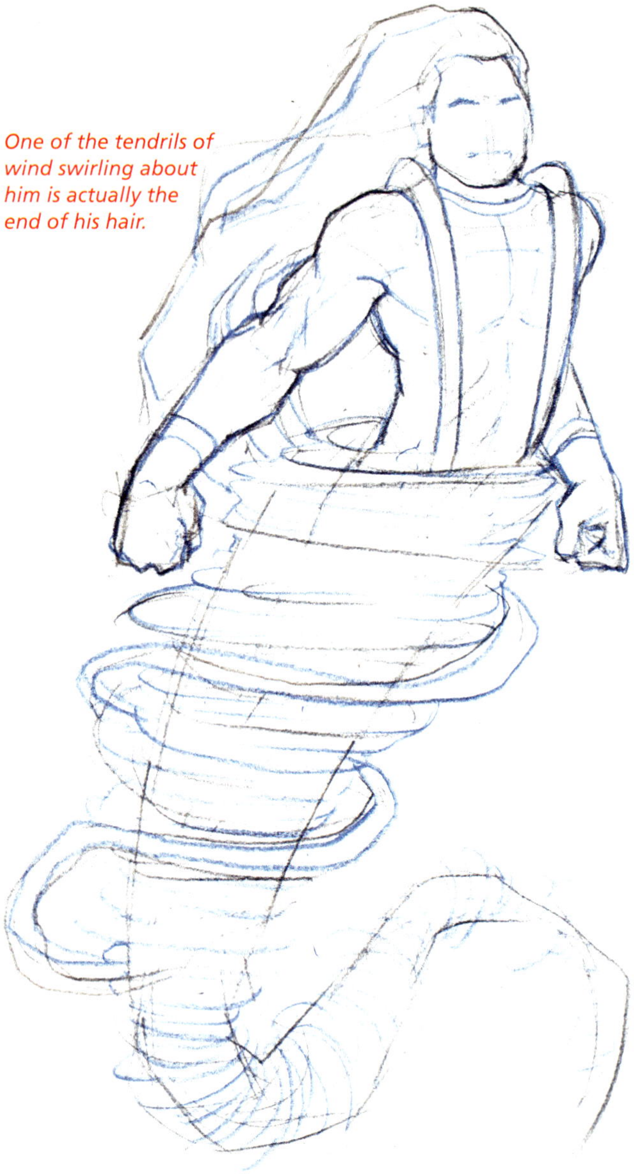

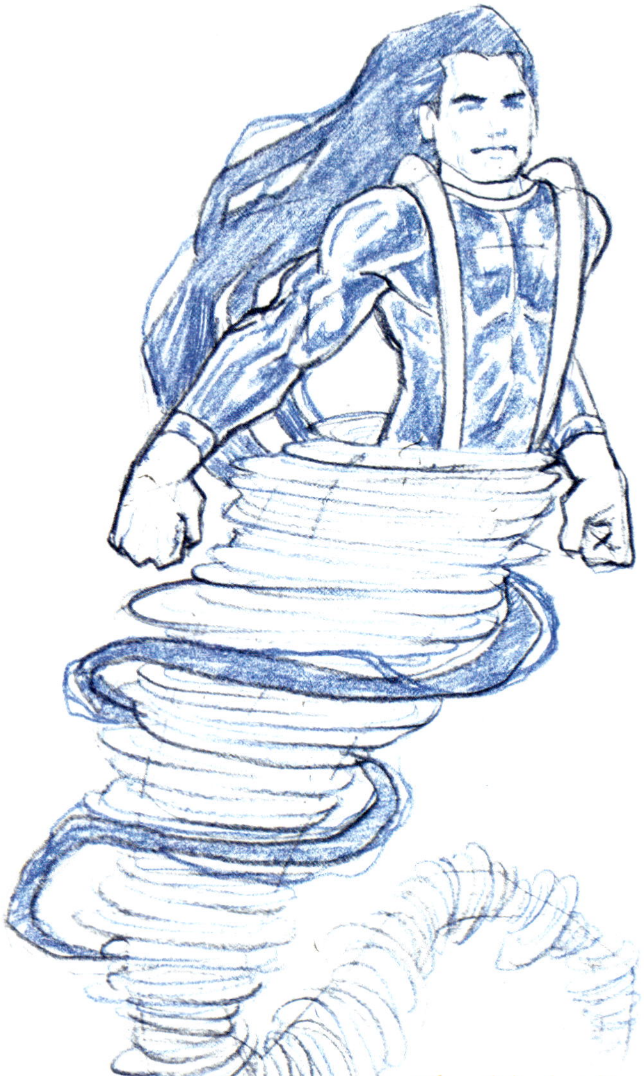

A funnel cloud might not look exactly like this, but the form shows your viewer what you mean.

3. Give Windswept some eyebrows and add some texture to the hair. Define his musculature, and work up the thickness of the funnel cloud on which he flies.

4. Black out the hair and bodysuit, as well as the length of hair running through the funnel cloud. Define his eyes, nose, and mouth. Define the funnel cloud even more.

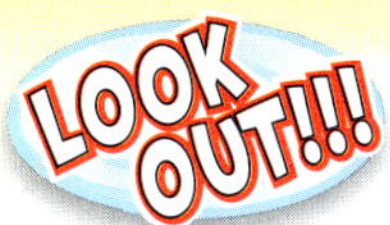

Don't worry too much about realism in superhero comics. A real funnel cloud around a man's waist would look nothing like this, assuming you could put one there and get it to stay there in the first place. The funnel cloud there looks cool and effectively tells the viewer all about how Windswept's powers work, which is just what's supposed to happen.

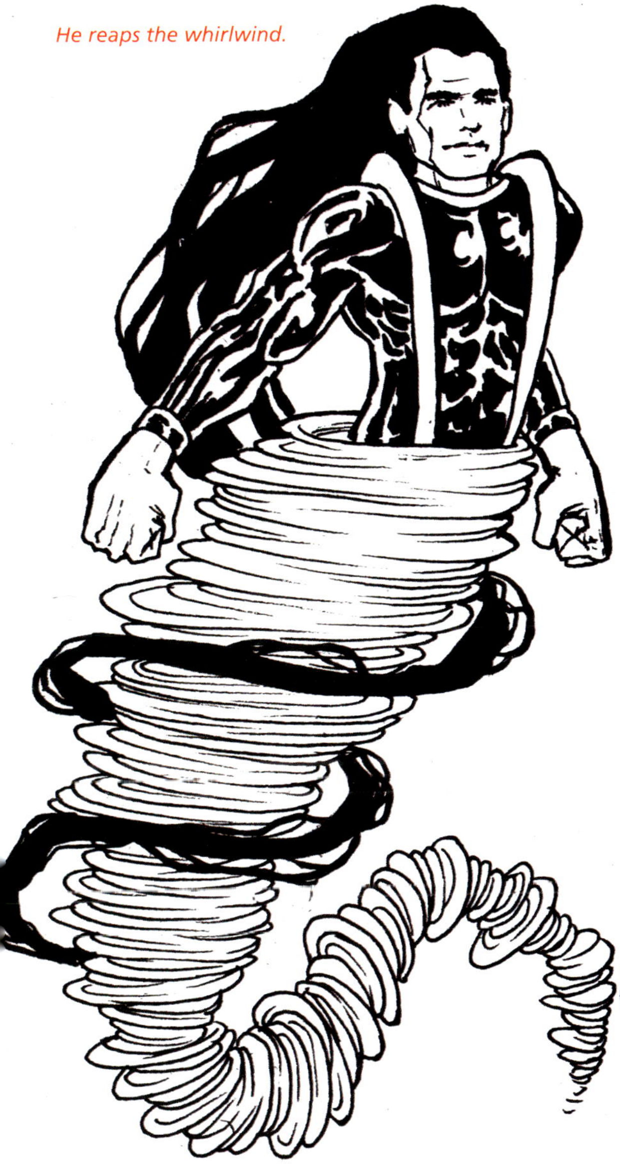

He reaps the whirlwind.

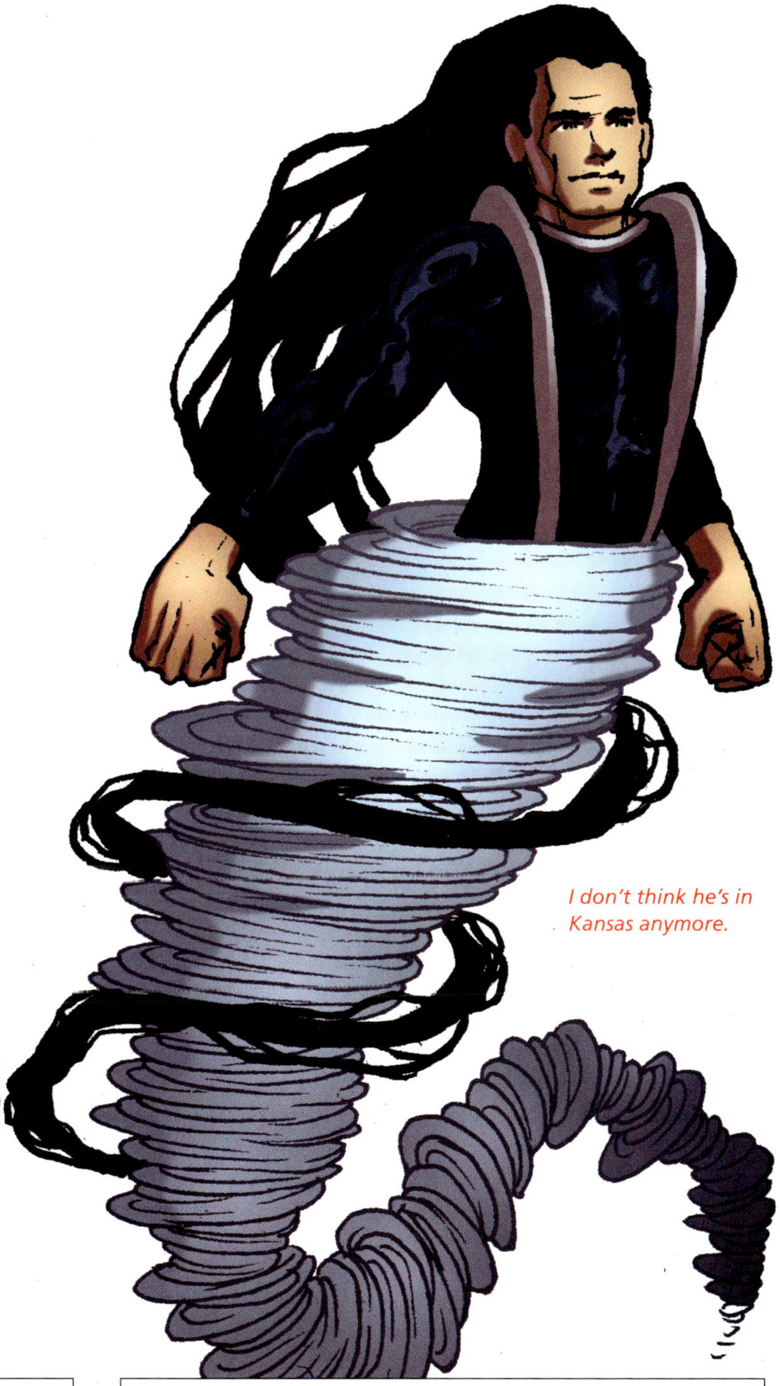

I don't think he's in Kansas anymore.

5. Use solid blacks on the hair, but outline the costume and his muscles in white to offer them definition. Running the black hair through the funnel clouds gives the illustration a three-dimensional feel. Use thinner lines for the whirlwind, but not too thin.

6. Choose midnight blue for the costume, plus violet for the guidance fins. A bluish gray works well for the funnel cloud, especially if it's paler in the middle and darker to the sides.

ROCKET

Rocket was once of the greatest daredevils the world had ever seen, but her determination to push herself harder to win caused her to slip. She paid the price with her legs. Now a rocket-powered villain, she prefers the hit-and-blast strategy, in which she hits a bank and then blasts away.

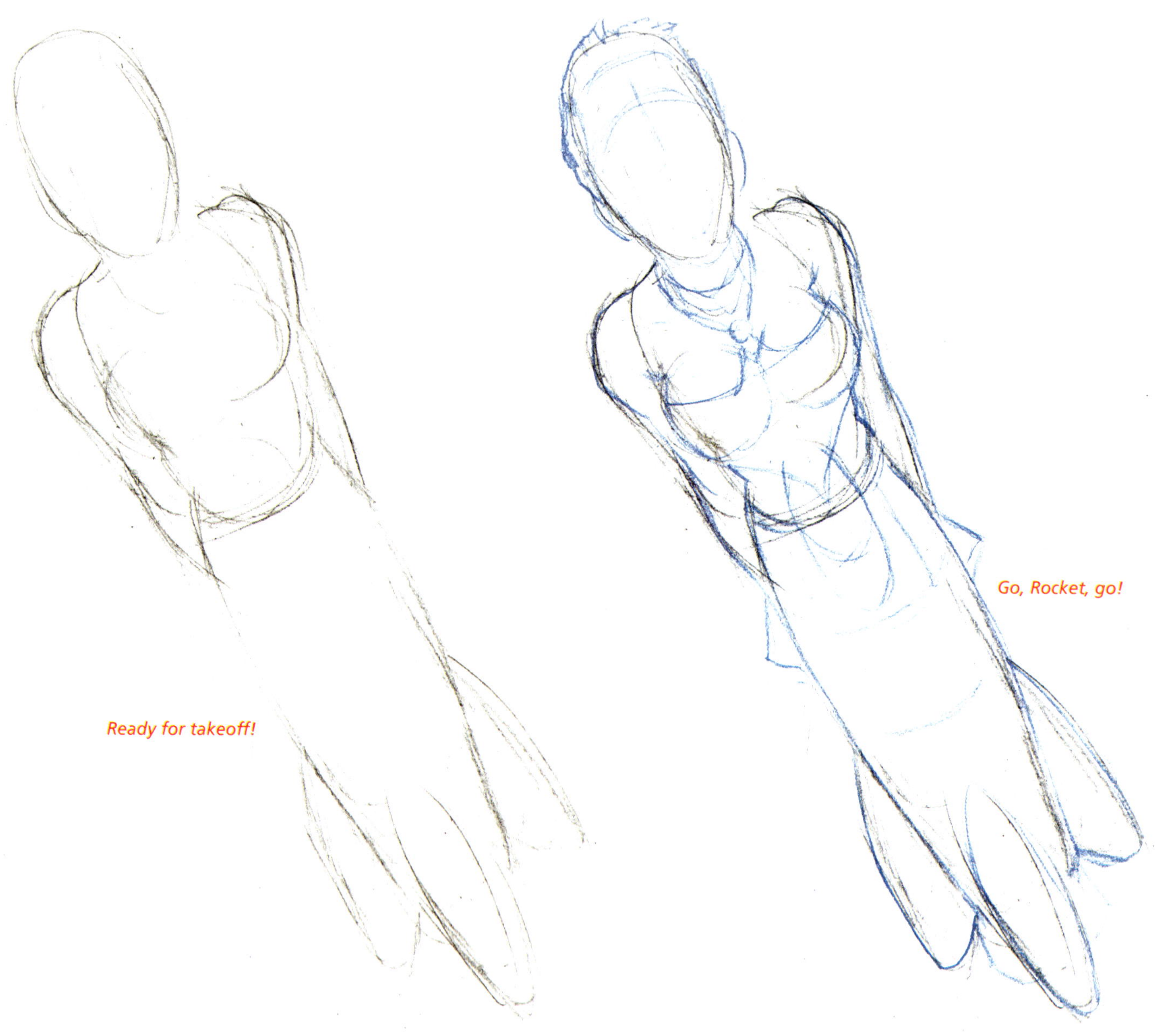

Ready for takeoff!

Go, Rocket, go!

1. Rocket is a human rocket, so break down her stance that way. Draw her zooming into the air, but put rocket fins in place of feet. Remember to account for perspective, so make her head larger and her feet smaller.

2. Add her short hair and dress her in simple clothes: a halter top stretched between a necklace and the top of her rocket-legs. Ovals around the base of the rocket show that it's round throughout its entire length. Use guidelines to show where her eyes will be.

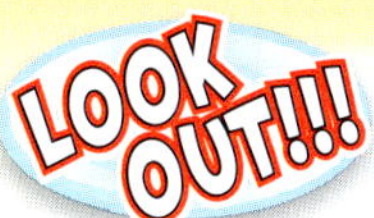

Working with a simpler stance like this can be tricky when it comes to perspective. The simplicity of the silhouette exposes any mistakes you might make, so take the time to get the breakdown right the first time through.

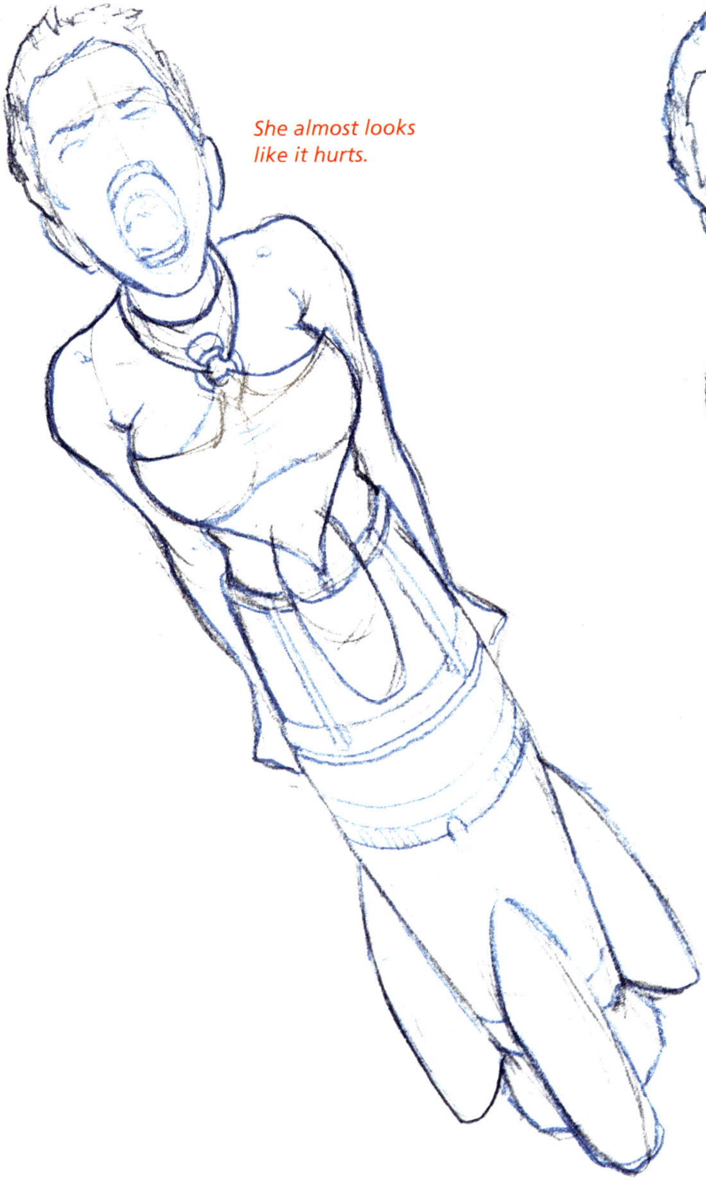

She almost looks like it hurts.

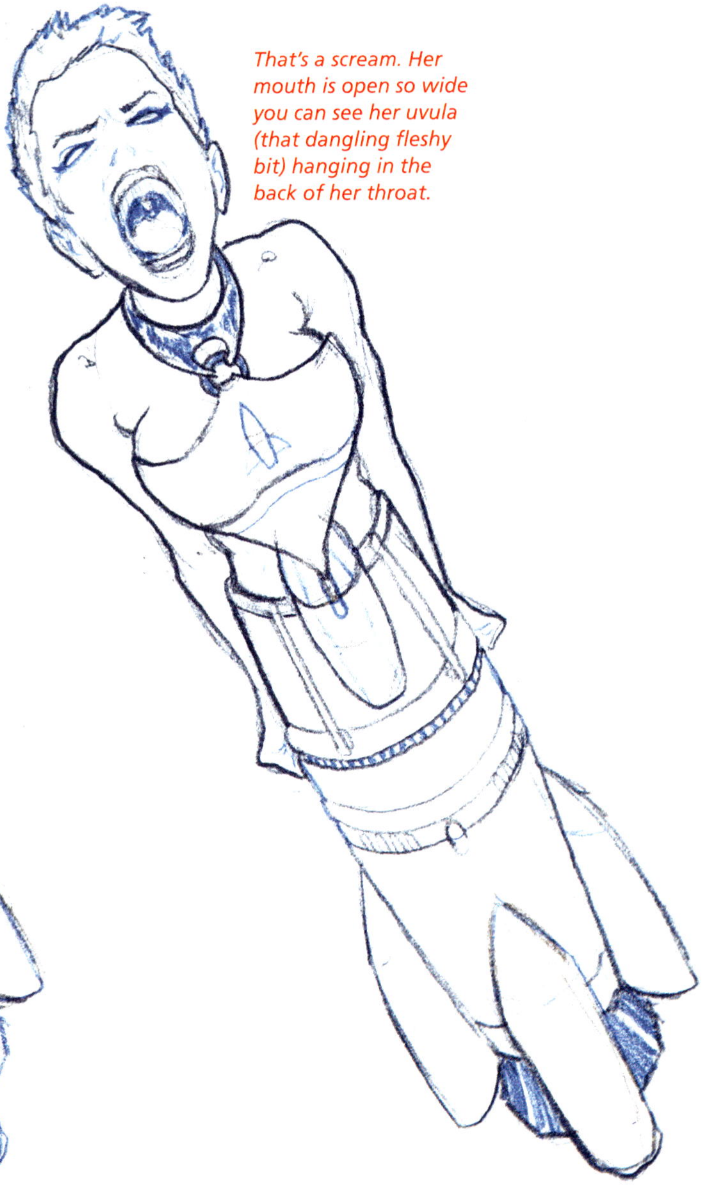

That's a scream. Her mouth is open so wide you can see her uvula (that dangling fleshy bit) hanging in the back of her throat.

3. Work on her face. Give her a screaming-wide mouth and squinty eyes. Put more details on the rocket, including some vertical details. These should bend slightly to show the curve of the rocket's central barrel.

4. Finish her face and teeth. Place the rocket icon on her shirt. Black out the exhaust on the bottom. Define her eyes and lips, and sketch in her nostrils.

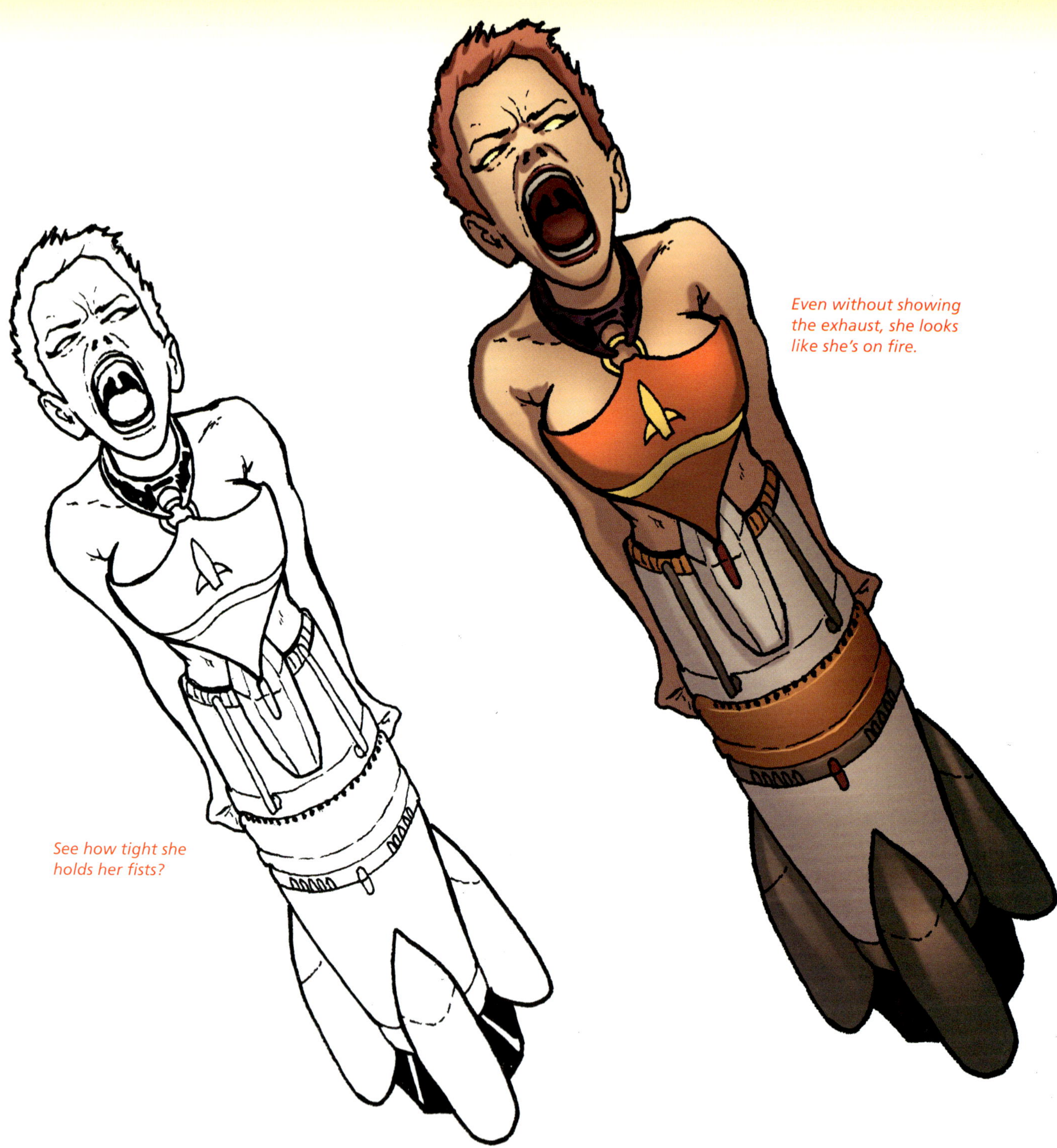

5. Use clean, uniform lines here, especially on her metallic bits. Use lighter, broken lines on her face and exposed skin, emphasizing the humanity in what's left of her.

6. Use fiery tones throughout here, from her bright yellow eyes to her glowing skin to her red hair and top. Even the grays of the rocket should have an orange tint to them, plus orange and red accents.

THE SKY PILOT

In an earlier age, the Sky Pilot would have flown a Sopwith Camel against the Red Baron. Now he barrel rolls a jet-bike of his own design straight through the clouds. Part gadgeteer, part madman, and all hero, the Sky Pilot dispenses justice from above, raining down righteousness from the heavens.

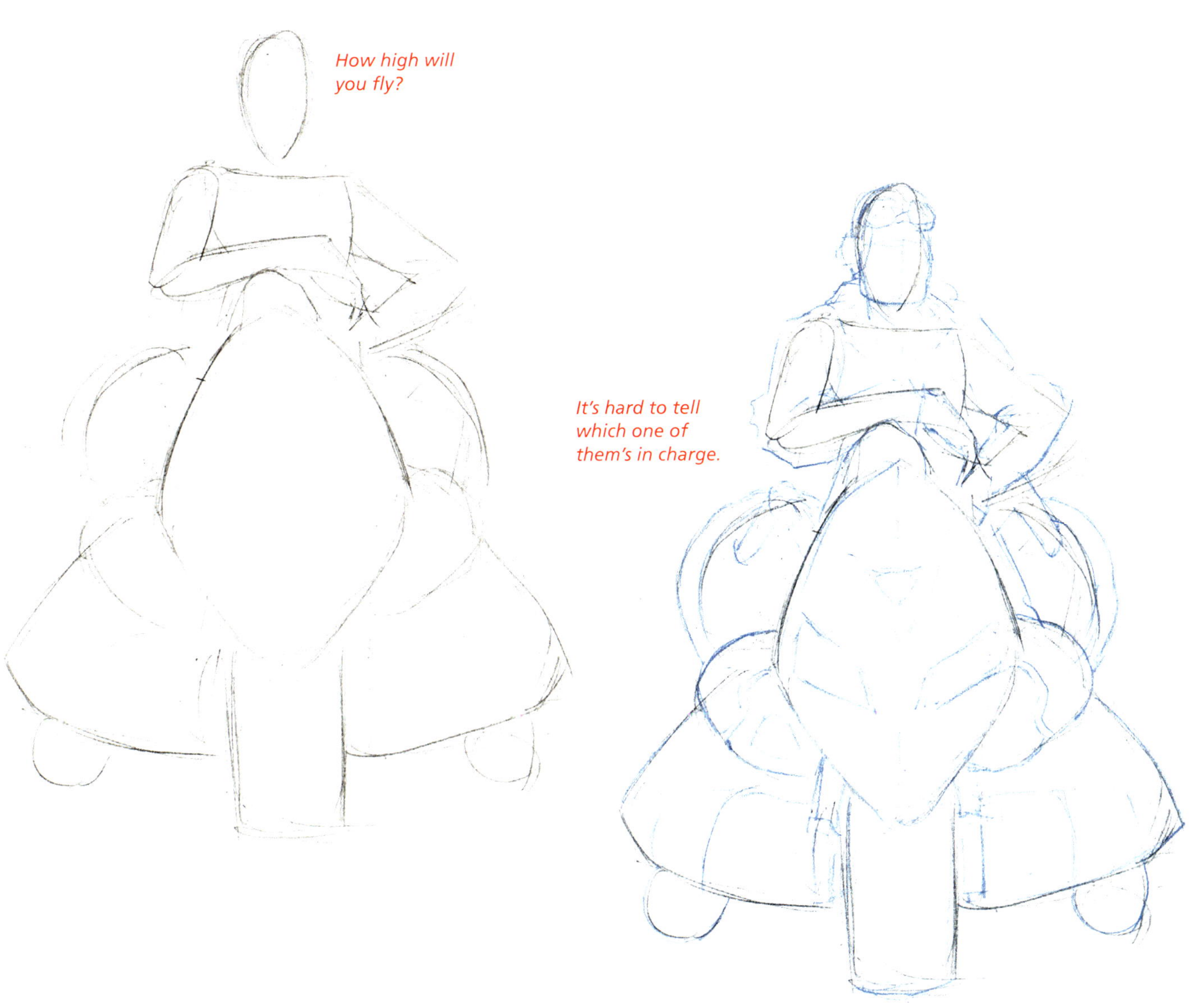

1. Break down the Sky Pilot's pose. He sits jauntily atop his jet-bike, which stares straight out at you as if you're dinner. Notice the rough pyramidal shape of the entire image, which lends it a feeling of stability and strength.

2. Add details to the jet-bike. It's actually the star of this image, so concentrate on it and make it come alive. Put a bomber jacket and goggles on Sky Pilot.

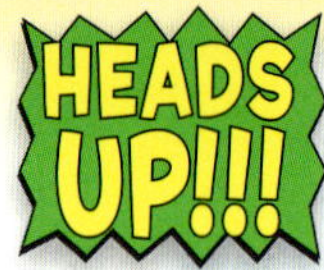

When composing an image's breakdown, you use simple shapes to build your complex picture. However, you can also put those shapes within a simple silhouette to give the image even more power. Circular, triangular, and square silhouettes all give an image a different feel. Experiment with different shapes and subjects to find the exact combination that works best in each situation.

His squinty eyes make him look like he spends a lot of time scanning the skies.

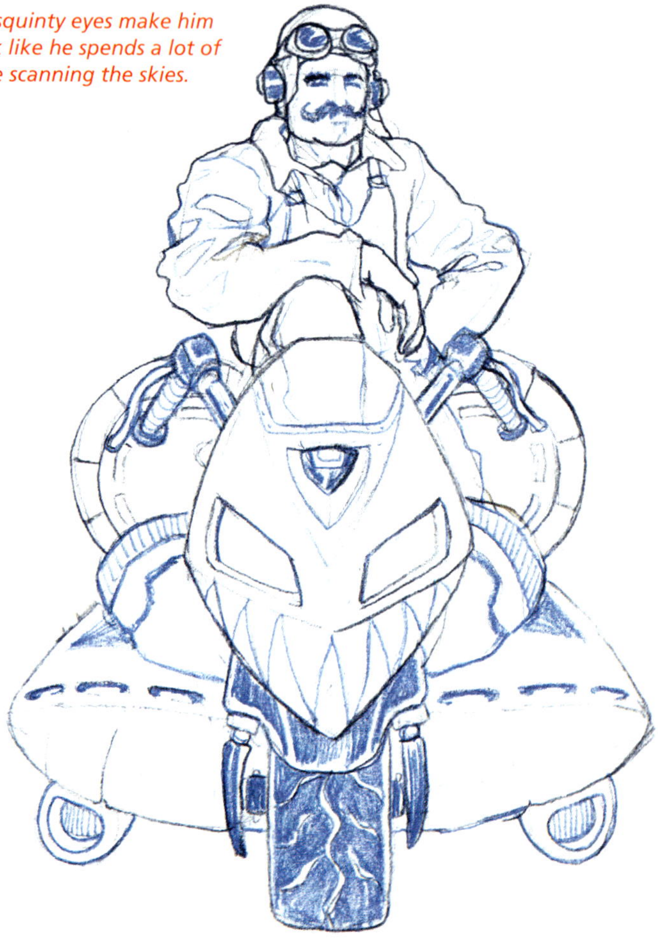

Notice the retro handlebar mustache on Sky Pilot's face.

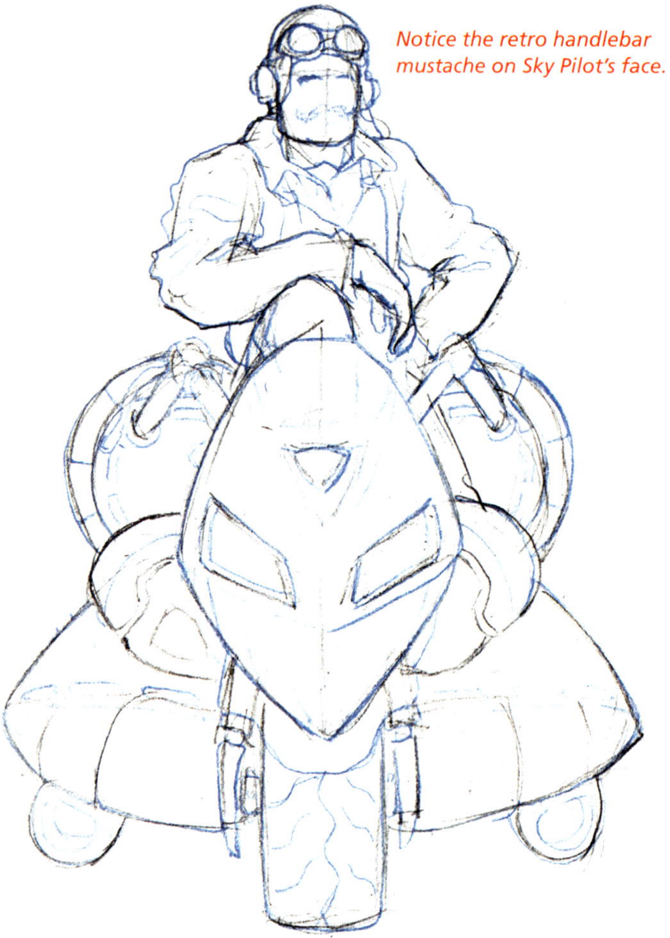

3. Add a leather helmet to Sky Pilot, plus a collar to the jacket. Refine the jet-bike's handlebars and twin jets, plus add some treads to the front tire. Define the angles a bit better all around the jet-bike, too.

4. Black out the tire but leave white for the treads. Add final details to the bike's surface, and lay down wrinkles on the Sky Pilot's jacket. Note how Yair uses lighter lines to show the Sky Pilot's leg through the jet-bike's windshield.

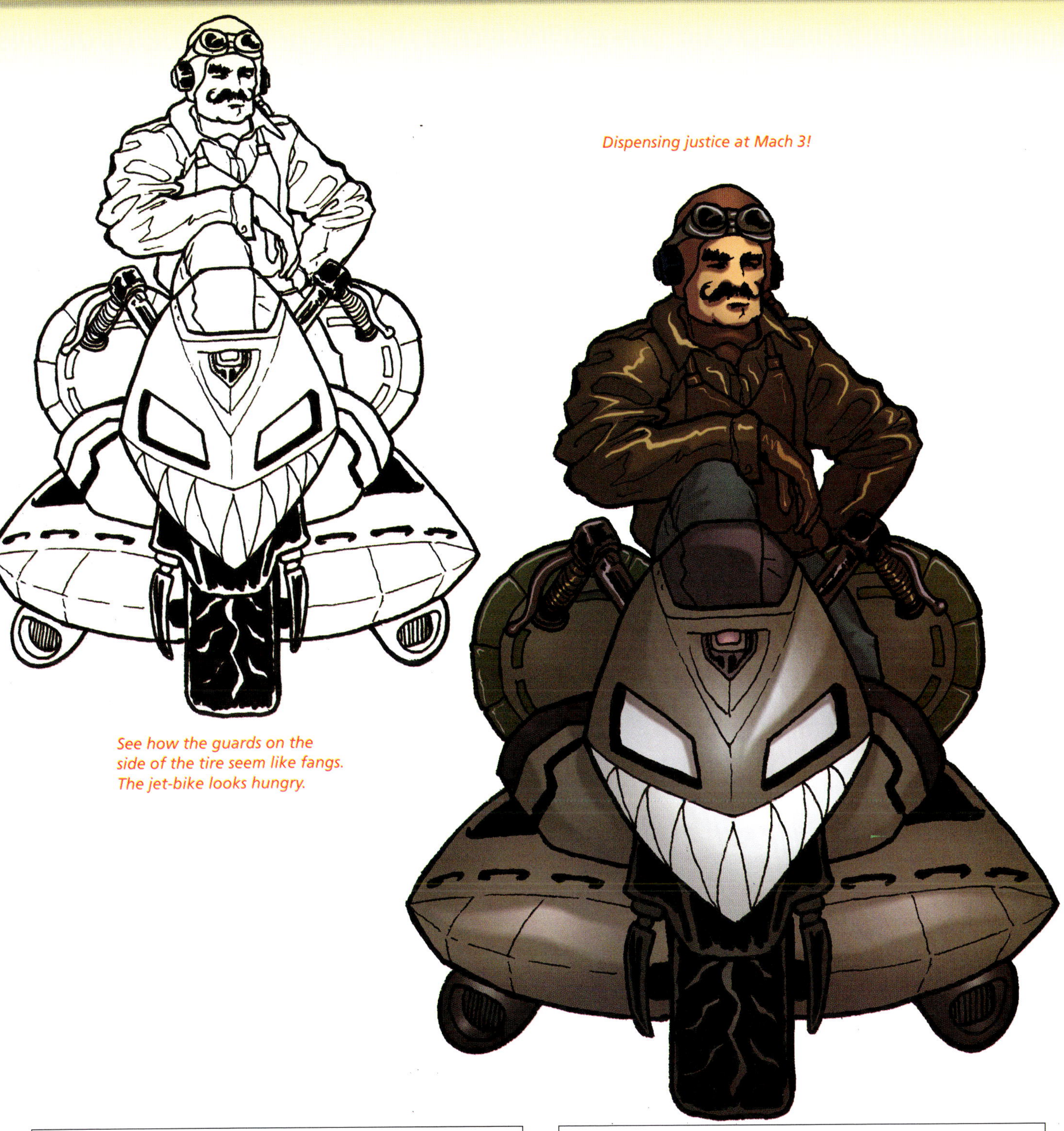

Dispensing justice at Mach 3!

See how the guards on the side of the tire seem like fangs. The jet-bike looks hungry.

5. Lay down a wide variety of inks here, to emphasize the different materials in use throughout the image. The jet-bike is sleek and clean, while the Sky Pilot is rumpled and unshaven, with bushy eyebrows.

6. Go with warm grays throughout the jet-bike, even just using paler hues on the toothy grille and the headlight-eyes. Use earth tones for Sky Pilot, mostly different shades of brown. This shows that he's of the earth, although he's conquered and rides a steely piece of the sky.

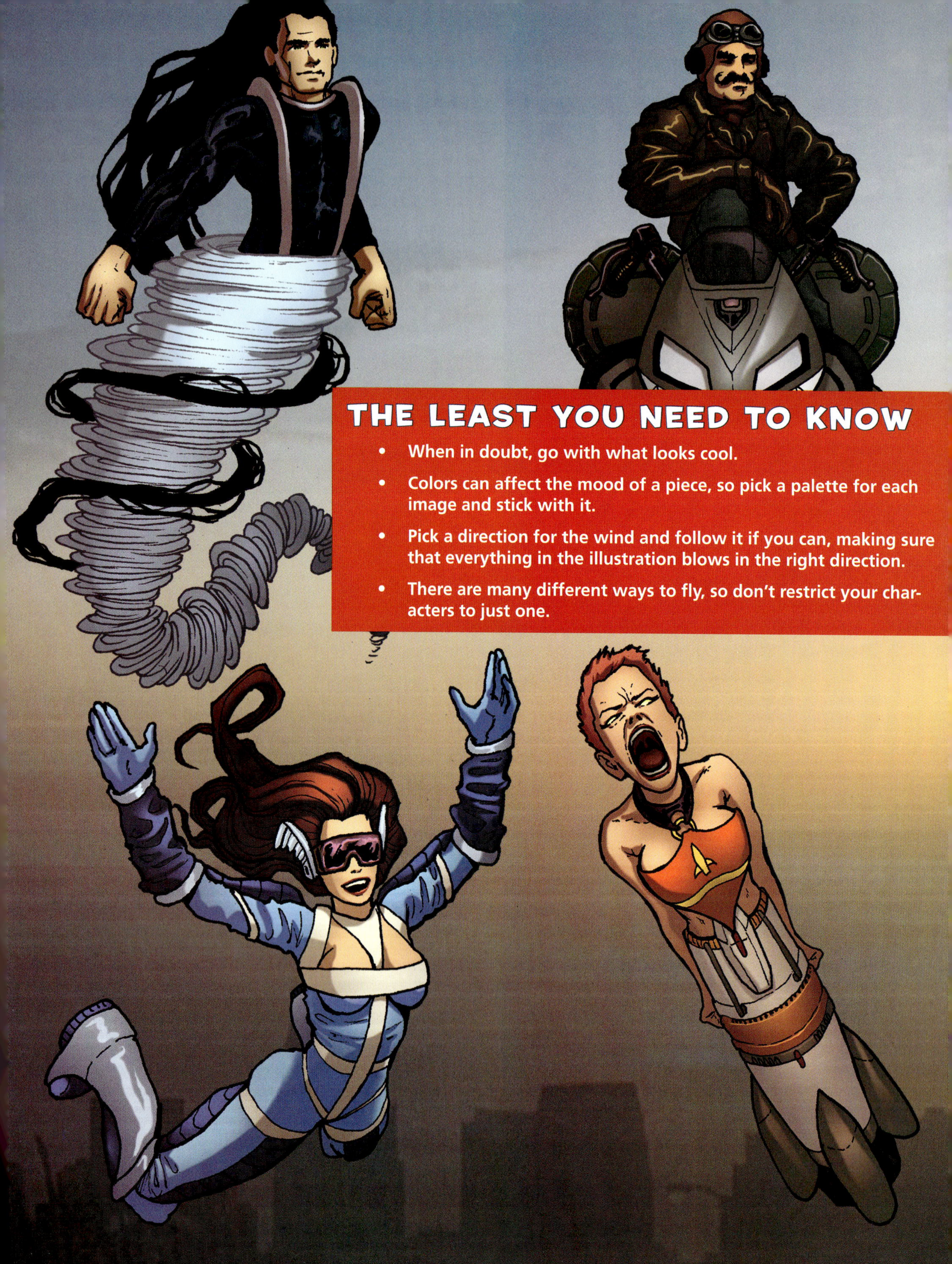

THE LEAST YOU NEED TO KNOW

- When in doubt, go with what looks cool.
- Colors can affect the mood of a piece, so pick a palette for each image and stick with it.
- Pick a direction for the wind and follow it if you can, making sure that everything in the illustration blows in the right direction.
- There are many different ways to fly, so don't restrict your characters to just one.

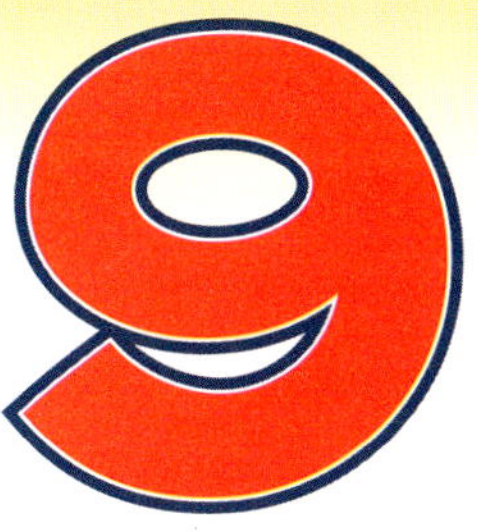

9 Fast Ones: Blink and You'll Miss 'Em

In This Chapter

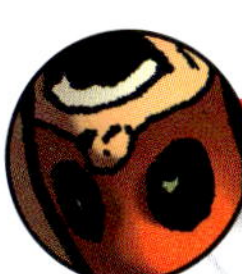

- A rubber-band man

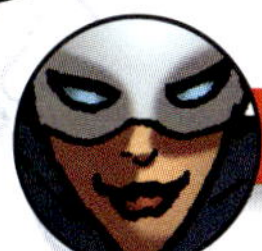

- A blazing-fast woman

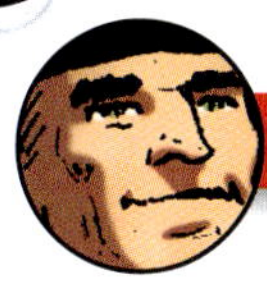

- A road warrior

Another common power fantasy is that of speed. It's why people like to drive fast and watch NASCAR. There's nothing like a good race to bring out the competitive edge in anyone.

In the lead we find the Bouncer, an acrobatic speedster who can careen around a landscape faster than the eye can follow. He was once a wealthy high-school student with the world at his feet, but when his parents cut off his trust fund he invested every last dollar he had into developing his bouncing powers. Now he uses them to rob banks so he can live the luxurious life to which he wishes to remain accustomed.

Speedster comes up fast from behind, ready to overtake Bouncer while he's bouncing around. Once a 500-pound couch potato, she submitted herself to an experimental weight-loss program that sped up her metabolism to superhuman levels. Now her ability to burn off calories has finally surpassed her appetite.

Just in back of her races Biker, a man with the kind of lightning-fast reflexes you'd need to be able to ride a motorcycle down a city street at 200 miles per hour. After getting into an accident without a helmet, he had to have a supercomputer replace a large portion of his brain. He no longer needs a helmet, as his entire replacement skull is made out of steel.

BOUNCER

Bouncer spent every last dime he could wheedle or steal from his parents on making himself as resilient and bouncy as a red rubber ball. He succeeded all too well, but he needs to keep paying for the treatments that give him his powers, or they fade away. To finance this, he's turned to the only kind of work he knows: crime.

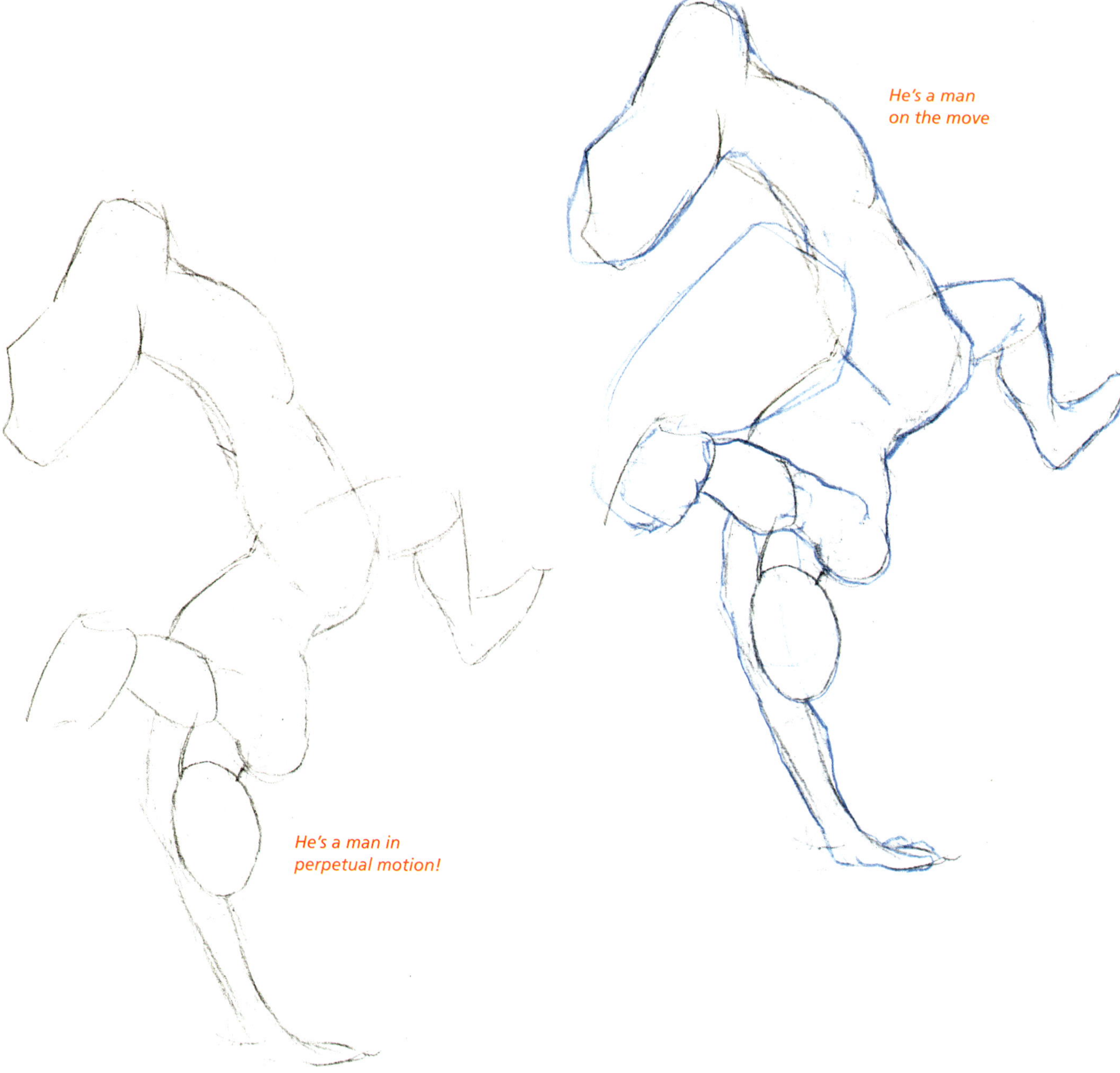

1. Rough out Bouncer's figure with simple shapes. Yair turns him upside down on one hand and poses his other limbs at dynamic angles. The forced perspective of both his hand and foot give the image a strong sense of motion.

2. As an acrobat, Bouncer has a reason to wear skin-tight spandex. It's embarrassing when your clothes catch on something as you zip by it, after all. Rough in his outfit and put a bag of cash in his hand. Swing it up and around, showing how his momentum makes it defy gravity.

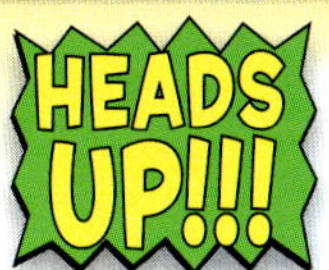

Drawing figures with their heads turned upside down can be tricky to wrap your brain around, but it doesn't have to be. If you can't master the perspective while the figure is inverted, turn your paper upside down and work that way for a while. Once you're comfortable enough, just turn the paper back the other way, and you're all set.

Perhaps we should have called him Ricochet.

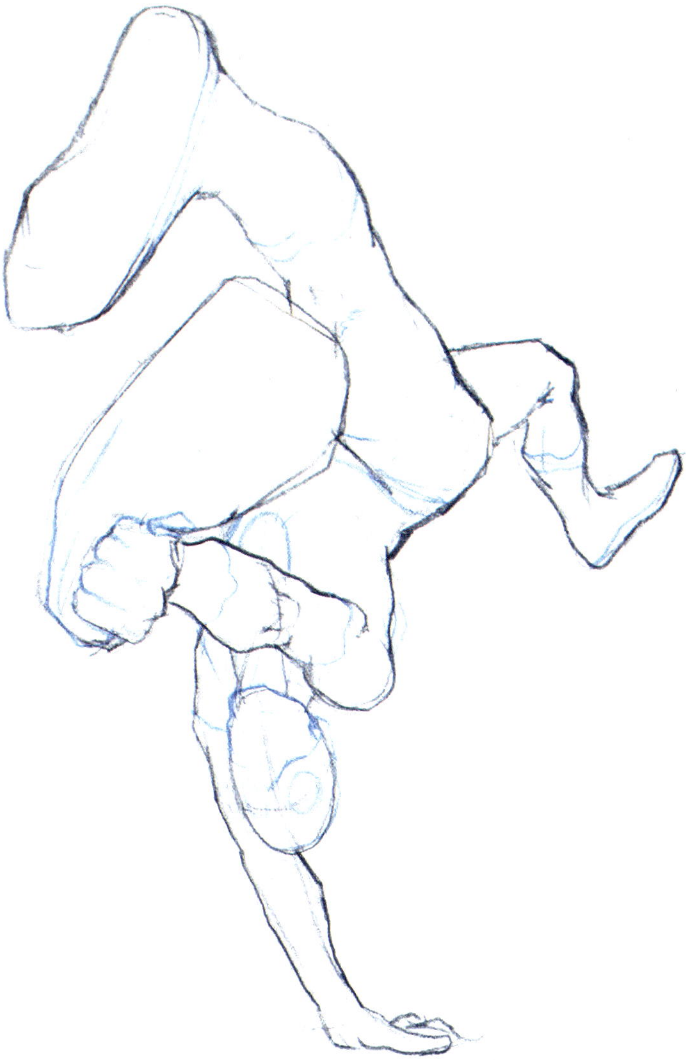

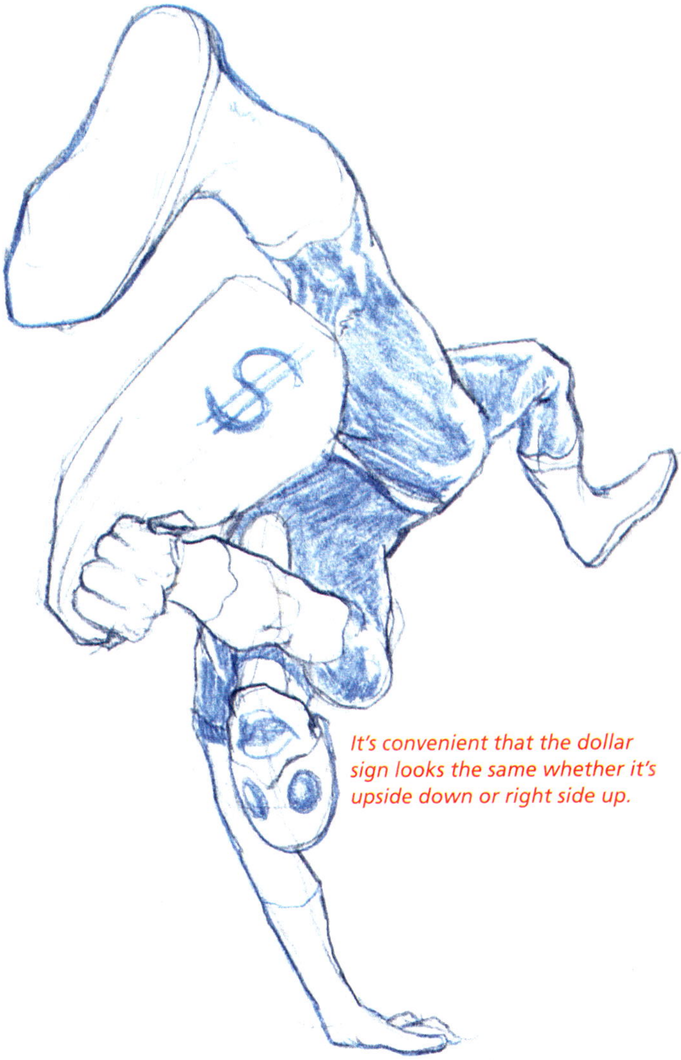

It's convenient that the dollar sign looks the same whether it's upside down or right side up.

3. Give Bouncer a mask, boots, and gloves. Put a red rubber-ball icon on his chest. Add some trim to those boots, especially the one closest to us.

4. Black in his outfit, using white space to outline the edges. Place a dollar sign on that bag so people know what's in it. Give him a wide grin in an open mouth.

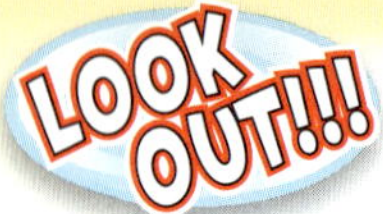

It's tempting to treat every element of a drawing equally, but it's smarter and looks better to give the parts closest to the viewer the most attention. With Bouncer, add more details to the foremost foot, and let such focus slack on the rear foot. It helps draw the eye to the focal point of the illustration rather than forcing it to choose between many interesting spots.

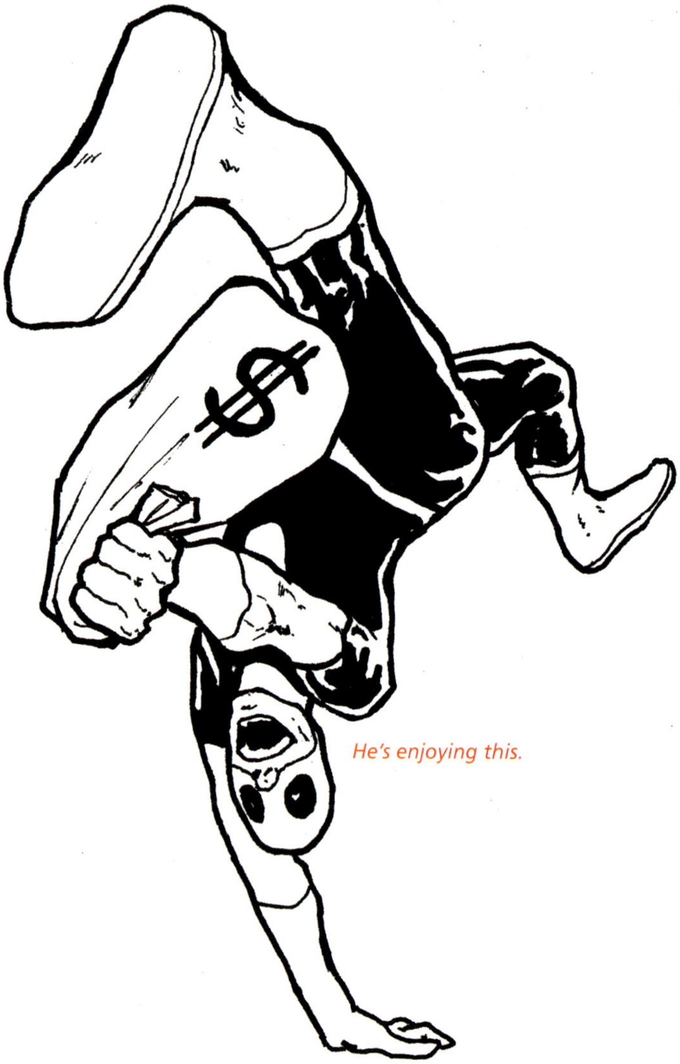

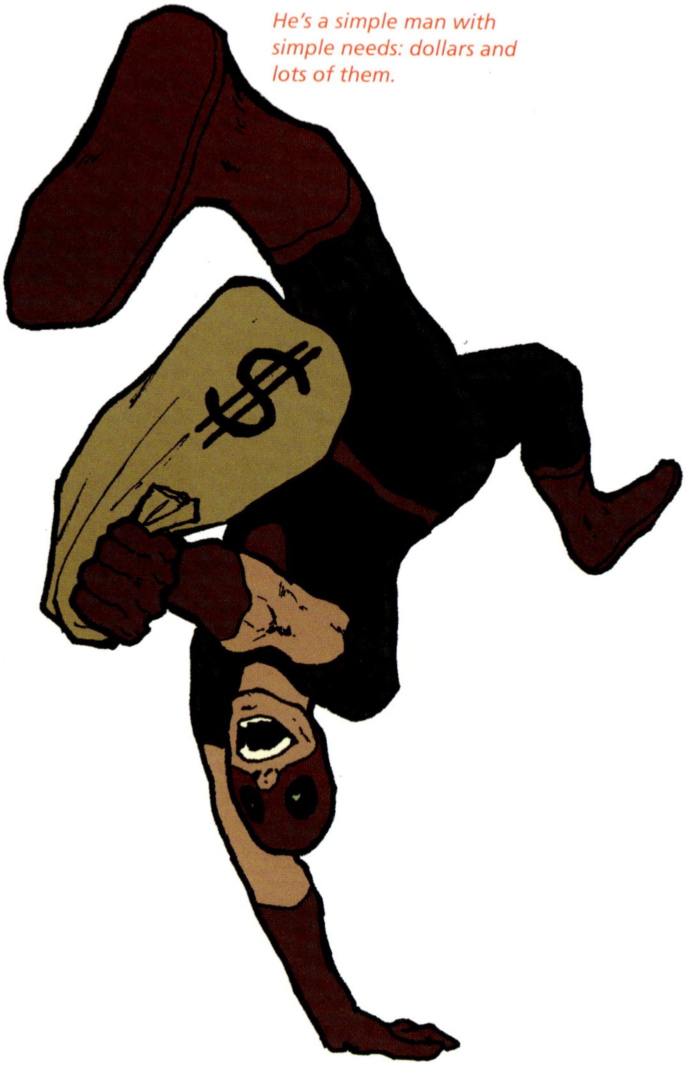

He's a simple man with simple needs: dollars and lots of them.

He's enjoying this.

5. Use fairly even lines here. If you like, you can add motion lines to indicate a direction in which Bouncer is moving, although Yair does a fine job of conveying this without resorting to such tropes.

6. Go with red on his boots, mask, and gloves, as well as his icon and belt. The tan of the bag resembles burlap just fine. Go with a dark gray over the black on the uniform for subtle highlights.

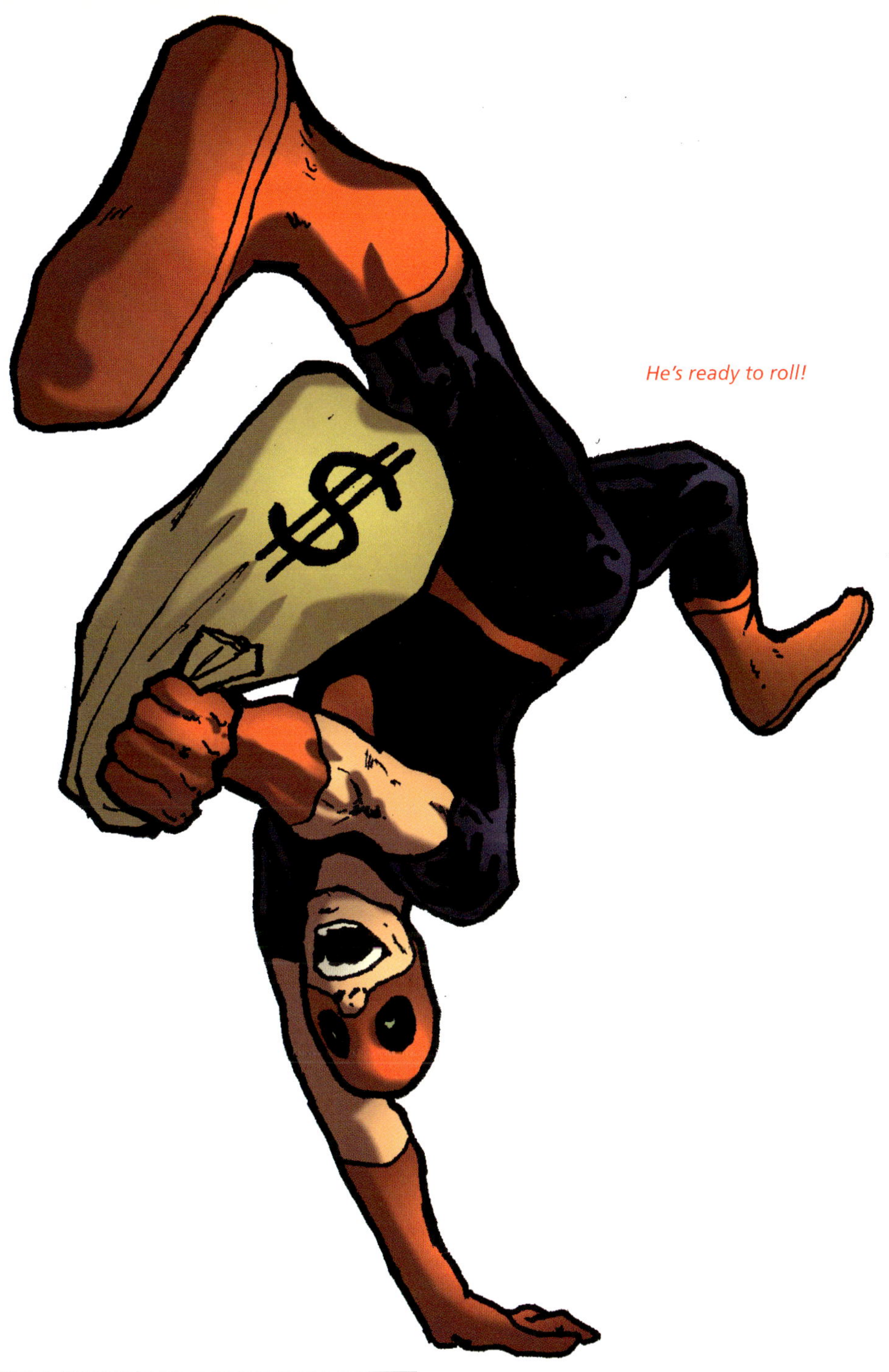

He's ready to roll!

7. Brighten up those reds so they nearly glow. Leave the black of the outfit flat. The brights of the shadow on the bottom of his boot really draws the eye right to it, too.

SPEEDSTER

Speedster once resembled the "before" photo for the most dramatic weight loss programs around. Determined to get into shape, she agreed to test out an experimental treatment that sped up her metabolism—and everything else about her. Now she races around, putting an end to crime and burning off all those calories she still puts down.

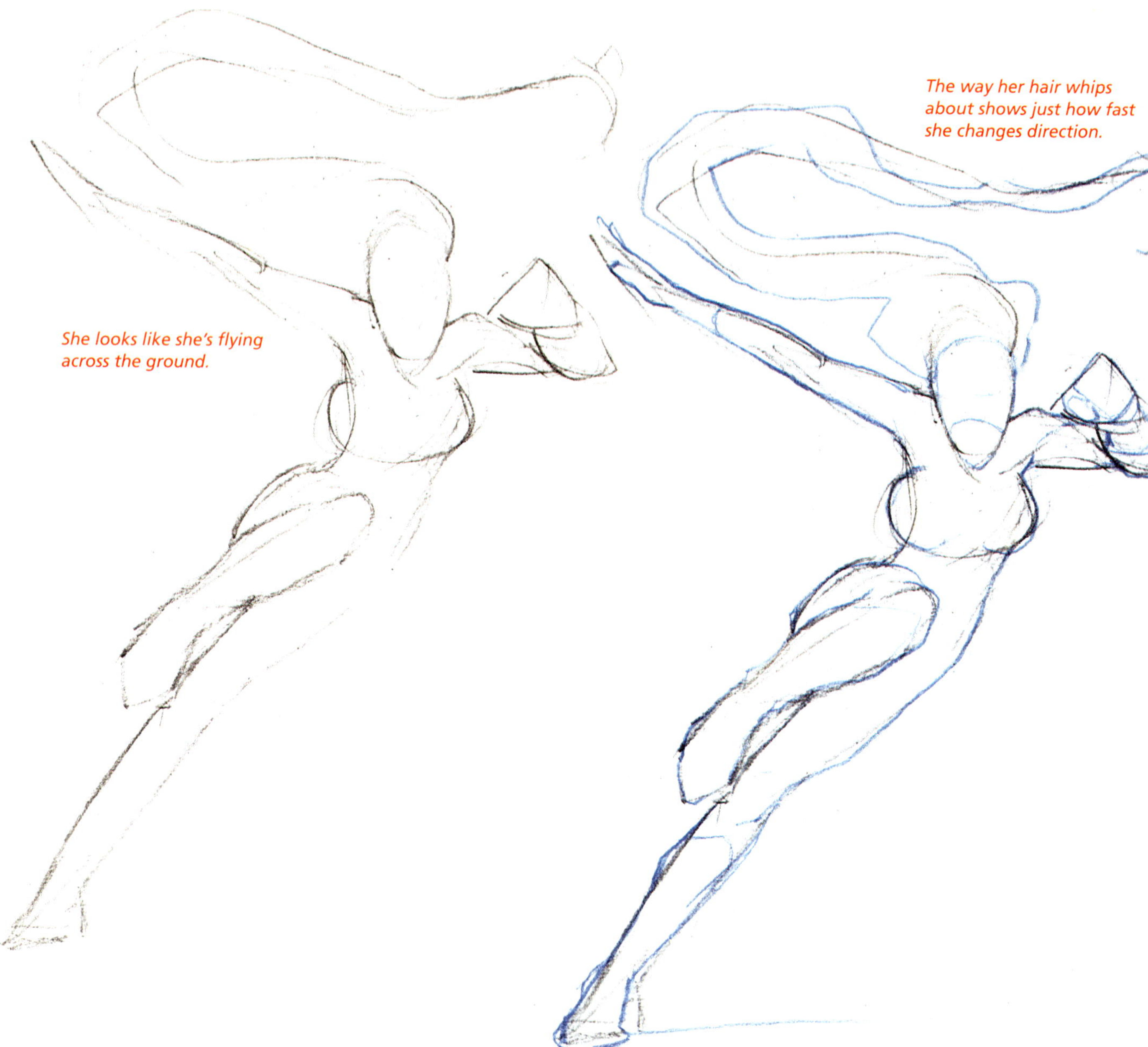

She looks like she's flying across the ground.

The way her hair whips about shows just how fast she changes direction.

1. Break down Speedster's pose. Yair chooses to show her sliding into a fast change of direction. It's a dynamic pose and a challenge to show a swift alteration in her momentum.

2. Add hair. Round out her breasts. Take care with the anatomy on her raised leg. The foreshortening can be tricky, but the look is worth it if you can pull it off.

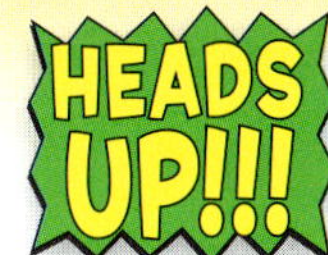

When hunting around for a proper pose, don't be afraid to look for resource images. Here, Speedster resembles nothing so much as a speed skater coming around a turn. For those who watch the Winter Olympics, her pose makes sense and connotes high speed.

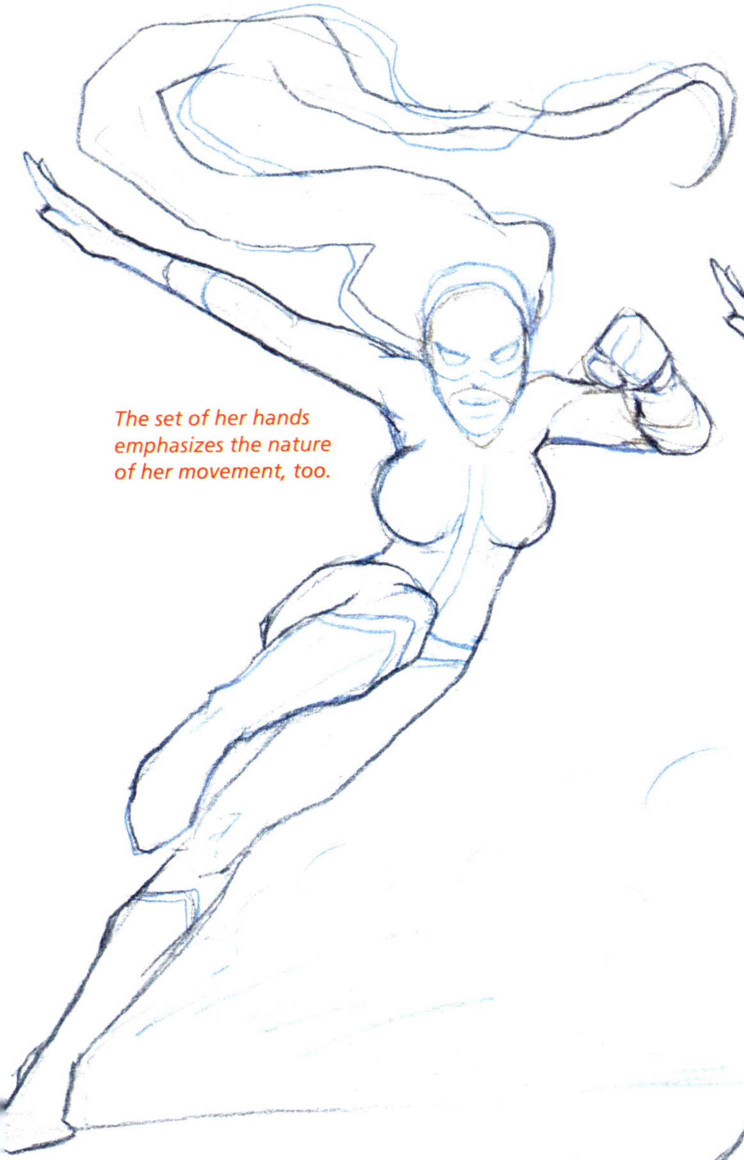

The set of her hands emphasizes the nature of her movement, too.

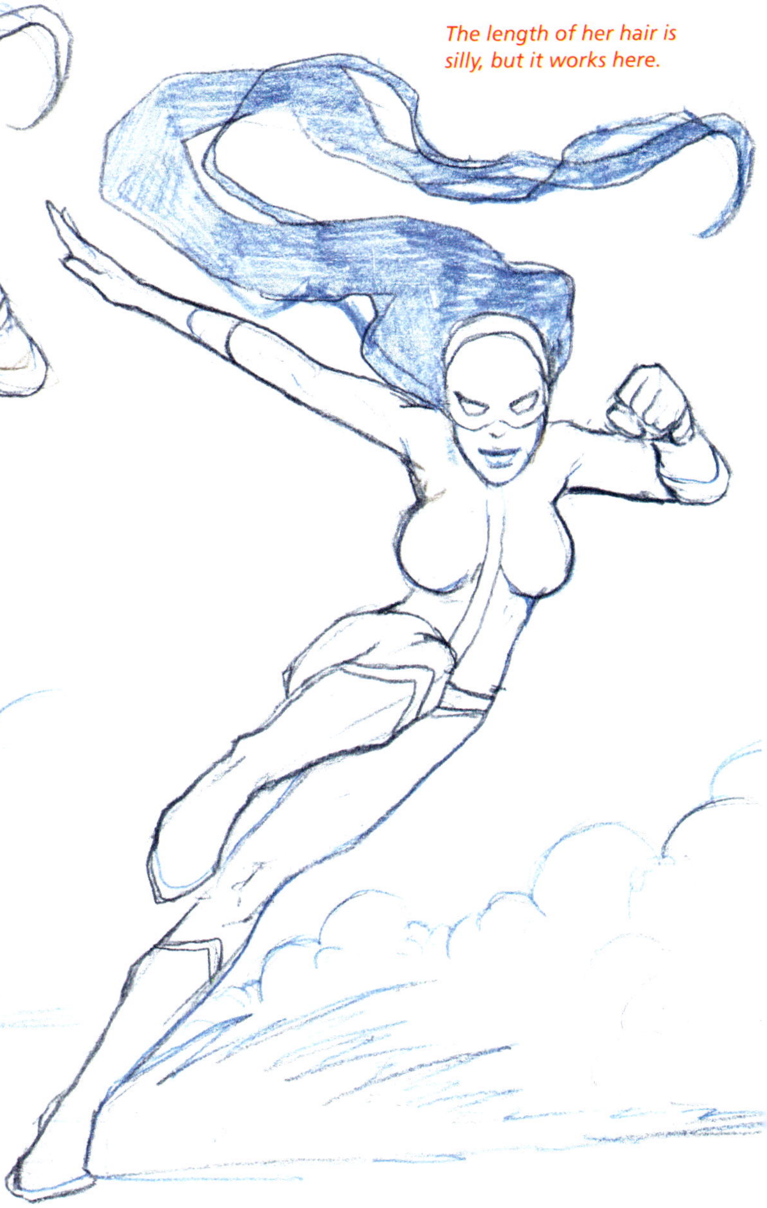

The length of her hair is silly, but it works here.

3. Put a mask on her and show the edges of her belt, boots, and gloves. Sketch in the dust she kicks up as she skids along the ground. Give her a confident and determined mouth.

4. Black out her hair. Work on the details of the skid. Show sharp edges of it near the ground, but allow dust to billow upward from it. Make the dust cloud grow larger the farther away from her it gets.

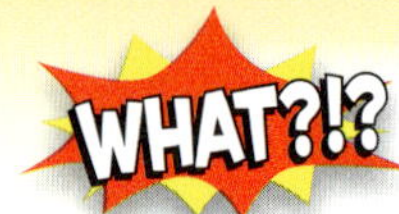

A **visual effect** stands in for something that you could not normally see. The fiery jaggies spurred up in the path of Speedster's skid, for instance, wouldn't be seen in reality, but in a comic book they provide a visual cue as to what's happening. They make it look like she's sliding sideways, even though she's in a static drawing.

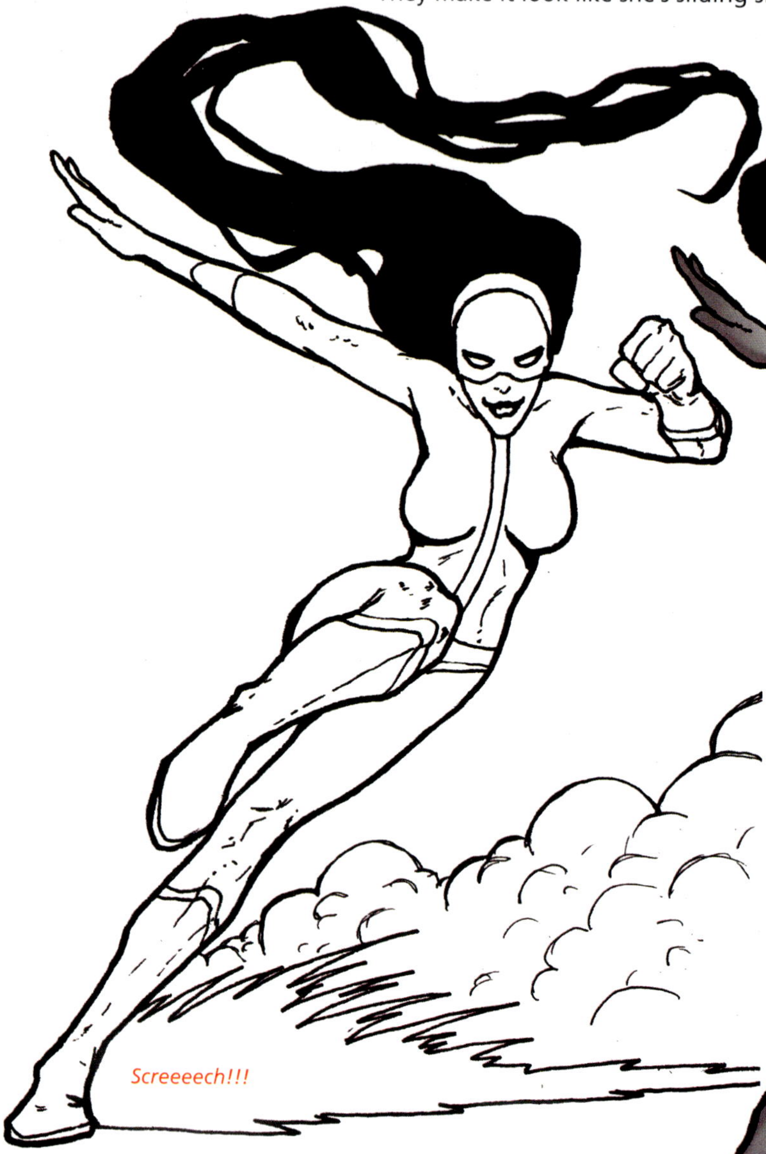

Screeeech!!!

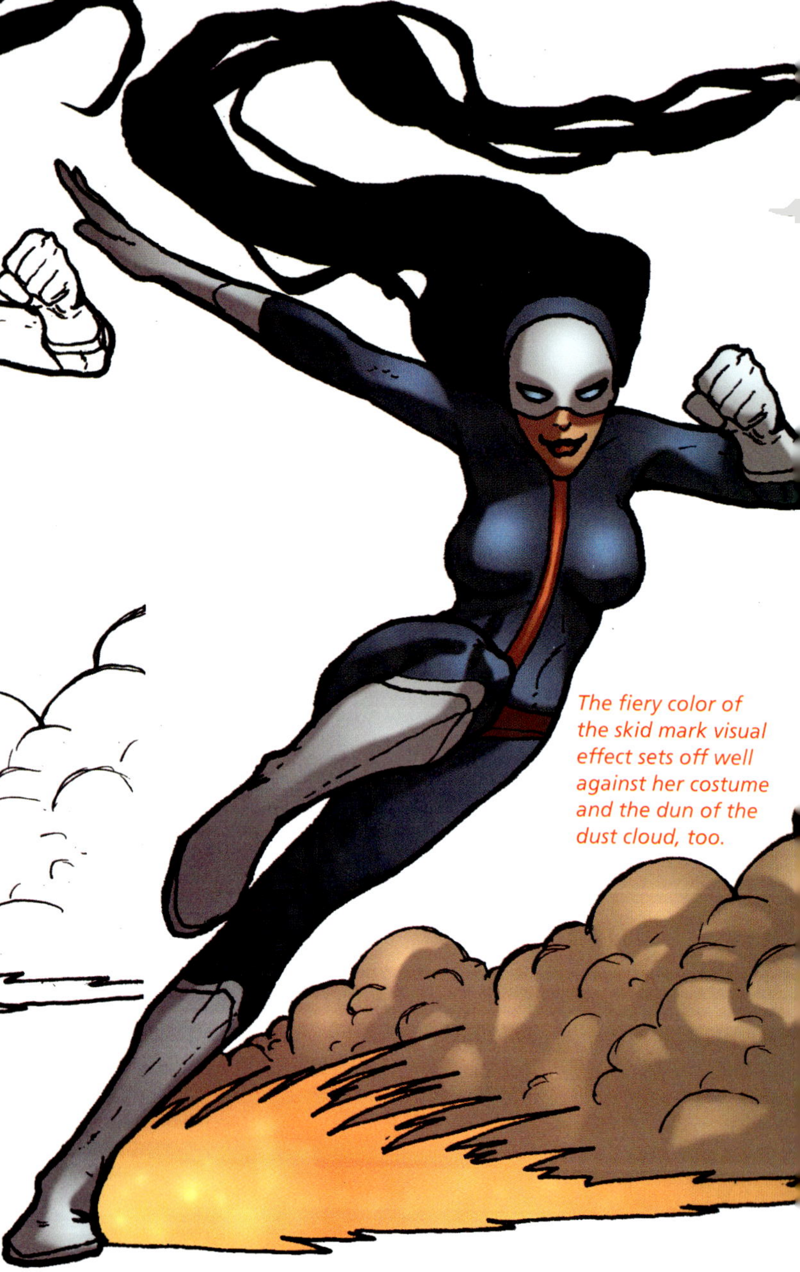

The fiery color of the skid mark visual effect sets off well against her costume and the dun of the dust cloud, too.

5. Use solid blacks on the hair, and vary the lines normally on her figure. For the skid, use solid lines on the jagged skid and thinner lines only on the interior of the billowing dust. This makes the skid seem harder and more real.

6. Use a vibrant blue for her suit, with red accents. The gloves and boots are a ghostly gray, as is her mask. Tint the lenses over her eyes a sky blue to give her a sharper look.

BIKER

Biker rode with a Harley Owners Group right up until the day a member of a rival HOG forced him off the road. When he awakened from the accident, he found his brain—much of which had been replaced with an experimental microchip—worked faster than ever. His reflexes made it seem like everyone around him was standing still. Back on his bike, he often rides in excess of 200 miles per hour, trusting his reflexes to keep him out of the same sort of trouble that gave him such powers in the first place.

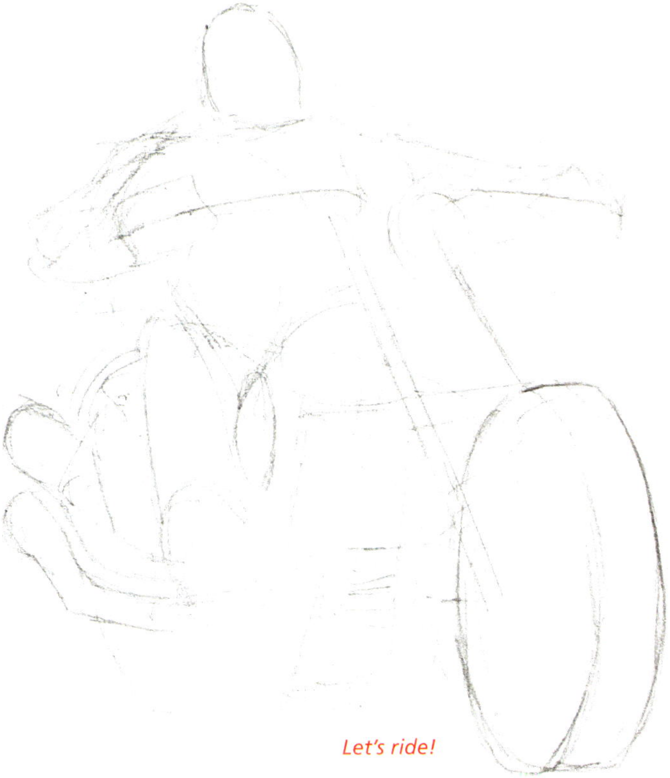

Note how the ends of the bandana flap behind him in the wind, helping show he's moving fast.

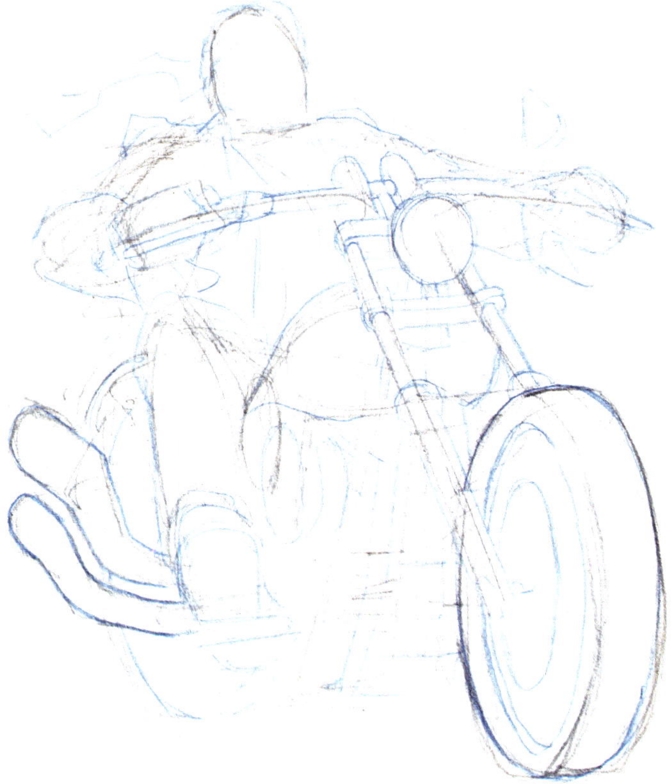

Let's ride!

1. Place Biker on a Harley-style motorcycle, slung low and covered with chrome and black leather trim. Angle the bike aggressively and rough in the wheels, frame, and exhaust pipes.

2. Put a bandana on Biker's head, and outfit him with a leather jacket and pants, plus a pair of riding boots. Add more details to the bike, including the headlight, mirrors, chassis, and more.

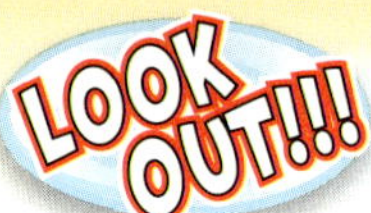

It's easy to think of a hero like Biker or Sky Pilot (from Chapter 8) as almost a part of his vehicle. Don't let him get stuck there, though. Separate the two from time to time and see how they fare on their own.

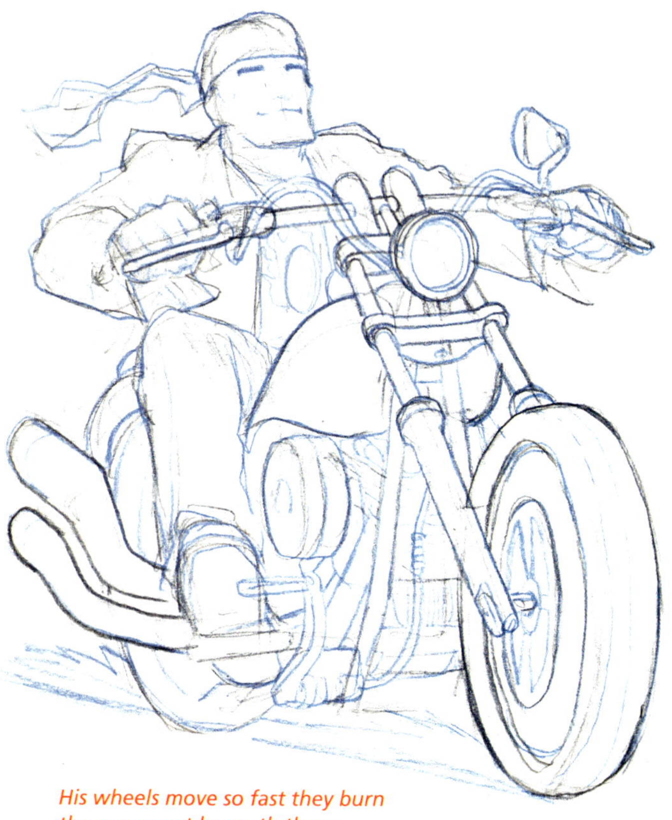

His wheels move so fast they burn the pavement beneath them.

It's good to be alive—even with a new brain.

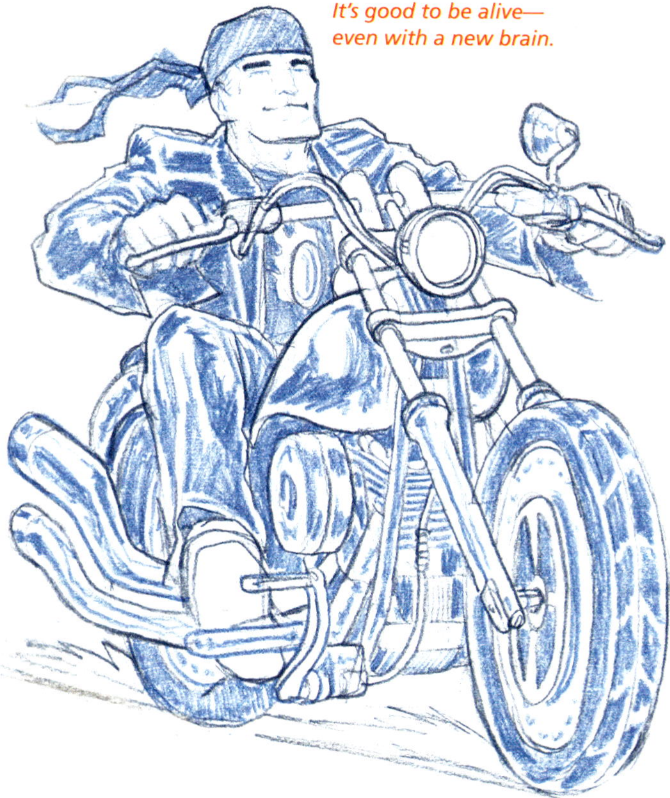

3. Add more details. Put the engine in the bike and show the shape of the tires and the brake and accelerator controls. Put a burning wheel icon on his shirt. Give him a thick set of eyebrows, a wide smile, and a square jaw.

4. Black out Biker's clothes, leaving ample white space to show texture and edging. Do the same for the front tire and its treads. Less black and more white space makes the mirror and the exhaust pipes look like shiny chrome. Give the man serene eyes and just the hint of a smile.

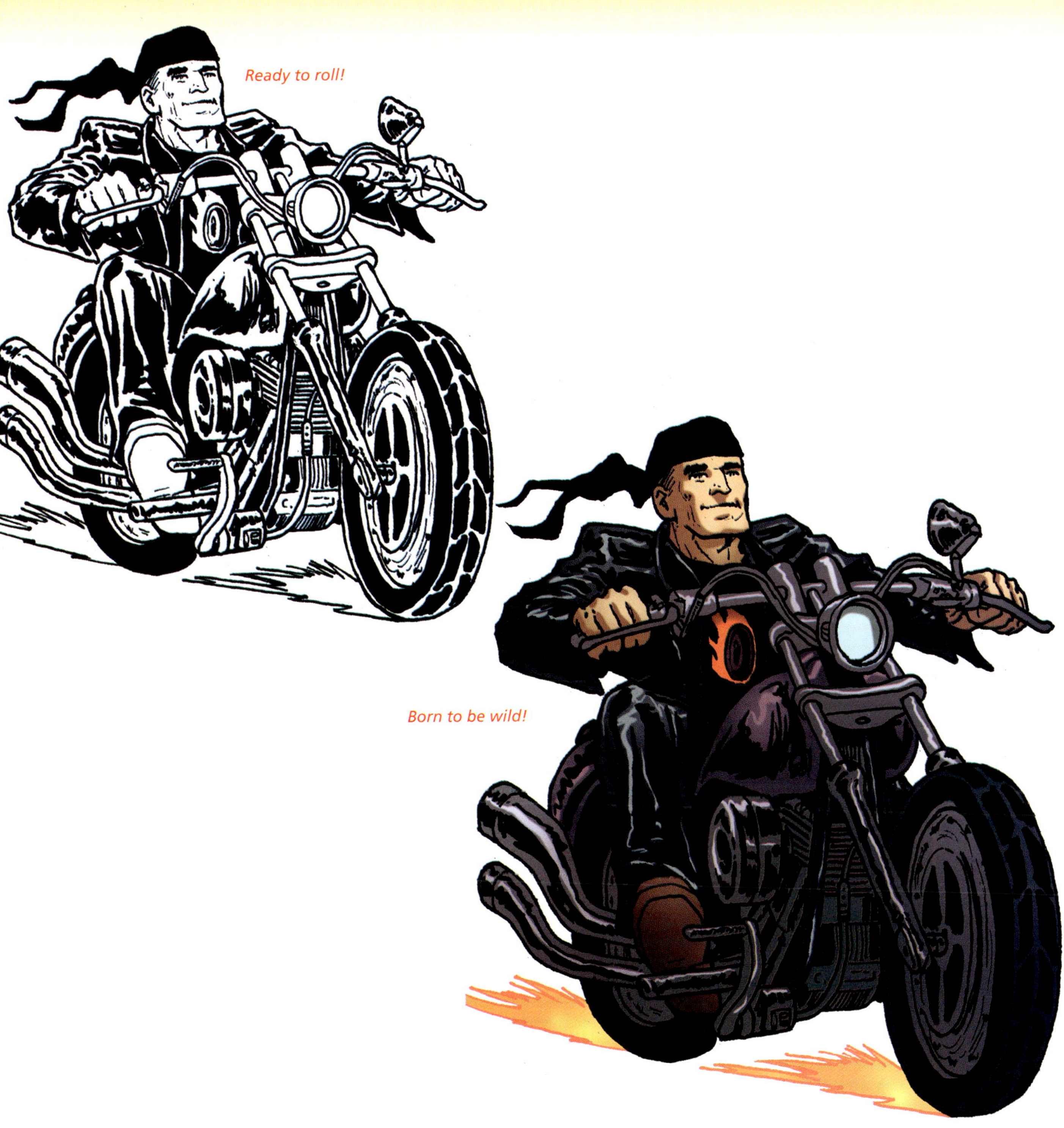

5. Use uniform lines here and lots of areas of solid black. Use white space to keep him from turning into a silhouette. The only thinner lines should be on his face. The black bandana emphasizes the fact his head isn't fully human any longer.

6. Go with grays on Biker's clothes and motorcycle. The only splashes of bright color come from the flames under his tire and the icon on his chest. The light blue of the headlight helps draw your eye to the center of the illustration.

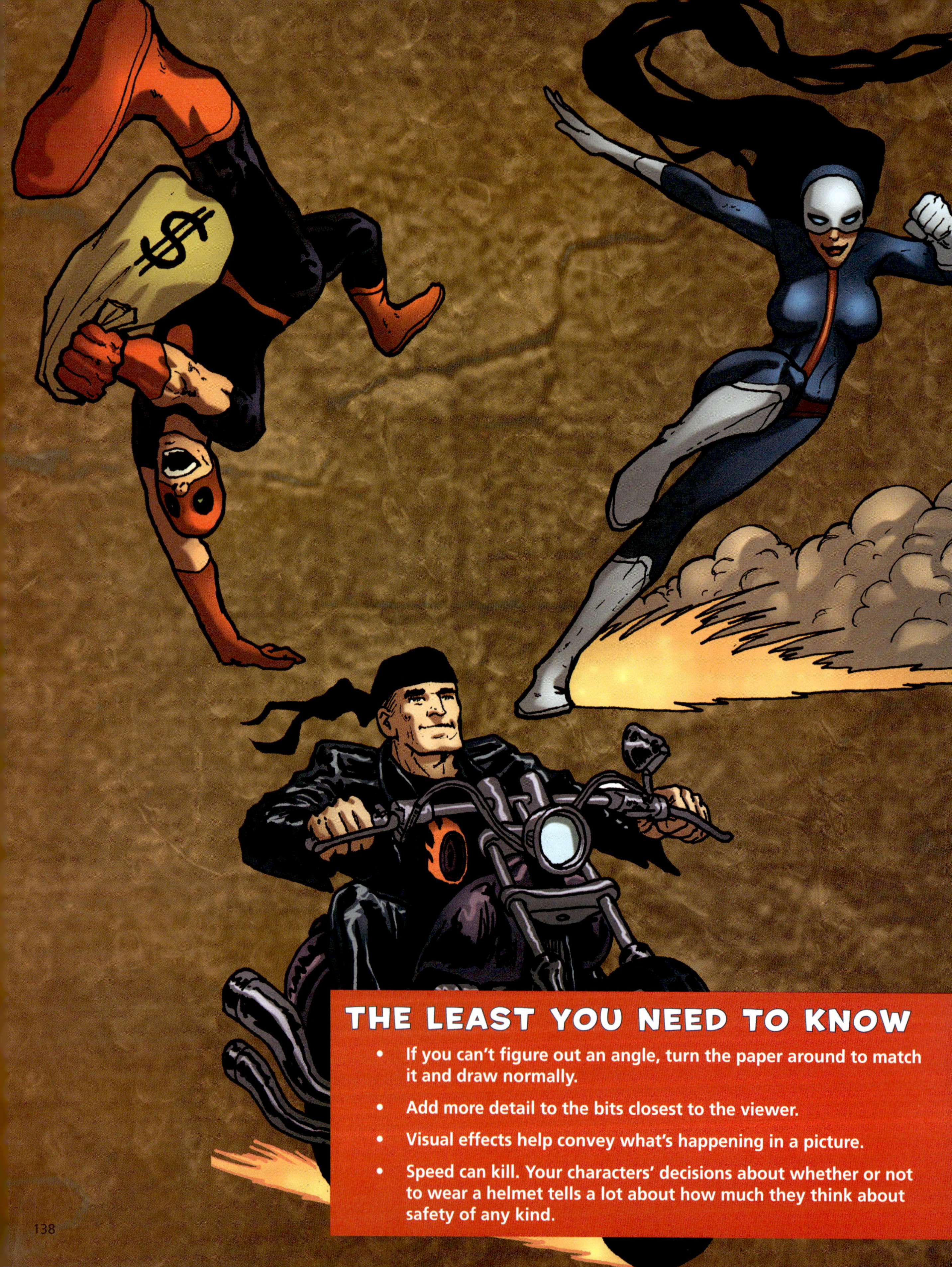

THE LEAST YOU NEED TO KNOW

- If you can't figure out an angle, turn the paper around to match it and draw normally.
- Add more detail to the bits closest to the viewer.
- Visual effects help convey what's happening in a picture.
- Speed can kill. Your characters' decisions about whether or not to wear a helmet tells a lot about how much they think about safety of any kind.

10 SHIFTERS: TIME FOR A CHANGE

In This Chapter

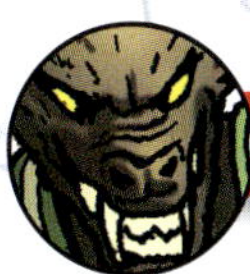

- A friendly werewolf

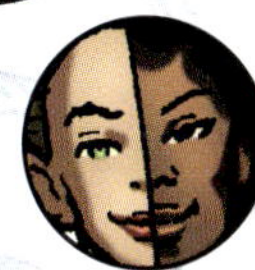

- A morphing supermodel

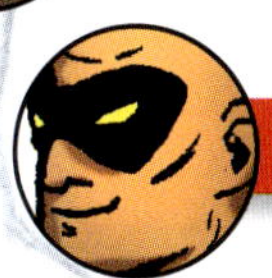

- A giant of a man

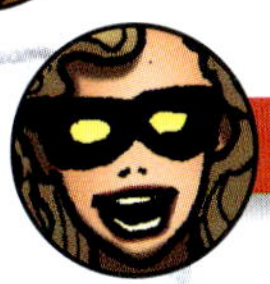

- A (very) little woman

From time to time, we'd all like to be someone other than who we actually are. Shifters get to make that kind of change all the time, morphing from one form into another. If life is change, then these people live life large.

We begin with Like-Anthrope, the friendliest werewolf you'd ever want to meet. While others may hate turning into a werewolf once a month, he's embraced the event. It gives him a chance to go out and help people in a way that he can't manage most other nights.

The Shaper can control every aspect of her appearance from her hair down to her dress. Is it any wonder she's almost always gorgeous? We catch her mid-change, between one face and another.

Giant stands taller than a 10-story building, and he's as strong as you might expect. Fortunately he doesn't stay this way all the time, or he'd have a hard time finding an apartment.

Shrinker is the polar opposite to Giant, a woman who can reduce her size down to smaller than a doll. She stays just as strong as ever, though, giving her a wicked punch for such a small person.

LIKE-ANTHROPE

Like-Anthrope took an unusual approach to becoming a *lycanthrope*. He sought out a werewolf and arranged to be bitten under the light of a full moon. Perhaps for this reason, he seems to have a great deal more control over his shapeshifting than usual. Even better, he enjoys it.

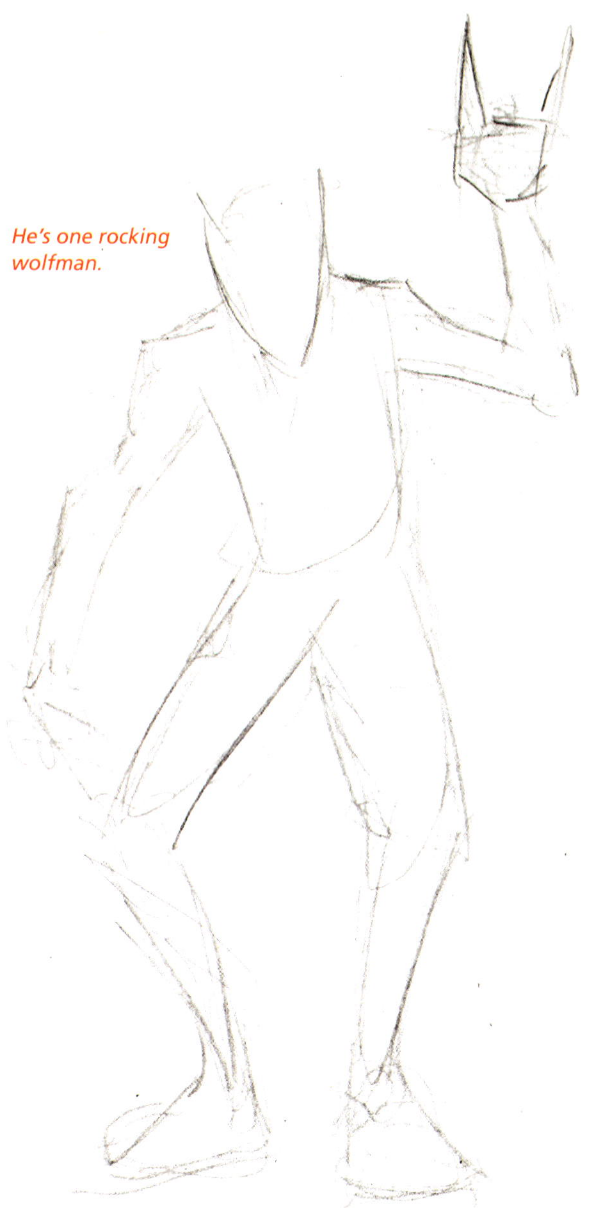

He's one rocking wolfman.

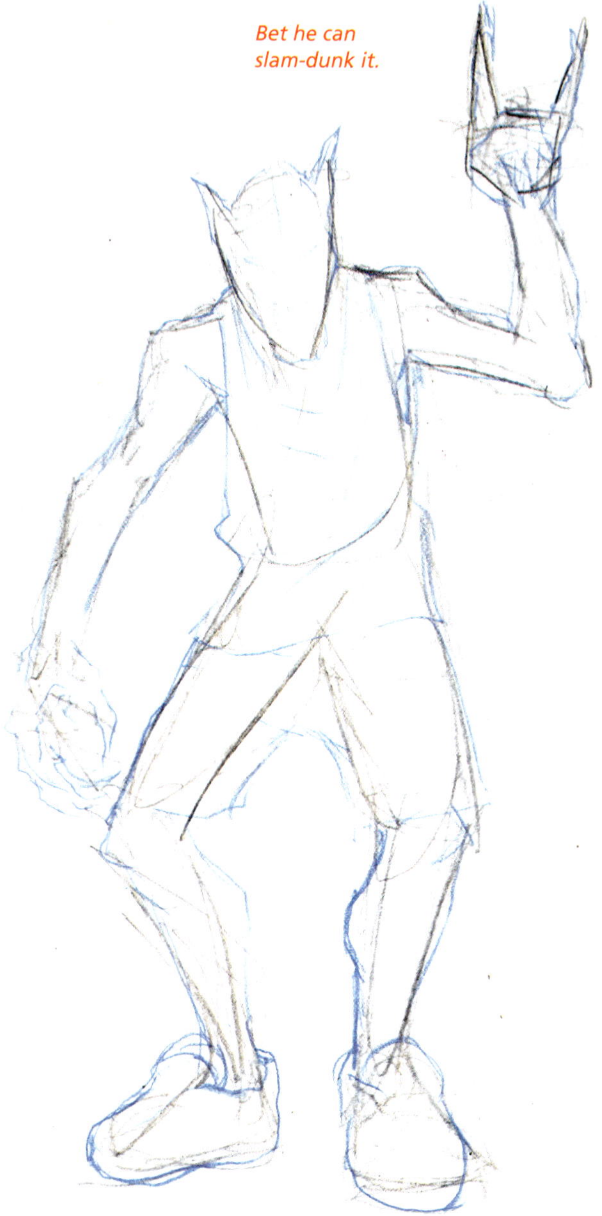

Bet he can slam-dunk it.

1. Break down Like-Anthrope's stance. He's a relaxed kid, dressed casually. He holds up his left hand to throw the goat ("Rock on!"). Yair gives him a gangly, wolfish pose, which you can see even in this rough state.

2. Dress Like-Anthrope in a street basketball outfit and put some low-top street ball shoes on his feet. Notice how the loose fabric hangs on his frame. Refine his hands and sketch in the barest basics of his face.

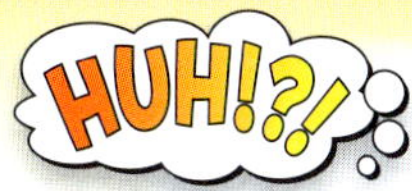

A **lycanthrope** is werewolf, a person who can shift into the shape of a wolf or, often, half-man/half-wolf forms. Many other animalistic shapeshifters exist in legends and stories too, including werebears, weresharks, etc. Traditionally, being a lycanthrope is seen as a curse, an inability to control basic, animalistic urges.

My, what big teeth you have.

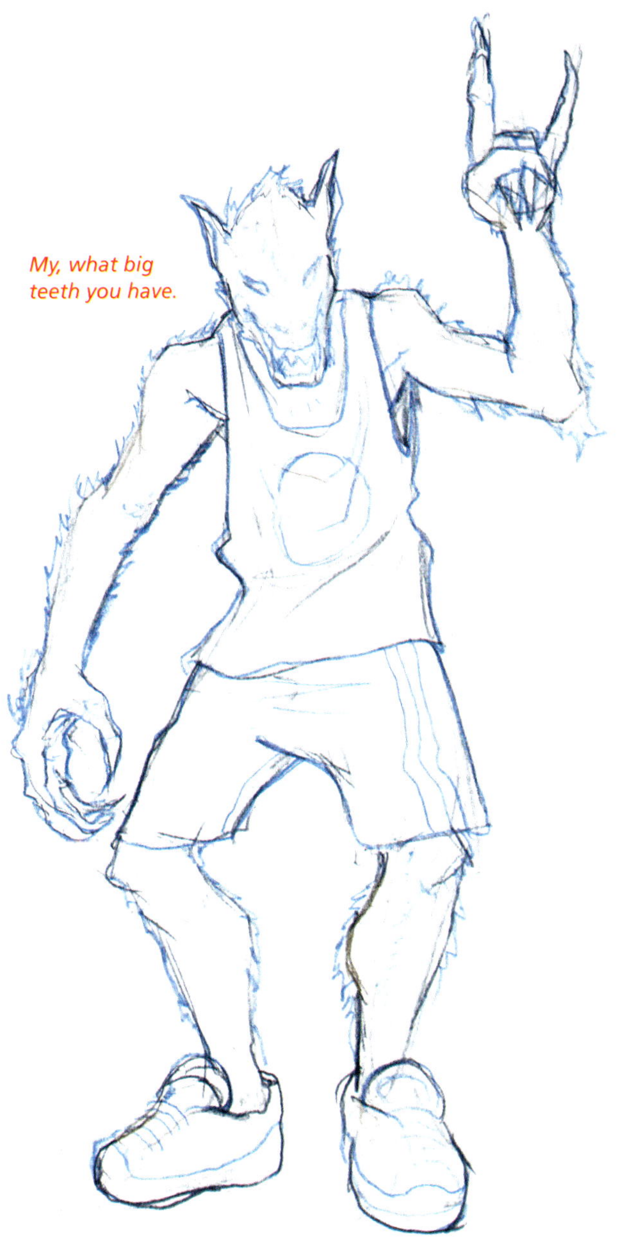

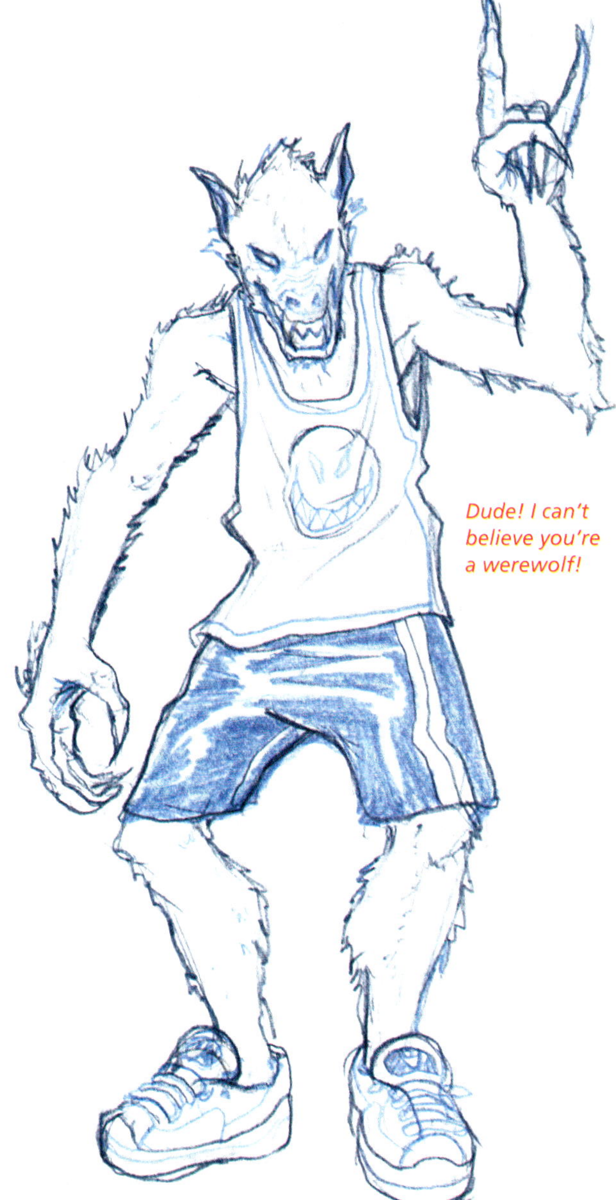

Dude! I can't believe you're a werewolf!

3. Give him a wolfish face and add a furry ridge to the edges of his silhouette. Notice how Yair extends his mouth, ears, and fingers to make him seem more like a wolf.

4. Black out the shorts, leaving white for wrinkles and for stripes along one side. Put a smiley face with teeth on his chest as his icon. Work on the details of the face and his shoes.

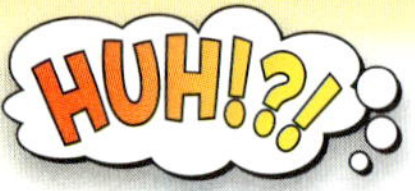

Throwing the goat (or making the devil's horns) is considered a vulgar insult in Italy and elsewhere around the Mediterranean. In America, it's come to mean "Rock on!" as popularized by heavy metal bands that swiped devilish iconography at every chance.

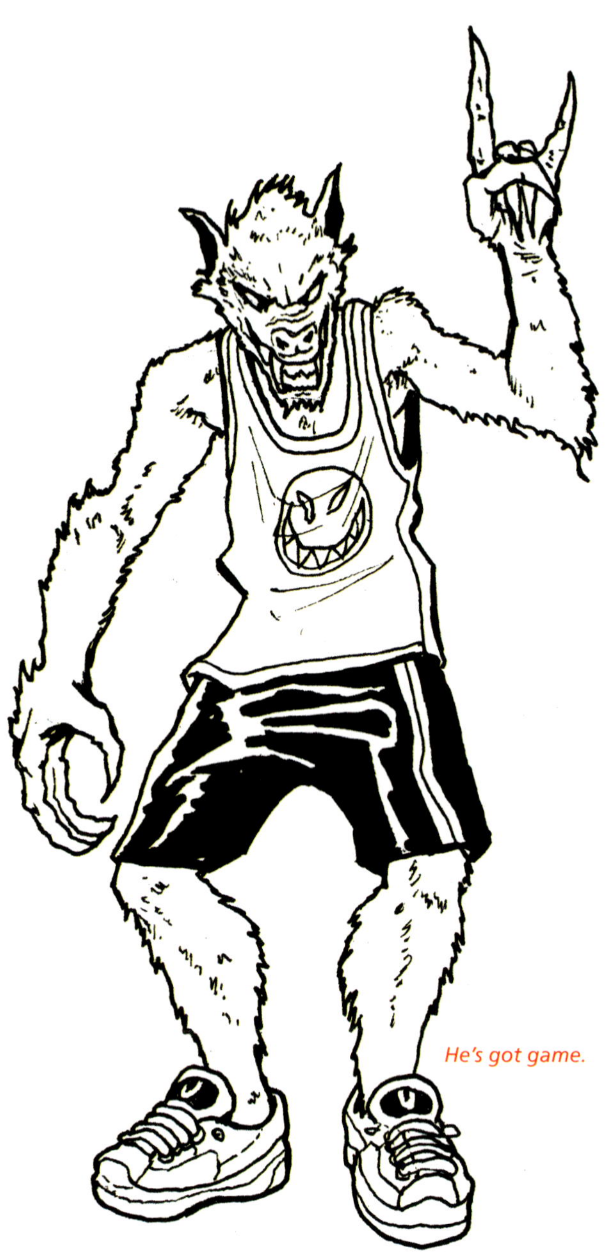

He's got game.

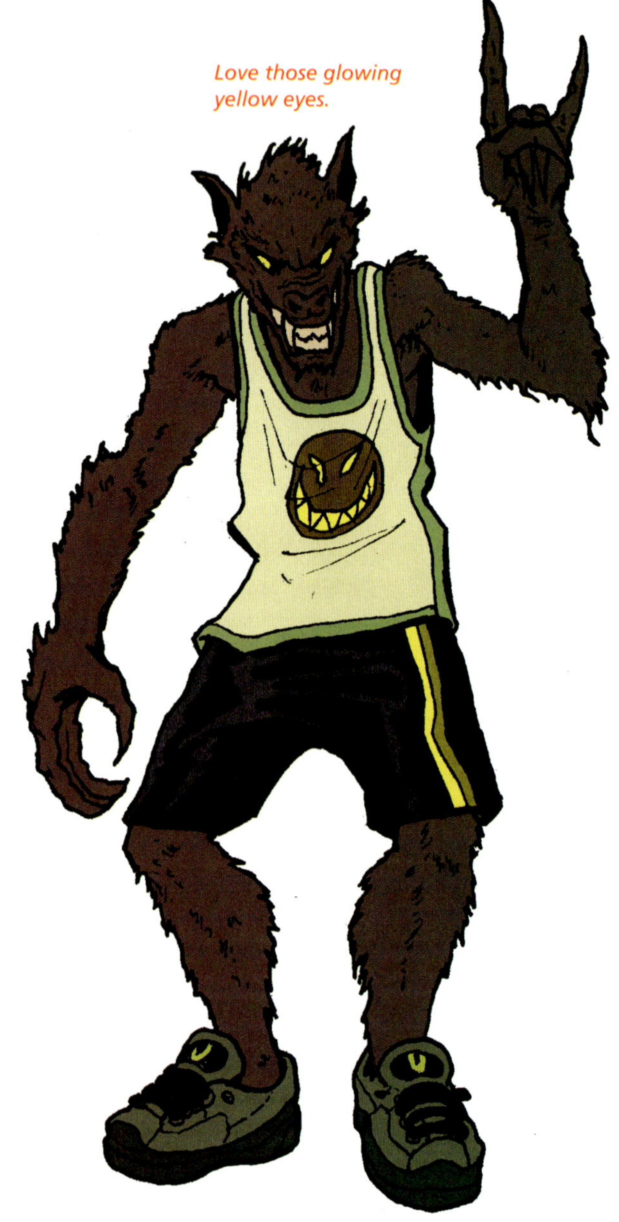

Love those glowing yellow eyes.

5. You don't have to vary your ink lines much for this guy. Use slightly lighter lines for interior fur hatching, but otherwise you can go fairly uniform with your line weight.

6. Color the fur brown and the shirt and shoes yellow and green. Make the smiley face the same color as his fur. Use dark gray on the highlights on the shorts.

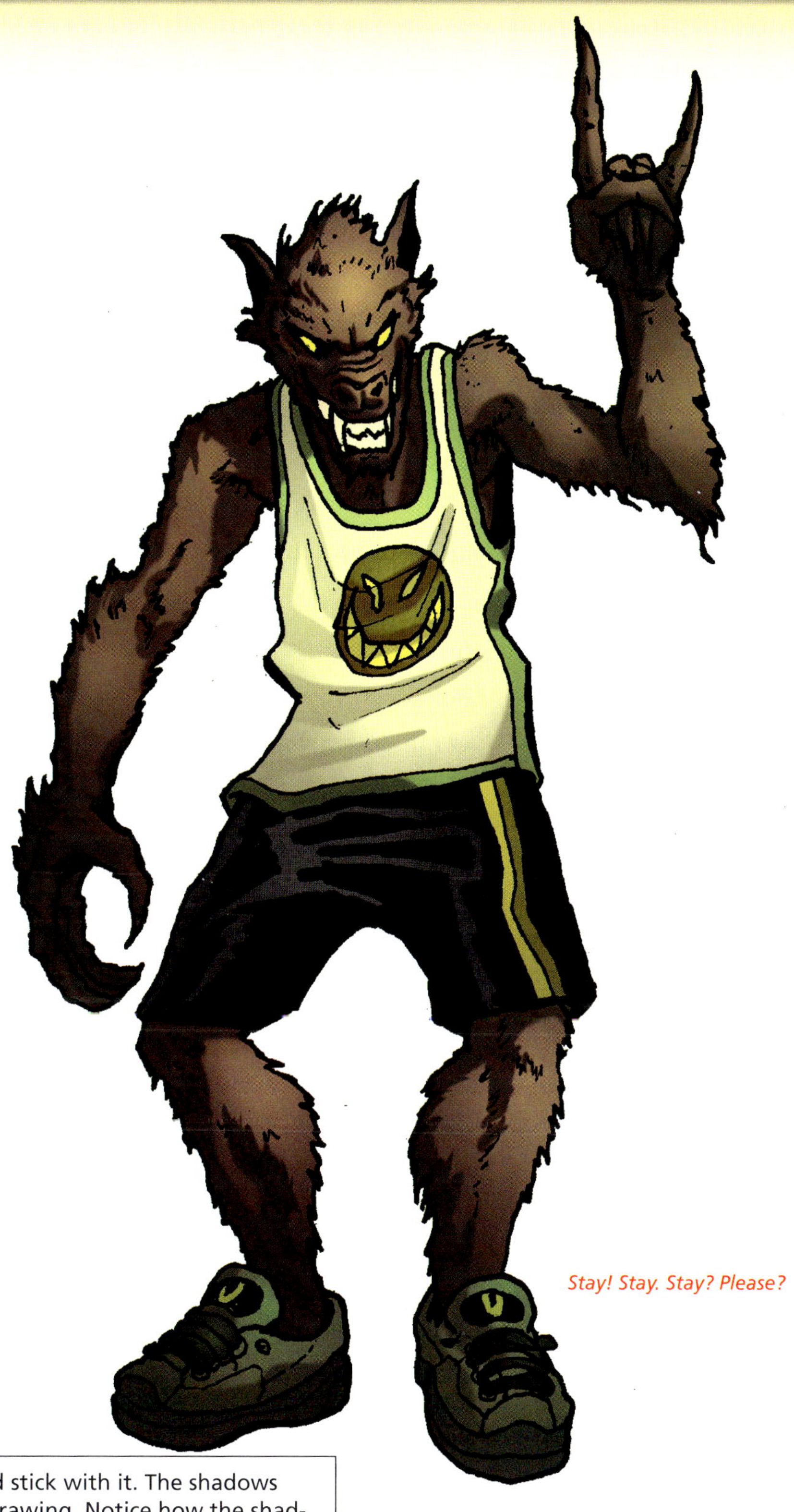

Stay! Stay. Stay? Please?

7. Pick a light source and stick with it. The shadows will really make this drawing. Notice how the shadows on the shirt emphasize the folds in the cloth and the direction of the light.

SHAPER

The Shaper was once the ugly duckling of her entire school. She dedicated herself to the study of appearances, struggling to find the Holy Grail of total, mentally activated control over her appearance. She succeeded, but the treatments mentally unbalanced her, and she now only uses her powers for personal gain.

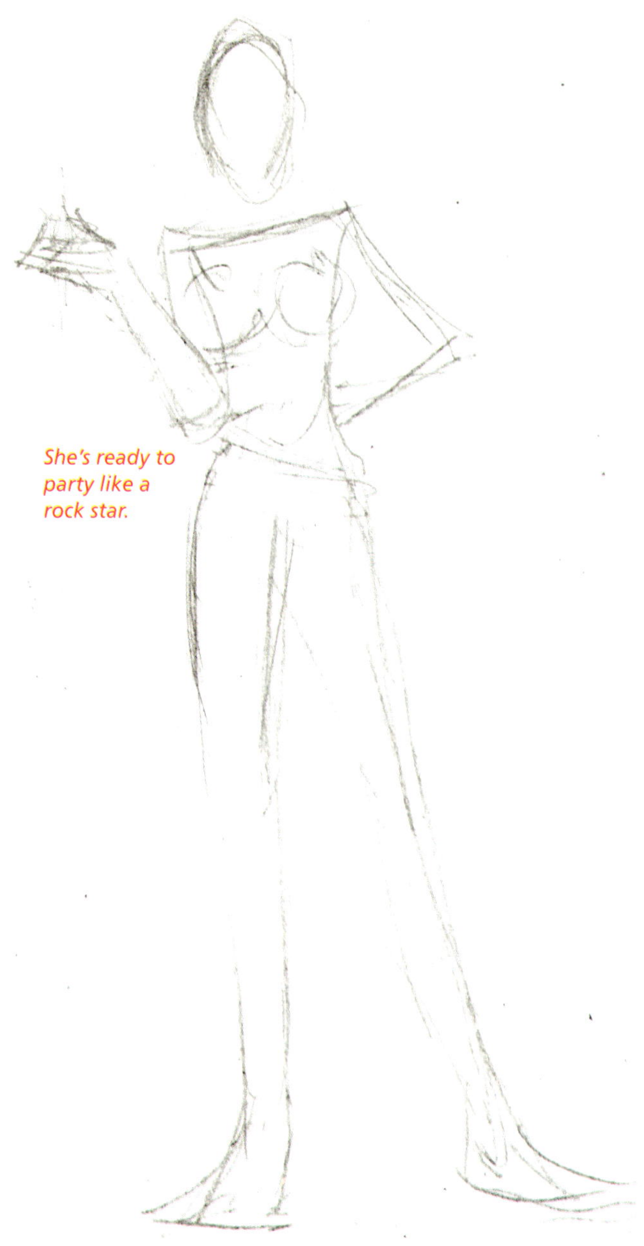

The guidelines will come in handy here.

1. Use a standard stance. With the Shaper, the fun will not be in the pose but the particulars. Yair makes her thin and leggy, with round breasts, like a supermodel.

2. Split the figure in half, right down the middle. Put her in two different dresses, two different hair styles, two different shoes, and so on. Place a champagne flute in her right hand.

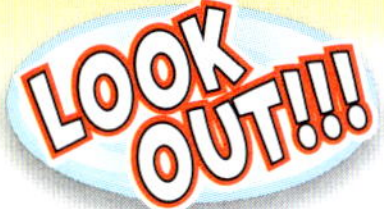

With a morphing character, it's tempting to try to capture her face, clothes, and so on in mid-change, in an image in which she looks not like one form or the other but something in between. This almost never satisfies, though, since you're working with static images. It's better to craft a bifurcated image like this and let the readers' imagination take care of the morphing details.

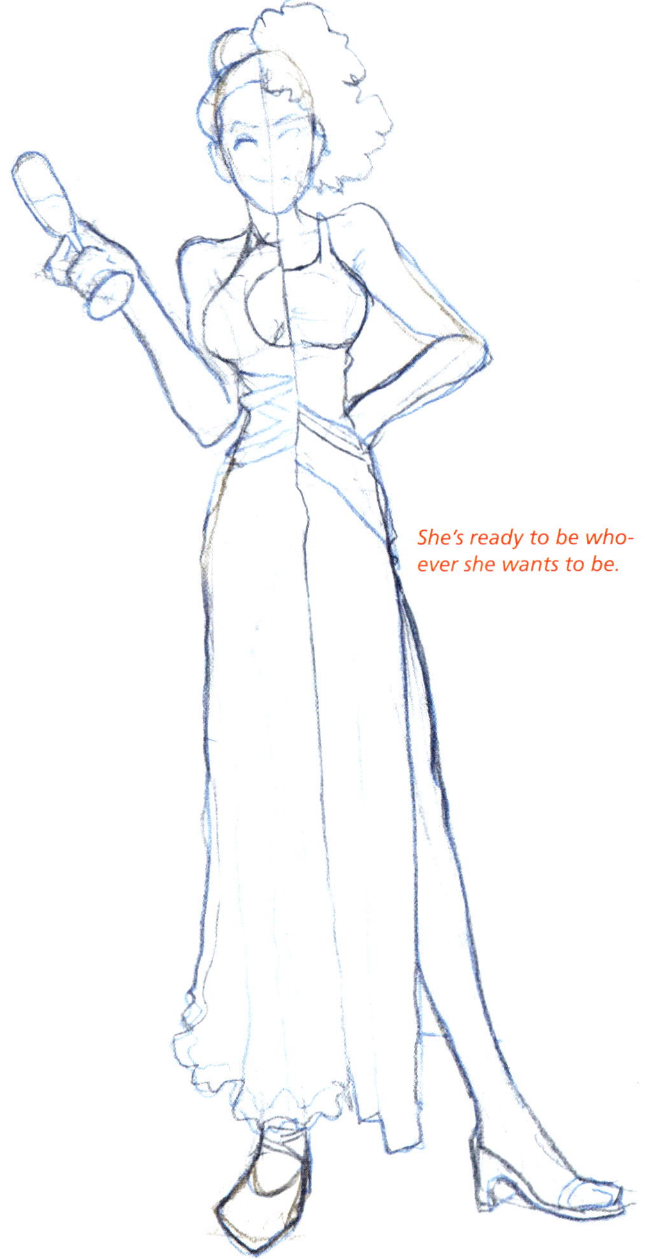

She's ready to be who-ever she wants to be.

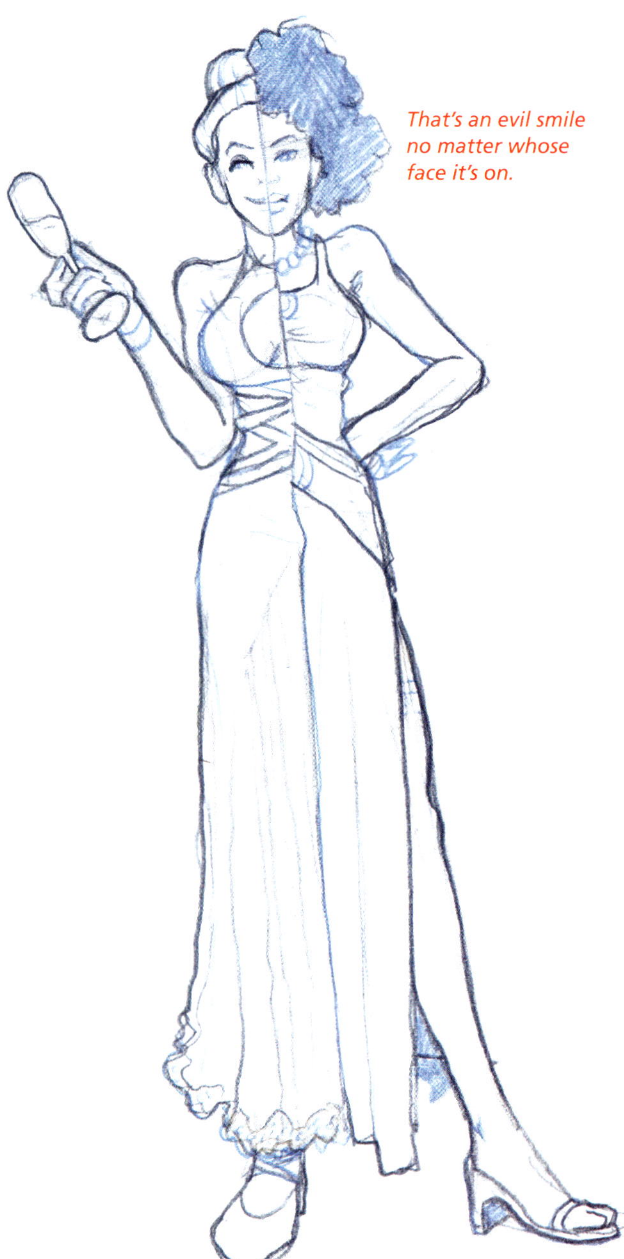

That's an evil smile no matter whose face it's on.

3. Add details to her face and her clothes. Take care to make each half distinctly different. The differences can be subtle, but it's important to even make each of her eyebrows a slightly different shape.

4. Black out her afro on the right side. Finish off the details on her dress, shoes, hands, and face. Note that even though she has two different faces, they are united by the same expression.

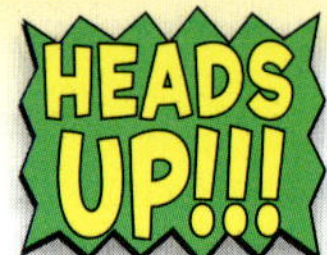

The tones and shadows here unite both halves of the image and make it work. While the two forms that Shaper takes are different from each other, the sun falls on them the same way. Show the same consistency in all of your drawings, and you'll go far.

Who would you like to talk with?

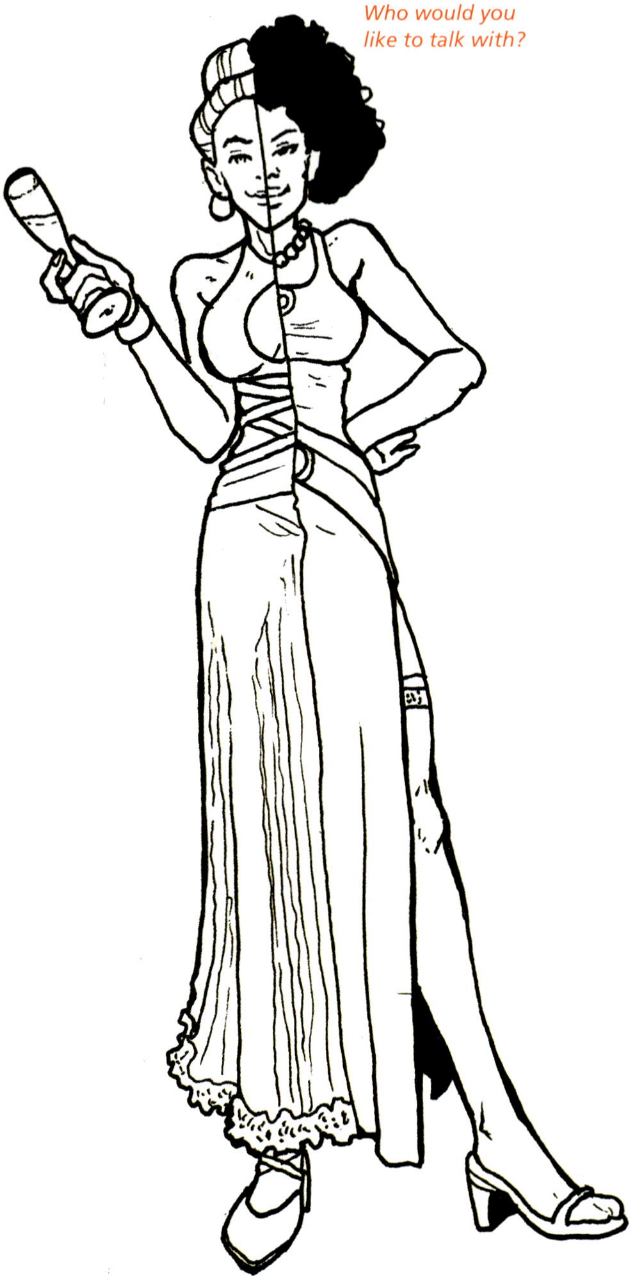

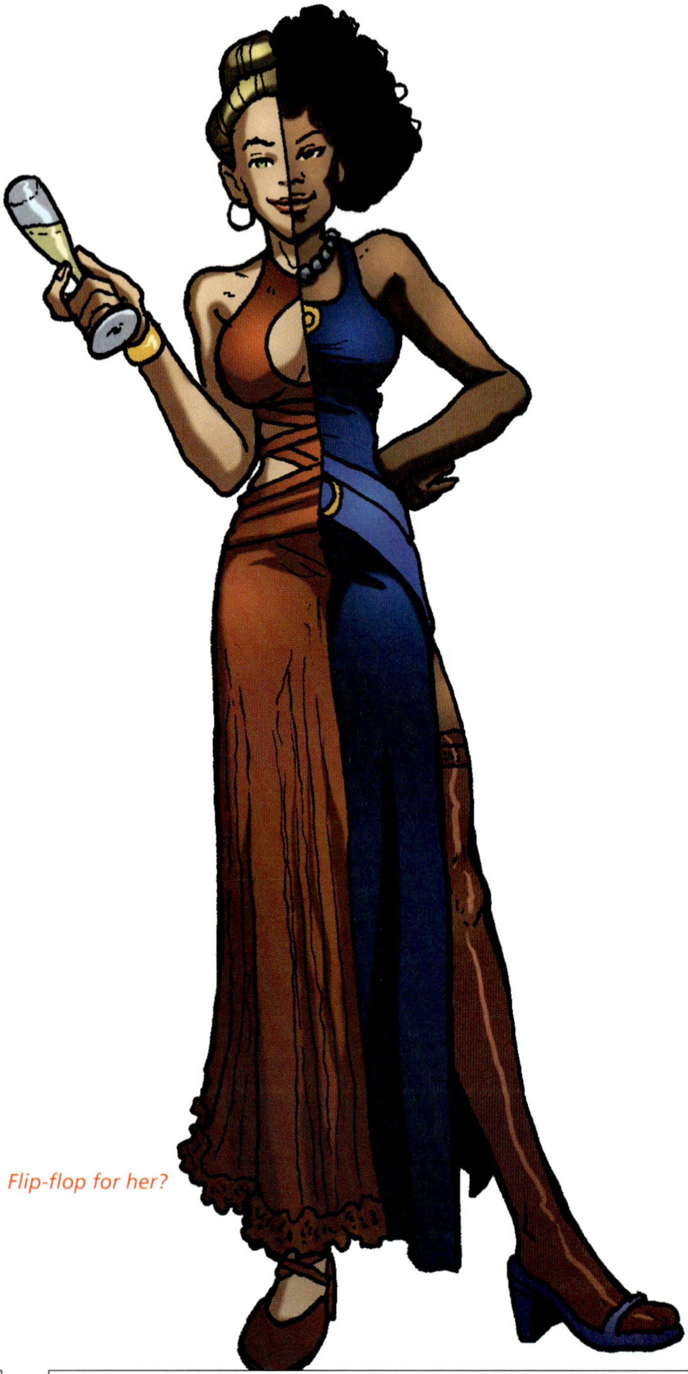

Flip-flop for her?

5. Use gentle lines throughout. The skirt on the left calls for lighter lines on its surface, although the one on the right does not.

6. Think contrasts. Go with Caucasian skin on one side and African American on the other. Put one in blue and the other in red. Give one black hair and the other blonde. Have fun with the differences.

GIANT

Giant's mother is the world's leading researcher into size changing. She used both him and his sister as her first human experiments when villains attacked her lab and tried to steal her secrets. She was killed, but Giant and his sister Shrinker lived on to exact their revenge on their mother's killers.

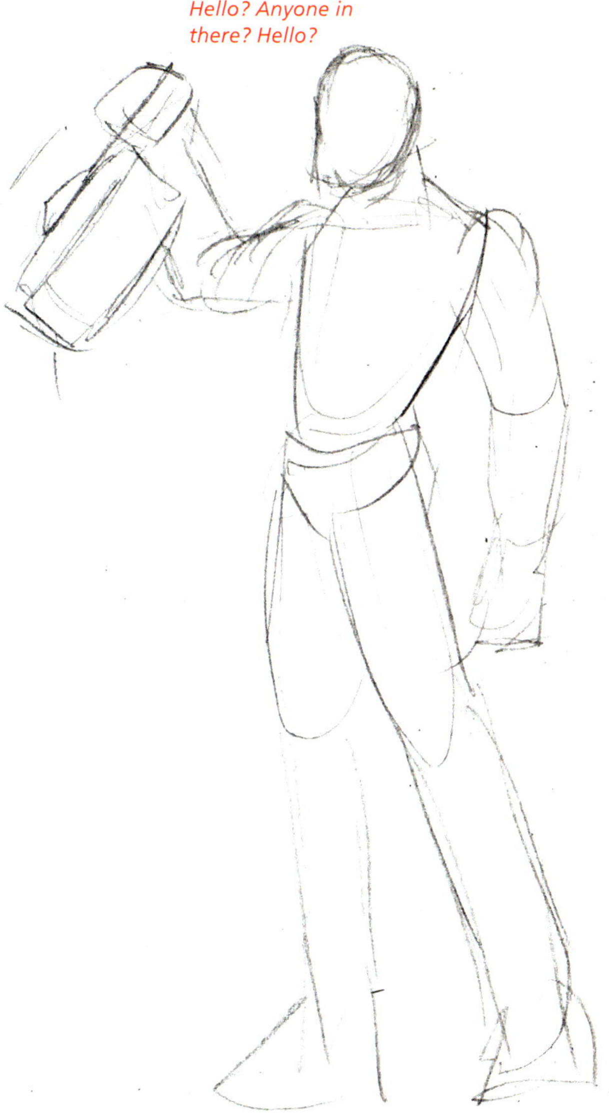

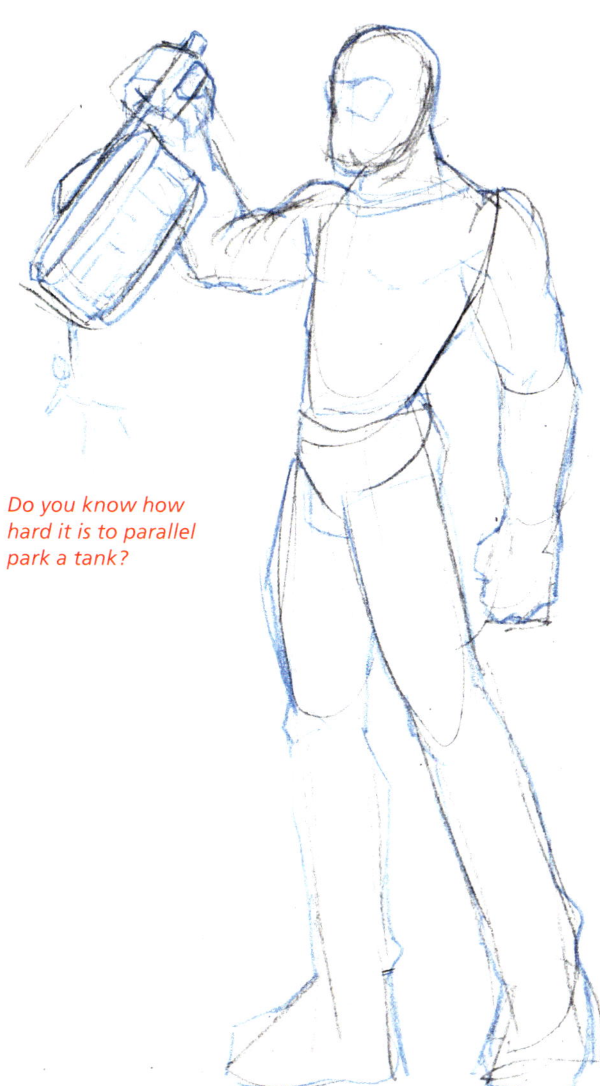

1. Break down Giant's pose. While he is thick of limb, he merely looks muscular. To give a sense of scale, we need to put a tank in his hand and let him shake it around like a toy.

2. Add clothes and a domino mask. With some refinements, we can now see that the vehicle Giant is shaking is a tank. Its driver hangs from the bottom for his life.

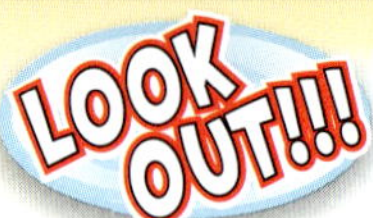

It's not enough to say that a character is particularly short or tall. You have to provide some kind of standard against which the viewer can measure the character. Otherwise, there's no way to tell what size a character may be.

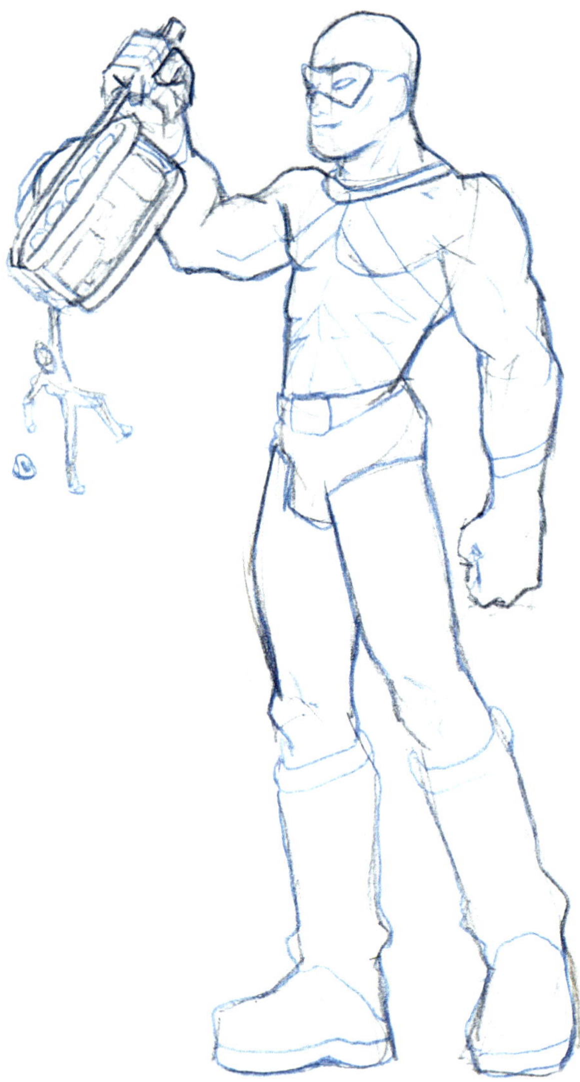

He's a big boy now.

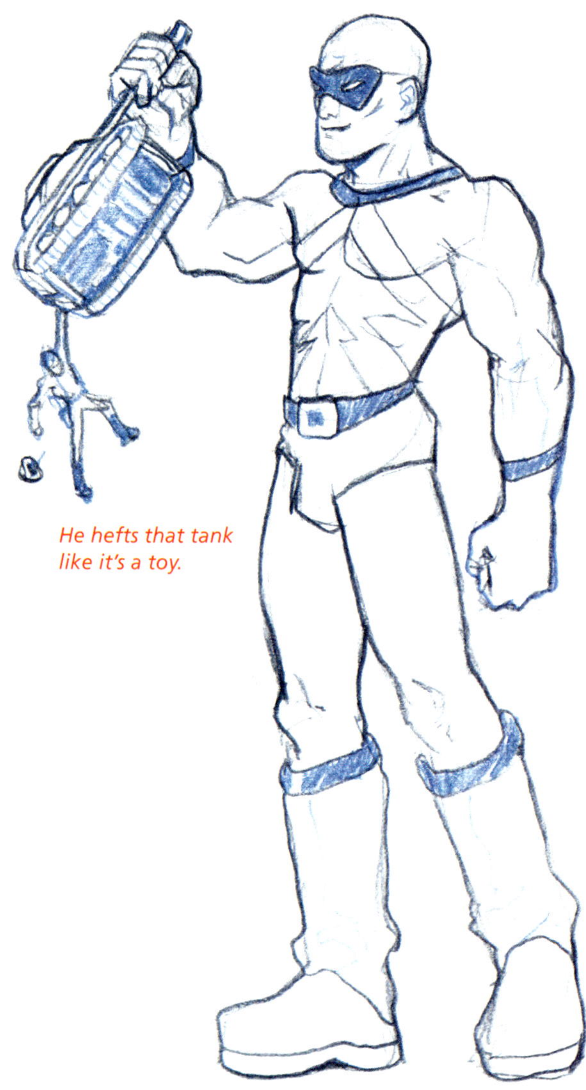

He hefts that tank like it's a toy.

3. Add more details, like the treads on the tank and the eyes in the mask. Notice the icon on his chest, which is a series of up-pointing arrows that grow larger as you go along. Having the soldier drop his helmet is a nice touch, as it emphasizes the danger he's in.

4. Black out the mask and the trim on the costume, as well as the underside of the tank. Refine the Giant's musculature.

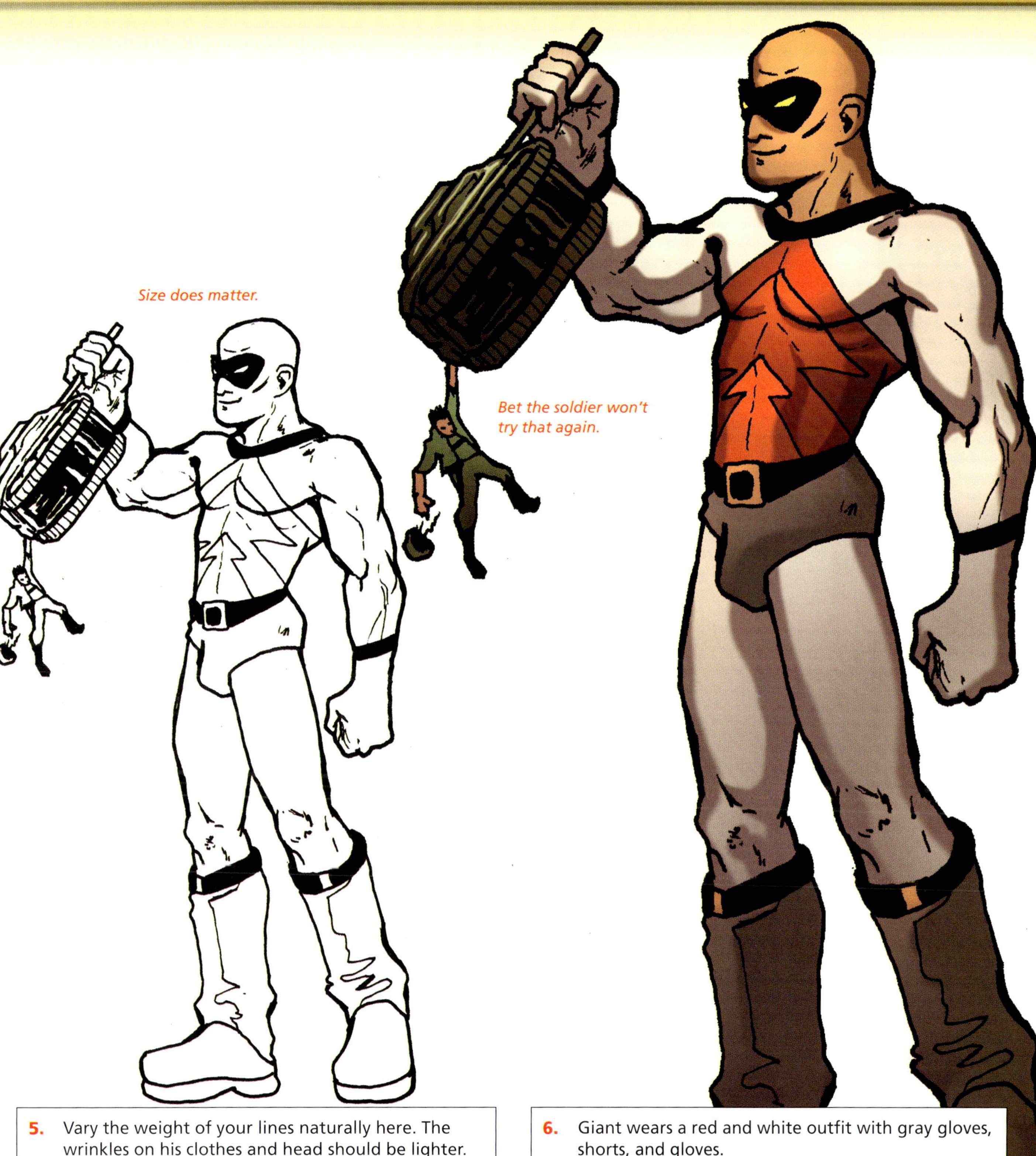

5. Vary the weight of your lines naturally here. The wrinkles on his clothes and head should be lighter.

6. Giant wears a red and white outfit with gray gloves, shorts, and gloves.

THE SHRINKER

The Shrinker is the Giant's little sister—literally. She's worked with him to discover the identity of the people behind her mother's murder, but exacting their revenge has not made up for her loss. Sometimes she just wants to shrink away to nothing.

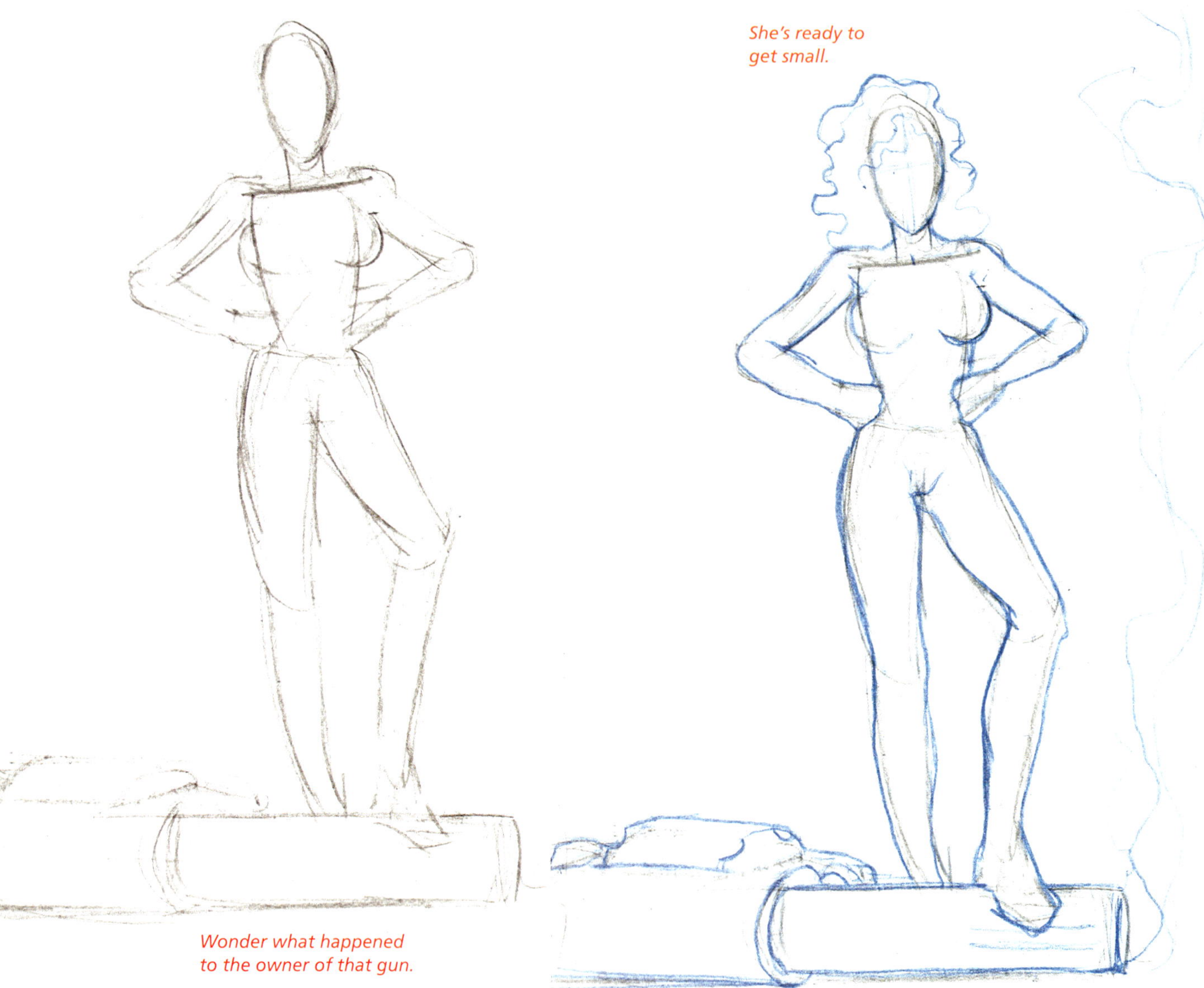

She's ready to get small.

Wonder what happened to the owner of that gun.

1. Break down the Shrinker's pose. She stands with one foot on top of a smoking gun, her hands on her hips in a traditionally heroic pose. The weapon gives us a sense of her scale: tiny.

2. Give Shrinker long, curly hair and a skintight outfit. Add a line of smoke curling up from the barrel of the gun. Note the guidelines on the face.

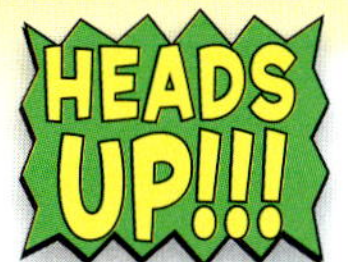

The best way to show scale with a small character is to take a standard item—something everyone can recognize—and enlarge it. Draw it bigger, replicating details that you normally wouldn't. Then place the figure in the same scene and show off your skills.

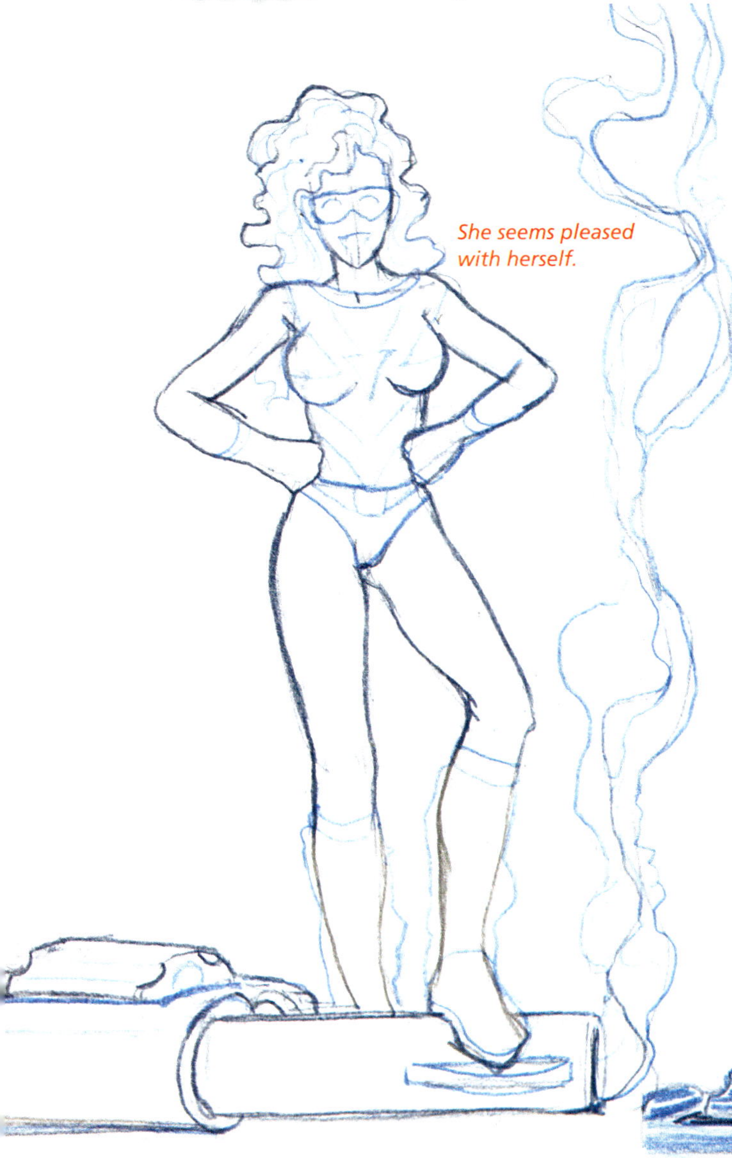

She seems pleased with herself.

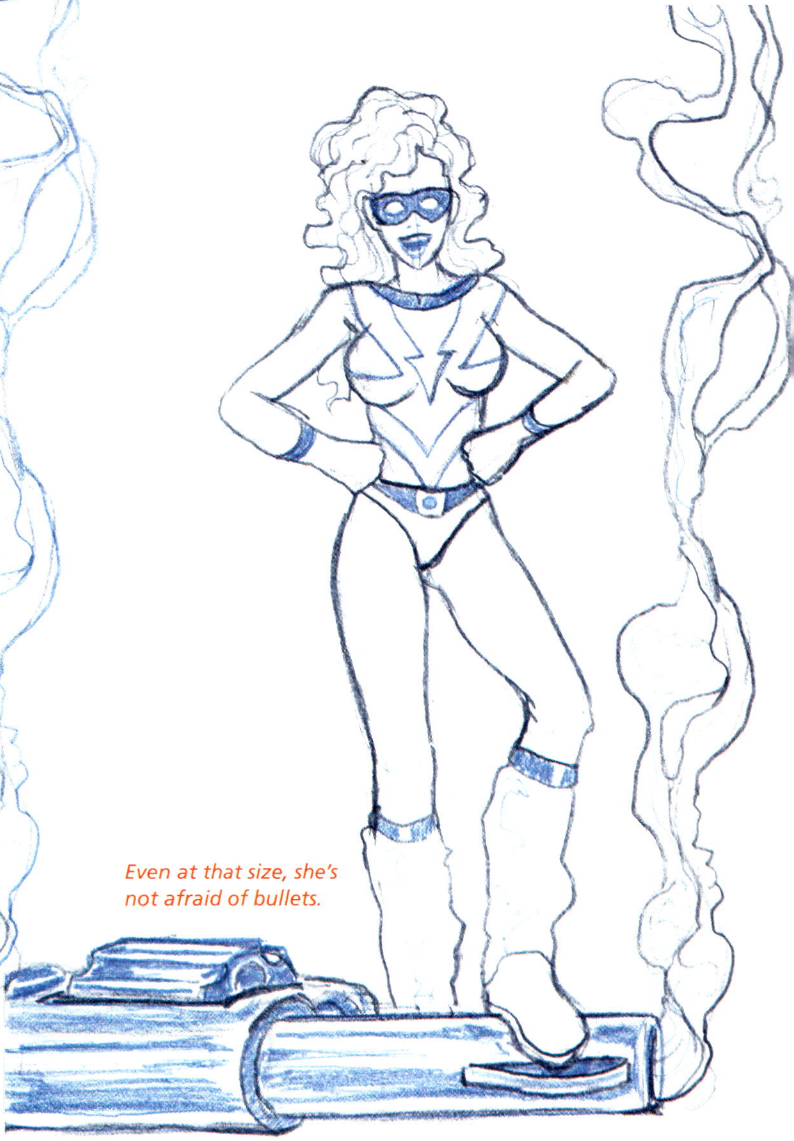

Even at that size, she's not afraid of bullets.

3. Add her icon to her outfit's chest. It's the exact opposite of her brother's symbol. Put some loose boots on her, and a set of tiny goggles as well.

4. Black out her domino mask, too, and blacken all over the gun. Add some wrinkles to her boots and some depth to the curling smoke.

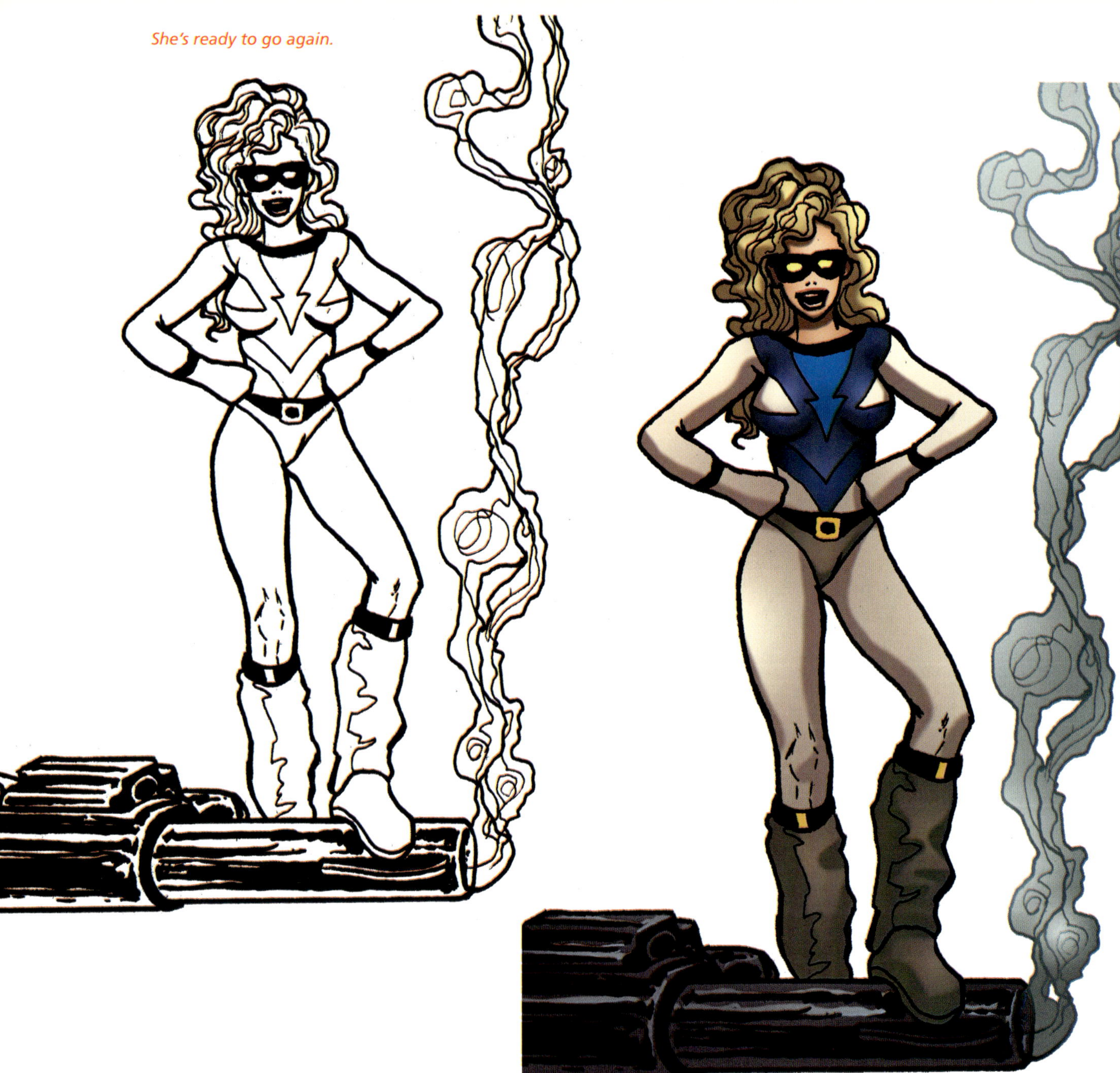

She's ready to go again.

Tiny but tough!

5. Use mostly consistent ink lines here. This time around, Yair even uses heavier lines in Shrinker's hair and in the smoke from the gun. It's a different style, but it's just as effective, especially given the relative size of the bits involved.

6. Use similar colors to Giant. This time go with a blue icon instead of red, though. Use grays on the bits of the gun that aren't entirely blacked out.

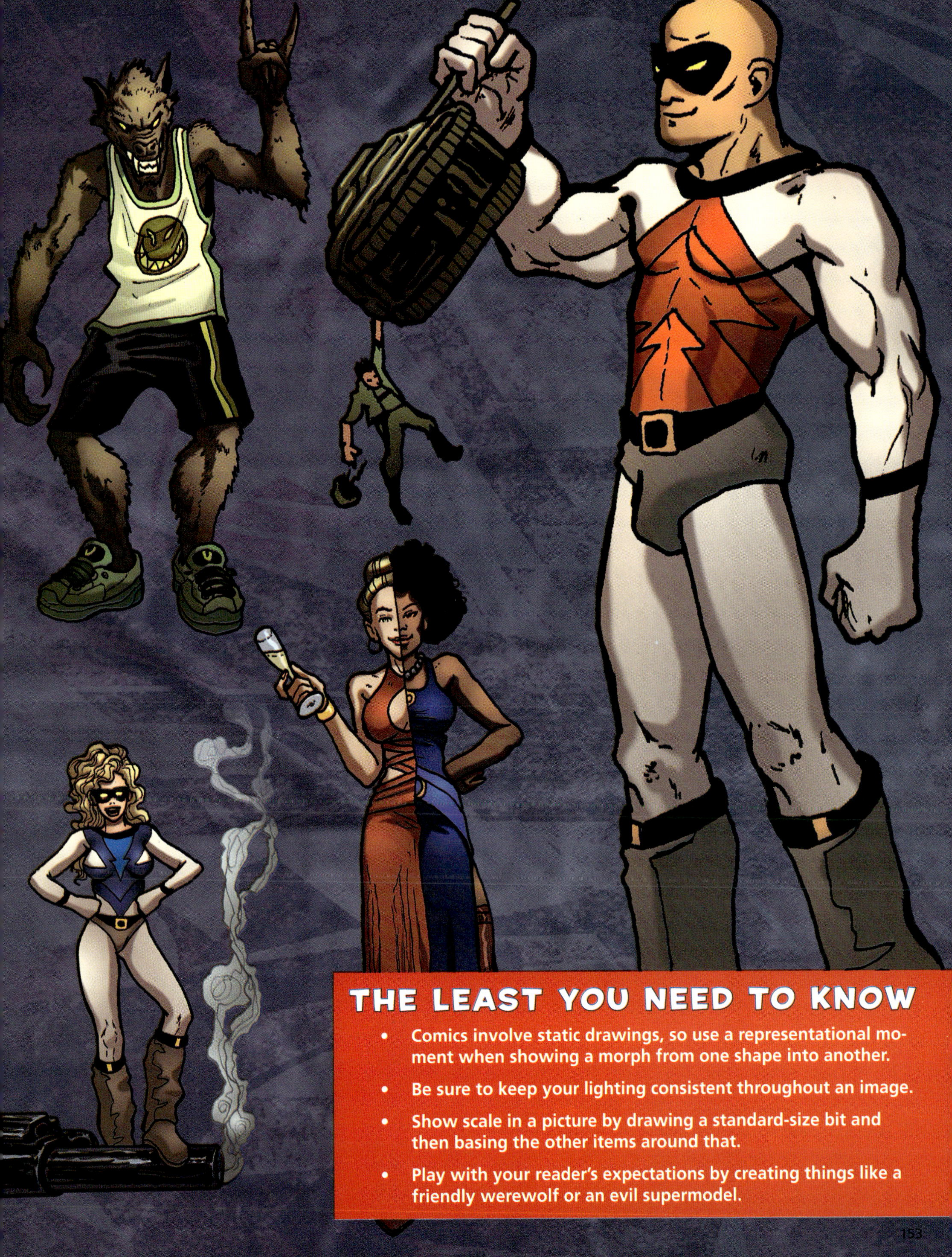

THE LEAST YOU NEED TO KNOW

- Comics involve static drawings, so use a representational moment when showing a morph from one shape into another.
- Be sure to keep your lighting consistent throughout an image.
- Show scale in a picture by drawing a standard-size bit and then basing the other items around that.
- Play with your reader's expectations by creating things like a friendly werewolf or an evil supermodel.

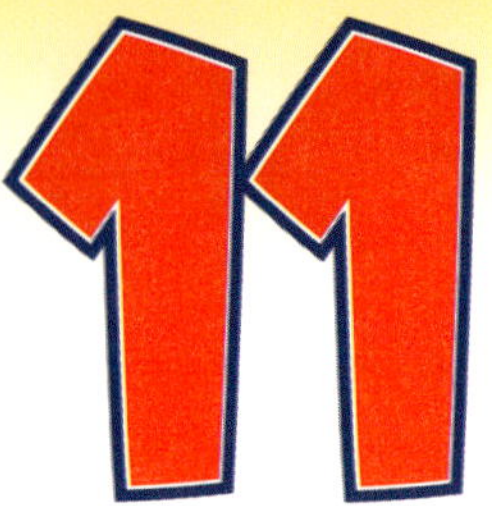

NATIONAL ICONS: THOSE WHO REPRESENT

In This Chapter

- American tech at its best
- America at its worst
- A silver hero from Argentina
- A blast from the Soviet past

Some people with superpowers have a well-developed sense of patriotism. Perhaps it has something to do with the source of their powers, or maybe they've always been a patriot and now have the means to display that. Either way, they fly their chosen flag proudly.

We start off with a modern American hero: the USAndroid. This combat-ready robot represents the pinnacle of American know-how when it comes to blowing things away. It moves like a walking tank and fights like one, too.

Then we move on to a rough-hewn hero: the Real American. This patriotic gunman has an answer for those who are afraid to stand up for their Constitutional rights. Fight harder! He never met a trouble he didn't like to shoot.

From there, we head south to meet the Argentine, the national hero of Argentina. This silver-skinned gaucho commands the power of the blazing sun in his hands. (Here's to Yair's homeland, too!)

We wrap up with the Supreme Soviet. This relic from the Cold War flies on the wings of the Russian eagle but wields the hammer and sickle from the Soviet flag. Take care around this bloodthirsty comrade.

THE USANDROID

While the vast majority of supers are power-mad villains or freelance vigilantes, the United States government decided that it needed to line up some powers of its own. To that end, it began the USAndroid project, a multibillion-dollar effort to create a powerful, artificially intelligent machine unquestioningly under United States control. From that effort sprang the national *icon* known as the USAndroid.

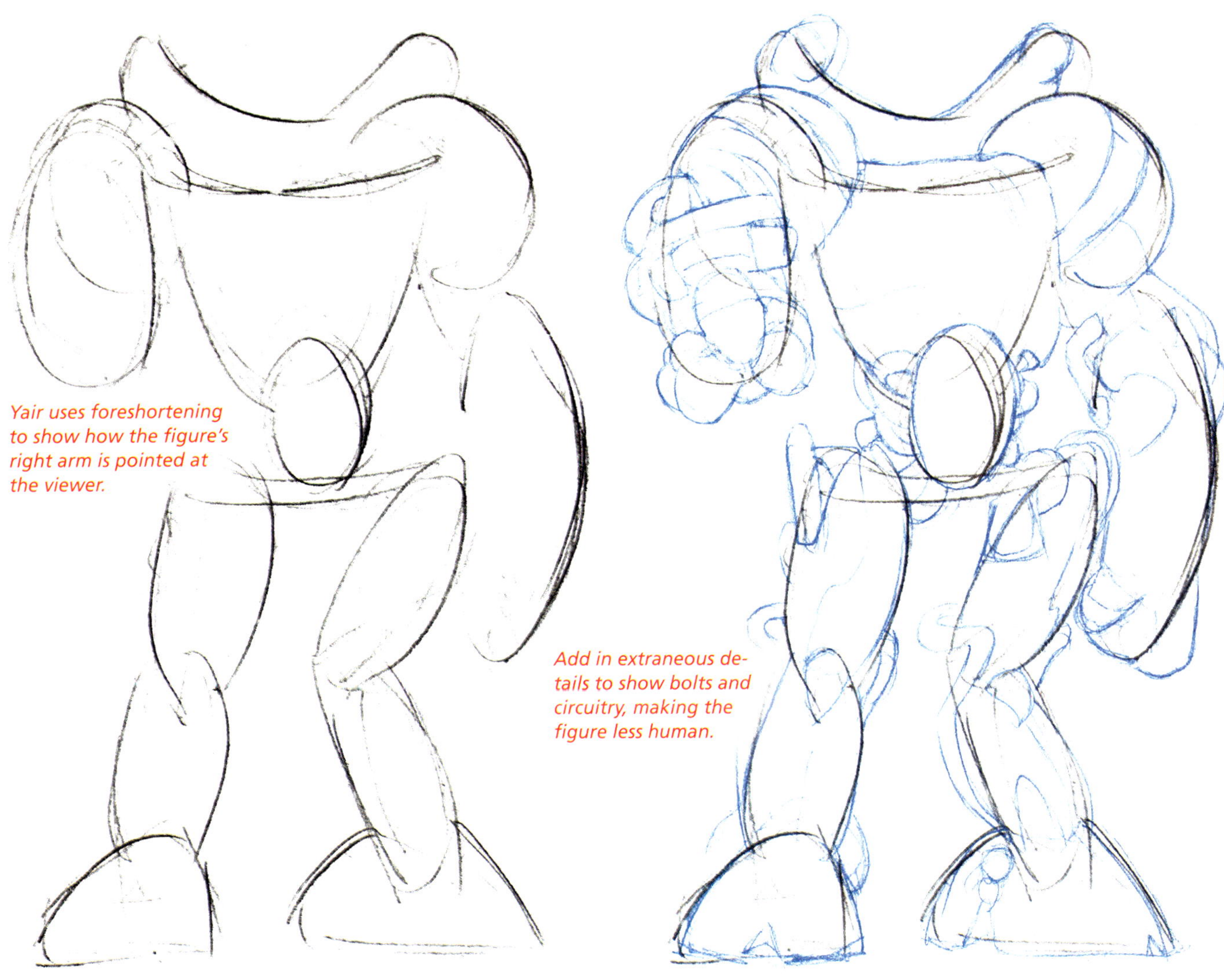

1. Sketch out the USAndroid's basic shapes. Its figure is based upon human anatomy but not limited to it. Note the lack of a head.

2. Rough in some more details. Note how the legs bend backward, like those of a dog. Work out the three-fingered hands, and show the rocket-launcher tubes over the figure's shoulders.

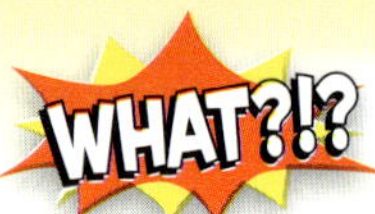

An **icon** is a symbol. In the case of a national icon, it represents the spirit of the nation in question. This can be a heavy load for a person to bear.

Ready to mete out justice!

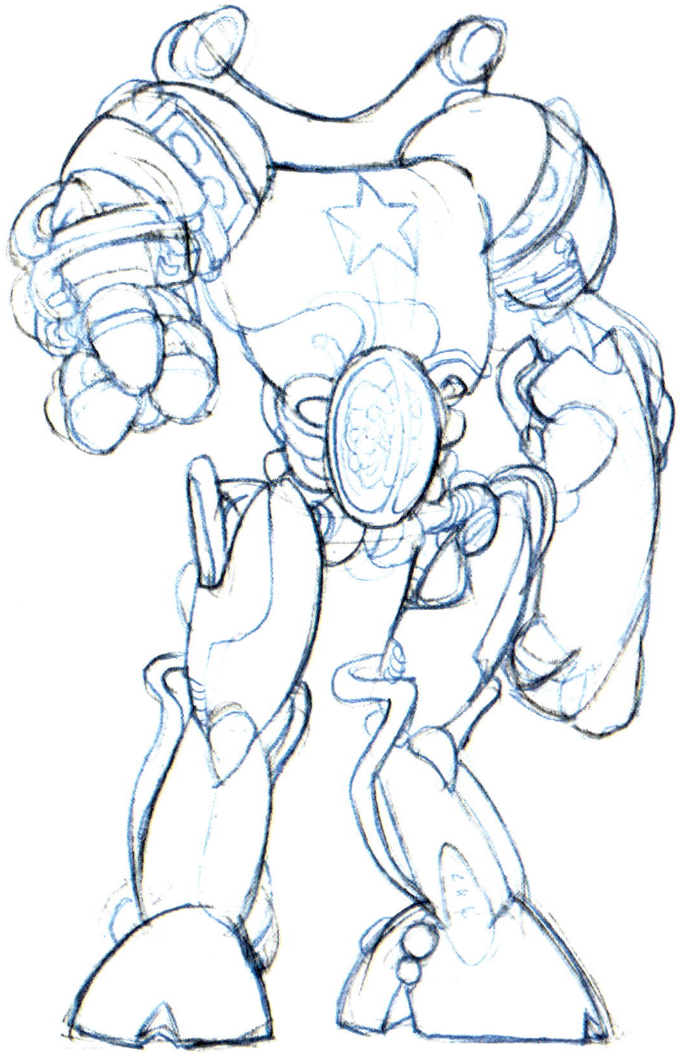

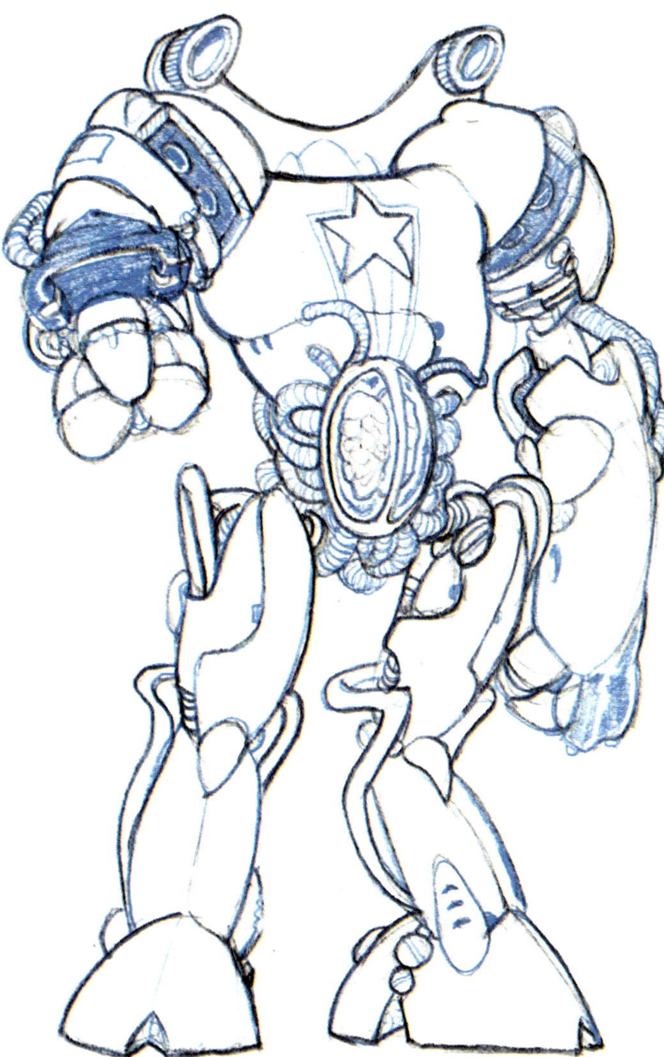

This thing must weigh tons.

3. Add more detail to the hydraulic tubes and machinery. Show the brain inside the armored housing on the USAndroid's belly. Place a shooting American star on the figure's chest.

4. Work on the details here. Add ribbing to the tubes and the softer parts of the machine. Trim the edges with hatching, and darken in deeper bits. Make it look more like a machine.

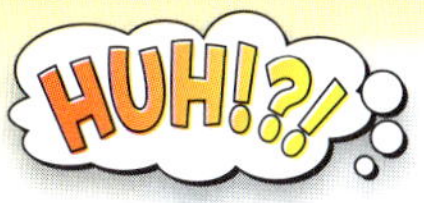

The USAndroid has what looks like a human brain encased in an armored pod on its belly. This is actually a computerized brain composed of self-aware nanites that form a hive mind. It's virtually indestructible, as long as the tiny nanites (microscopic machines) survive.

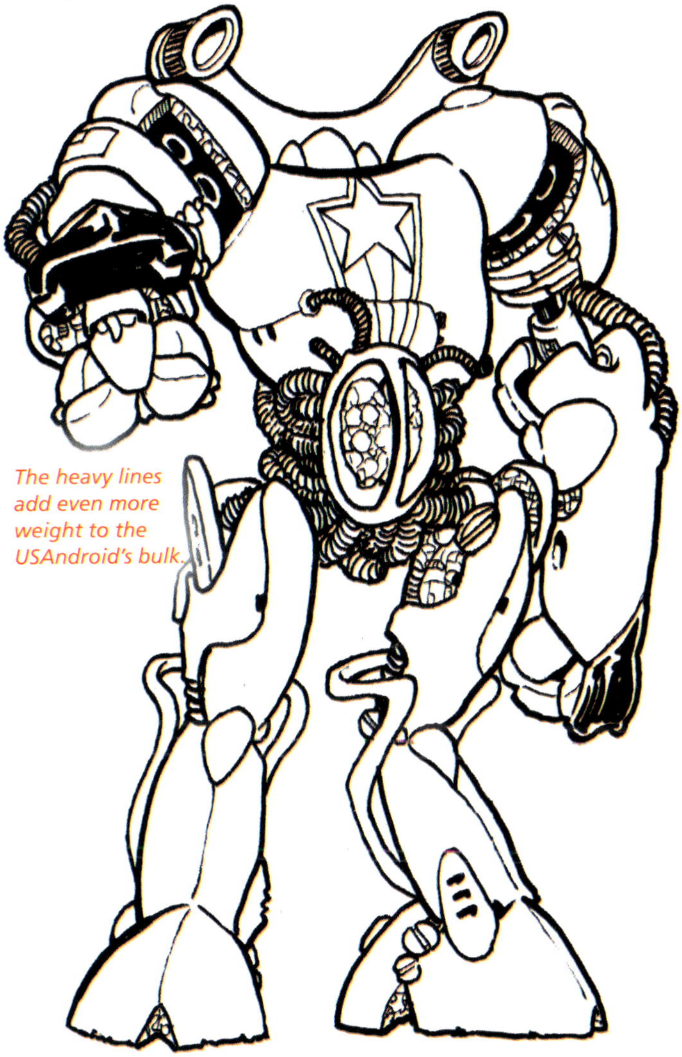

Don't forget to add the Stars and Bars on each shoulder.

The heavy lines add even more weight to the USAndroid's bulk.

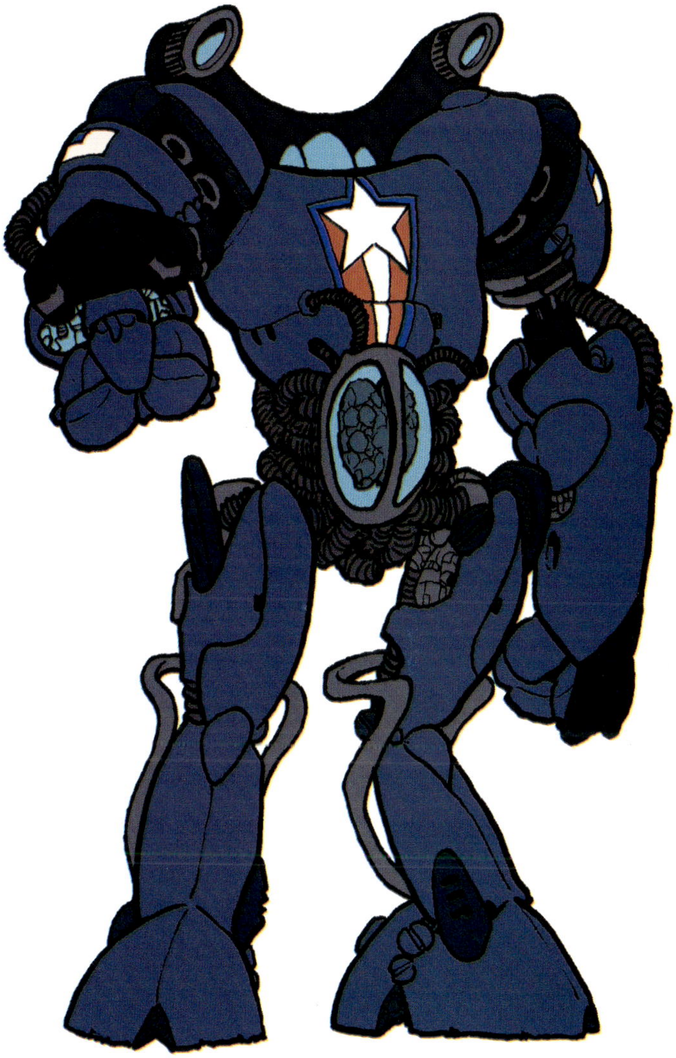

5. Use heavy ink lines on the outer edges of the figure, but go with lighter ones to show seam lines, decorations, and so on. Black out the darkest areas. You can handle the shading when you move to add colors.

6. Go with a navy blue for most of the figure, just like you'd find on the starry field of an American flag. Leave the star white, and color the three stripes zooming up to it red-white-red. Use a lighter blue for highlighted areas, and go with a couple shades of gray for tubing and hydraulics.

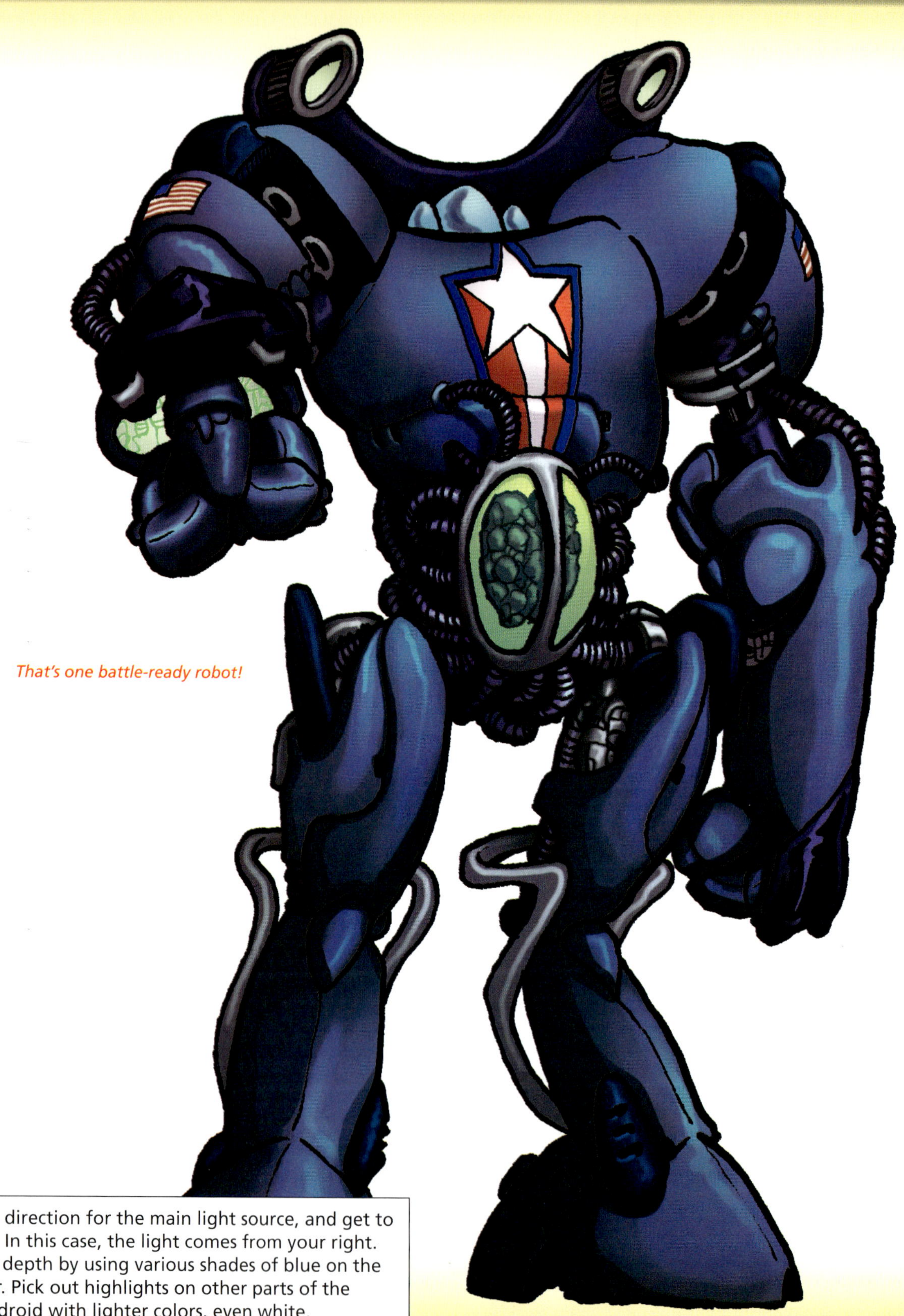

That's one battle-ready robot!

7. Pick a direction for the main light source, and get to work. In this case, the light comes from your right. Show depth by using various shades of blue on the armor. Pick out highlights on other parts of the USAndroid with lighter colors, even white.

THE REAL AMERICAN

The Real American loves his country and works hard to stand up for it. He's risked his life on battlefields from Afghanistan to LA, and he's ready to do the same to ensure the basic liberties of all Americans are protected for when they need them most.

If he could hold more than two guns at a time, he would.

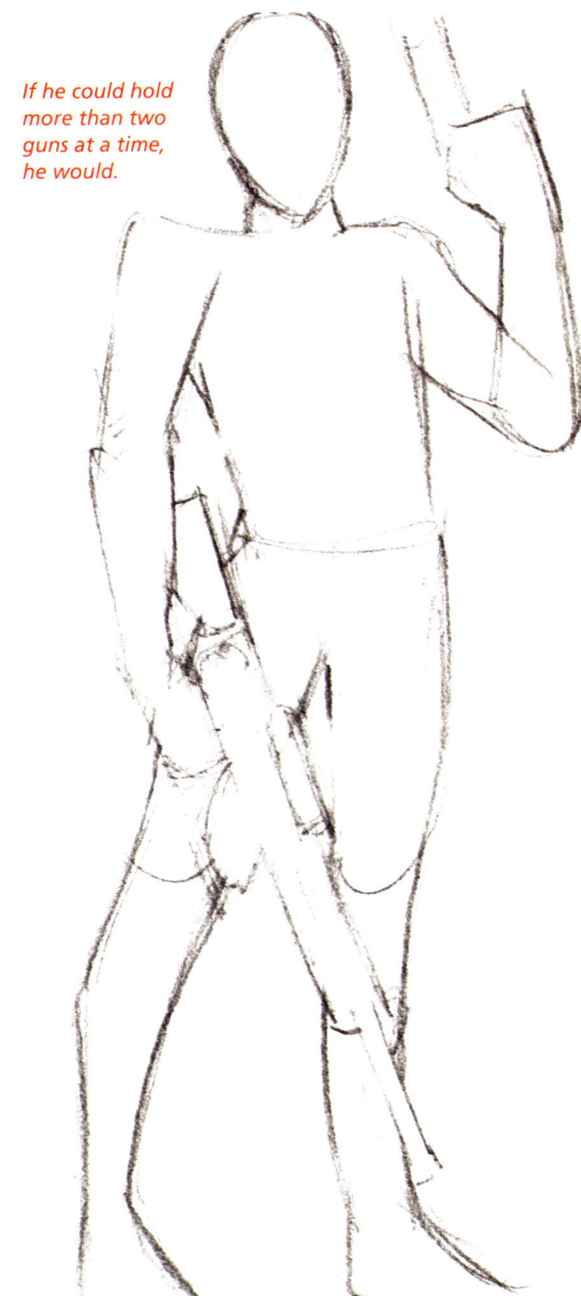

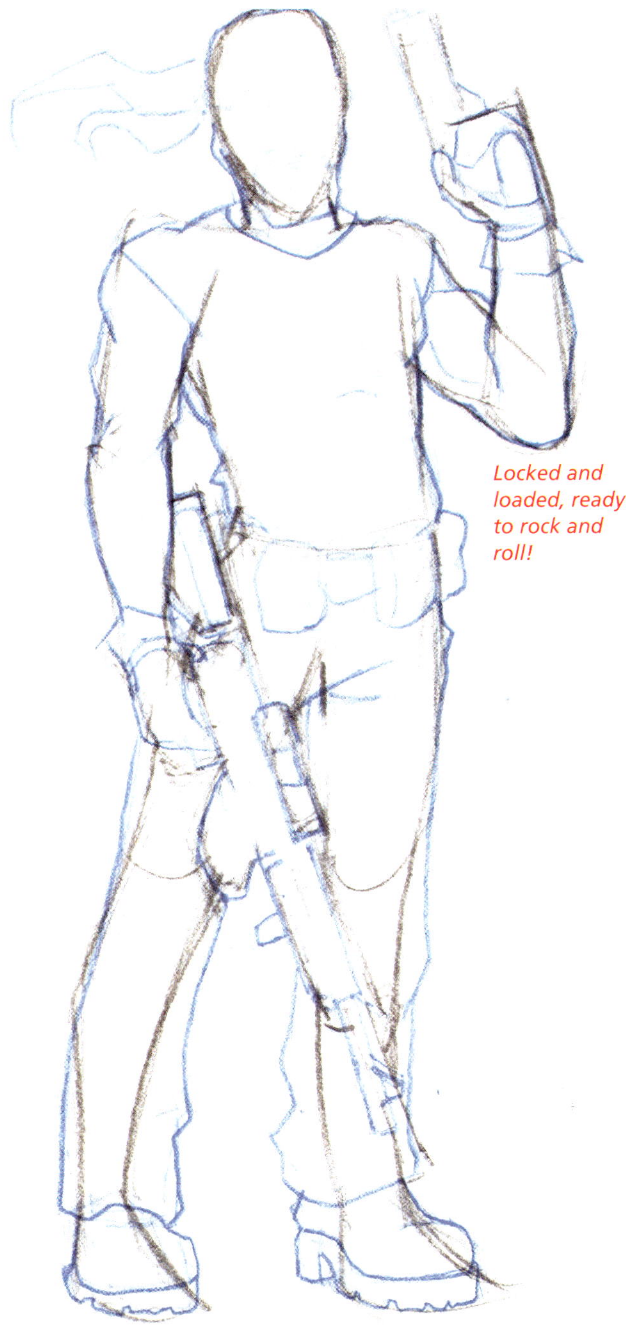

Locked and loaded, ready to rock and roll!

1. Work out the rough shape of the figure. He doesn't have a heroic build, although he is trim. To make his points, he relies on guns instead of fists, and his physique represents that. Put a gun in each hand.

2. Rough in some details. Put him in pants and a sleeveless shirt. Add some ammo pouches to his belt. Put a bandana around his head and let its tails fly.

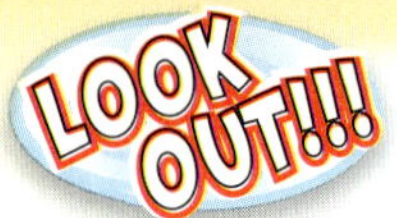

Some who disagree with the Real American might see him as overzealous, but he's okay with that. After all, he's fighting to preserve their rights, no matter what they may wish to do with them.

This is your basic, American, one-man army.

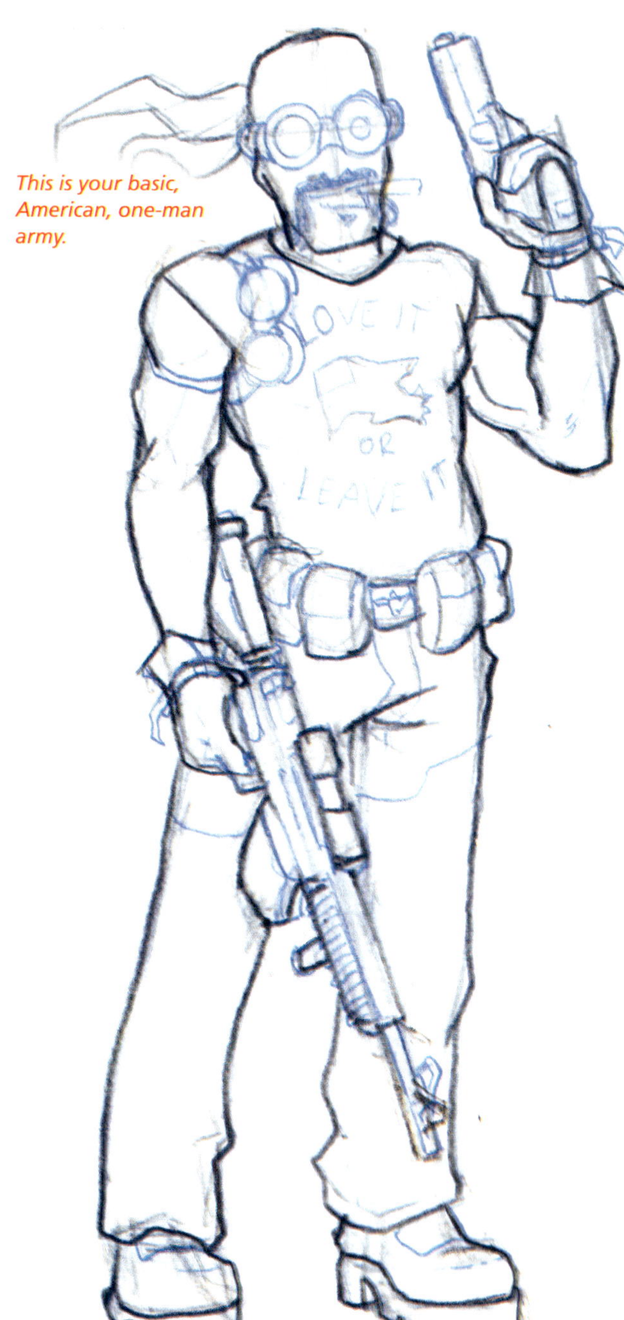

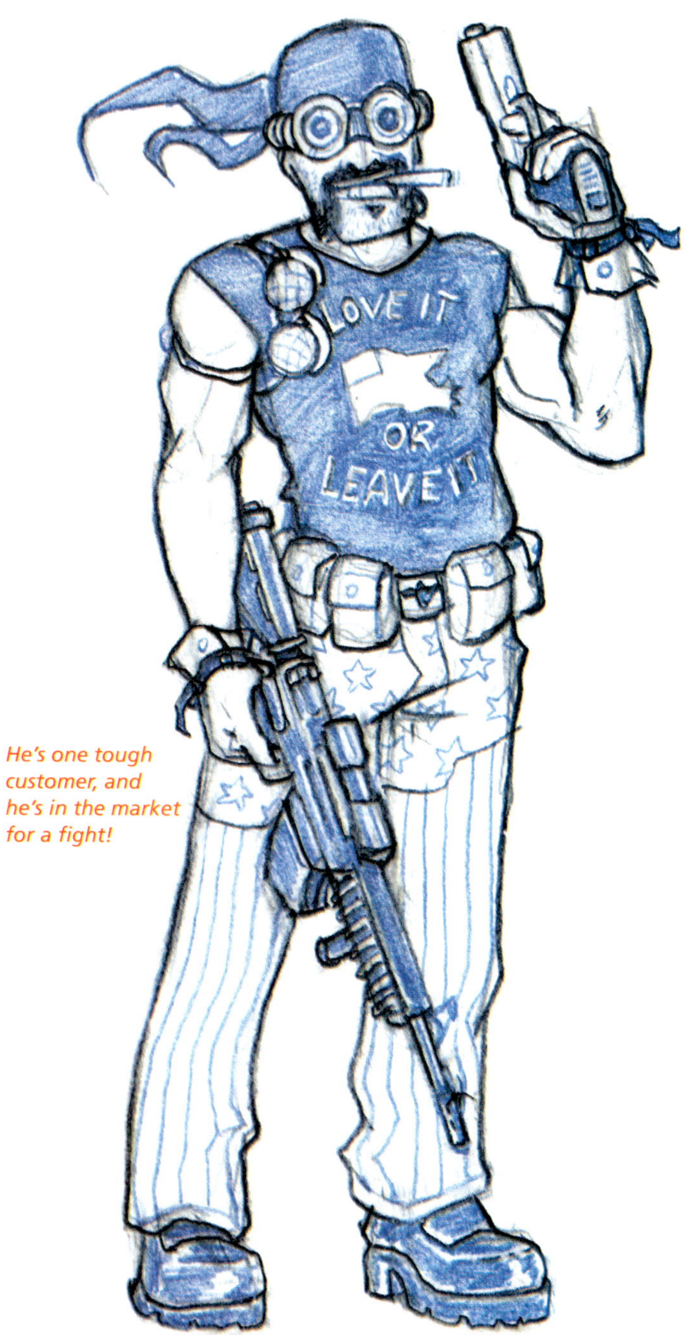

He's one tough customer, and he's in the market for a fight!

3. Detail the weapons a bit more. Use photo references if you like. Give him some night-vision goggles and slap a patriotic slogan on that shirt. Strap a couple grenades around his shoulder, too.

4. Black in the shirt and the bandana. Give him some United States flag pants and a Fu Manchu mustache. Put a cigarillo in his mouth to give him something to chew on between villains.

The stubble on the chin and the hair on the arms add to the machismo.

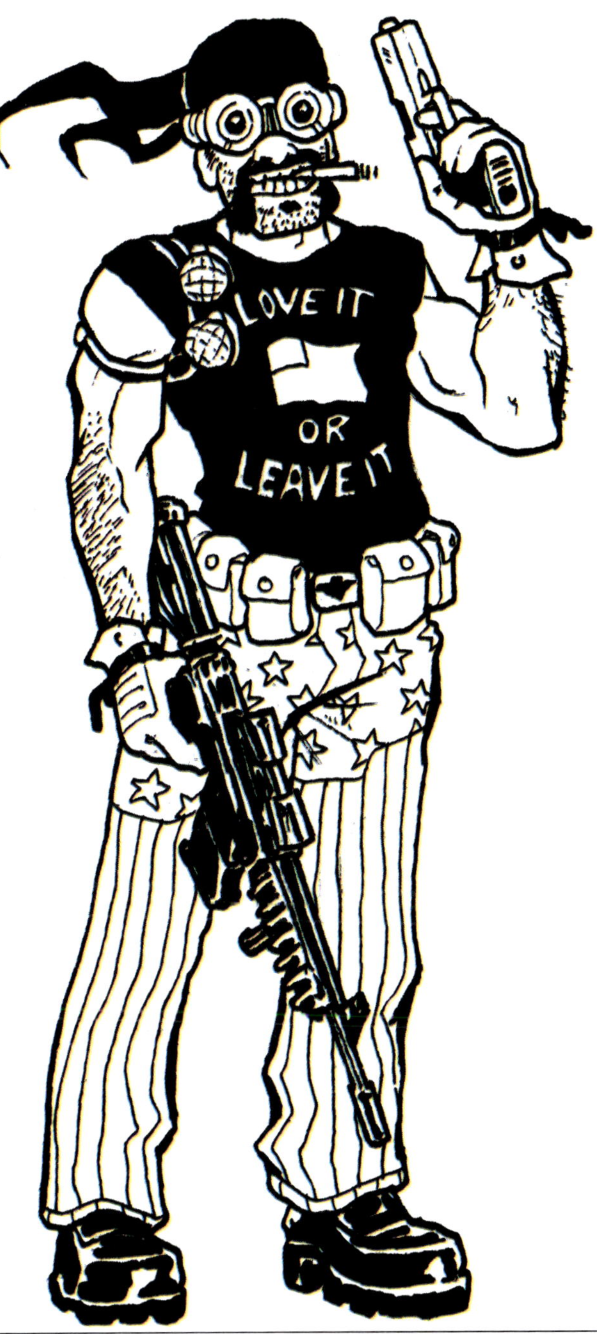

The single gold tooth is a nice touch.

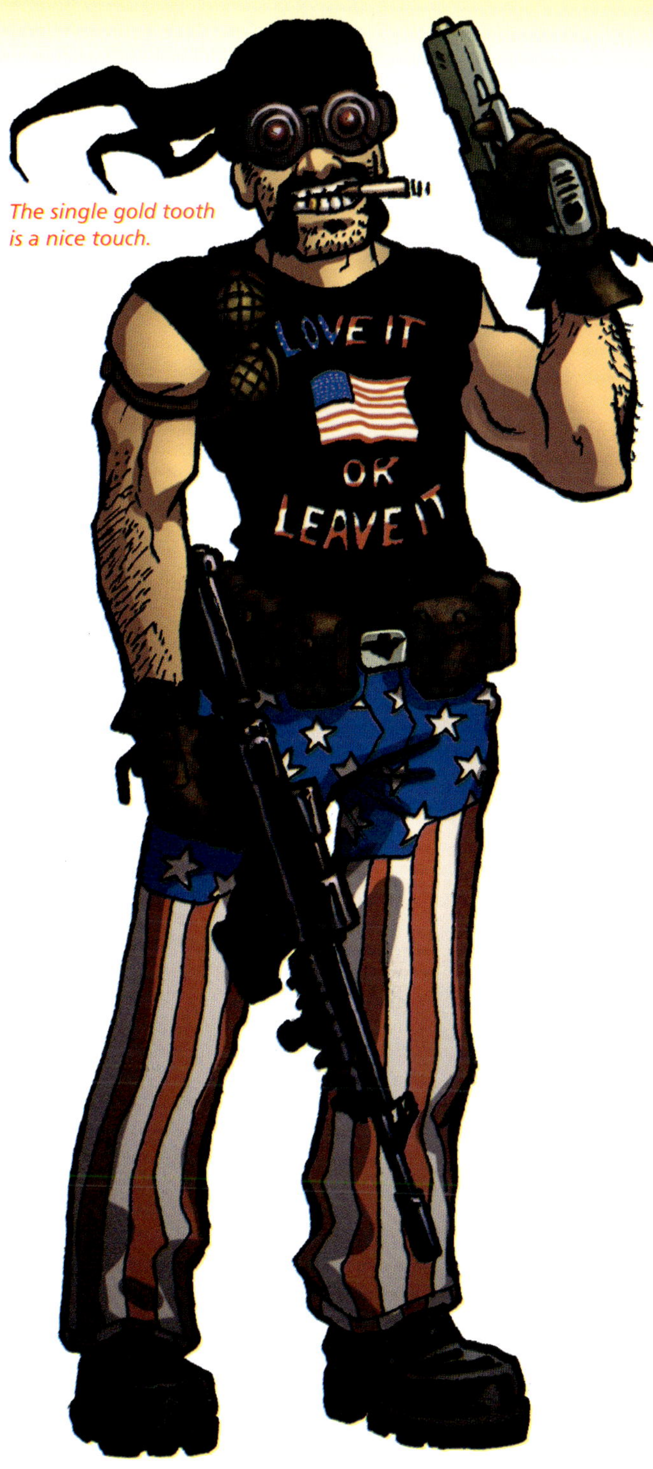

5. Go thick with the inks here. The Real American should be gritty and grimy. A few oil stains from his motorcycle wouldn't hurt his look at all.

6. The pants are red, white, and blue, of course. Go with black for the shirt and bandana, but use American flag colors again for his slogan's lettering, and for the flag on his chest. Gray works great for the guns, goggles, and boots, as well as for shading throughout.

THE ARGENTINE

For the Argentine, we're going to hit the classic elements of Argentine culture. "Argent" means silver, so that's what we use for the Argentine's skin. The Argentine flag features the sun on a field of white surrounded by bars of light blue, and Yair does a great job of working this into the *gaucho*-inspired design.

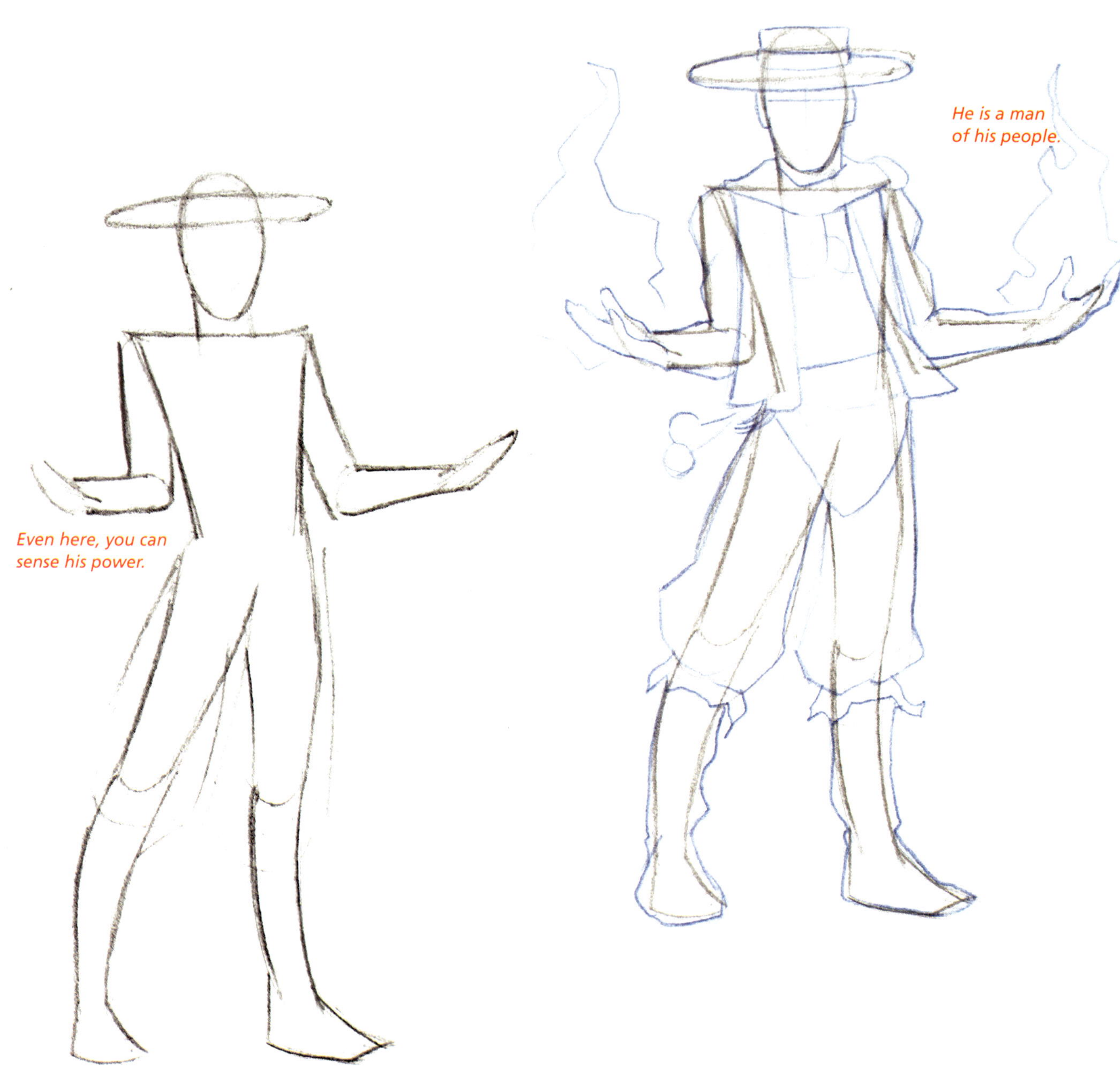

1. Break down the Argentine into basic shapes. Give him a heroic stance with his palms out and up, as if cupping the rays of the sun. Put a ring around his head to represent the rim of his hat.

2. Add in the outline of the Argentine's clothes. Include his hat, pants, boots, vest, and so on. Place fire around his hands and attach a set of bolos to his belt.

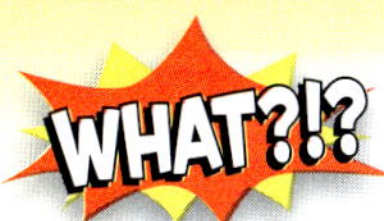

A **gaucho** is a South American version of a cowboy, a cattle rancher who lives in the country and spends much of his time wrangling animals. Argentina still has a large gaucho population, although their numbers dwindle every year. Their characteristic outfits, though, mark them for who they are, and we make use of that here.

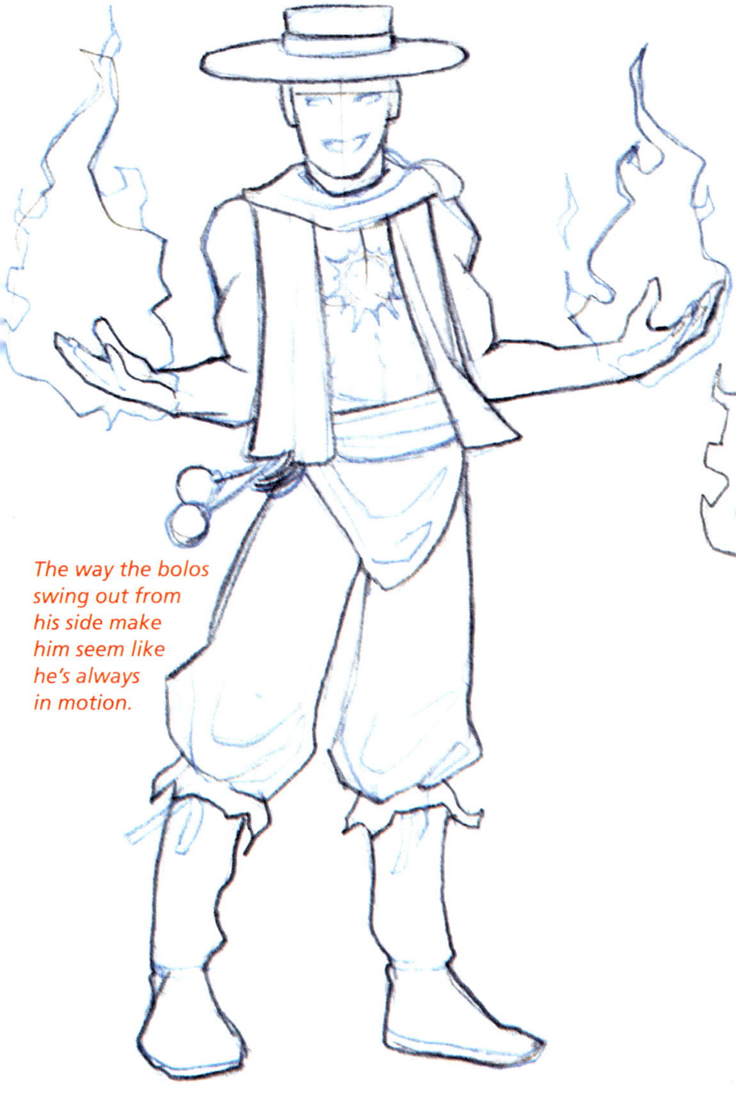

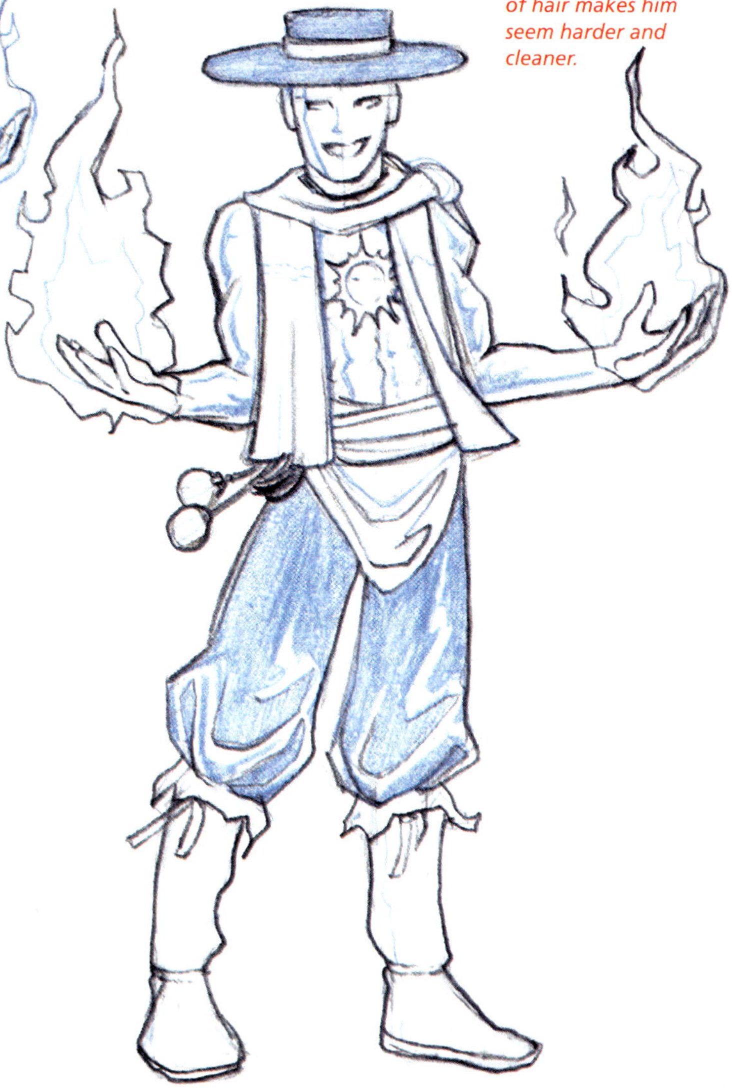

The total absence of hair makes him seem harder and cleaner.

The way the bolos swing out from his side make him seem like he's always in motion.

3. Show his face and eyes. Add the symbol of the sun to his chest. Use the Argentine flag as a reference. Add folds to the clothing. Pay attention to his sash and vest and to how the pants bunch around his knees.

4. Finish the details. Since his skin is silvery, use reflective lines to show its metallic sheen. Add another layer to the fire to show that the center is a different temperature than the edges.

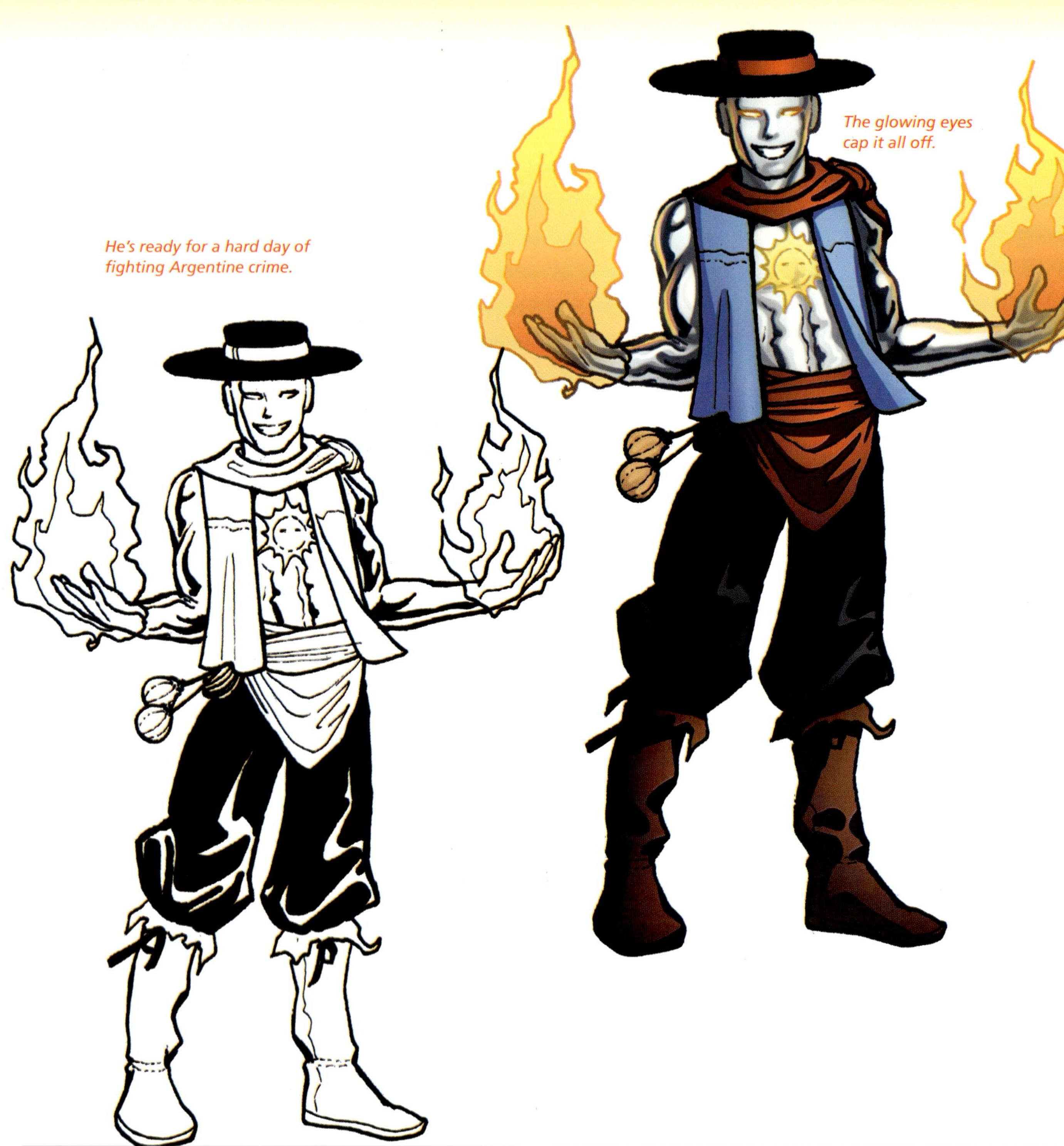

5. Black out the jeans and hat. Use heavy lines on his metallic skin to emphasize its weight. Don't forget to remove the guidelines, like the ones that divided his face.

6. Use varying shades of gray to give the skin a silvery look. The boots are brown, and the pants and hat are black. The hatband and sash are red, while the vest is blue. The way the light blue of the vest frames his chest, upon which the Argentine sun rests, makes him look like a living flag.

THE SUPREME SOVIET

Just because the Soviet Union fell doesn't mean it's not still dangerous. Case in point: the Supreme Soviet, superpowered servant of the Kremlin. Now a patriot without a nation, she continues to work for the restoration of the massive communist state that bestowed such fantastic abilities upon her.

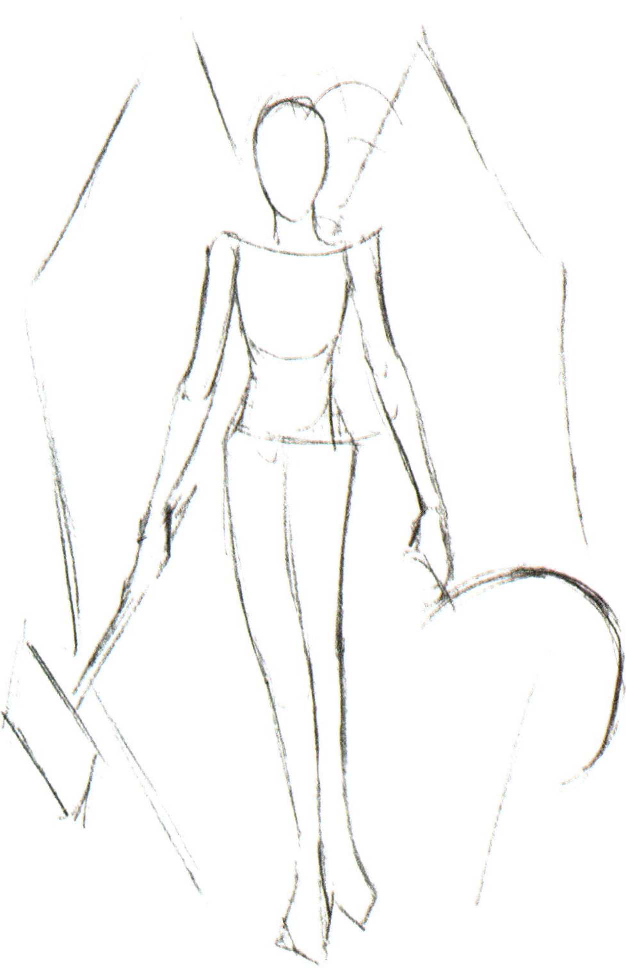

She already looks like the angel of death.

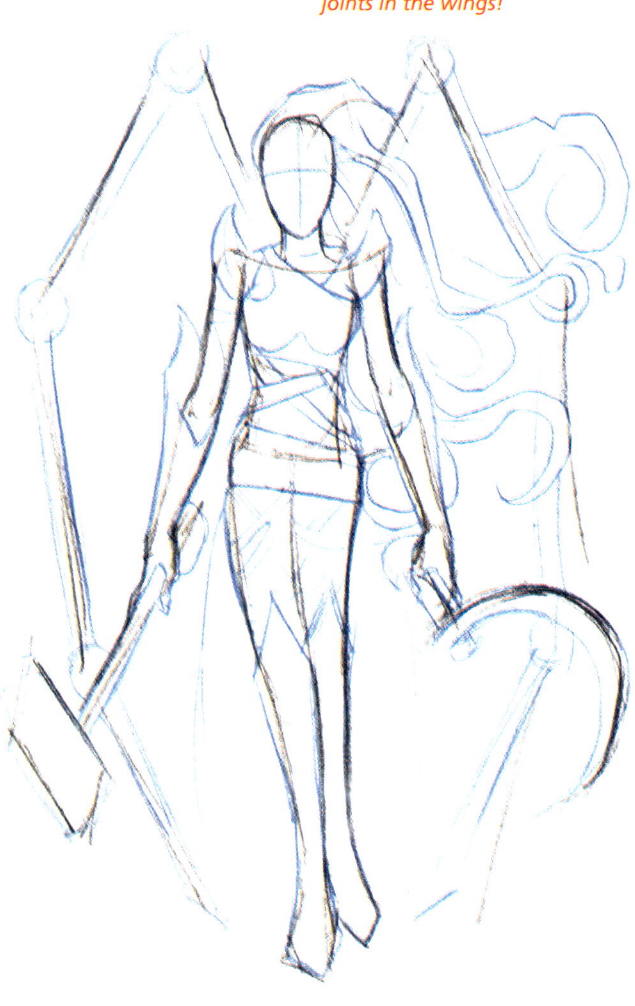

Notice the mechanical joints in the wings!

1. The Supreme Soviet is a different kind of icon. Block out her shapes as if she was an eagle-winged angel, armed with the classic Soviet hammer and sickle. Because her powers are years old, we'll go for a dated, bulky feel. Despite her image, nothing about her is elegant.

2. Add in the Soviet's long, swirling hair. Her outfit is made of tattered strips of crimson leather. Her boots are tall and vicious. Give her arm guards that work the same way, and add some spiked shoulder pads, too.

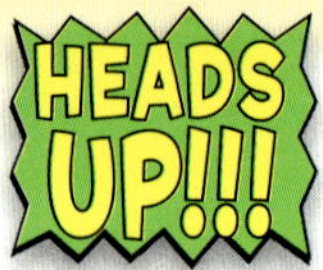

For quick rivets and such, use semicircles rather than full circles. Point the open end toward your established light source. That way, the curve that's left represents the shadows the rivets cast.

She looks like fifteen kinds of trouble.

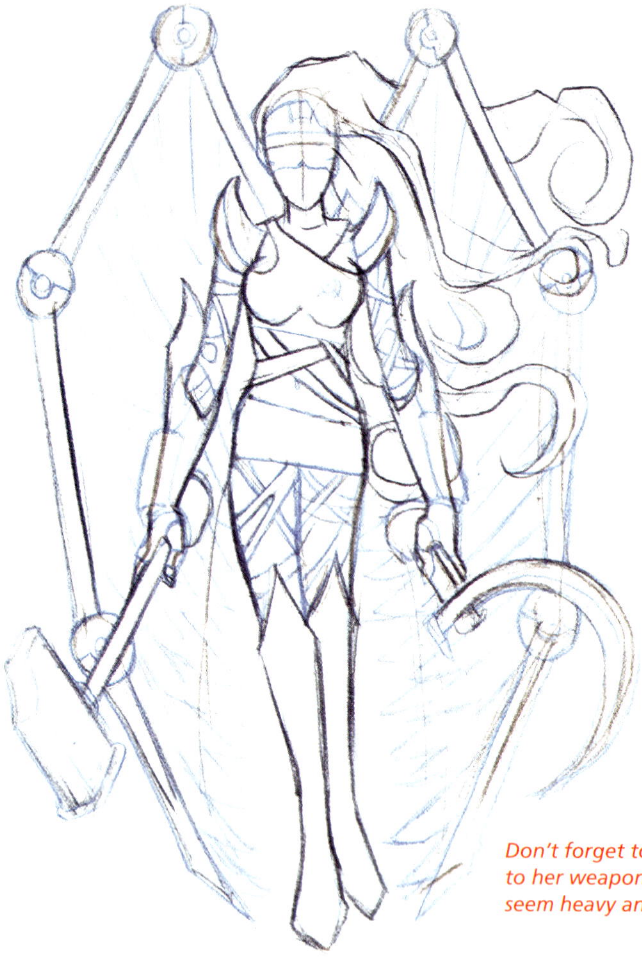

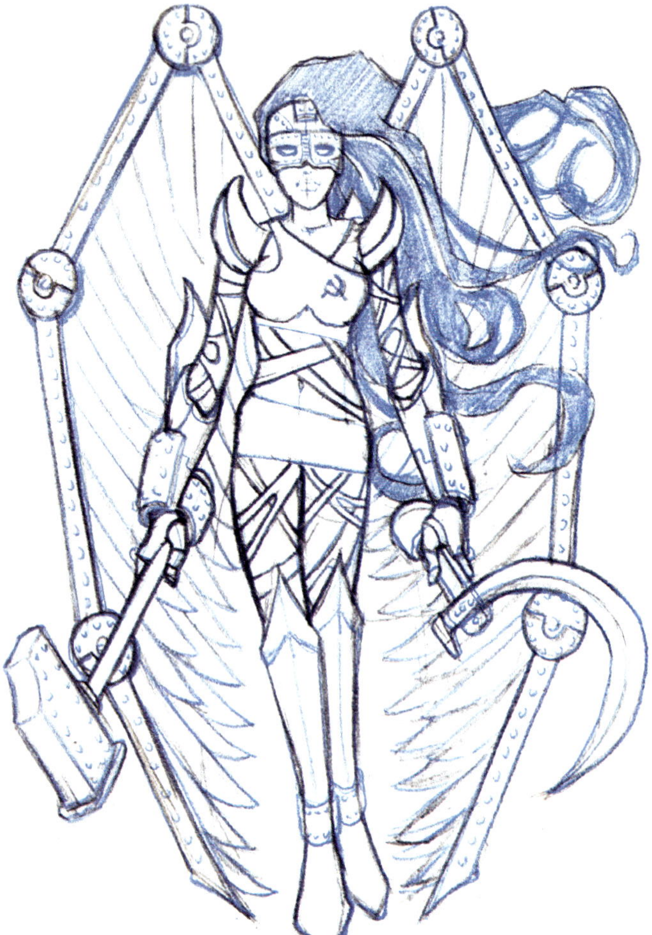

Don't forget to add a bit of depth to her weapons to make them seem heavy and real.

3. Sketch out the feathers in the wings. Make them long and thick, each like a blade. Add more straps to the costume and work out the details of her metallic mask.

4. Black out the hair. Add rivets to everything, along the edges of the wings, on the anklets, on her wrist armor, on her mask, and on the hammer, too.

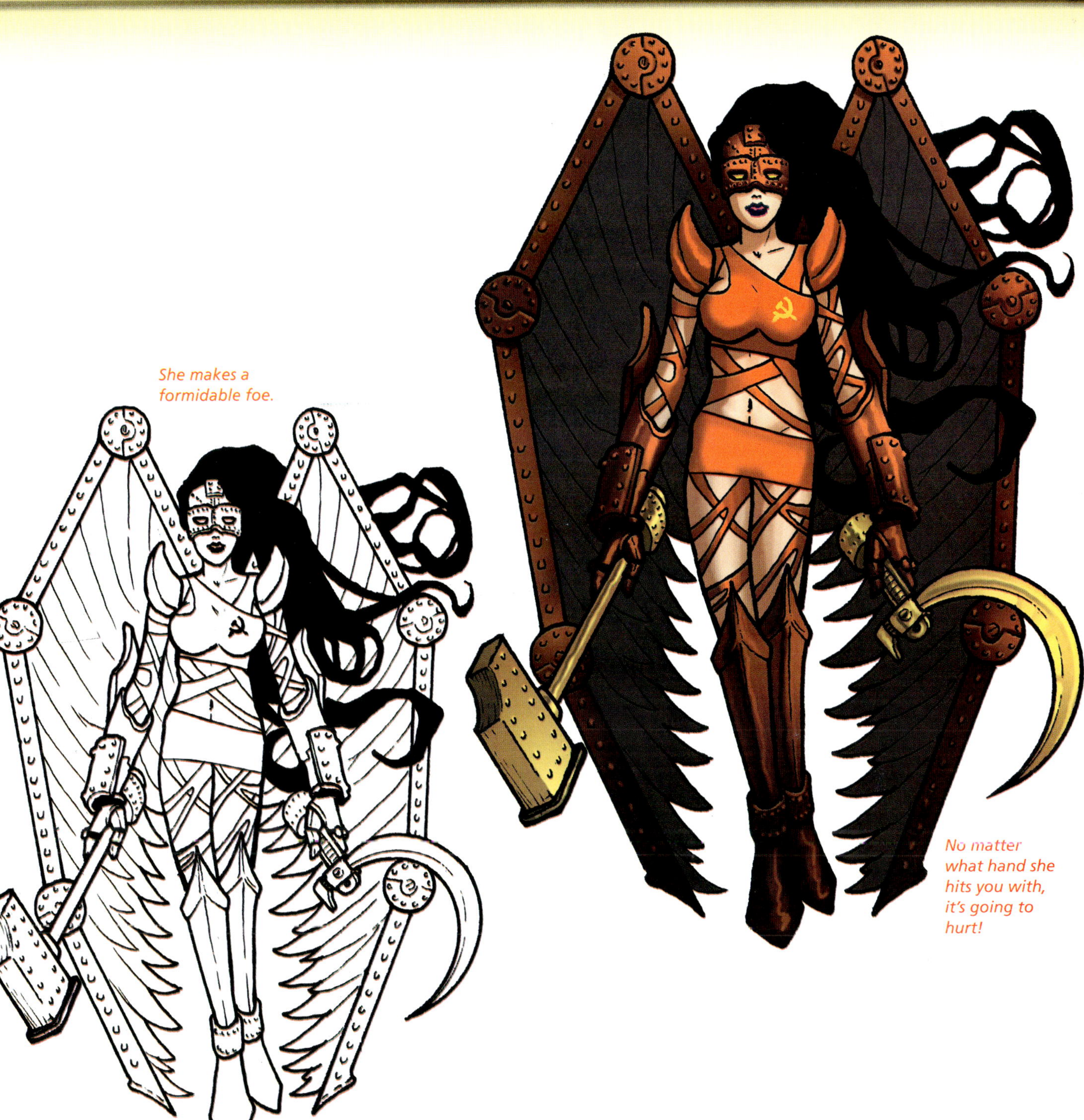

5. Use varied lines for inks. Go thicker around the edges, and black out the Soviet's hair. Use lighter lines on her feathers and on the rivets.

6. Use the Soviet Union's colors—crimson and gold—as the basic colors for her outfit. Use the gold only for a Soviet symbol over her right breast, and for the golden weapons lifted from that symbol. A purplish gray for the feathers and a flat black for her hair give her a sinister look.

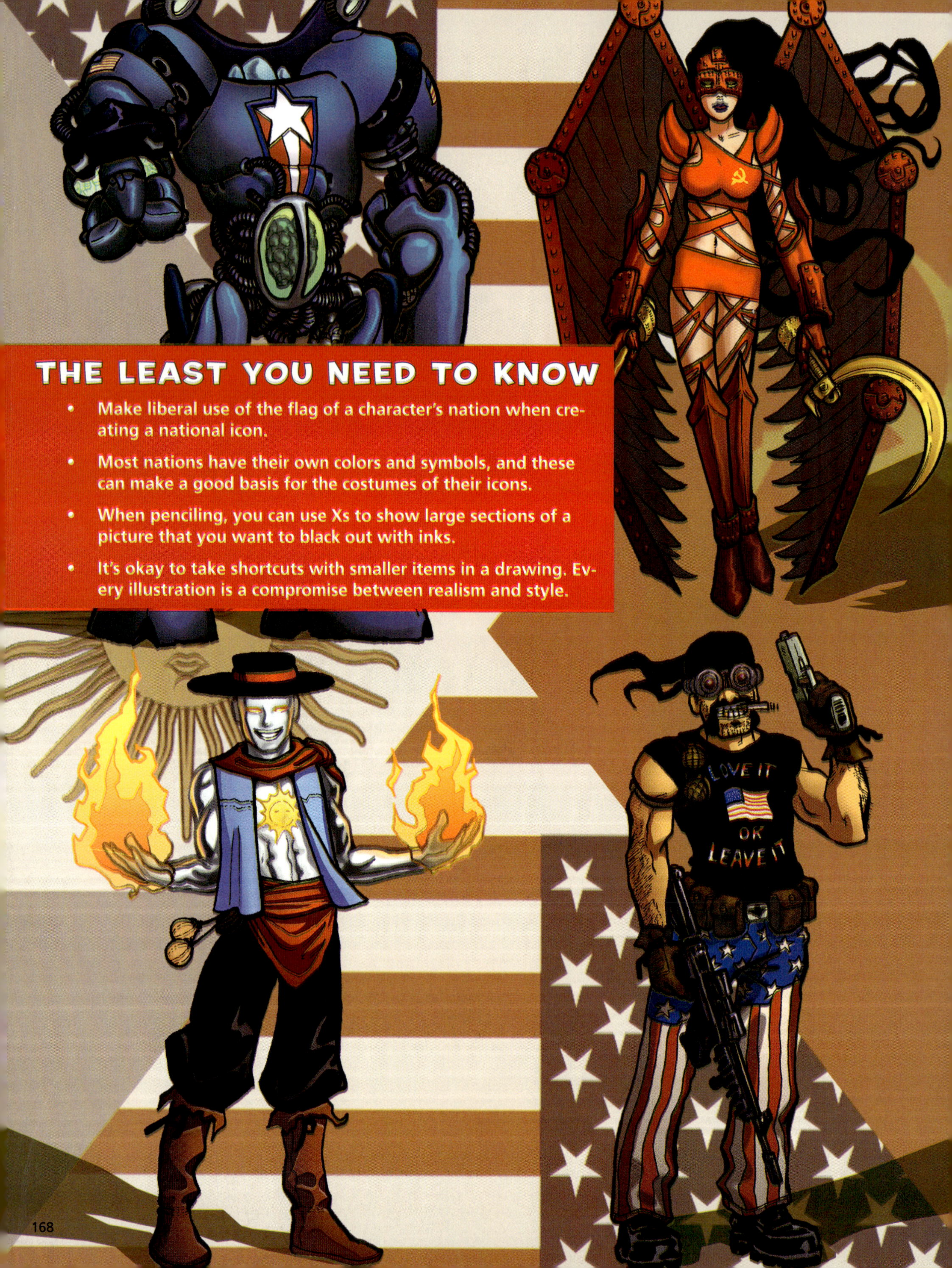

THE LEAST YOU NEED TO KNOW

- Make liberal use of the flag of a character's nation when creating a national icon.
- Most nations have their own colors and symbols, and these can make a good basis for the costumes of their icons.
- When penciling, you can use Xs to show large sections of a picture that you want to black out with inks.
- It's okay to take shortcuts with smaller items in a drawing. Every illustration is a compromise between realism and style.

12 Sidekicks: Powers in Training

In This Chapter

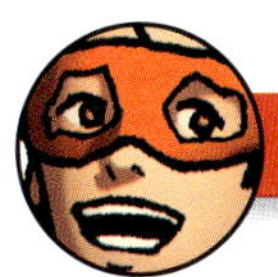

A young hero gets his start

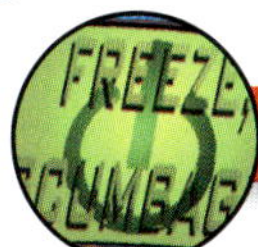

An electronic interventionist

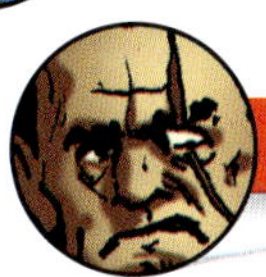

A minion for a master

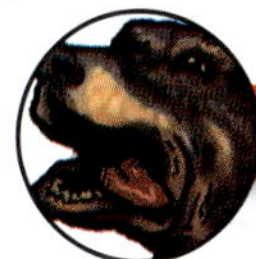

A hero's best friend

Comic books aren't filled with just superheroes and villains, of course. Besides all the regular folks, a number of other types of people fill the pages of the monthly tales. We can't possibly cover them all here, but we can tackle the highlights.

The Kid wants nothing more than to grow up to be a superhero himself, and he figures the best way to manage this is to attach himself to one of his favorites. He has a good heart and really wants to be helpful. He might even make a great superhero someday—if he survives that long.

The Robot was built to help a hero—in this case, Power, from Chapter 3. Despite his lack of blood, lungs, etc.—or perhaps because of it—the Robot excels at this job. This machine also maintains Power's contact database and daily schedule. He plays wicked games, too.

The Minion isn't much of a villain himself. A career criminal, he works for whichever mastermind offers him the better deal at the time. He spends more time in jail than out, it seems.

The Dog is more than just a superhero's pet. He has full powers of his own. Despite his brains, though, he's still a dog. Woe to any innocent cat that crosses his path.

THE KID

The Kid loves superheroes. He follows them on the news, in the comics, and anywhere else he can learn more about them. He wants to be one more than anything, and he thinks he's figured out a way to make that happen—if only the heroes let him hang around.

There's a hero to be!

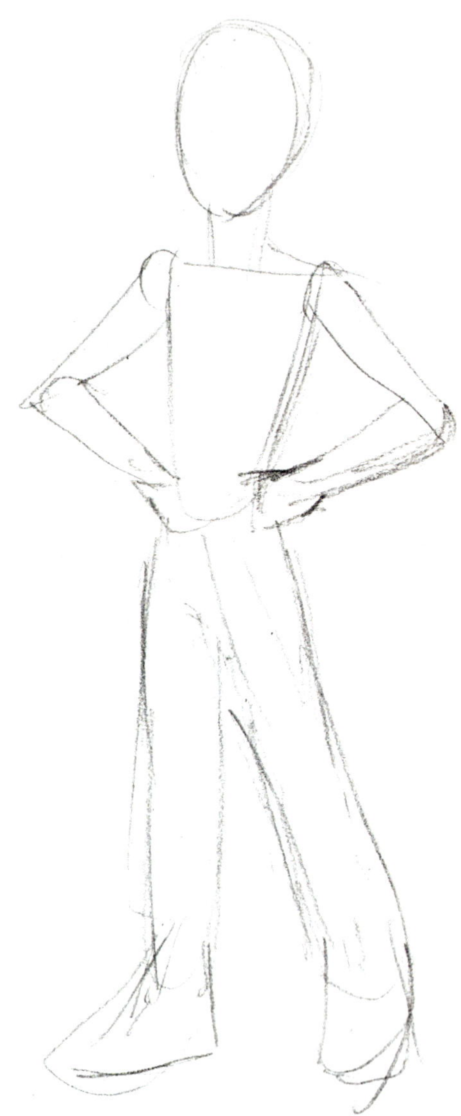

If only he could fly.

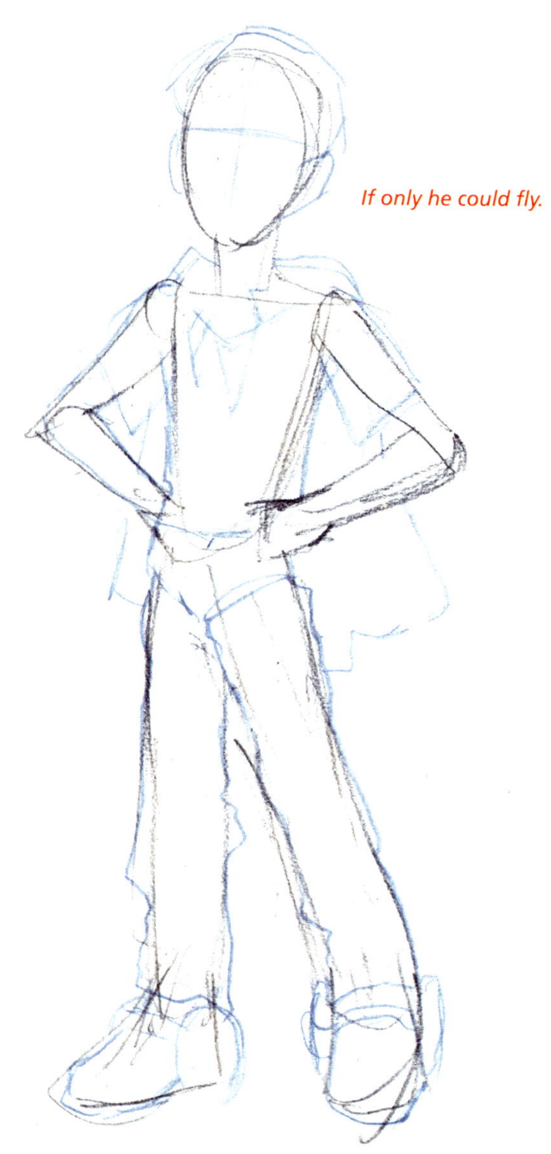

1. Break down the Kid's stance. Make his head a little bigger than normal and his body slimmer. Give him a heroic pose like that of his favorite supers.

2. Dress the Kid in street clothes, but tie a homemade cape around his shoulders. Make sure it only comes halfway down so that no one can take it too seriously. Notice the sketched-in hair and the guidelines on the face, too.

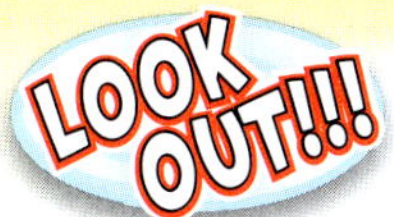

A child's anatomy differs a bit from an adults. It's not enough to just draw a shorter person. In general, give a child a head he or she still needs to grow into, and you should do fine.

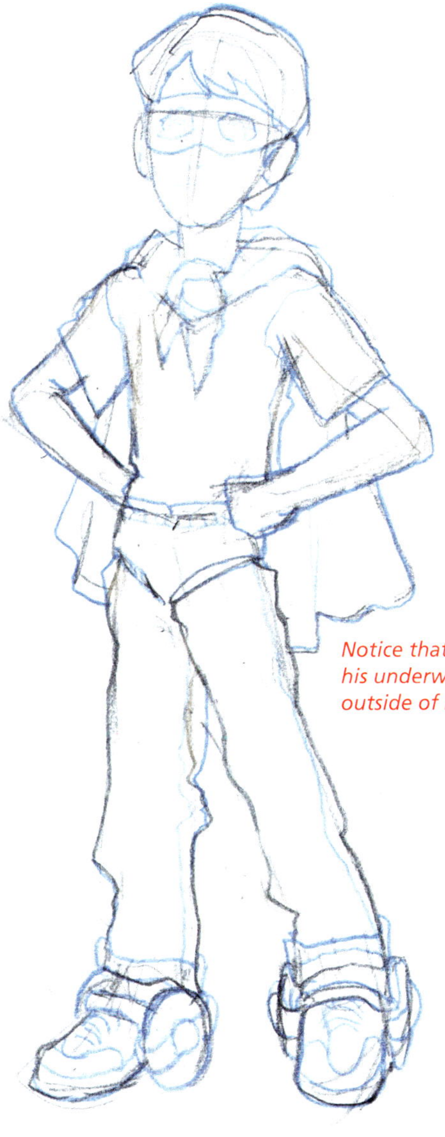

He's ready for anything—or so he thinks.

Notice that he's wearing his underwear on the outside of his pants.

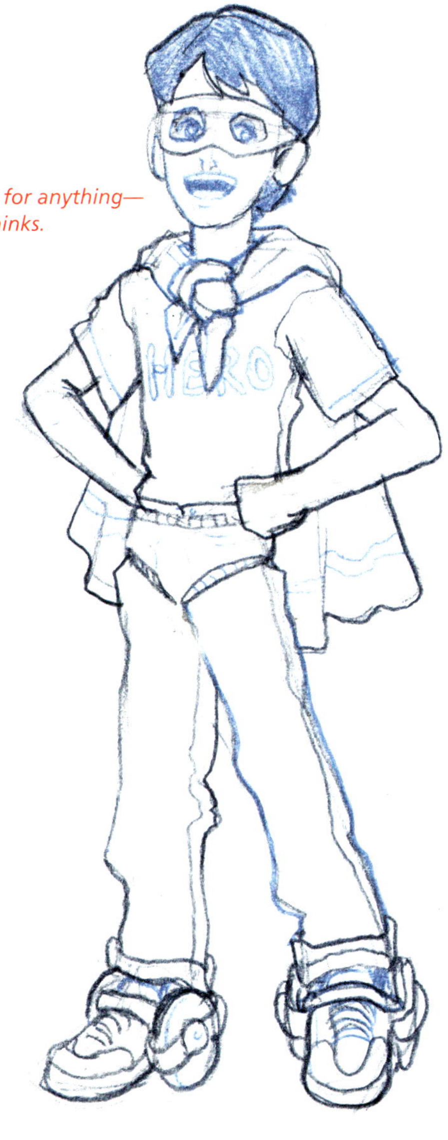

3. Tie a domino mask around his eyes. Put wheels on his shoes to help him get around. Cap him off with a dashing mop of hair.

4. Blacken his hair. Give him a set of wide eyes and a big, happy mouth. Write the word "Hero" on the Kid's shirt as his chosen icon. A fringe near the end of the cape shows that it's actually a towel.

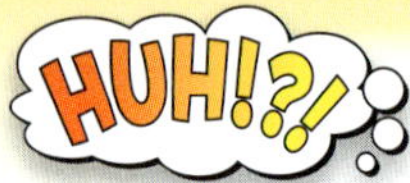

For some reason, the classic heroes look like they're not only running around in their underwear but putting their briefs on outside of their long pants. It's silly, of course, but it's become a bit of a tradition, and few people complain about it.

Just give him a few years. Please!

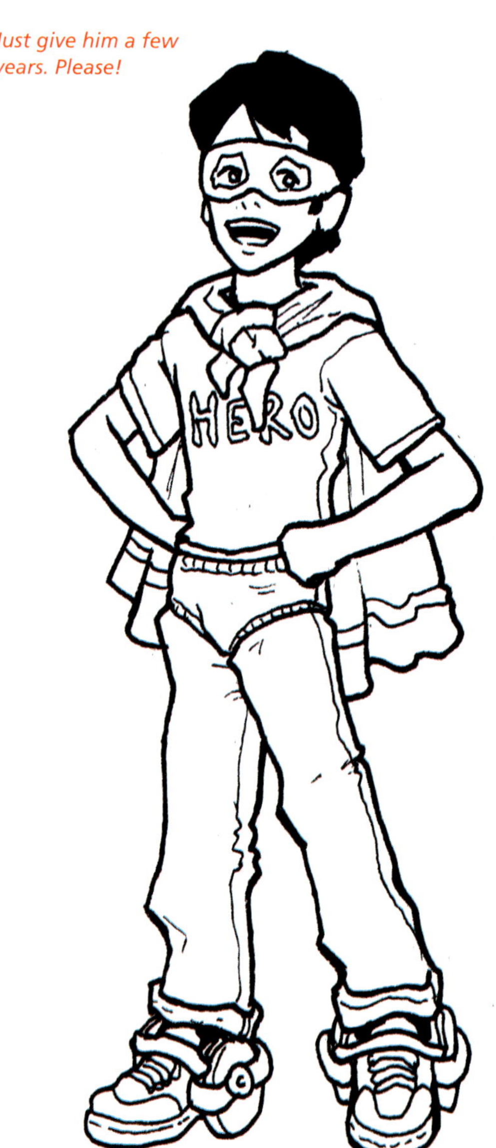

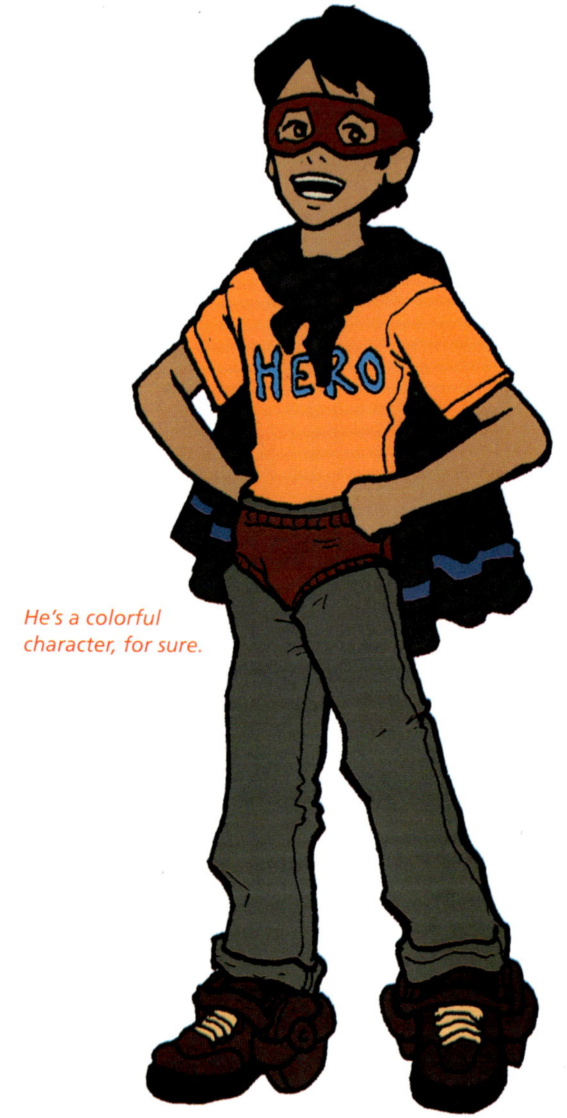

He's a colorful character, for sure.

5. Use varied lines here. Employ heavier lines around the perimeter and on the edges of his clothes. Use fainter lines for seams and wrinkles.

6. Give him a dark cape, gray pants, and brown shoes. Color his mask and underwear a bright red. Use orange for his shirt, with blue writing.

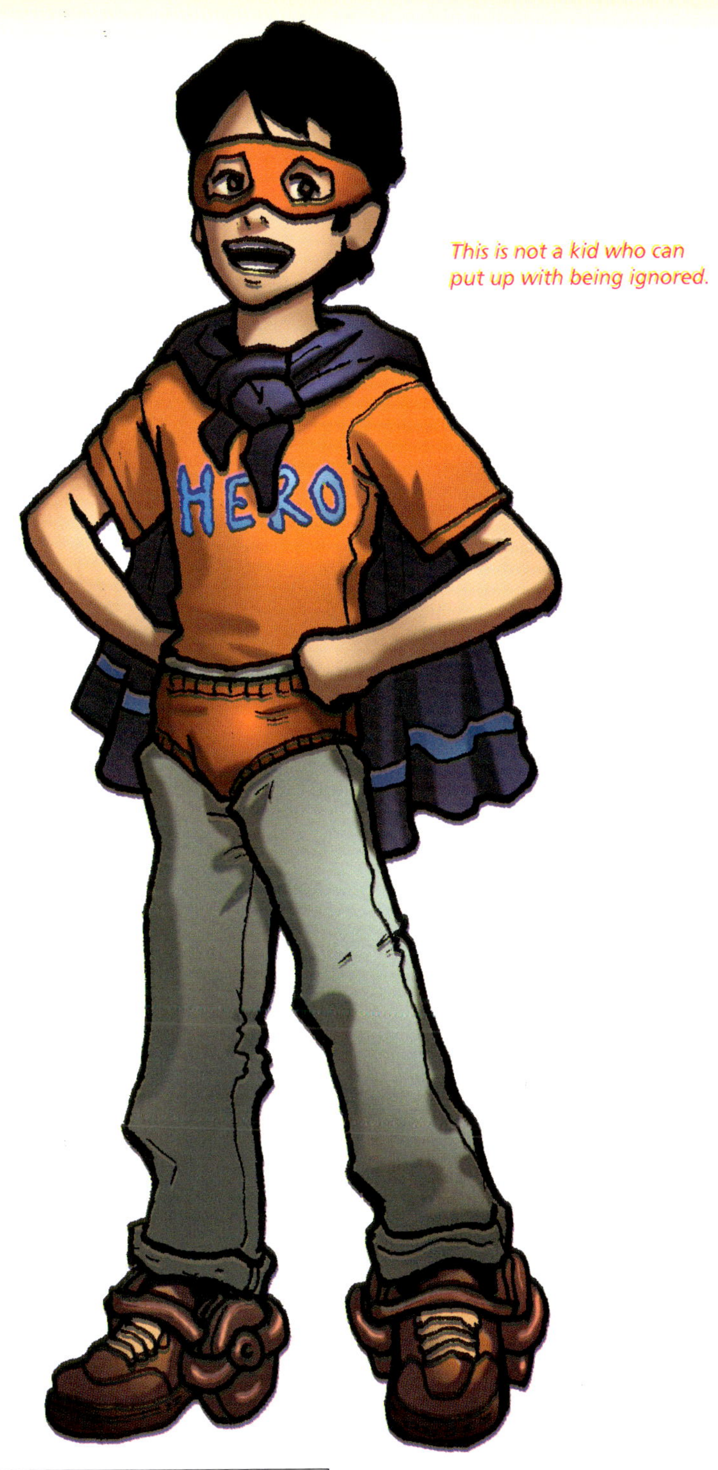

This is not a kid who can put up with being ignored.

7. Add highlights and brighten up some of those bits of clothing. Lighter lines on the shoe-wheels give them a bright, plastic look. Keep that smile bright and white.

ROBOT

Power built the Robot early on in his career, to give himself an edge against the criminal element in town. He took a flat-panel monitor and gave it arms, the ability to fly, and a serious attitude. The Robot has served him faithfully ever since.

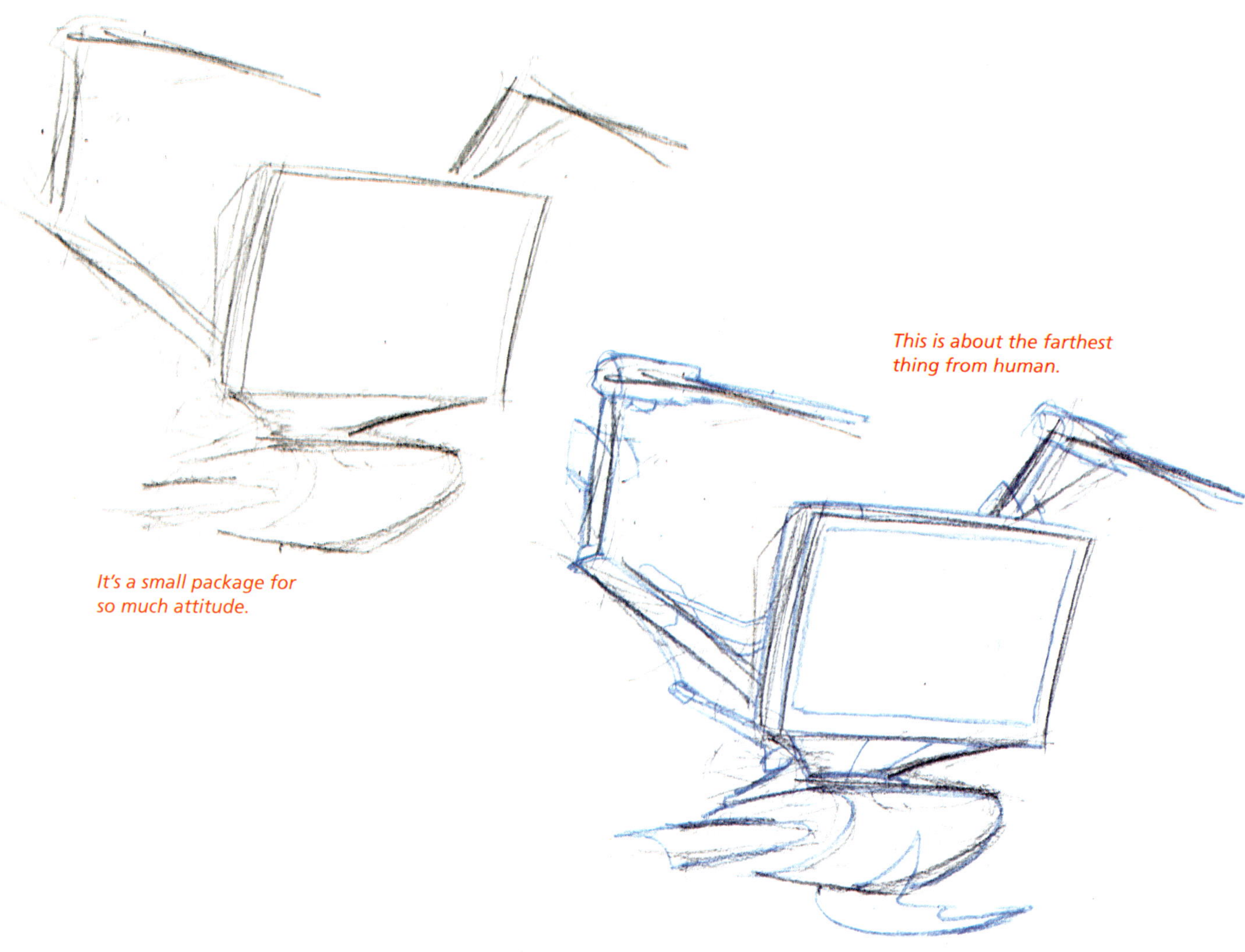

This is about the farthest thing from human.

It's a small package for so much attitude.

1. Break down Robot's stance. Essentially, it's a rectangle with arms and its flying base hanging off of it.

2. Thicken the screen a bit and work out just how those arms look. Fashion a base for it, based upon the idea that it can make the thing more aerodynamic.

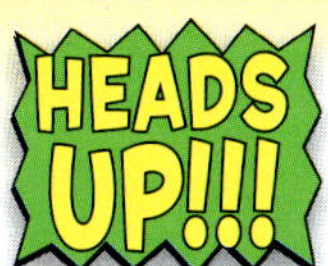

Because a robot doesn't have any facial features—or very few depending on who you're working with—you must convey its attitude with various angles. You can tilt the screen forward or arrange the arms aggressively. As important, though, is how you choose to frame the Robot in any images you make.

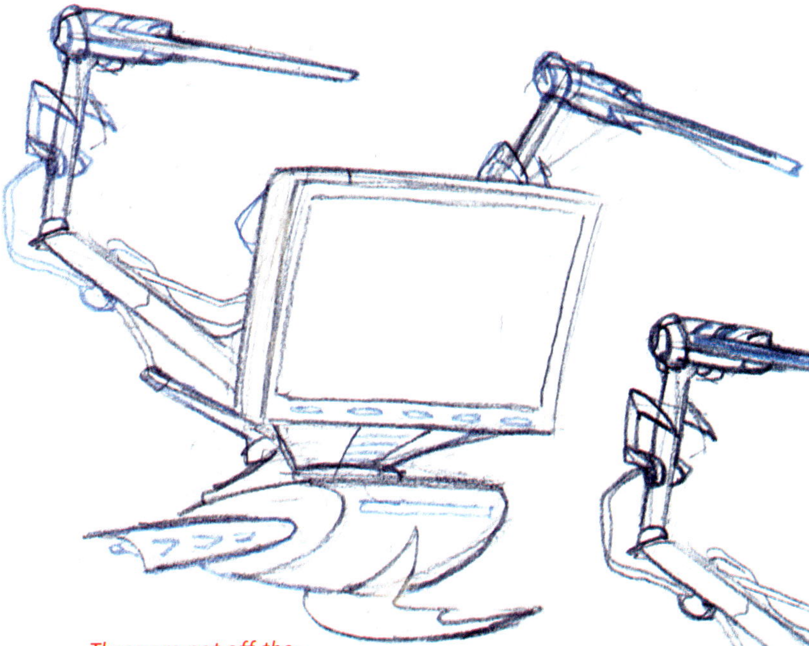

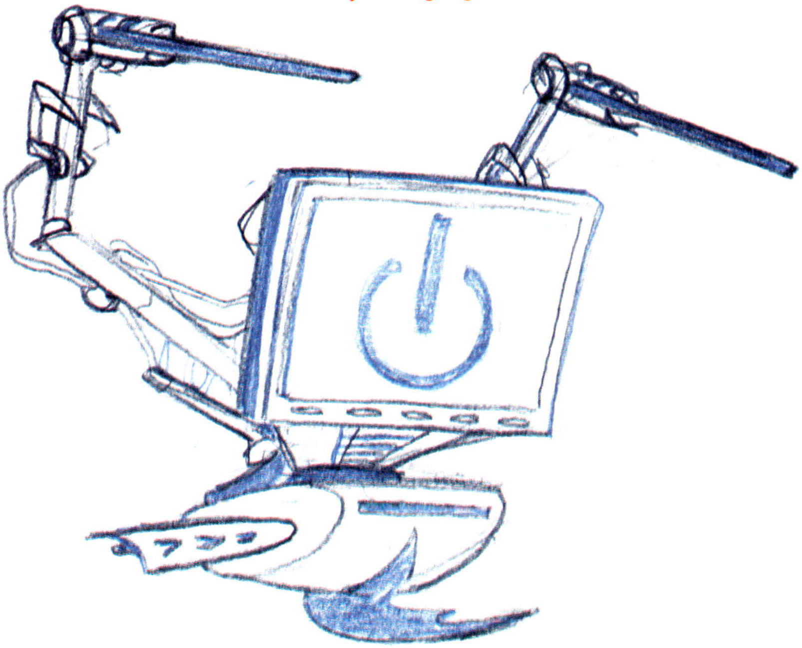

It's really coming together.

These are not off-the-shelf products.

3. Define the arms and the base better. Include a jagged fin jutting out from the bottom, perhaps as an antenna. Place a line of buttons along the bottom of the screen.

4. Put Power's icon on the screen and black out the tips of the arms and the fin below the screen. Firm up the details on the rest of the picture as well.

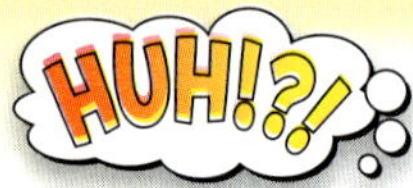

While comics are rife with robots, such creatures come in a dizzying array of samples. Don't restrict yourself to things you've seen before. Be as innovative as you'd guess their people would be, given the chance.

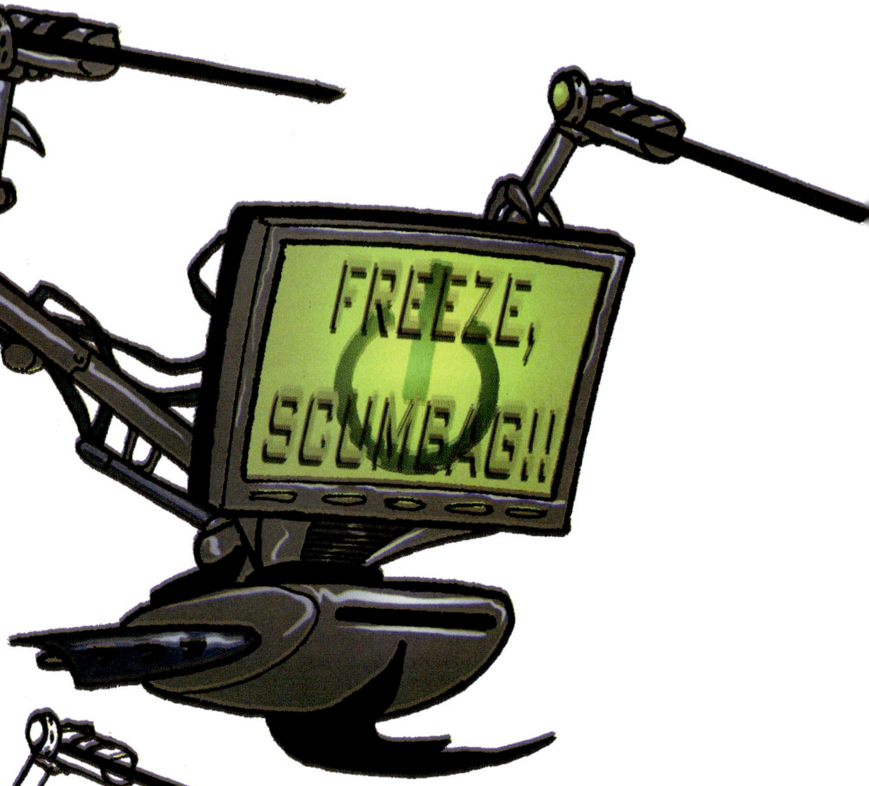

Who's the scumbag here?

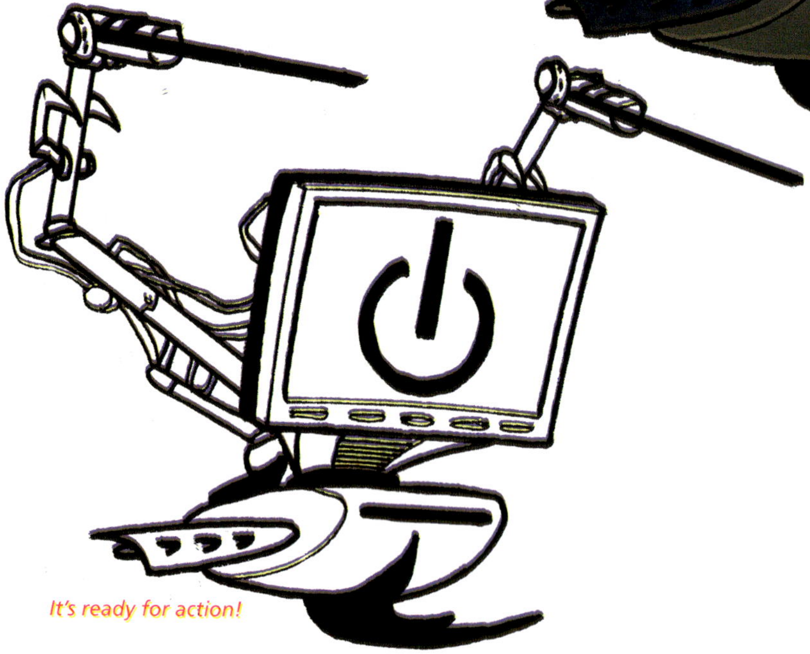

It's ready for action!

5. Use consistent lines throughout here, and make use of a straightedge if you'd like to. Blacken out the housing of the screen, as well as the tips of the arms and the fin resting below the main stand.

6. Color most of the robot a steel gray. Use a light blue-gray for highlights. Yair adds in a message on the Robot's screen, showing just how intimidating such a creature can be.

THE MINION

The Minion would just be a low-level thug on his own. Somehow, though, he's had a run-in with the wrong people and found himself working for a villain. He's no real challenge to anyone with powers, although he might give regular folks a run for their money. If he could just hit it big once, he'd retire, he tells himself. Sure.

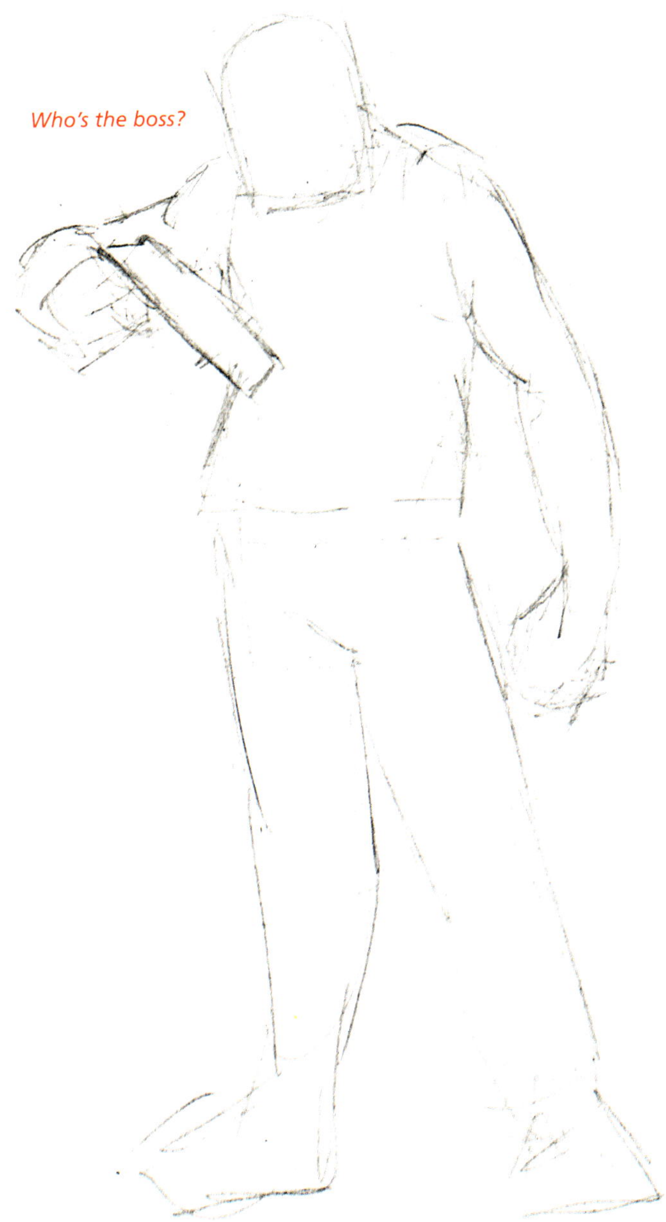

Who's the boss?

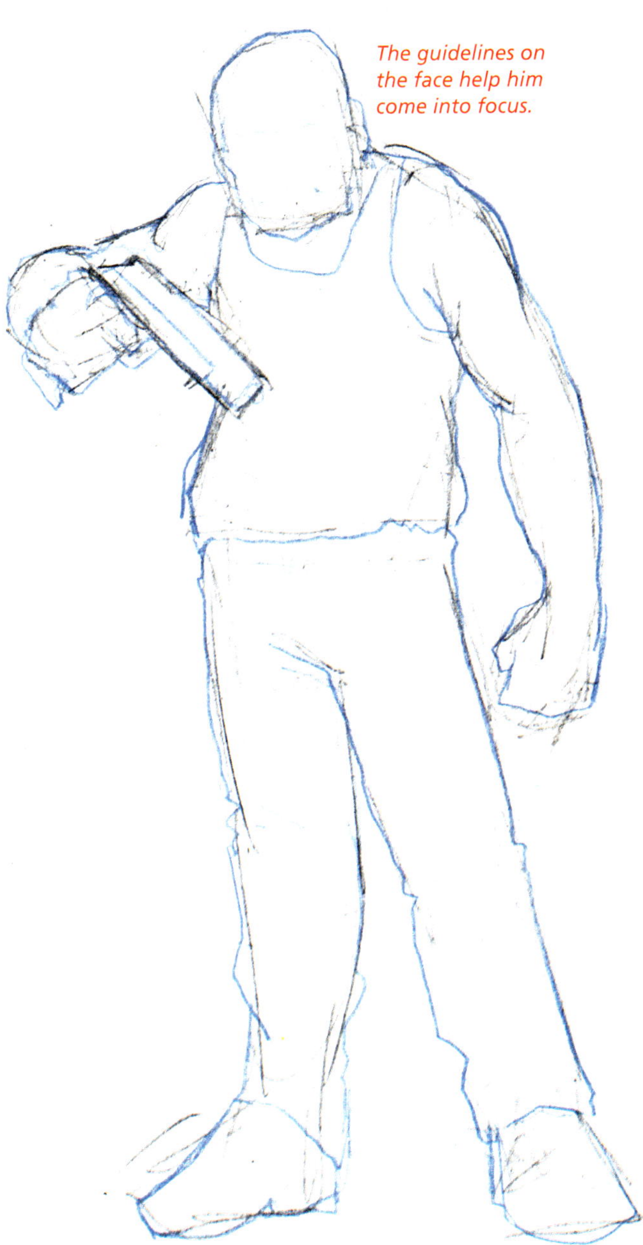

The guidelines on the face help him come into focus.

1. Break down the Minion's stance. He's a bit of a slob and a bully, so play up the belly and the slouch. Put a gun in his hand, too. Minions always go for guns when all else fails, which it often does.

2. Refine the Minion a bit. Put a tank top and slacks on him, along with basic shoes. Note that he's not holding the gun very well, but he's likely never had any formal training with one.

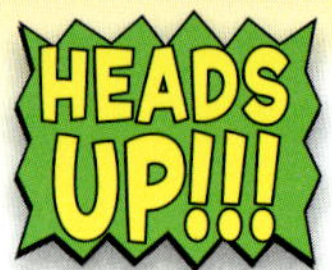

Minions rarely work for a villain out of love or a sense of loyalty. They care about money and power, probably in that order. They're brutes who are there to do a job and—if they're lucky—go home.

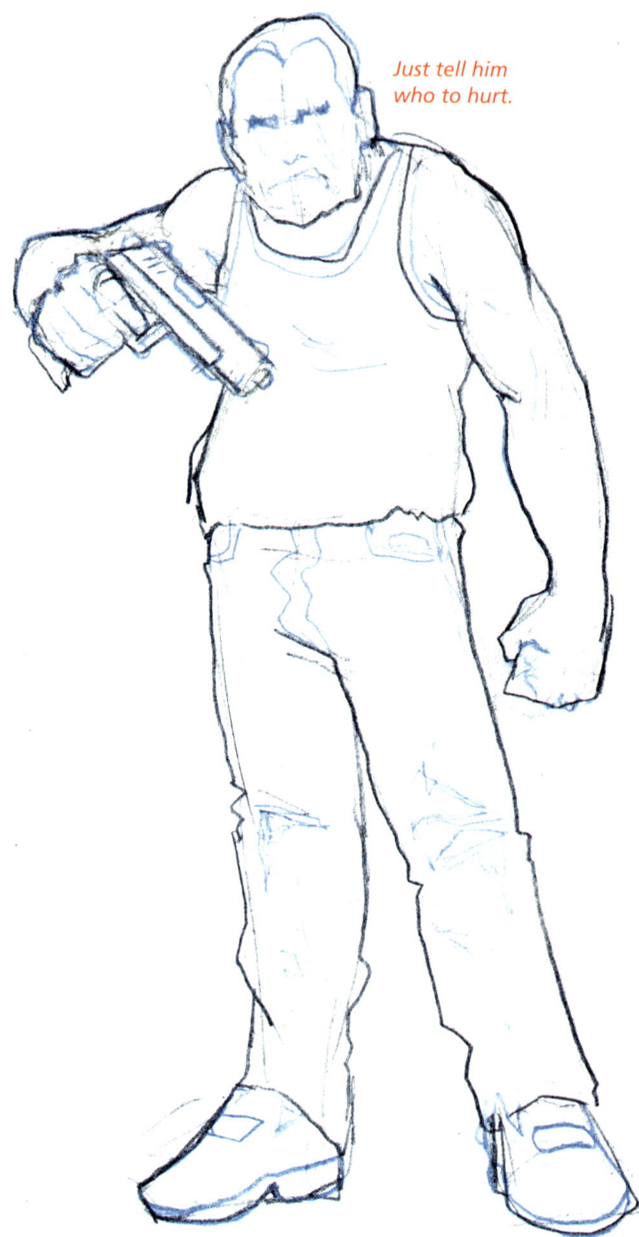

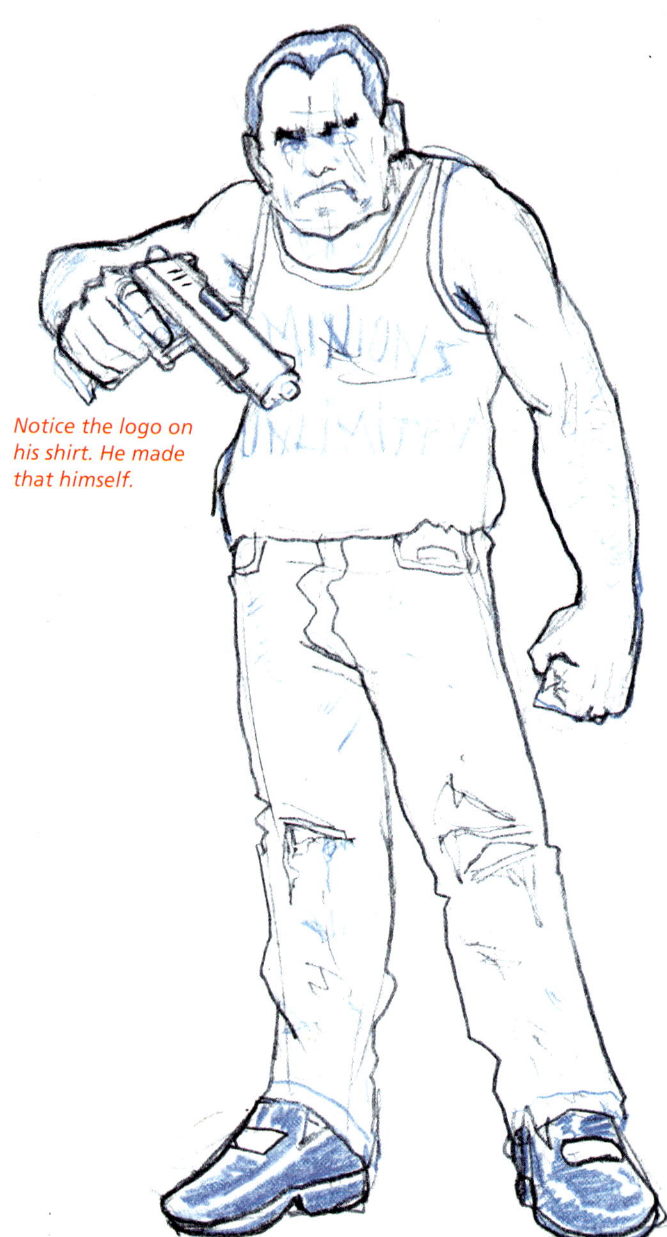

3. Add hair, plus a snarl and several scars to the Minion's face. Tear out the knees of his jeans. Show his wrinkled fly on his pants. Give him a bushy set of eyebrows.

4. Work on the Minion's eyes. Blacken his shoes. Write Minions Unlimited on his shirt as a joke for him.

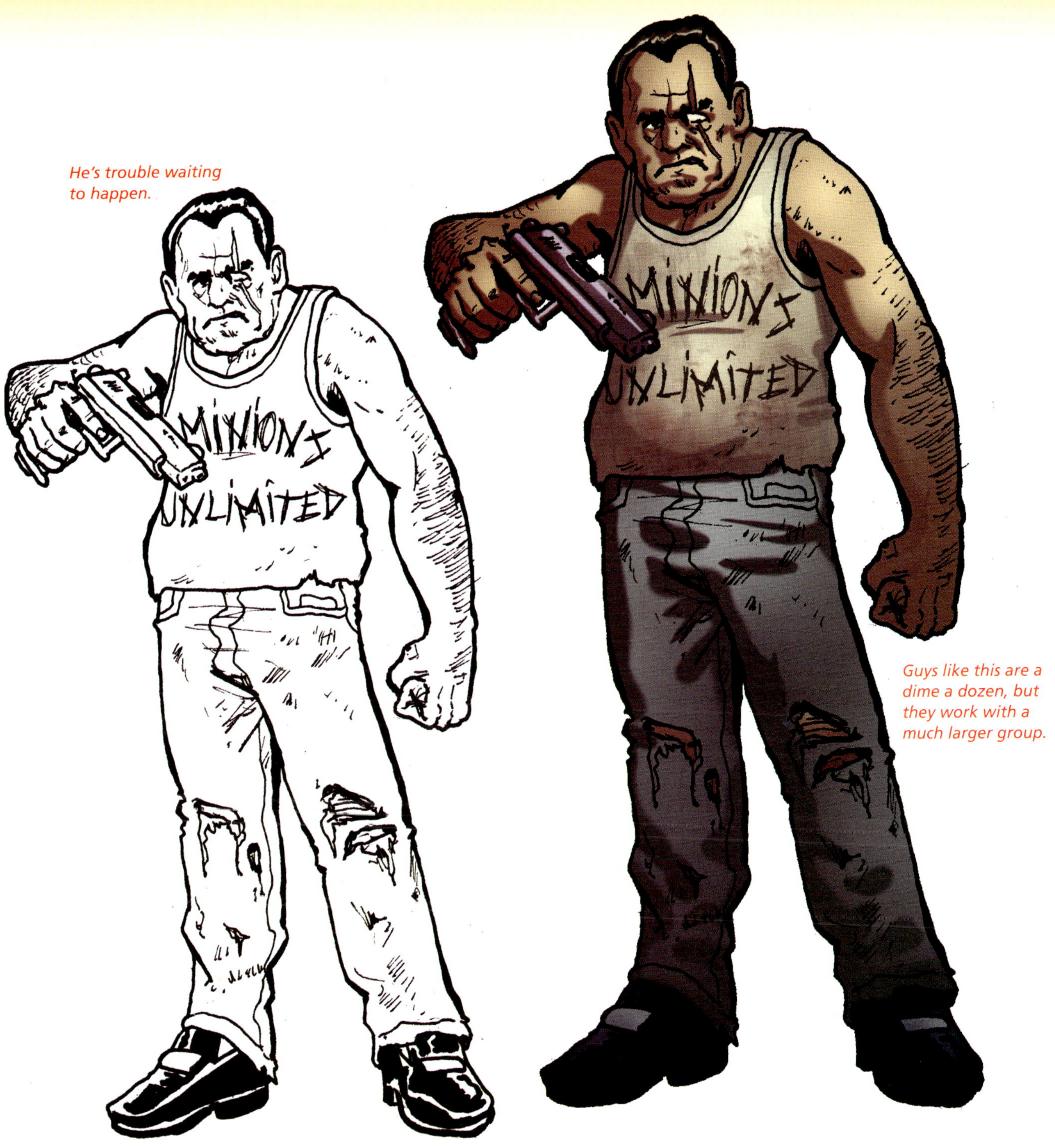

He's trouble waiting to happen.

Guys like this are a dime a dozen, but they work with a much larger group.

5. Use dirty, nasty lines on the Minion's silhouette. Save the lighter lines for the details of the scum crusted on him.

6. Color the Minion in a half-dirty cream for his shirt and a tattered blue for his pants. Everything about him seems to be covered in a layer of dirt, so include that, too.

THE DOG

Not every superhero or villain is human—or even humanoid. When a hero needs a hand, who better to turn to than humanity's best friend: the dog. Of course, the Dog isn't just any mutt. He's got powers of his own, too.

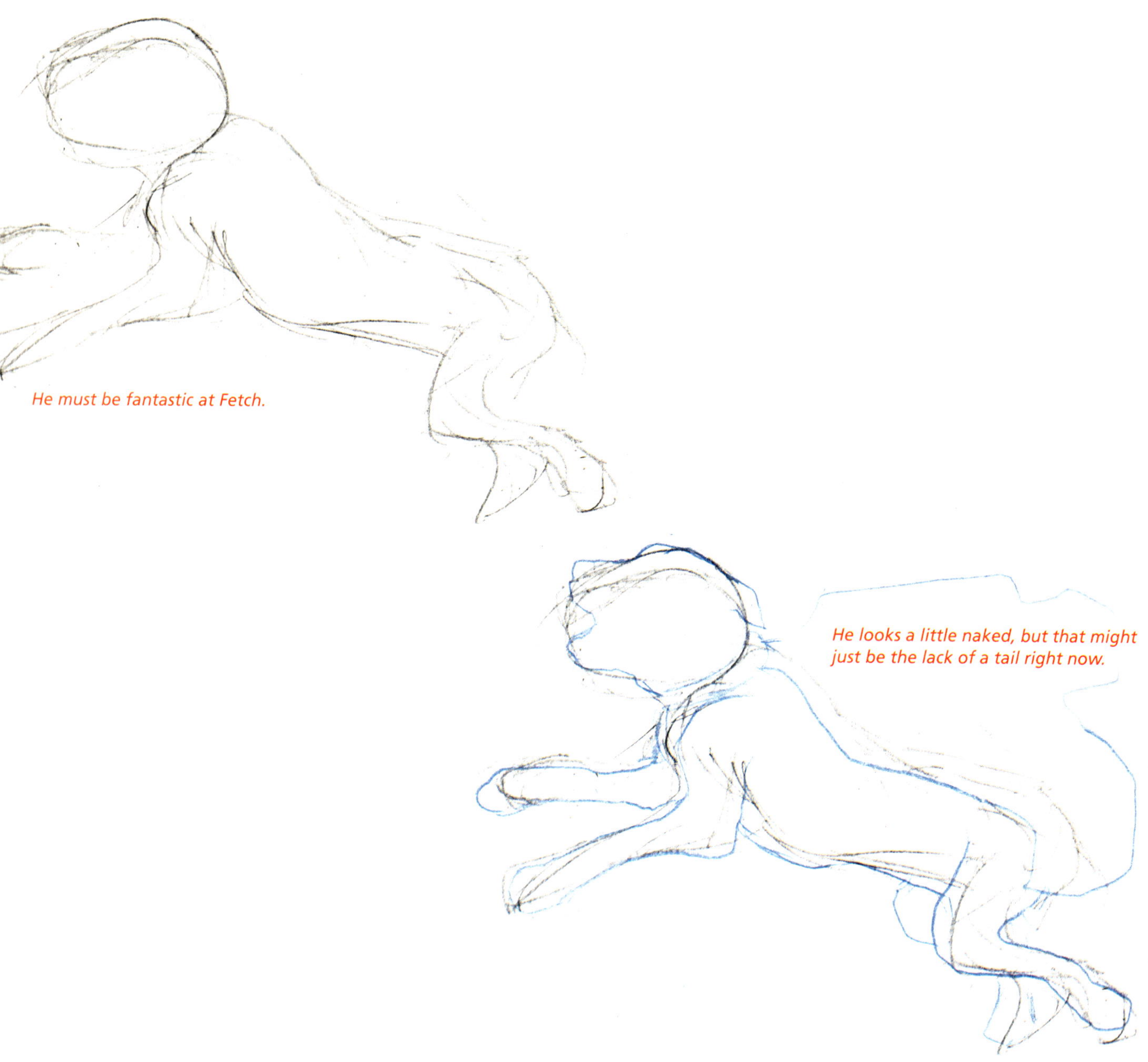

He must be fantastic at Fetch.

He looks a little naked, but that might just be the lack of a tail right now.

1. Break down the Dog's pose. He's flying through the air, going from right to left.

2. Add a cape and collar to the Dog. Open up his mouth a bit, not for a snarl but perhaps for a bark. Arrange his legs just the way you want them.

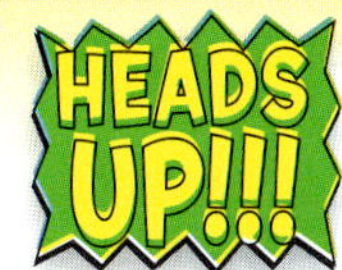

If you don't understand canine anatomy, pick up a book about drawing animals or find an actual creature you can study. It's okay to specialize in drawing certain things like people, but you should be able to learn how to draw anything else—from a dog to a tank—on the fly if need be.

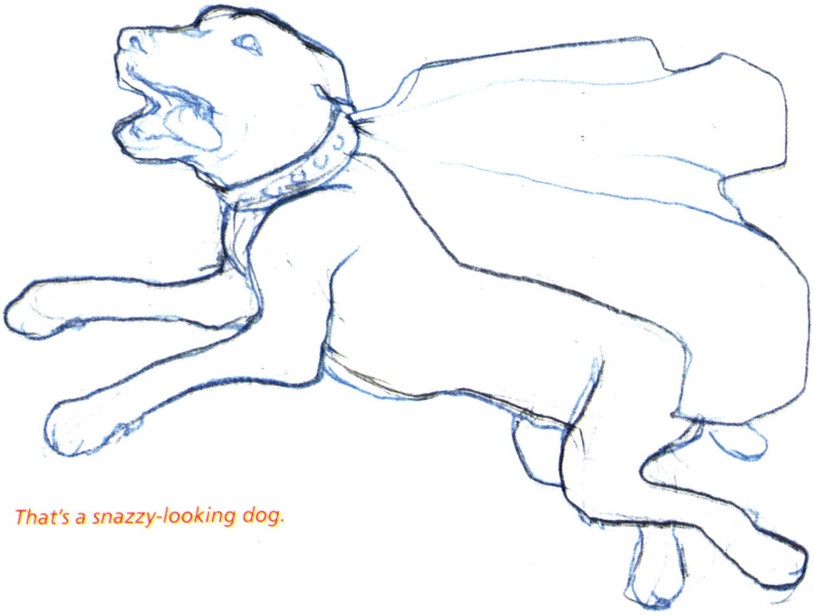

That's a snazzy-looking dog.

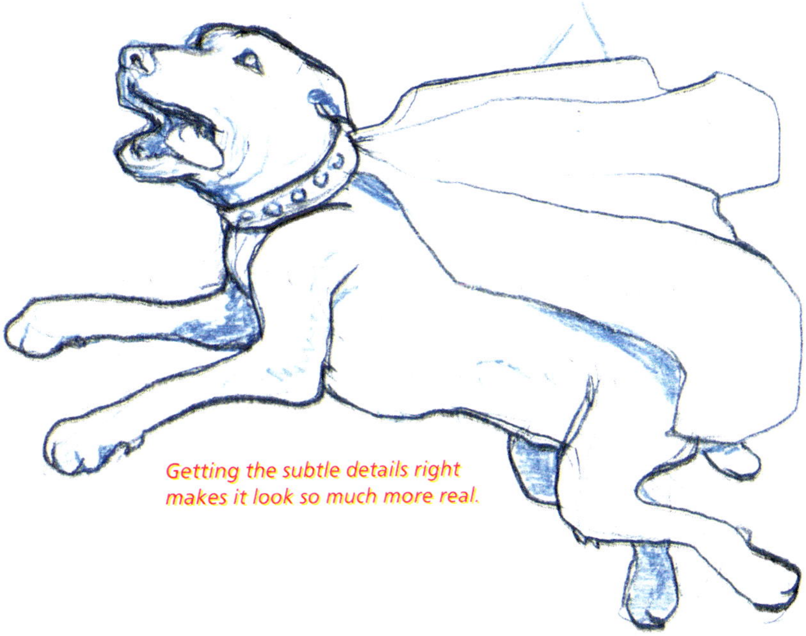

Getting the subtle details right makes it look so much more real.

3. Give the Dog a short tail and work on his face. Give him deep eyes, a wet nose, and a tongue that hangs from his mouth as he flies. Put studs on his collar and put some folds in his cape.

4. Add shadows with your pencil. Also refine the Dog's mouth. Pay close attention to his paws and dew-claws.

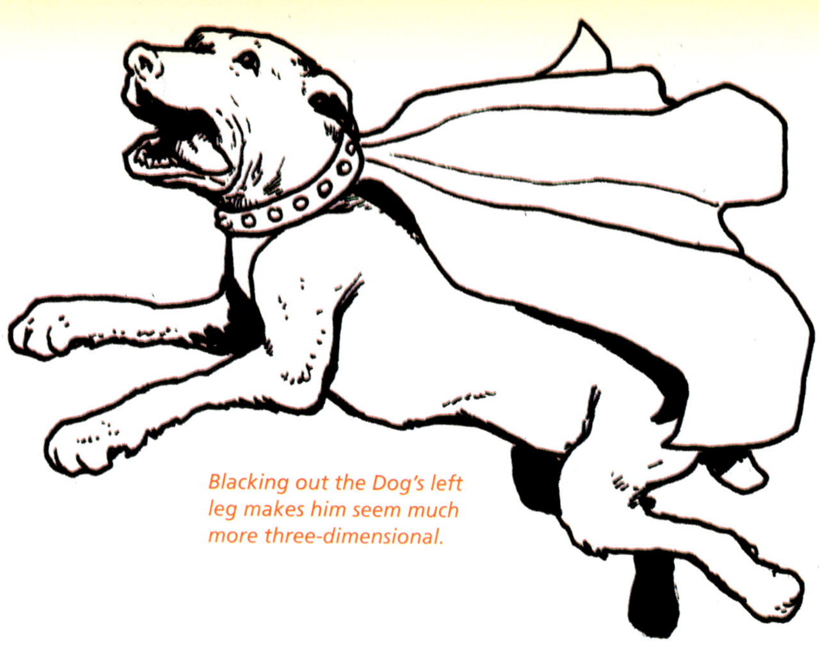

Blacking out the Dog's left leg makes him seem much more three-dimensional.

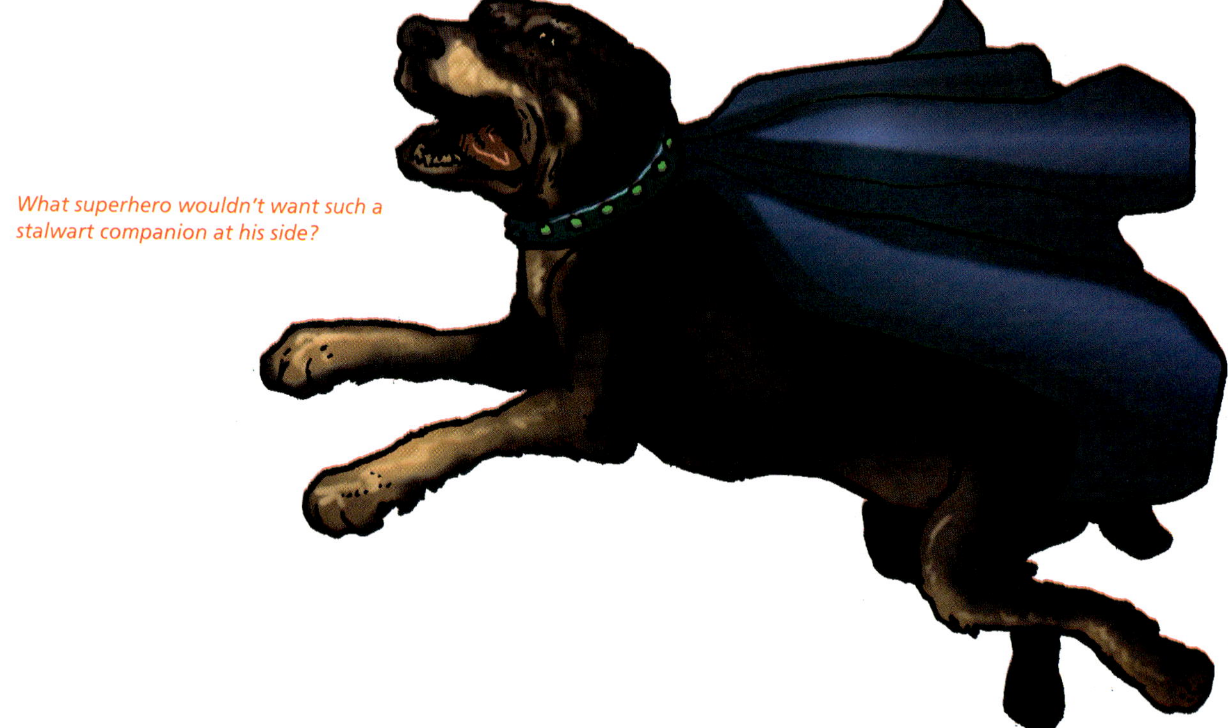

What superhero wouldn't want such a stalwart companion at his side?

5. Use a consistent line here. Only the interior hatching on the Dog's fur and the folds of his cape should have lesser lines.

6. The Dog is a Rottweiler, so go with a dark brown coat with the characteristic brindling, including the markings on the face. Add a turquoise collar and a royal blue cape, and you're done!

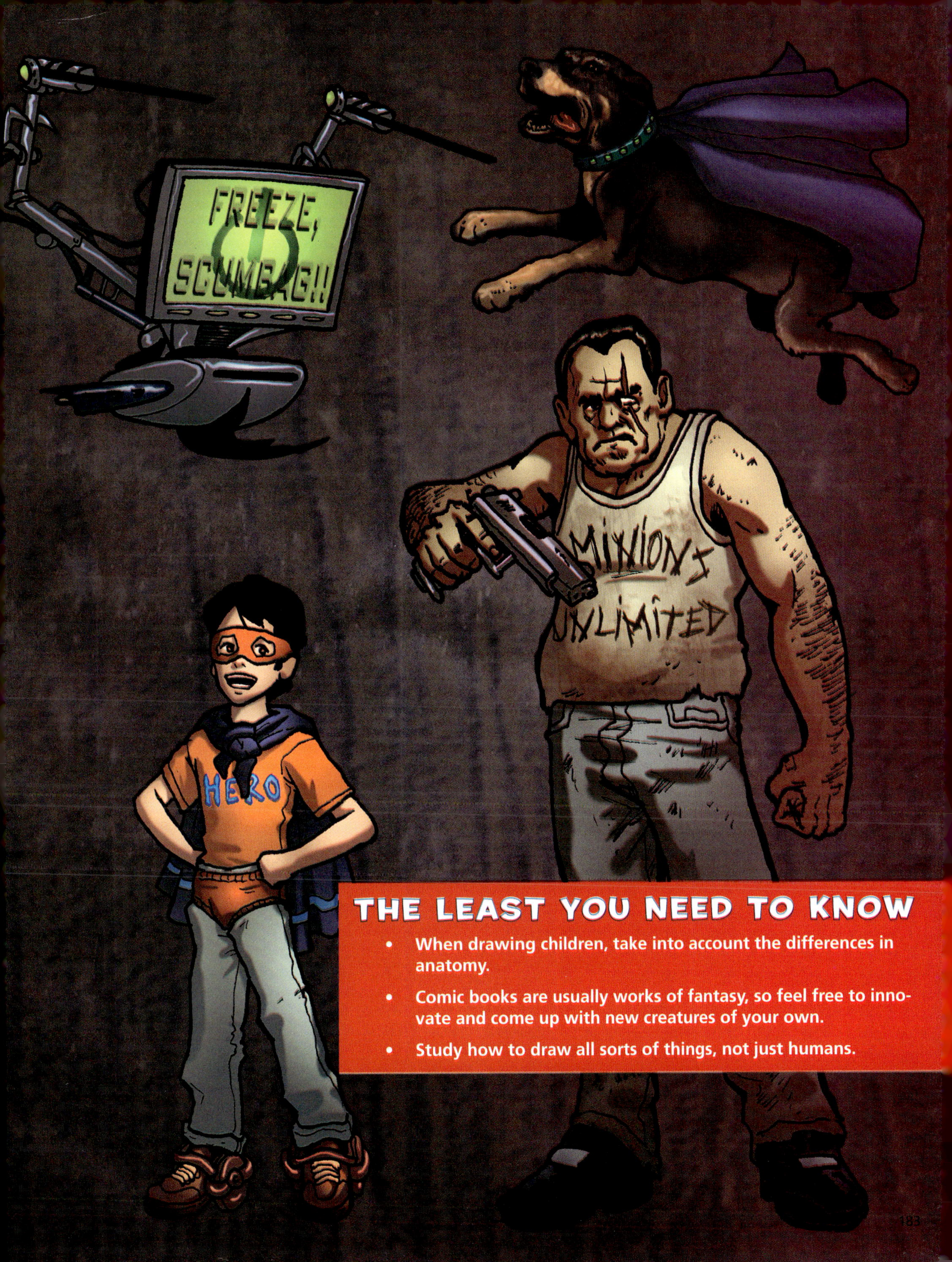

THE LEAST YOU NEED TO KNOW

- When drawing children, take into account the differences in anatomy.
- Comic books are usually works of fantasy, so feel free to innovate and come up with new creatures of your own.
- Study how to draw all sorts of things, not just humans.

APPENDIXES

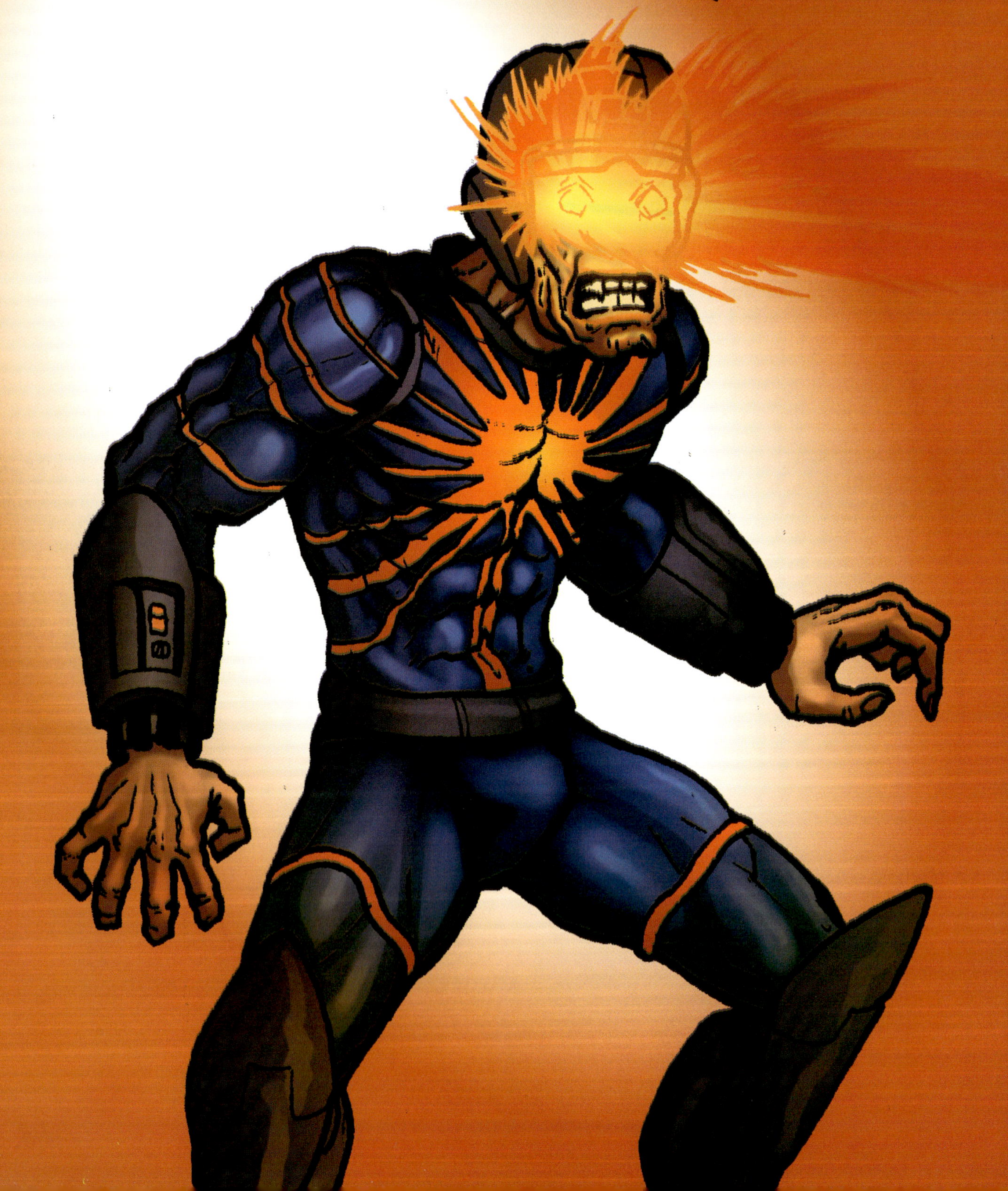

Appendix A

Glossary

alien A person from another place, often (in comics) another planet.

antihero A protagonist who commits unheroic acts, often in the pursuit of heroic ends.

archetype A classic sort of superpowered character that can be recognized by its salient traits.

breakdown The roughest stage of a drawing. Here, you put down simple shapes in pencil, figure out the poses of the creatures and items involved, and determine the angle at which the viewer sees the contents of the picture.

coloring After a drawing is inked, it is often colored. Originally, this was done with paints, markers, or colored pencils. Today, most comics are colored on a computer.

comic (or comic book) A pamphlet or book that tells a story using sequential art and often words.

curvilinear perspective A process that uses five vanishing points and curved perspective lines to show depth in a drawing.

finished pencils A pencil drawing that is as complete as you can make it. Often such drawings are then inked and colored.

foreshortening The forced use of perspective to make things closer to you appear larger.

Golden Age A period of comics history that stretches from the 1920s through the 1950s, usually distinguished by idealistic heroes and stilted dialogue.

graphic novel A comic book published in book form, usually containing either a complete story or a substantial arc of a larger story.

hero A character who acts in valiant or helpful ways, often at great personal risk.

inking Going over finished pencils with ink to make the art permanent and sharp.

manga Originally, comics published in Japan, but the term now encompasses any comics work that uses the artistic styles and tropes that originated in Japan.

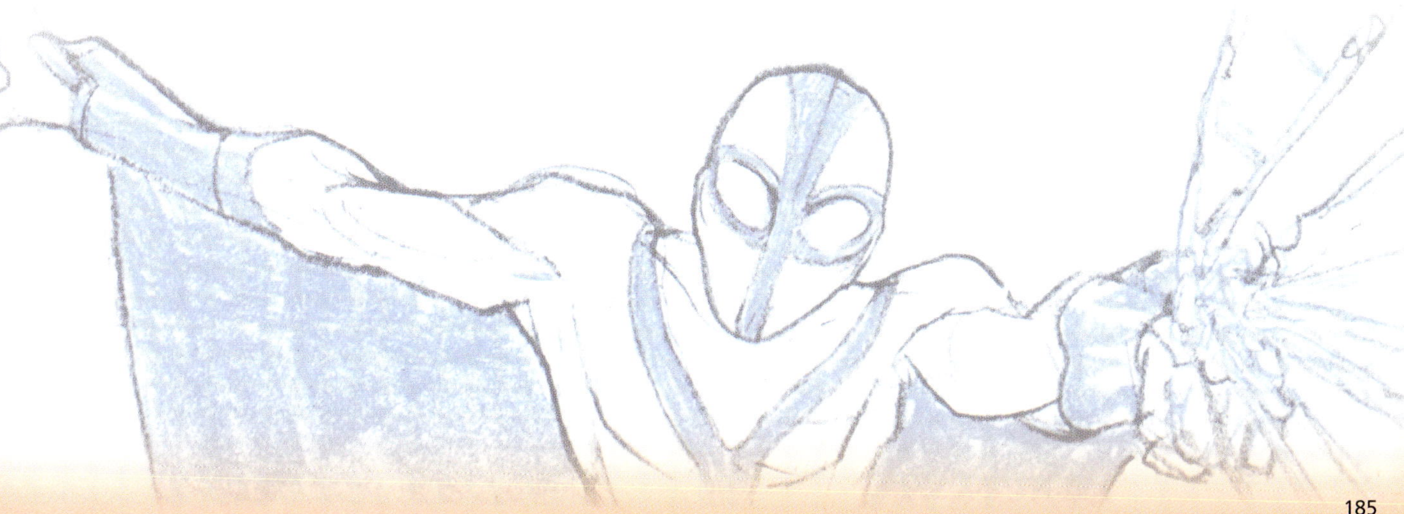

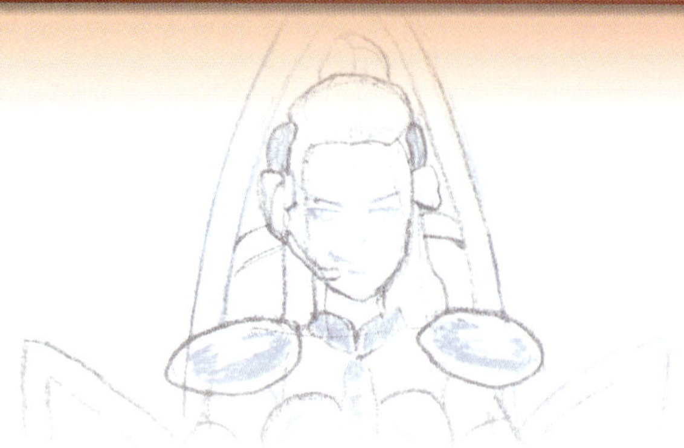

Modern Age A period in comics history stretching from the mid-1980s to the present, usually distinguished by morally ambiguous stories and characters and a more realistic (and darker) approach to both.

mutant A person who derives superpowers from a genetic mutation.

penciling Drawing a picture with a pencil. Artists often start with breakdowns and work their way up to finished pencils, which are then inked and colored.

perspective The fact that things farther from the eye look smaller than those that are closer. Artists mimic this in two-dimensional drawings to give their work the perception of depth.

perspective lines Straight lines that meet at a vanishing point and are used to help mimic three-dimensional depth on a page. They can seem almost parallel at first but they eventually meet somewhere, even off the page.

radiation A common source of superpowers in older comics.

rough A drawing in a preliminary stage, after you've got down the breakdown and the skeleton but before the finished pencils.

screentone A rub-on pattern—often simply dots or lines—used to add shading, depth, and texture to a drawing.

Silver Age A period in comics history stretching from the 1960s through the mid-1980s, usually distinguished by characters with personal lives and the problems that go with them.

skeleton The underlying framework of any creature, whether it has bones or not.

superhero A hero (see the entry for "hero") with superpowers.

superpowers Unusual personal abilities that do not exist in modern reality.

vanishing point The point at which the perspective lines in a drawing meet. Look to the end of a long, straight road to see this effect in real life.

villain A character who seeks to better himself at the expense of others. A villain often acts as a foil to the hero.

APPENDIX B

VISUAL GLOSSARY

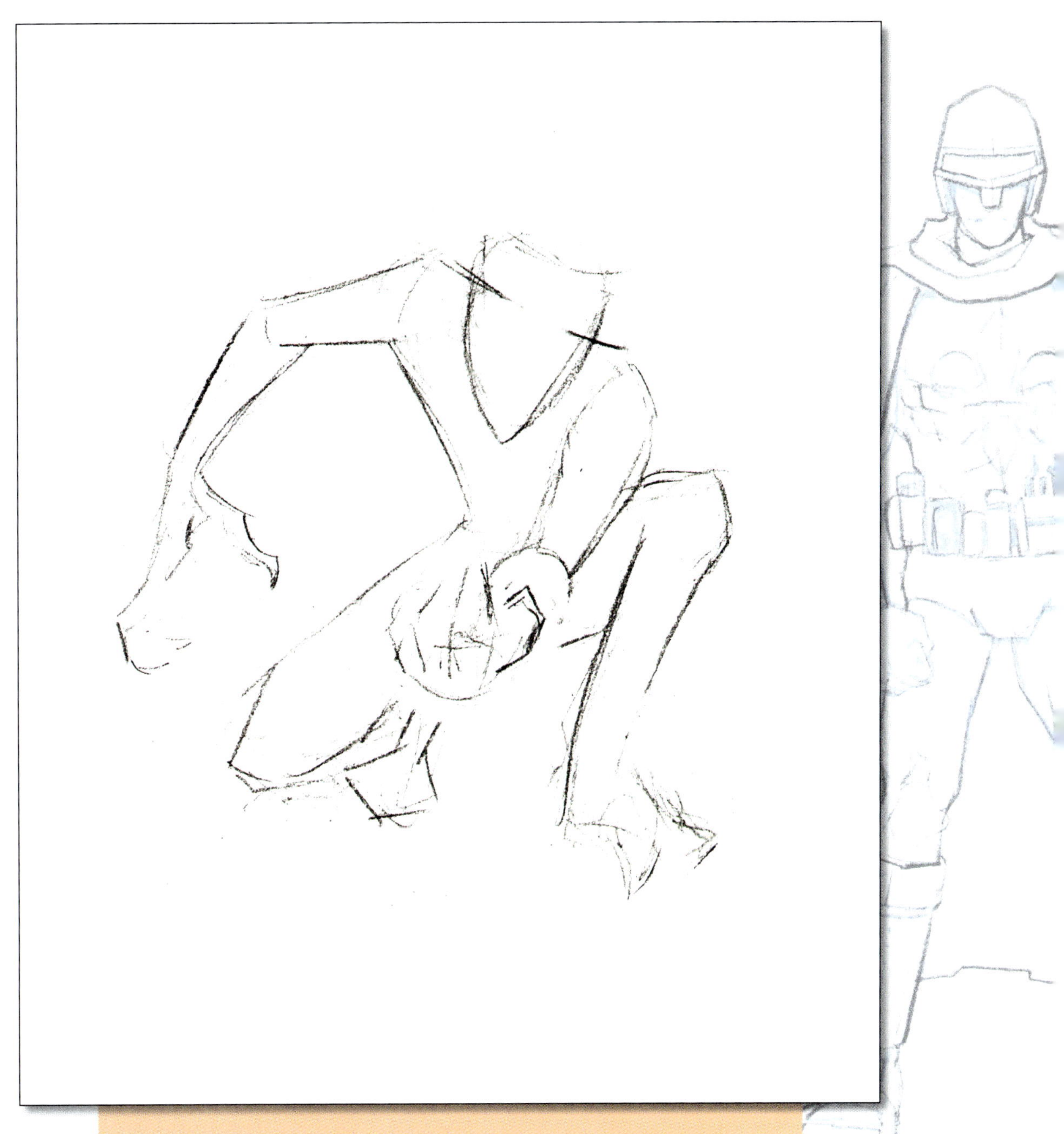

breakdown The roughest stage of a pencil drawing. You use basic shapes to show the rough position of each element in the drawing, including the poses of each figure.

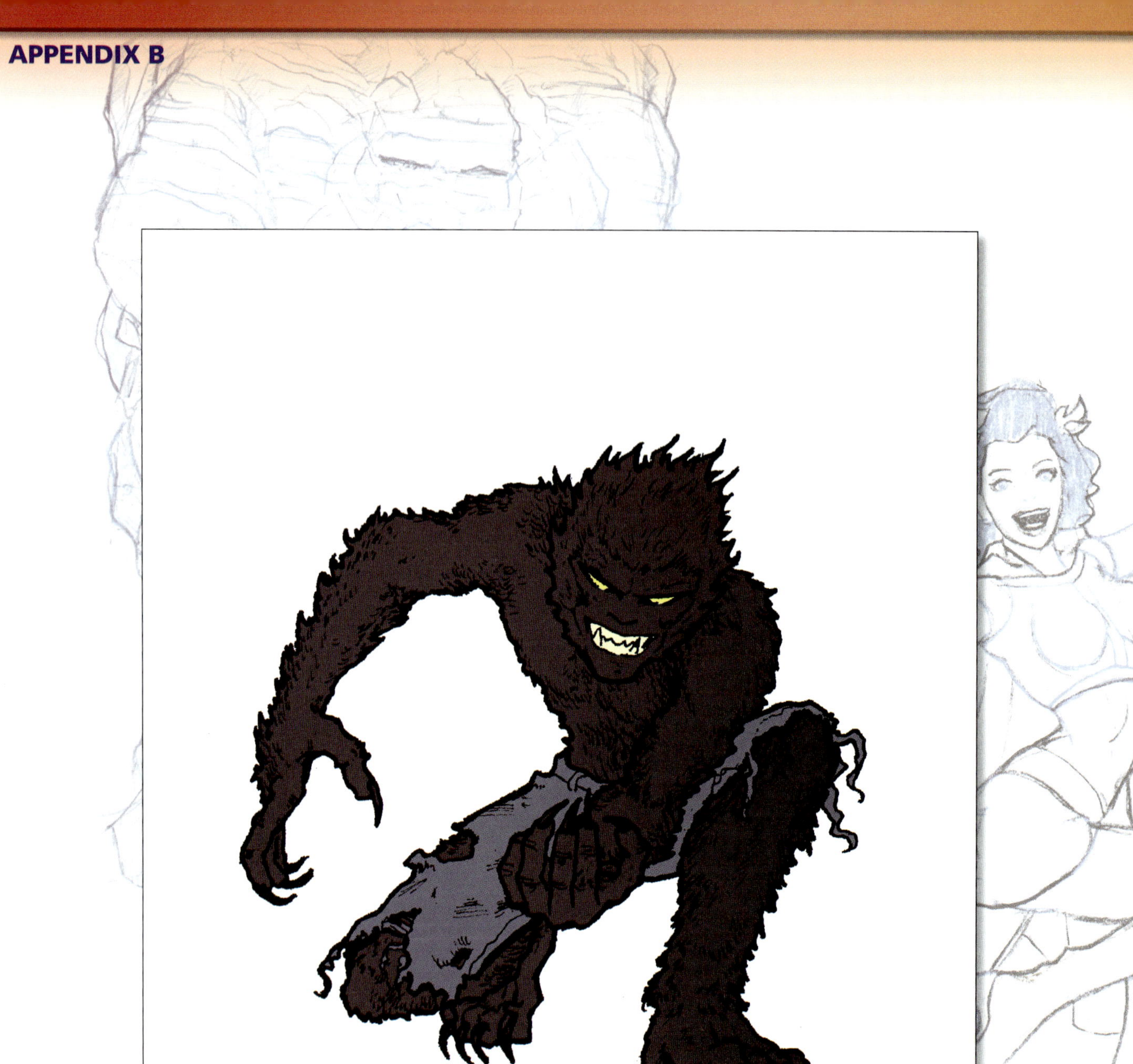

colors The final stage of a drawing, in which you color it in whatever fashion you like. Most American comics are produced in full color.

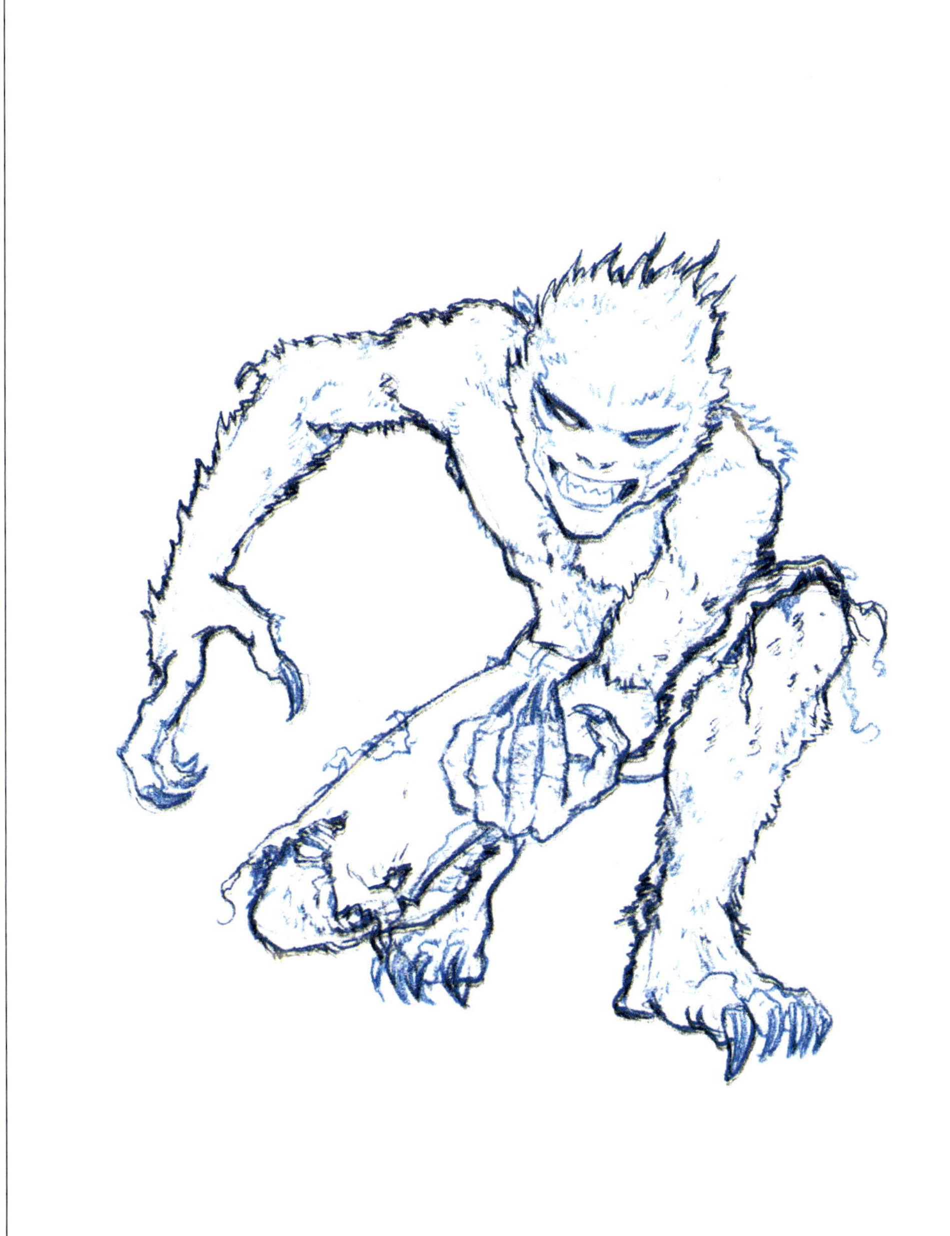

finished pencils A pencil drawing that is as complete as you can make it. Often such drawings are then inked and colored.

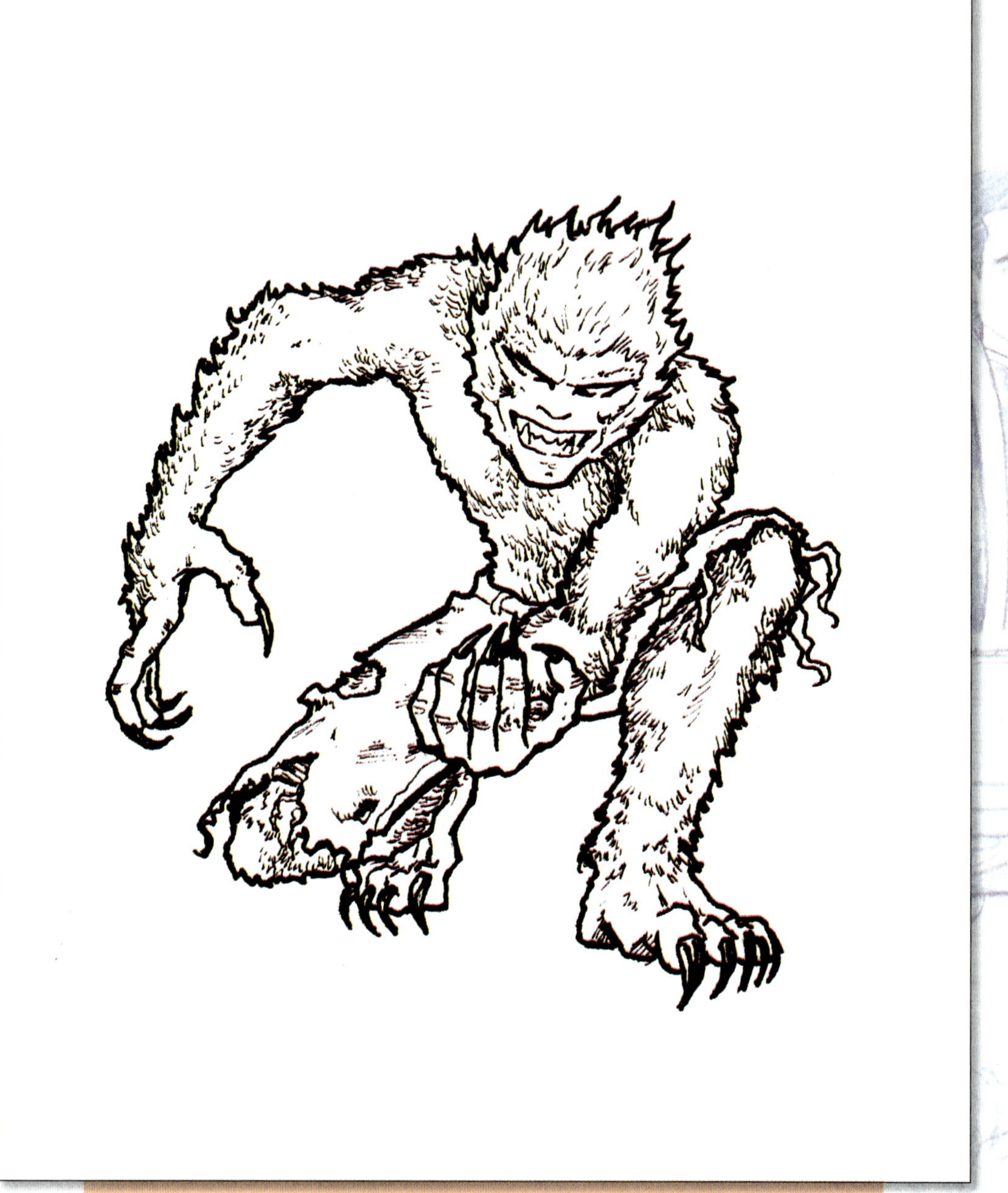

inks The stage of a drawing at which you go over your pencils with ink to make them more permanent. Some artists skip this step, preferring the look of the finished pencils instead.

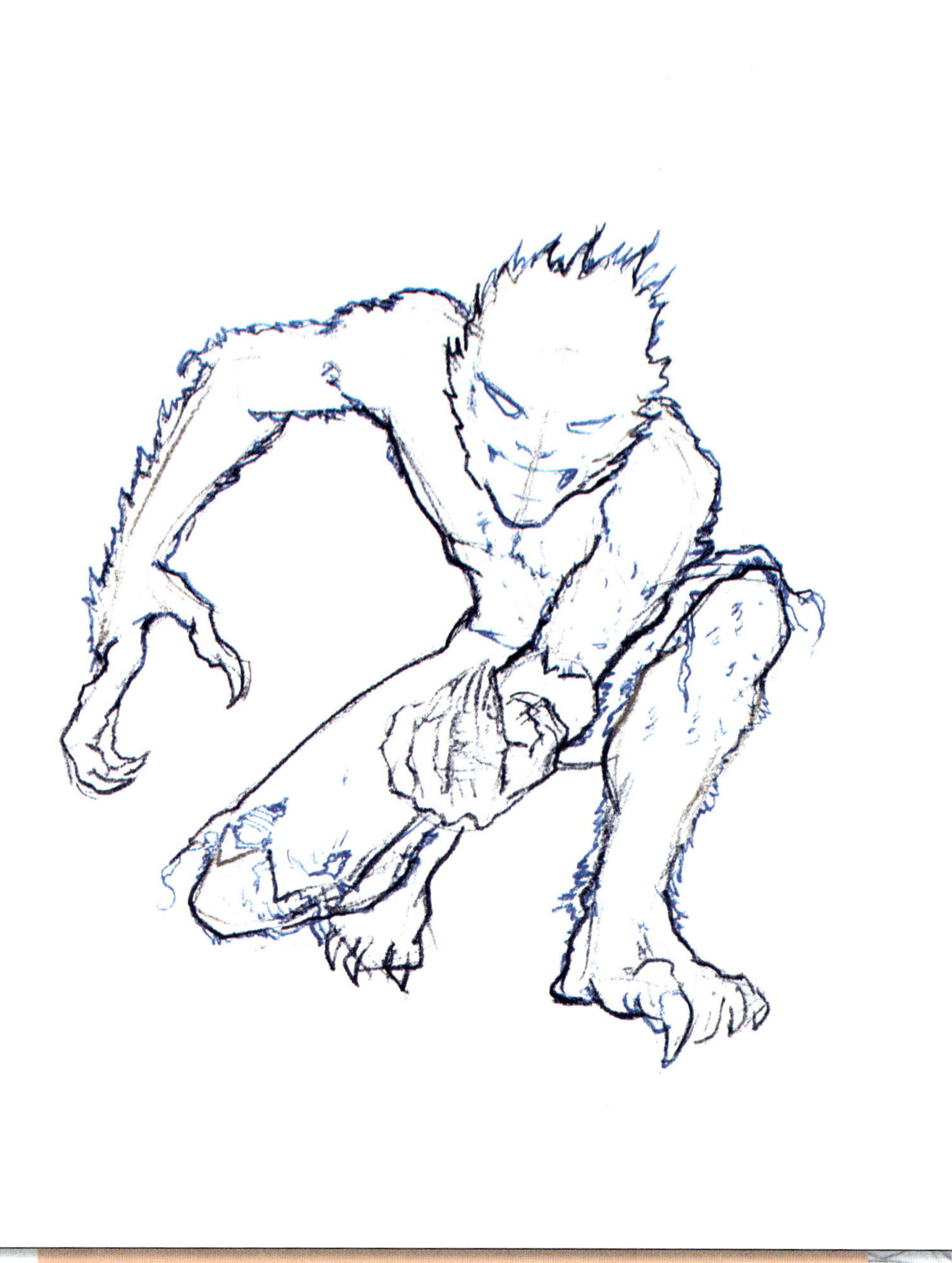

rough A drawing in a preliminary stage, after you've got down the breakdown and the skeleton but before the finished pencils.

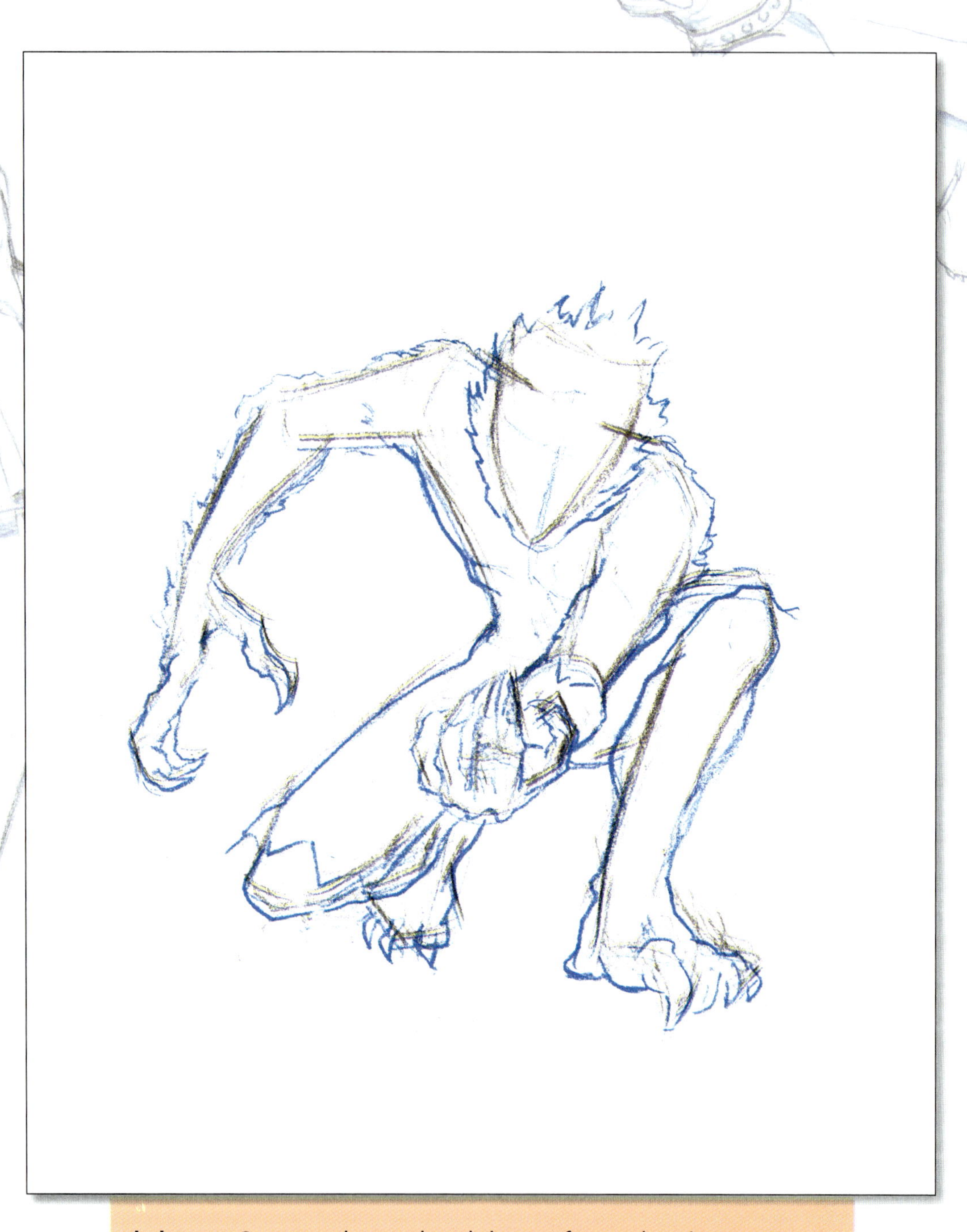

skeleton Once you have a breakdown of your drawing, you move to the skeleton, making sure the figures each comply with their underlying framework.

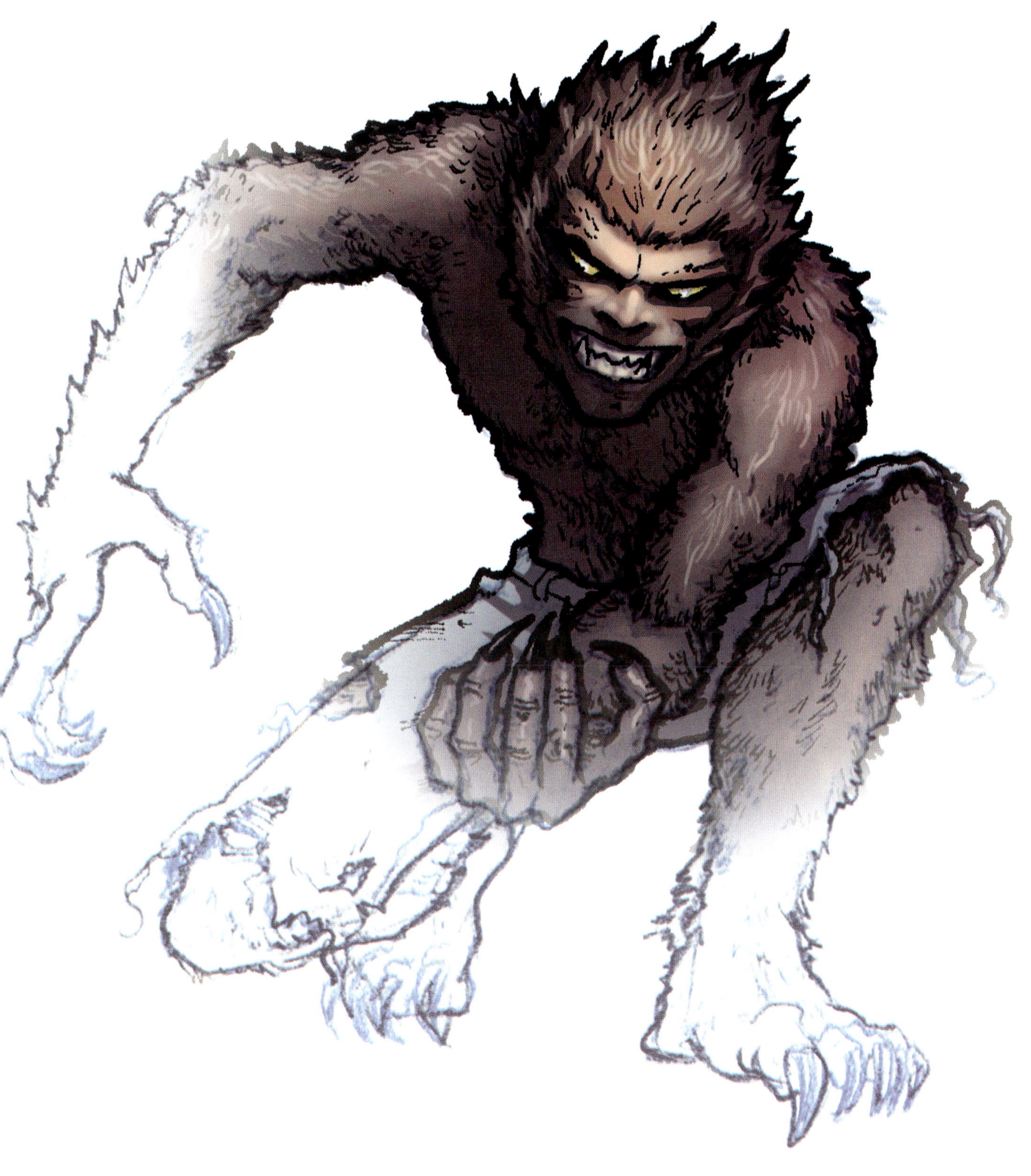

Appendix C

Further Reading

Our Drawing Books

As you know by now, this book is not meant for those new to drawing. It's an intermediate-level course for people who want to know more about drawing superheroes and villains.

If you're just getting your feet wet, we suggest you start out with another *Complete Idiot's Guide* to get a good, solid grounding on how to create this sort of art:

Fradella, Frank, for Idea + Design Works. *The Complete Idiot's Guide to Drawing Basics Illustrated.* Indianapolis: Alpha, 2006.

Once you've read this book, come back here and we'll show you how to do things the superpowered way.

Also, if you're interested in manga (Japanese-style comics), be sure to pick up the two other *Complete Idiot's Guides* that Matt wrote with Tomoko Taniguchi:

Forbeck, Matt, and Tomoko Taniguchi. *The Complete Idiot's Guide to Manga Fantasy Creatures Illustrated*. Indianapolis: Alpha, 2007.

Forbeck, Matt, and Tomoko Taniguchi. *The Complete Idiot's Guide to Drawing Manga Illustrated: Shoujo*. Indianapolis: Alpha, 2008.

A couple other guides in *The Complete Idiot's* series should prove useful, too. These are:

Gertler, Nat, and Steve Lieber. *The Complete Idiot's Guide to Creating a Graphic Novel.* Indianapolis: Alpha, 2004.

Hoddinott, Brenda. *The Complete Idiot's Guide to Drawing People Illustrated.* Indianapolis: Alpha, 2004.

Layman, John, and David Hutchinson. *The Complete Idiot's Guide to Drawing Manga Illustrated.* Indianapolis: Alpha, 2005.

Other Drawing Books

Now that you've plumbed *The Complete Idiot's Guides*, here are a number of other books you might find useful. They range from books that cover the same subject as this work to intellectual examinations of exactly how comics work. Dip in deeply, and enjoy liberally.

Chiarello, Mark, and Todd Klein. *The DC Comics Guide to Coloring and Lettering.* New York: Watson-Guptill Publications, 2004.

Dean, Martyn. *The Guide to Fantasy Art Techniques*. New York: Paper Tiger, 1988.

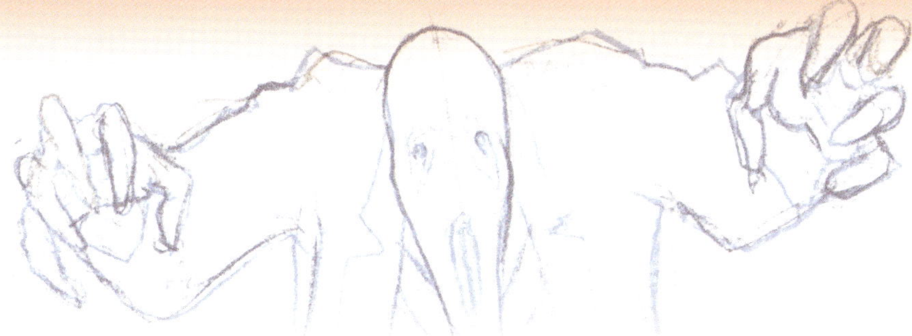

Edwards, Betty. *The New Drawing on the Right Side of the Brain.* New York: Tarcher, 1999.

Eisner, Will. *Comics and Sequential Art, Expanded Edition.* Tamarac, FL: Poorhouse Press, 1985.

———. *Graphic Storytelling and Visual Narrative.* Tamarac, FL: Poorhouse Press, 1996.

Giordano, Dick. *Draw Comics with Dick Giordano.* Cincinnati: Impact Books, 2005.

Hart, Christopher. *Drawing Cutting Edge Anatomy: The Ultimate Reference for Comic Book Artists.* New York: Watson-Guptill Publications, 2004.

———. *Simplified Anatomy for the Comic Book Artist.* New York: Watson-Guptill Publications, 2007.

Hogarth, Burne. *Dynamic Figure Drawing*. New York: Watson-Guptill Publications, 1996.

Janson, Klaus. *The DC Comics Guide to Pencilling Comics*. New York: Watson-Guptill Publications, 2001.

Lee, Stan, and John Buscema. *How to Draw Comics the Marvel Way.* London: Titan Books, 1986.

Martin, Gary. *The Art of Comic Book Inking.* Milwaukie, OR: Dark Horse Comics, 1997.

McCloud, Scott. *Making Comics: Storytelling Secrets of Comics, Manga and Graphic Novels*. New York: Harper Paperbacks, 2006.

———. *Reinventing Comics: How Imagination and Technology Are Revolutionizing an Art Form*. New York: Harper Paperbacks, 2000.

———. *Understanding Comics: The Invisible Art*. New York: Harper Paperbacks, 1994.

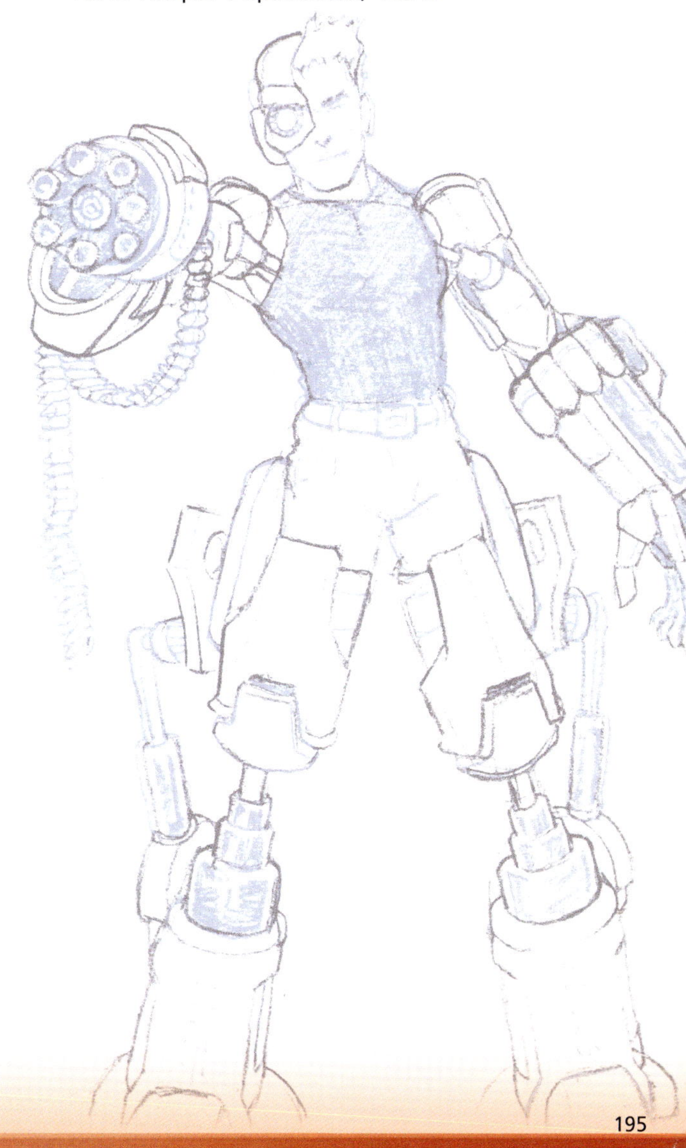

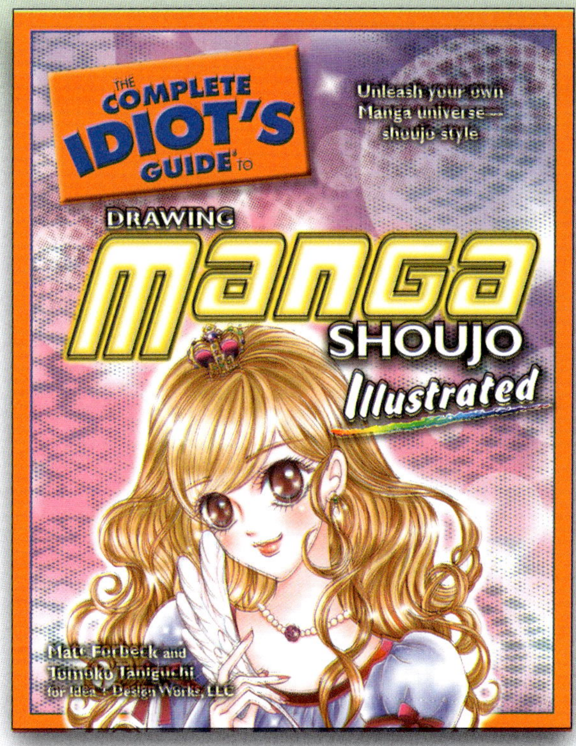

ISBN: 978-1-59257-738-5

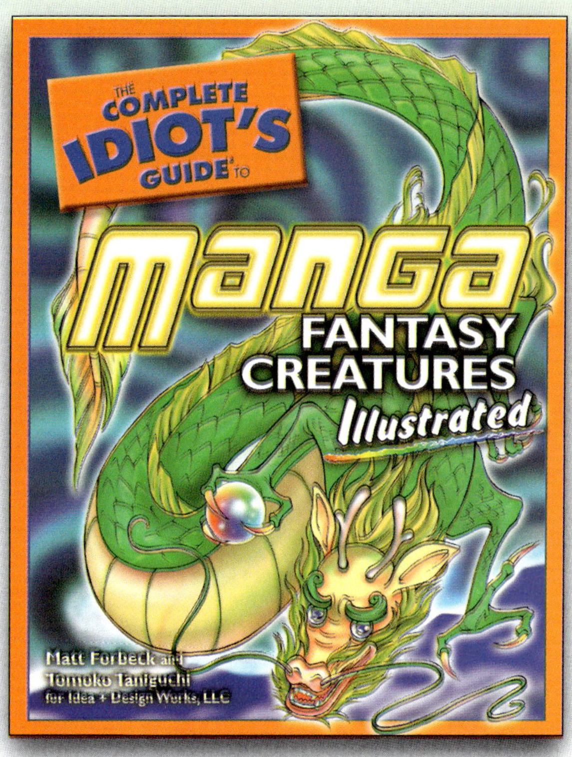

ISBN: 978-1-59257-636-4

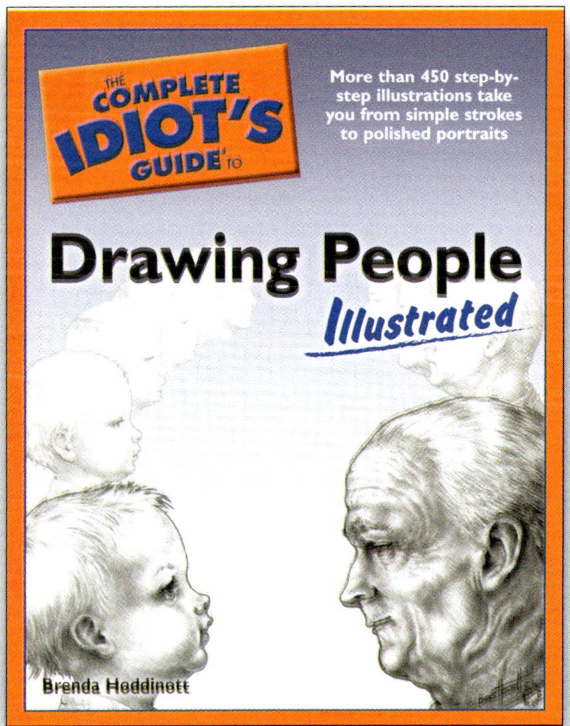

ISBN: 978-1-59257-223-6

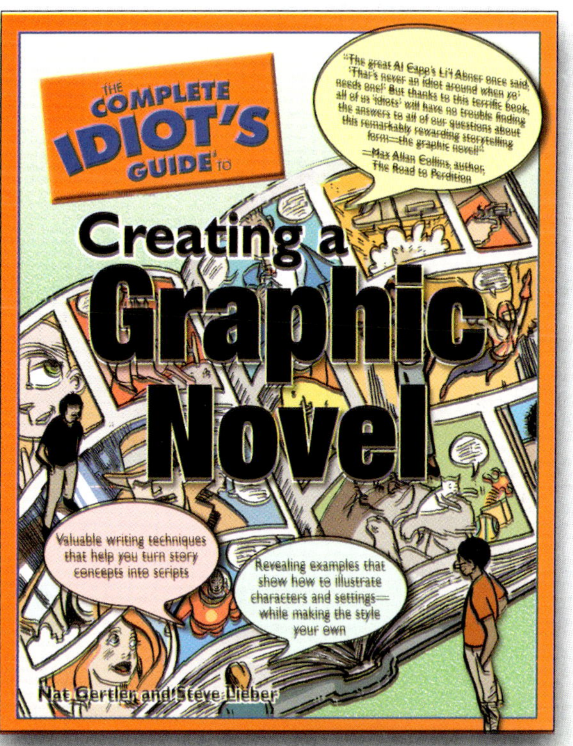

ISBN: 978-1-59257-233-5